New Casebooks

SHAKESPEARE'S TRAGEDIES

New Casebooks

Further titles are in preparation

New Casebooks Series
Series Standing Order ISBN 0–333–69345–0
(*outside North America only*)

You can receive future titles in this series as they are published by placing a standing order. Please contact your bookseller or, in case of difficulty, write to us at the address below with your name and address, the title of the series and the ISBN quoted above.

Customer Services Department, Macmillan Distribution Ltd
Houndmills, Basingstoke, Hampshire RG21 6XS, England

New Casebooks

SHAKESPEARE'S TRAGEDIES

EDITED BY SUSAN ZIMMERMAN

Introduction, selection and editorial matter
© Susan Zimmerman 1998

First published 1998 by
MACMILLAN PRESS LTD
Houndmills, Basingstoke, Hampshire RG21 6XS
and London
Companies and representatives throughout the world

ISBN 0-333-63218-4 hardcover
ISBN 0-333-63219-2 paperback

A catalogue record for this book is available from the British Library.

This book is printed on paper suitable for recycling and made from
fully managed and sustained forest sources.

10   9   8   7   6   5   4   3   2   1
07 06 05 04 03 02 01 00 99 98

Typeset by EXPO Holdings, Malaysia

Printed in Hong Kong

Published in the United States of America 1998 by
ST. MARTIN'S PRESS, INC.,
Scholarly and Reference Division,
175 Fifth Avenue, New York, N.Y. 10010

ISBN 0-312-21272-0 cloth
ISBN 0-333-21273-9 paperback

Contents

Acknowledgements

The editor and publishers wish to thank the following for permission to use copyright material:

Janet Adelman, for material from *Suffocating Mothers: Fantasies of Maternal Origin in Shakespeare's Plays*, Routledge, pp. 147–61, first published as, 'Anger's My Meat': Feeding, Dependency, and Aggression in *Coriolanus*', in David Bevington and Jay L. Halio (eds), *Shakespeare: Pattern of Excelling Nature*, Associated University Presses (1978), by permission of Associated University Presses; Philip Armstrong, for material from 'Spheres of Influence: Cartography and the Gaze in Shakespearean Tragedy and History', *Shakespeare Studies*, 23 (1995), by permission of the author; Michael Bristol, for material from '"Funeral Bak'd Meats": Carnival and the Carnivalesque in *Hamlet*', in Suzanne L. Wofford (ed.), *Hamlet: Case Studies in Contemporary Criticism* (1994). Copyright © 1994 St. Martin's Press, by permission of St. Martin's Press; Catherine Belsey, for material from 'The Name of the Rose in *Romeo and Juliet*', *The Yearbook of English Studies*, 23 (1993), by permission of The *Yearbook of English Studies*; Karin S. Coddon, for '"Suche Strange Desygns": Madness, Subjectivity and Treason in *Hamlet* and Elizabethan Culture', *Renaissance Drama*, NS, 20 (1989), by permission of Northwestern University Press; John Drakakis, for '"Fashion it Thus": *Julius Caesar* and the Politics of Theatrical Representation', *Shakespeare Survey*, 44 (1992) by permission of Cambridge University Press; Margreta de Grazia, for 'The Ideology of Superfluous Things: *King Lear* as period piece', in Margreta de Grazia, Maureen Quilligan and Peter Stallybrass (eds), *Subject and Object in Renaissance Culture* (1996), by permission of Cambridge University Press; Jonathan Goldberg, for material from 'Dover Cliff and the Conditions of Representation: *King Lear* 4:6 in

Perspective', *Poetics Today*, 5:3 (1984). Copyright © 1984 Porter Institute for Poetics and Semiotics, Tel Aviv University, by permission of Duke University Press; Stephen Greenblatt, for material from 'Shakespeare Bewitched', in Jeffrey N. Cox and Larry J. Reynolds (eds), *New Historical Literary Studies: Essays on Reproducing Texts, Representing History* (1993). Copyright © 1993 by Princeton University Press, by permission of Princeton University Press; Patricia Parker, for 'Fantasies of "Race" and "Gender": Africa, *Othello*, and bringing to light', in Margo Hendricks and Patricia Parker (eds), *Women, 'Race' and Writing in the Early Modern Period* (1994), by permission of Routledge; Peter Stallybrass, for material from 'Transvestism and "the body beneath"' in Susan Zimmerman (ed.), *Erotic Politics: Desire on the Renaissance Stage* (1992), by permission of Routledge; Marion Wynne-Davies, for material from '"The Swallowing Womb": Consumed and Consuming Women in *Titus Andronicus*', in Valerie Wayne (ed.), *The Matter of Difference: Materialist Feminist Criticism of Shakespeare* (1991). Essay copyright © Marion Wynne-Davies 1991, by permission of Harvester Wheatsheaf and Cornell University Press.

Every effort has been made to trace the copyright holders but if any have been inadvertently overlooked the publishers will be pleased to make the necessary arrangement at the first opportunity.

General Editors' Preface

The purpose of this series of New Casebooks is to reveal some of the ways in which contemporary criticism has changed our understanding of commonly studied texts and writers and, indeed, of the nature of criticism itself. Central to the series is a concern with modern critical theory and its effect on current approaches to the study of literature. Each New Casebook editor has been asked to select a sequence of essays which will introduce the reader to the new critical approaches to the text or texts being discussed in the volume and also illuminate the rich interchange between critical theory and critical practice that characterises so much current writing about literature.

In this focus on modern critical thinking and practice New Casebooks aim not only to inform but also to stimulate, with volumes seeking to reflect both the controversy and the excitement of current criticism. Because much of this criticism is difficult and often employs an unfamiliar critical language, editors have been asked to give the reader as much help as they feel is appropriate, but without simplifying the essays or the issues they raise. Again, editors have been asked to supply a list of further reading which will enable readers to follow up issues raised by the essays in the volume.

The project of New Casebooks, then, is to bring together in an illuminating way those critics who best illustrate the ways in which contemporary criticism has established new methods of analysing texts and who have reinvigorated the important debate about how we 'read' literature. The hope is, of course, that New Casebooks will not only open up this debate to a wider audience, but will also encourage students to extend their own ideas, and think afresh about their responses to the texts they are studying.

John Peck and Martin Coyle
University of Wales, Cardiff

Introduction: Shakespeare's Tragedies in Postmodern Perspective

SUSAN ZIMMERMAN

I

The purpose of this new collection of essays[1] is to demonstrate how postmodern theory[2] has radically reconfigured critical approaches to Shakespeare's tragedies. As the essays themselves make clear, this is not a simple demonstration. Because Shakespearean tragedy and postmodernism are both extremely fluid categories, there is no single model for either. Thus we can speak only, on the one hand, of Shakespearean trage*dies*, that is, of ten plays that focus on the suffering and deaths of their protagonists and that do not lend themselves, collectively, to formulaic description;[3] and, on the other, of a range of postmodern theoretical frameworks by which any of these tragedies may be examined. But if theory is able to inform tragedy in multiple and complex ways, the converse is also true: one of the liberating features of postmodern criticism is that it engages in a reciprocal exchange with the texts it examines.

Shakespeare's tragedies have a particular relevance to the post-modern project because they explore so compellingly one of its primary concerns – that is, how and according to what dictates the human subject is constituted. If, as Catherine Belsey argues, fiction is the pre-eminent mode for addressing the social and intrapersonal relations which shape human identity, then tragedy is the genre that represents these relations in their starkest and most terrifying dimensions. Comedy may move toward 'final reconciliation' of the human struggle, but 'tragedy is subject to no such imperative':[4] that which the taboos of civilised life would deny – death, violence, illicit sexuality – is the very stuff of tragedy. And because the 'stuff' or representations of Shakespeare's tragedies are so richly particularised, these plays occupy a privileged position in the postmodern scrutiny of early modern subjectivity.

But Shakespeare's dramatic representations are privileged also because of the *mode* in which they were staged in the early modern public theatre. There is, in fact, a homology between the physical structure and formal dictates of this theatre and the postmodernist project itself: that is, both can be said to resist closure and fixity, and to foreground heterogeneity and indeterminacy. As I shall suggest in more detail later, postmodernism (of whatever stripe) has at least one foundational principle: that language is unstable because meaning is an effect of difference, not identity; therefore, there can be no determinate, absolute 'truth', no clear and ordered system for apprehending reality. To the extent that Shakespeare's representations *as representations* – as constituted by historical contingencies of stage, conventions, location and audience – are not intelligible by means of 'commonsensical' notions of coherence, they exemplify this principle. Thus to examine the representations of subjectivity in Shakespeare's tragedies is simultaneously to focus a special lens on the function of representation itself.

It has, of course, long been recognised that theatres such as the Globe were not conducive to the unified, coherent drama that we have come to associate with realism (that is, drama constructed on the premise that the illusion must seem 'real'). In the absence of artificial lighting, performances at the Globe were at mid-day, whatever the supposed time of a play's action, with most of the elevated platform stage open to the elements; scenery was minimal, and suggestive in a literal way (for example, a tree-like prop for a forest); and the spectators, whether standing in the pit, or seated in the circular galleries that ascended to the roof of the structure, surrounded the stage on three sides, precluding 'a comprehensive vision of the events dramatised'.[5] In addition, poetic language (including soliloquies and asides), emblematic and stylised modes of acting, unlocalised settings, anachronistic costuming, the mixing of genres, disparities of time and place, and perhaps most importantly, the use of boy actors for women, militated against illusionistic representation. All of this

'gallimaufry', to use the encapsulating term of early modern anti-
theatricalists, positioned Shakespeare's plays at a considerable distance from the self-contained, ordered drama that was later accom-
modated by the Restoration proscenium stage.

But if the structures and conventions of early modern theatres
helped shape a distinctive mode of representation, so did their location outside the jurisdictional precincts of London – across the
Thames on the Bankside, or in the northern suburbs. A commercial
enterprise dependent on attracting spectators from all classes of
society, public theatre offered 'an escape ... from surveillance of attitude, feeling, and expression'[6] – in Bakhtinian terms, a carnivalesque
locus for interrogating and contesting hegemonic discourses.[7] Thus
the theatrical industry that included Shakespeare's Globe participated
(at times subversively) in 'the circulation of social energy'[8] that constituted early modern culture. And Shakespeare's tragedies, among the
most popular plays of the period, both appropriated and transformed
discourses from many sectors (politics, religion, law, science, to name
a few) for the purposes of theatrical representation. In tracking this
transformative process, the postmodern scholar is able to discern not
only particular features of Shakespeare's cultural landscape, but also
that culture's interactive modes of production.[9]

For these reasons it can be said that the London public theatre,
and Shakespeare's tragedies in particular, foreground the problem
that engages all postmodern theory, that is, the relationship
between subjectivity and representation. This is the concern that,
inevitably, pervades this collection – specifically, the subject of
early modern tragedy as inscribed by language and by culture.
Nonetheless, the essays in this volume are most notable for their
disparateness – their individual modes of theorising the terms of the
problem. As a way of organising such heterogeneity, it has been
common in recent practice to divide postmodern criticism roughly
according to whether its primary focus is language *or* culture, even
though these are profoundly interdependent phenomena. According
to this dichotomy, deconstruction and psychoanalysis focus primarily on ways in which surplus in signification – the discontinuities
and excesses of language itself – constitute the subject of tragedy
and intensify the representation of tragic experience. And cultural
history (which may be said to include 'cultural materialism', 'the
new historicism', and 'the poetics of culture') focuses primarily on
the subject of tragedy as ideological construct, the destination of
culturally specific discourses.[10]

In some respects, the language/culture dichotomy is a useful one, if only because it provides a framework for describing the postmodern project (I invoke it myself for these purposes in the next section, which describes some of the major concepts of postmodernism as a way of introducing the essays). But it is worth remembering, as the essays themselves prompt us to do, that postmodern criticism does not arrange itself tidily along an arbitrary categorical divide – that psychoanalysis is compatible with history, history with deconstruction, and so on in a virtually endless sequence of combinations and permutations. The postmodern project, like Shakespeare's tragedies, is complex and multiform: in the last analysis, as Greenblatt suggests, there *is* no last analysis.

II

During the last several decades, the use of the term 'postmodern' in literary theory has become increasingly elastic, accommodating a wide range of argument and critical practice. Most simply, the term signifies that which follows upon and contests the interpretive traditions of modernism, and for most scholars of early modern literature, modernism is customarily identified with 'essentialist humanism' or 'liberal humanism'. As a new category of critical reference, 'essentialist humanism' (which I will subsequently refer to simply as 'humanism') has itself been stretched to trace a lineage from the eighteenth-century Enlightenment to the early twentieth century. The humanist position is thus rooted in a rationalist tradition of consistency and coherence, one that assumes a teleologically conceived natural order. According to this tradition, there are constants in the natural order (whatever is *natural* is axiomatically *ordered*) that connect present to past despite the vagaries of human history. Particularities of time and place – what we call historical contingencies – are subsumed in the shaping force of a larger design.

In such a system the human subject functions, first, as the crucial constant, the essentially unchanged locus of signification, that which connects present to past. Thus the humanist views the early modern subject and the modern subject as linked in a 'profound continuity',[11] and subjectivity itself as a 'pre-social essence'[12] which may be understood in terms of universal principles. Moreover, the essentialist, transhistorical subject of humanism figures as the determining factor in the teleological scheme, the 'unconstrained *author* of meaning and action'.[13] Paradoxically, then, humanism would inscribe human agency at the centre of human history at the same time that it would exempt this agency from the materiality of historical process.[14]

Postmodernism takes a very different view of human subjectivity and its relationship to historical process. Eschewing all totalising narratives, including that of humanism, it is committed to the anti-idealist principle that the human subject 'is never an indivisible unity, never an autonomous, self-determining centre of consciousness';[15] and that human subjectivity does *not* transcend the material conditions of its own existence. On the contrary, because 'the meanings in circulation at a given moment specify the limits of what can be said and understood',[16] human subjectivity derives from historically specific social practices and discourses. A totalising philosophy such as that of humanism, one that suppresses plurality and difference in order to reify a transcendental subject, is an exercise in metaphysics, not in historical scrutiny.

Postmodern strategies for scrutinising the past without the metaphysical superstructure of humanism – for approaching historical process synchronically rather than diachronically – have been heavily influenced by the theories of Michel Foucault. In *The Archaeology of Knowledge*, Foucault contends that human societies are *dis*continuous, that history should be a way of 'conceiving of difference, [of] describing separations and dispersions, [of] disassociating [from] the reassuring form of the identical'.[17] This principle applies not only to relationships among societies, but also to the discontinuous structures of individual societies. Thus the task of the cultural historian is to isolate whatever a society attempts to marginalise, demonise, or deny, and to search for what seems *alien* or unfamiliar in the past, notwithstanding the enormous difficulties implicit in 'recognising' strange or unknown historical formations. Foucault's own studies of madness, sexuality, and prisons, to cite only a few of his works, provide methodological models for the application of his theory.[18]

A compelling example of a Foucauldian perspective on early modern subjectivity may be found in recent scholarship on the medical discourse of early modern England. The seminal research by Thomas Laqueur on this discourse purports to show that the concept of sexual dimorphism – that is, the biological separation of the sexes which renders the categories of male and female 'essential' and 'natural' – developed in the late seventeenth century and was later sanctioned by developments in biological science.[19] During the time of Shakespeare, medical discourse constructed bodies differently. The Galenic model for gender differentiation, probably the most influential, described a developmental process in which male and female sexual organs derived from the same source, and in which males passed through a female stage in the course of establishing sexual identity. Presumably, then, it was not 'natural' for the early modern subject to conceive of his/her body as biologically 'opposite' that of another sex, however self-evident such a concept may seem to a modernist. The notion that sexual identity in Shakespeare's time may not be part of an historical continuum – that it was a function of specific, time-bound discourse – is precisely the kind of Foucauldian insight that challenges the humanist ideology.[20]

Foucault's chief influence, however, lies in his theory of the relationship of ideology to power, the strategies by which ideological discourses such as that of early modern medicine might be appropriated and disseminated by social forces. According to Foucault, ideology functions so as to enable a hegemony, or site of consolidated power, to mask its own complexity, to appear simple, self-evident, all-encompassing. Thus, to return to our example, if, as Laqueur argues, the Galenic model of biological development dominated early modern medicine, it did so for specific, power-related purposes that would not be readily apparent in the social deployment of this ideology. On the contrary, Galenism would be made to appear as 'natural', as inevitably *true*, in much the same way that the concept of sexual dimorphism operates in modern societies. Further, in each case the fiction of transparent 'truth' reinforces another fiction: that the hegemony which promotes it is univocal, *all*-powerful.[21]

Although the followers of Foucault are sometimes accused of describing the deployment of power as if 'the hegemony' were a single entity, the emphasis in recent historical studies has been on power as a function of hegemon*ies* – discursive structures frequently in conflict. Any society produces multiple discourses which intersect in the subject, and although taken collectively they specify the limits within which subjectivity may be constituted at a given time, they also make possible a plurality of shifting ideological positions. Thus even the assumed dominance of the Galenic model for sexual development in early modern England would not have excluded other contestatory models, and the cultural historian is enjoined to examine not only the radical implications of Galenic theory for this society, but also its position within a complicated network of intersecting ideologies.[22] In pursuing this inquiry, the following questions might be asked: Did the varieties of early modern medical discourse represent alternative sites of power? Were they directed at different groups or classes? Do their representations of 'male' and 'female' identify their origins and intended audiences? How do they intersect with each other and with non-medical discourses? And how, finally, do the circulations of these discursive ideologies help to frame the possibilities for early modern subjectivity – and ultimately, for the subject of early modern tragedy?

There are, of course, many kinds of discourse that impinge directly on the construction of early modern subjectivity (those of madness and witchcraft, for example, are scrutinised in this volume). But for the cultural historian who would examine the representation of subjectivity in the public *theatre*, historical inquiry is further complicated by issues specific to theatrical representation. Because the theatre participates in the circulation of social discourses, theatrical representations are, in effect, representations of other representations – another level of mimesis, as it were. Thus we may say, for example, that Shakespeare's tragic protagonists can never be synonymous with their models in Shakespeare's sources, or, for that matter, with historical personages; nor can the ideological positions of a play be identical to those in antecedent discourses. Both Hamlet and *Hamlet* are *fictions* with *localised* habitations, and it is the business of the cultural historian to anatomise the transformative modes through which Shakespeare's fictions become 'originals' that, in turn, contribute to the construction of new social discourses.

There is, inevitably, a political dimension in any transaction between social discourse and theatrical representation, and for this reason a considerable body of criticism on Shakespeare's tragedies has focused on ways in which these plays subvert or reinforce hegemonic values. Feminist cultural history, for example, has concerned itself largely with Shakespeare's representations of women. In this instance, the problematic of theatrical representation is further complicated by the virtual absence of women in the ranks of early modern playwrights, actors, investors, and regulators. Female figures in Shakespeare's tragedies are, in effect, products of a male-dominated industry which has appropriated male-dominated discourses for impersonations by male actors. This cultural phenomenon complicates the potential for feminist subversion in Shakespeare's plays, and multiplies the analytic screens through which feminist scholars must sift the evidence for early modern female subjectivity.

The difficulties of feminist scholars exemplify a theoretical crux common to all postmodern historical inquiry. If human subjectivity is constituted by ideological formations, then what becomes of human agency, individual and collective; and what, in turn, are the conditions for the representation of such agency in Shakespeare's theatre? Or, to put it another way, what are the possibilities of *resistance* to the formative power of social discourses (in the feminist case, patriarchal discourses) in early modern England, and how might the theatre be implicated in this resistance? Although, as we have seen, ideology makes possible a plurality of subject positions, it does not seem to allow for a subject position that resists ideology itself, a position that is imaginable, presumably, only *outside* ideology, outside representation.

This paradox, which foregrounds a seeming contradiction in the concept of the subject as socially constituted, is fundamentally about language: it is impossible to imagine anything outside representation because we imagine by *means* of representations – the signifiers of our linguistic systems. And because language and social discourse *precede* the speaking subject, who is 'the destination of meaning',[23] subjectivity is ultimately a function of the way language works. Thus many postmodern scholars, including Shakespeareans, choose to focus on the function of linguistic structures within texts, and on the relationship of these structures to the representation of subjectivity. Such analysis might be termed Derridian/deconstructive or Lacanian/psychoanalytical, depending on its theoretical assumptions. As theories of language, however, both deconstruction and psychoanalysis challenge Ferdinand de Saussure's system of structural linguistics, to which they are also indebted.

Saussure argues that signifiers (acoustic or written symbols) are arbitrary; and that because meaning, the signified, is determined by its differences from other meanings, it derives from what it is *not*.[24] There is no necessary connection between the signifier 'cat' and our concept of the whiskered animal that cries 'meow': this concept might, after all, be just as readily signified by the word 'dog'. Further, 'cat' signifies a particular concept because it does *not* signify another, such as our concept of 'dog', or of 'computer'. Thus in order to function as a signifier, 'cat' depends on the relations of difference between one term and another within the language, the gap between what is present and what is absent.

As a system of symbolisation based on differentiation, on presence and absence, language cannot fix meaning – the relationship between signifier and signified is unstable.[25] Structuralism, while acknowledging the differential structure of meaning, would at the same time deny it, contending that the sliding signifiers of language are ultimately fixed by underlying principles of unity and intelligibility, principles which govern all semiotic systems. As a consequence, it is possible for a structuralist linguist to envisage human subjectivity (as a humanist would) as an intelligible essence, discoverable by means of the invariant structures, or universals, of language.

The *post*structuralist, deconstructive project of Jacques Derrida would dismantle 'a concept of "structure" that serves to immobilise the play of meaning in a text'[26] by exposing the internal contradictions in Saussure's own text – the meanings implicit in its gaps or *aporia*. According to Derrida, slippages in signification set in motion an endless displacement of meaning which never comes to rest in self-authenticating 'truth'. That such 'truth' is discoverable through language is, in fact, 'the ruling illusion'[27] not only of structural linguistics but also of Western metaphysics. Derrida argues, instead, that the signifier has no final destination; its meaning is a function of difference and of deferral (thus the anomalous spelling of Derrida's term 'differance'). Contrary to the logocentric assumptions of Western metaphysics, language cannot guarantee truth, plenitude, identity.[28]

The deconstructionist focusing on Shakespearean tragedy would, then, examine the text in terms of the play of 'differance' within it. This exercise might focus on small units, such as words or phrases, or on longer patterns of meaning, but in either case the purpose of the critique would be to locate contradictions within the text which transgress both its principles of construction and the intentions of its author, much as Derrida did with Saussure's work. The author is 'dead', as Roland Barthes has argued,[29] because signification in language always exceeds authorial intentionality. Thus, rather than decode a text conceived of as a self-contained unit, as a modernist would, the deconstructionist creates new textual meanings and displaces old ones. This generative approach to critical practice results in a metalanguage that is itself subject to deconstruction – and so on through a regression as infinite as language itself.

Although it might seem, at least initially, that the Derridean concept of indeterminacy in language would preclude the possibility of human agency (a primary problem, as we have seen, in the postmodern interrogation of human subjectivity), this is not necessarily the case. On one hand, the principles of deconstruction affirm that the subject is not the autonomous origin of meaning – in any given utterance, she cannot say all that she intends or intend all that she says; moreover, because the subject is inscribed by the linguistic structures of social discourse, identity is always unstable, decentred. At the same time, however, linguistic instability can be said to militate against ideological determinism: the gaps, or *aporia*, in language suggest that human identity can never be wholly fixed, nor wholly controlled. Thus the deconstructionist who examines surplus in signification is, in a sense, simultaneously exploring sites of possible resistance within language. And the deconstructionist who explores such sites in Shakespeare's tragedies is focusing on a genre whose direct concern is with the representation of human subjectivity itself.

Lacanian psychoanalytic theory, like deconstruction, borrows heavily from Saussurean linguistics, but Lacan would connect the infinite regressions of language – its *aporia* – to the phenomenon of human desire.[30] For Lacan, language, sexuality, and subjectivity are inextricably related in a single developmental process. The human subject enters into consciousness, and simultaneously the unconscious, through the agency of language, and in so doing experiences a radical split or division.[31] All the mental impulses prohibited by what Lacan terms the symbolic order – language and the Law which it constitutes – must be repressed: thus the function of the unconscious. Desire is 'the effect in the subject of the condition imposed by the division between conscious and unconscious',[32] a sense or misrecognition that an originary, non-differentiated, pre-linguistic being has been lost.[33] Because desire aspires to reclaim this imagined plenitude of originary being (Lacan's *objet a*), it – like language – is structured as an endless process of substitution and deferment.[34]

The Lacanian scholar of Shakespeare's tragedies would, then, examine these texts in terms of their representations of desire, that is, their symbolic substitutes, or stand-ins for the unsignifiable, unknowable *objet a*. Not surprisingly, these 'stand-ins' are often constructed in terms of social and sexual prohibitions, because the tragic protagonist would reach beyond division, alterity, and the prescriptions of the symbolic order toward an illusion of perfect plenitude.[35] But tragedy denies such illusion: the hero's struggle against the constraints of subjectivity is by definition doomed. From the Lacanian perspective, this denial exposes the impossibility of desire on two levels: first, through the representation of the failure of the tragic protagonist; and second, through the 'unconscious' of the text, that is, its underlying recognition that originary presence can never be reconstituted, that representation itself can only point to the lack which constitutes language and gives rise to human desire.

Because Lacanian literary analysis presupposes a theory of psychical development, it is frequently criticised as a kind of postmodern humanism, that is, a methodology which appropriates postmodern linguistics in order to reinstate the transhistorical subject. Lacanians argue that, on the contrary, the principles of indeterminacy which underlie Lacanian theory are precisely what make it possible to 'trace the constraints and resistances of desire in their historical *dis*continuity',[36] and that the unconscious as a structure need not imply an organisation of particular meanings at a given historical moment. In this view, to label psychoanalysis as 'essentialist' in contradistinction to other kinds of historical inquiry is to misunderstand the liberating potential of the Lacanian analytical paradigm.[37]

Interestingly, the epistomological problem that challenges psychoanalysis – to identify synchronicity within structure – is the converse of that which challenges cultural history – to identify a non-essentialising structure for change within synchronicity. This means that psychoanalysis and cultural history may be understood as mutually reinforcing, rather than as oppositional.[38] One might argue further that there are commonalities which connect *all* forms of postmodern theory, such as the repudiation of the humanist concept of the subject as autonomous. As we have seen, the postmodern subject – whether viewed primarily as an ideological, linguistic, or psychic construct – has nonetheless been redefined as 'a *process*, perpetually in construction, perpetually contradictory, perpetually open to change'.[39]

Since all postmodernists, including Shakespeareans, subscribe to this concept of subjectivity, perhaps we should expect that their most exemplary work is interdependent, at least collectively. The essays in this volume are a case in point: individually distinctive, they intersect, both wittingly and unwittingly, in multiple (and multiplying) ways.

To my mind, these reciprocal tensions suggest the vitality of the post-modern project, its ongoing potential for generating fresh critical insights, especially, as we shall see, when the critical lens is focused on the subjects of Shakespeare's tragedies.

III

It would be easy enough to classify the essays in this volume in terms of the type of theory most prevalent in each, a common editorial practice in scholarly collections. Thus Adelman's, Armstrong's, and Belsey's work might be described as psychoanalytical (or, more properly in the case of Armstrong and Belsey, Lacanian); Bristol's and Drakakis's as Marxist; Goldberg's as deconstructionist; and Coddon's, Greenblatt's, and Wynne-Davies's as materialist, or new historicist. But, as I have already suggested, such labels, although useful, can also mislead. 'Marxist' is a case in point: as a category, it is far too broad to be meaningful, and in this instance would collapse the quite dissimilar theories of Bakhtin and Volosinov. 'New historicist', on the other hand, delimits the essays of Greenblatt and Coddon, which are profoundly concerned with psychic process; as does 'psychoanalytical' as a descriptor for Armstrong's analysis, which is rooted in the discoveries of early modern science. And so on: there is, finally, no critical category or single theoretical system which adequately describes the work of any Shakespearean in this volume.

Accordingly, it seems to me that a more profitable approach to this body of criticism – one that respects both its pluralities and its intersections – is to extrapolate a cross-section of critical opinion on issues of common concern. Those issues on which I will focus (already identified in a more general theoretical context in the previous section) include the theatrical representation of early modern subjectivity; the representation, specifically, of early modern women; and the potential of the public theatre for political agency.

Although all the essays in the volume deal in some way with theatrical representation, several focus closely on the *structure* of this representation. John Drakakis (essay 6), for example, argues that *Julius Caesar* may be read as a kind of metatheatre: by figuring Caesar, Brutus, Cassius, and others as actors, self-consciously fashioning Roman politics as competing theatrical performances, the play enacts the relationship of representation itself to ideology, and of ideology to subjectivity. Moreover, if the subjects within the fiction of *Julius Caesar* are radically unstable by virtue of their representations, then so is the theatre whose function is to stage this instability, and whose own liminality is thereby figured in this play.

Theatrical liminality is also the foremost issue in Stephen Greenblatt's essay (5) on *Macbeth*, in which theatre and witchcraft are shown to be similarly constituted by means of the mystification of boundaries. As 'immaterial figures of the mind made flesh', witches break down the mind/body duality that constitutes post-Cartesian identity; like ghosts, or madmen, they straddle categories of being, occupying an unfixed, interstitial space outside categorisation.[40] The polemical writings of Reginald Scot would attack witches, and witchcraft, as *mis*representations, that is, fictions that result from a deliberate blurring of 'real' and 'illusory'. But the early modern theatre – pre-eminent trafficker in fantasy – denies Scot's metaphysical distinctions. Thus in *Macbeth* Shakespeare can fashion witches that serve (not unlike the figurations in *Julius Caesar*) as a meta-commentary on his own function as playwright, and on the function of his industry.

Although their interpretive strategies are different, Philip Armstrong (essay 3) and Jonathan Goldberg (essay 7) both examine the fashioning of theatrical illusion in terms of early modern theories of perspective, in particular, the emergence of Albertian linear perspective. Armstrong argues that developments in optics, mathematics and cartography afforded the early modern subject a new, monocentric position in relation to his world which was, in Lacanian terms, a delusion. The cartographic metaphors of *King Lear* and *Antony and Cleopatra* emblematise the tensions of this new position, as do the physical constraints of the early modern stage. Goldberg, also attentive to the spatial requirements of the early modern stage, would connect the illusions of visual perspective to those of language. In deconstructing the Dover scene from *King Lear*, Goldberg demonstrates how the impossibility of desire can be staged as the impossibility of representation: the mad Lear and the blind Gloucester are each unable to arrive at 'the place of desire', conceived of simultaneously as a physical site and as a metaphysical presence.[41]

For Armstrong and Goldberg, the specularity of Shakespeare's tragedies – that is, the 'ocular recognising' enacted both by the spectators in the theatre and by the figures within the drama – is basic to the theatrical dynamic. Patricia Parker (essay 8) and Peter Stallybrass (essay 9), also concerned with this dynamic, focus in particular on its sexual and erotic dimensions in *Othello*. Stallybrass argues that the stage convention of using boys to impersonate women operates as the specular site of contradictory sexual fixations: on one hand, the audience is asked to envisage the female in terms of prosthetic devices worn by the boy; on the other, in terms of 'essential' features (vagina, breasts) which are absent from the boy's body. In the erotically inflected bedroom scene in which Desdemona is unpinned prior to her murder, *Othello* stages the radical uncertainty of these fetishistic fixations. Parker, focusing on specularity as a structural principle *within* the play, describes Othello's destruction in terms of his obsession to see pruriently, to 'dilate' or expose more fully to view the hidden, sexualised 'chamber' of Desdemona. Othello would 'grossly gape' at what should remain private, what belongs *off*-stage, what may, finally, be too monstrous or unnatural to 'bring to light'.[42]

It is, in fact, the concept of the monstrous in *Othello*, especially as figured by Desdemona, that Parker would herself 'dilate'. By analysing the tropes for gender and race found in early modern medical discourse and in travel narrative (including cartographic illustration), Parker demonstrates that the 'asymmetrical crossings' in *Othello* between domestic and exotic, civil and barbarous, render both Othello and Desdemona as monstrous, but it is Othello's imaginings of 'female hideousness' that the play foregrounds. In her essay on *Titus Andronicus*, Marion Wynne-Davies (essay 10) also finds the 'destructive depersonalisation' of the female to be linked to discourses of race, as well as to current legislative controversies concerning rape and the status of women as property. As in *Othello*, the female is complexly figured, but demonised nonetheless.[43]

Janet Adelman's essay (1) on *Coriolanus* would situate the demonised woman in an explicitly psychoanalytical framework. As the cannibalistic mother who denies nurture to her son yet feeds on the heroic persona her deprivations have generated, Volumnia 'stands at the darkest centre of the play'. Yet because the play stages the impossibility of Coriolanus's effort to construct his manhood according to Volumnia's prescription, in isolation from the female principle, it thereby interrogates sexual polarities themselves – male/female, active/passive. In her Lacanian analysis of *Romeo and Juliet*, Catherine Belsey (essay 2) examines this compulsion to polarise in terms of the post-Cartesian disjunction between mind and body. The lovers would fantasise their bodies as pure sensation, natural organisms independent of nomenclature, but this is their tragedy: 'Romeo is *not* Romeo with another name.' Paradoxically, however, the meanings of the differential signifier (including those inscribed on the bodies of the lovers) cannot be confined. Desire itself is endless because it is 'hollowed out' in the 'unspeakable excess' of language.

According to Karin Coddon (essay 4), the post-Cartesian mind/body duality is also subverted by madness, seen in Hamlet (and in the Earl of Essex) as the 'internalisation of disobedience'. If the subject's identity depends on the tenuous relationship between 'inward and outward adherence to prescriptions of authority', then treason, which collapses this distinction, is akin to madness, and *Hamlet* can be said to enact 'the political-isation of subjectivity'. Moreover, the *theatricalising* of Hamlet's madness/treason precludes its containment, so that the theatre itself participates in 'a larger crisis of authority'.[44] In a Bakhtinian analysis of the same play, Michael D. Bristol (essay 11) also impli-cates the theatre in political subversion, as expressed through *Hamlet*'s carnivalesque valences. One such valence is the 'dooms-day merriment' of the gravedigger, which neutralises the power of death, at least momentarily, by inverting social hierarchies in the recognition of a common humanity. In Bakhtinian terms, this 'corrosive and clarifying' laughter gives voice to a plebian culture that would abolish social inequality and affirm the possibility of social transformation.

Whereas Bristol emphasises the plebian subtext in *Hamlet*, Margreta de Grazia (essay 12) argues that it is precisely the prospect of flattened hierarchies – a heterogeneous *polis* – that *King Lear* represents as threatening. In de Grazia's view, early modern subjectivity is, in fact, defined by property and possession, a concept that is virtually inaccessible to us: 'removing what a person *has* simultaneously takes away what a person *is*'. Unrestrained superfluity – in nature (the storm scene), or in the production and distribution of material goods – is represented in *Lear* as anarchic, even Apocalyptic. Thus, notwithstanding the fates of its protago-nists, the tragedy itself follows conservatively 'the precise course of primogeniture and succession'.

In directing attention to a concept of subjectivity that antedates the ideological framework of capitalism, de Grazia is issuing a caveat to postmodern Shakespeareans that extends beyond *Lear*. Fundamentally, she is challenging what she sees as the tendency to privilege the 'modern' in 'early modern', to make 'the nascent dominant before history does', to analyse Shakespeare's culture in a teleological continuum with our own. de Grazia's comments are apt because the universalising tendency is always a danger in studying the past, even when essentialism has been explicitly rejected: postmodern scholars are themselves as culturally conditioned as the historical subjects they would study, and, as we have seen, face enormous challenges in learning to recognise the unfamiliar. But there is a paradox here too, which is to say that the postmodern scholar, enjoined to study the past synchronically, knows that this past is impossible to access except through a series of analytic filters that necessarily keep it forever at a distance. Knowing this, however, doesn't change anything: the effort must still be made. In this sense it can be said that postmodernism, like desire, continually renews itself in its own impossibility.

NOTES

1. I would like to extend a special thanks to Martin Coyle, General Editor of the New Casebook series, for his excellent and generous advice throughout this project.

2. All of the theorists discussed in the second section of this introduction may be termed 'poststructuralist' in that they have contributed in some way to the dismantling of the conceptual foundation for Ferdinand de Saussure's system of structural linguistics (and of Claude Lévi-Strauss's system of structural anthropology). Nonetheless, I have decided to use the more generic term 'postmodern' throughout this essay to emphasise two points which I take up later: the interdependence of structuralism and poststructuralism, and the relationship between structure and indeterminacy.

3. It is difficult to differentiate Shakespeare's plays by genre; for example, *Richard II* and *Troilus and Cressida* are frequently considered to be tragedies. I have followed prevalent (if arbitrary) critical convention in designating only the following plays as tragedies: *Antony and Cleopatra, Coriolanus, Hamlet, Julius Caesar, King Lear, Macbeth, Othello, Romeo and Juliet, Timon of Athens, Titus Andronicus*. Except for *Timon of Athens*, this collection includes at least one essay on each of these plays.

4. Catherine Belsey, *The Subject of Tragedy: Identity and Difference in Renaissance Drama* (London, 1985), pp. 9–10.

5. Catherine Belsey, *Critical Practice* (London, 1980), p. 97.

6. Michael D. Bristol, *Carnival and Theatre: Plebian Culture and the Structure of Authority in Renaissance England* (London, 1985), p. 112.

7. Mikhail Bakhtin's theory of carnival provides a context for viewing Shakespeare's theatre as a site for masking, misrule, and bodily excess, the features traditionally associated with pre-Lenten carnival. According to Bakhtin, the purpose of carnival is to invert and thereby challenge hegemonic social structures, to give a communal, transgressive voice to disenfranchised classes. As carnivalesque theatre, Shakespeare's tragedies would, then, function subversively to suggest, at least implicitly, that early modern social hierarchies might be radically reconfigured. See *Rabelais and His World*, trans. Helene Iswolsky (Cambridge, MA, 1968). See also Bristol, *Carnival and Theatre*; and Peter Stallybrass and Allon White, *The Politics and Poetics of Transgression* (London, 1986).

8. See Stephen Greenblatt, *Shakespearean Negotiations: The Circulation of Social Energy in Renaissance England* (Oxford, 1988).

9. For recent critical works on Shakespeare's theatre and audience see Ann Jennalie Cook, *The Privileged Playgoers of Shakespeare's London, 1576–1642* (Princeton, NJ, 1981); Andrew Gurr, *Playgoing in Shakespeare's London* (Cambridge, 1986); Jean E. Howard, *The Stage and Social Struggle in Early Modern England* (London and New York, 1994); and Steven Mullaney, *The Place of the Stage: License, Play and Power in Renaissance England* (Chicago, 1987).

10. By using the term 'cultural history', I do not mean to minimise the differences between critical methodologies or between theories of historiography. For detailed examinations of these differences, see Jonathan Dollimore and Alan Sinfield (eds), *Political Shakespeare: Essays in Cultural Materialism*, 2nd edn (Ithaca, NY, and London, 1994); Stephen Greenblatt, *Shakespearean Negotiations: The Circulation of Social Energy in Renaissance England* (Oxford, 1988); Jean E. Howard, 'The New Historicism in Renaissance Studies', *English Literary Renaissance*, 16 (1986), 13–43; and H. Aram Veeser (ed.), *The New Historicism* (New York and London, 1989).

11. Catherine Belsey, *The Subject of Tragedy: Identity and Difference in Renaissance Drama* (London, 1985), p. 2.

12. Jonathan Dollimore, *Radical Tragedy: Religion, Ideology and Power in the Drama of Shakespeare and His Contemporaries* (Chicago, 1984), p. 250.

13. Catherine Belsey, *Subject of Tragedy*, p. 8 (my emphasis).

14. Perhaps the best exemplar (in many senses) of the humanist tradition in Shakespearean criticism is A. C. Bradley, whose *Shakespearean*

Tragedy (Oxford, 1904) became a model for a generation of scholars. Bradley developed a subtle form of characterological analysis based on the essentialist assumption that the conflicts of Shakespeare's tragic protagonists can be best understood in terms of the dictates of 'human nature', especially the moral crises occasioned by the exercise of free will.

15. Dollimore, *Radical Tragedy*, p. 269.

16. Catherine Belsey, *Subject of Tragedy*, p. 5.

17. Michel Foucault, *The Archaeology of Knowledge*, trans. A. M. Sheridan Smith (London, 1974), pp. 11–12, quoted by Dollimore in *Radical Tragedy*, p. 270.

18. See Michel Foucault, *Madness and Civilisation: A History of Insanity in the Age of Reason*, trans. Richard Howard (New York, 1973); *Discipline and Punish: The Birth of the Prison*, trans. Alan Sheridan (New York, 1979); and *The History of Sexuality*, Vol. 1, trans. Robert Hurley (London, 1979).

19. Thomas Laqueur, *Making Sex: Body and Gender from the Greeks to Freud* (Cambridge, MA, and London, 1990).

20. In recent decades, the construction of early modern sexuality has been a major concern of Shakespeareans. See, for example, Jonathan Dollimore, *Sexual Dissonance: Augustine to Wilde, Freud to Foucault* (Oxford, 1991); Jonathan Goldberg, *Sodometries: Renaissance Texts, Modern Sexualities* (Stanford, CA, 1992); and Jonathan Goldberg (ed.), *Queering the Renaissance* (Durham and London, 1994); Stephen Orgel, *Impersonations: The Performance of Gender in Shakespeare's England* (Cambridge, 1996); Bruce R. Smith, *Homosexual Desire in Shakespeare's England: A Cultural Poetics* (Chicago and London, 1991); Valerie Traub, *Desire and Anxiety: Circulations of Sexuality in Shakespearean Drama* (London and New York, 1992); and Susan Zimmerman's edition of essays, *Erotic Politics: Desire on the Renaissance Stage* (London and New York, 1992).

21. Critical studies of early modern societies themselves often reinforce the notion of univocal hegemonies. For example, E. M. W. Tillyard's highly influential works *The Elizabethan World Picture* (London, 1943), and *Shakespeare's History Plays* (London, 1944), purported to describe Shakespeare's milieu (and Shakespeare's plays) in terms of a single, rigidly hierarchalised social and cosmological structure.

22. Recent feminist criticism has, in fact, challenged Laqueur's privileging of Galenic theory, arguing on the basis of a wider range of early modern scientific discourse for other influential concepts of sexual development, and/or for differently inflected interpretations of Galen. See, for example, Janet Adelman, 'Making Defect Perfection:

Shakespeare and the One-Sex Model', in Viviana Comensoli and Anne Russell (eds), *Enacting Gender on the English Renaissance Stage* (Illinois, forthcoming); Heather Dubrow, 'Navel Battles: Interpreting Renaissance Gynecological Manuals', *ANO*, 5, N. S. (1992), 67–71; and Patricia Parker, 'Gender Ideology, Gender Change: The Case of Marie Germain', *Critical Inquiry*, 19 (1993), 337–64. For a reconsideration of Galenic humoral theory in terms of gender issues see Gail Kern Paster, *The Body Embarrassed: Drama and the Disciplines of Shame in Early Modern England* (Ithaca and London, 1993).

23. Catherine Belsey, *Subject of Tragedy*, p. 5.

24. See Ferdinand de Saussure, *Course in General Linguistics*, trans. Wade Baskin (London, 1974).

25. Moreover, contrary to what common sense might dictate, the signified, as an *imagined* presence, is not synonymous with an object in the 'outside world' which antedates the signifier: 'there are not ... two separate orders, the object on the one hand given in its pristine integrity, and a signifier on the other, a transcription of the object, secondary ... the piece of cheese we eat is always already named, with the consequence that its imagined presence independent of the deflecting, deferring, differing signifier is not an option.' See Catherine Belsey, 'Desire in Theory: Freud, Lacan, Derrida', in *Desire: Love Stories in Western Culture* (Oxford, 1994), pp. 64–5.

26. Christopher Norris, *Deconstruction: Theory and Practice*, rev. edn (New York, 1996), p. 2.

27. Ibid., p. 19.

28. Derrida is particularly critical of the privileging of speech, or voice, over writing in Western logocentrism because of the misapprehension that speech is closer to originating thought, to self-presence. In Derrida's system, writing precedes speech in that it foregrounds 'differance', the precondition of all language. See *Of Grammatology*, trans. Gayatra Chakravorty Spivak (Baltimore, 1976); and *The Post-Card: From Socrates to Freud and Beyond*, trans. Alan Bass (Chicago, 1987).

29. Roland Barthes, 'The Death of the Author', in *Image, Music, Text*, trans. Stephen Heath (New York, 1977), pp. 142–8. See also, Michel Foucault, 'What is an Author?' rpt. in *The Critical Tradition: Classic Texts and Contemporary Trends*, ed. David H. Richter (New York, 1989), pp. 978–88.

30. Lacan's theory of desire is, of course, heavily indebted to Freud's theory of sexual development. For the concept of desire as an infinite regression, see especially Freud's 'On the Universal Tendency to Debasement in the Sphere of Love', in *On Sexuality*, ed. Angela Richards (London, 1977), pp. 243–60.

31. '"I identify myself in language, but only by losing myself in it like an object."' See Jacques Lacan, 'Function and Field of Speech and Language', in *Ecrits: A Selection*, trans. Alan Sheridan (New York and London, 1977), p. 86.

32. Catherine Belsey, *Critical Practice* (London, 1980), p. 132.

33. Lacan's 'radical split' includes both the subject's induction into the symbolic order and a pre-linguistic experience (the imaginary) in which the infant (mis)recognises its mirror image as a unit, or coherent entity. The 'mirror stage' enacts an imperfect differentiation of self (infant) from 'other' (image), and at the same time a projected desire for wholeness. After the subject's induction into language, and the split between the conscious and the unconscious, the desire for wholeness represents an effort to *exceed* language – the very condition of human subjectivity. But the differential structure of language (I am not synonymous with my conscious self; I am not you) precludes the subject from ever becoming identical with itself, or with an other. See Jacques Lacan, 'The Signification of the Phallus', *Ecrits: A Selection*, trans. Alan Sheridan (New York and London, 1977), pp. 281–91.

34. In Lacan's system, *jouissance* is the excess or residue in the experience of desire over what can be experienced as pleasure or spoken as language, an excess that guarantees the re-enactment of desire. As concepts of excess deriving from absence or lack, Lacan's *jouissance* seems intimately related to Derrida's 'differance'. Derrida, however, resists such affinities: see especially 'Le Facteur de la verité', in *The Post-Card*, pp. 411–96.

35. Representations of the 'illusion of perfect plenitude' need not, of course, involve romantic love, or even human relationships. In his seminar 'Of the Gaze as *Objet Petit a*' Lacan describes the subject's illusory belief that vision can guarantee knowledge and possession of the world. Lacan's 'gaze' signifies precisely that which eludes or is absent in the subject's vision, including the 'world's' view of the subject herself. See Jacques Lacan, *The Four Fundamental Concepts of Psycho-analysis*, trans. Alan Sheridan (New York and London, 1981), pp. 67–119.

36. Catherine Belsey, 'Prologue: Writing About Desire', in *Desire: Love Stories in Western Culture* (Oxford, 1994), p. 9 (my emphasis).

37. Another problem in Lacanian theory that is a matter of particular concern to postmodern feminists, including, of course, Shakespeareans, is its phallocentrism. Throughout his narrative of the birth of desire, Lacan uses the phallus to signify language and the law (the symbolic order, the Other, the Name-of-the-Father), thereby privileging the male symbol and calling into question the agency of the female subject. In Lacan's system, woman is doubly constrained: first, by language itself

(as is man), and then by the organisation of language and society, at least in patriarchal societies, around the paternal metaphor, or phallus. This is the dilemma – or entrapment – that some feminists would try to circumvent or resist, and others would repudiate. See especially Hélène Cixous, *The Newly Born Woman*, trans. Betsy Wing (Minneapolis, 1986); Luce Irigaray, *Speculum of the Other Woman*, trans. Gillian C. Gill (Ithaca, NY, 1985); and *This Sex Which Is Not One*, trans. Catherine Porter (Ithaca, NY, 1977); and Julia Kristeva, 'About Chinese Women', 'Stabat Mater' and 'Women's Time', in *The Kristeva Reader*, ed. Toril Moi (New York, 1986), pp. 138–59; 160–86; 187–213, respectively.

38. In recent decades, several postmodern Marxist critics have convincingly demonstrated this interdependence. For example, in his influential essay, 'Ideology and Ideological State Apparatuses' (see *Lenin and Philosophy*, trans. B. Brewster [New York, 1971], pp. 127–86), Louis Althusser develops the concept of the 'interpellated subject' in which the Lacanian process of desire is seen to inhere in ideological formations. Fredric Jameson's theory of the 'political unconscious', which is indebted to Althusser's work, also links collective social formations and intersubjective phenomena (see 'Imaginary and Symbolic in Lacan: Marxism, Psychoanalytic Criticism and the Problem of the Subject', in Shoshana Felman (ed.), *Literature and Psychoanalysis: The Question of Reading: Otherwise* [Baltimore, 1982], (pp. 338–95). And in *The Sublime Object of Ideology* (New York and London, 1989), Slavoj Žižek elucidates Lacanian psychoanalytic theory as a '*break* with essentialist logic', a means of grasping 'the radical contingency of the social-historical process' as well as the plurality of ideological formations (p. 5, my emphasis).

39. Catherine Belsey, *Critical Practice* (London, 1980), p. 132.

40. In her essay on *Hamlet*, Karin Coddon discusses madness in a similar context. As a subversion of the mind/body duality, madness cannot be represented on the stage without disrupting a linear model of mimesis.

41. Although Goldberg does not invoke Lacan in his essay, his description of language as constitutive of desire is closely allied to the overtly Lacanian analysis of language in Belsey's 'The Name of the Rose'. Goldberg's essay also connects with Coddon's in their formulations of madness as a symptom of the divided self.

42. Parker implicitly associates theatrical transvestism (at least in terms of its function in *Othello*) with what is *un*natural. Stallybrass's quite different emphasis is on the way in which transvestism suggests a conception of early modern sexuality which challenges the Enlightenment fantasy of teleologically differentiated genders.

43. Wynne-Davies is also concerned with the conundrum by which Rome is represented at the beginning and the end of the play as a headless

female body, thus implicating the female in the failure of monarchal imperialism, at the same time that Lavinia (and Marcus) would seem to contest the excesses of this imperialism. The headless female body might also suggest the absence of a successor during the reign of Elizabeth and thus serve as an oblique criticism of the monarch herself. Patricia Parker takes up a similar issue in discussing the displacement of anxieties about imperial conquest (and about Elizabeth) in Shakespeare's representations of Cleopatra's Egypt and Dido's Carthage; and Philip Armstrong suggests that the new concept of monocentric subjectivity is implicated in perspectives of conquest and commodity that emerged during the reigns of Elizabeth and James.

44. For me, Coddon's essay, which is frequently cited as an example of new historicist criticism, resonates intriguingly with Lacan's 'Desire and the Interpretation of Desire in *Hamlet*' (in *Literature and Psychoanalysis: The Question of Reading: Otherwise*, ed. Shoshana Felman [Baltimore, 1982], pp. 11–52). Lacan speaks of Hamlet's moments of depersonalisation, when 'the imaginary limits between subject and object change' (p. 22), and his identity decomposes. Lacan borrows from Freud's concept of the uncanny (what is manifested as the in-between, what is both familiar and concealed) to elucidate what happens at these moments, invoking the ghost of Hamlet's father as uncanny signifier. Coddon also identifies madness with what exists in the margins, ambiguously, and at one point argues that the disintegration of subjective identity in Hamlet corresponds to the 'airy nothing of ghostly authority', and 'the dream of passion' by the players.

1

Escaping the Matrix: The Construction of Masculinity in *Coriolanus*

JANET ADELMAN

Coriolanus begins in the landscape of maternal deprivation.[1] It was written during a period of rising corn prices and the accompanying fear of famine; in May 1607, 'a great number of common persons' – up to five thousand, Stow tells us in his *Annales* – assembled in various Midlands counties, including Shakespeare's own county of Warwickshire, to protest the acceleration of enclosures and the resulting food shortages.[2] Shakespeare rewrites the popular uprising in Plutarch to make it reflect the contemporary threat: in Plutarch the people riot because the Senate refuses to control usury; in Shakespeare they riot because they are hungry. And if the spectre of a multitude of hungry mouths, ready to rise and demand their own, is the exciting cause of *Coriolanus*, the image of the mother who has not fed her children enough is at its centre. One does not need the help of a psychoanalytic approach to notice that Volumnia is not a nourishing mother. Her attitude toward food is nicely summed up when she rejects Menenius's invitation to a consolatory dinner after Coriolanus's banishment: 'Anger's my meat: I sup upon myself/And so shall starve with feeding' (IV.ii. 50–1). We might suspect her of having been as niggardly in providing food for her son as she is for herself, or rather suspect her of insisting that he too be self-sufficient, that he feed only on his own anger; and indeed, he is apparently fed only valiantness by her ('Thy valiantness was mine, thou suck'st it from me' [III.ii.129]). He certainly has not been fed the milk of human kindness: when Menenius later tells us that 'there is no more mercy in him than there is milk in a male tiger' (V.iv.28–9), he seems to associate Coriolanus's lack of humanity not only with the absence of any nurturing female element in him but also with the absence of mother's milk itself.[3] Volumnia takes some pride in the creation of her son, and when we first meet her, she tells us exactly how she has done it: by sending him to a cruel war at an age when a mother should not be willing to allow a son out of the protective maternal circle for an hour (I.iii.5–15). She elaborates her creation as she imagines herself mother to twelve sons and then kills all but one of them off: 'I had rather had eleven die nobly for their country, than one voluptuously surfeit out of action' (I.iii.24–5). To be noble is to die; to live is to be ignoble and to eat too much.[4] If you are Volumnia's son, the choice is clear.

But the most telling – certainly the most disturbing – revelation of Volumnia's attitude toward feeding comes some twenty lines later, when she is encouraging Virgilia to share her own glee in the thought of Coriolanus's wounds: 'The breasts of Hecuba/When she did suckle Hector, look'd not lovelier/Than Hector's forehead when it spit forth blood/At Grecian sword contemning' (I.iii.40–3). Blood is more beautiful than milk, the wound than the breast, warfare than peaceful feeding. But this image is more disturbing than these easy comparatives suggest. It does not bode well for Coriolanus that the heroic Hector doesn't stand a chance in Volumnia's imagination: he is transformed immediately from infantile feeding mouth to bleeding wound. For the unspoken mediator between breast and wound is the infant's mouth: in this imagistic transformation, to feed is to be wounded; the mouth becomes the wound, the breast the sword. The metaphoric process suggests the psychological fact that is, I think, at the centre of the play: the taking in of food is the primary acknowledgement of one's dependence on the world, and as such, it is the primary token of one's vulnerability. But at the same time as Volumnia's image suggests the vulnerability inherent in feeding, it also suggests a way to fend off that vulnerability. In her image, feeding, incorporating, is transformed into spitting out, an aggressive expelling; the wound once again becomes the mouth that spits 'forth blood/At Grecian sword contemning'. The wound spitting blood thus becomes not a sign of vulnerability but an instrument of attack.

Volumnia's attitudes toward feeding and dependence are echoed perfectly in her son. Coriolanus persistently regards food as poisonous (I.i.177–8, III.i.155–6); the only thing he can imagine nourishing is rebellion (III.i.68–9,116). Among the patricians, only Menenius is associated with the ordinary consumption of food and wine without an allaying drop of Tiber in it, and his distance from Coriolanus can be measured partly by his pathetic conviction that Coriolanus will be malleable – that he will have a 'suppler' soul (V.i.55) – after he has had a full meal. But for Coriolanus, as for his mother, nobility consists precisely in *not* eating: he twice imagines starving himself honourably to death before asking for food, or anything else, from the plebians (II.iii.112–13; III.iii.89–91).[5]

Coriolanus incorporates not only his mother's attitude toward food but also the transformations in mode implicit in her image of Hector. These transformations – from feeding to warfare, from vulnerability to aggressive attack, from incorporation to spitting out – are at the centre of Coriolanus's character and of our responses to him; for the whole of his masculine identity depends on his transformation of his vulnerability into an instrument of attack, as Menenius suggests when he tells us that each of Coriolanus's wounds 'was an enemy's grave' (II.i.154–5). Cominius reports that Coriolanus entered his first battle a sexually indefinite thing, a boy or Amazon (II.ii.91), and found his manhood there: 'When he might act the woman in the scene, /He prov'd best man i'th'field' (II.ii.96–7). The rigid masculinity that Coriolanus finds in war becomes a defence against acknowledgement of his neediness; he nearly succeeds in transforming himself from a vulnerable human creature into a grotesquely invulnerable and isolated thing. His body becomes his armour (I.iii.35, I.iv.24); he himself becomes a weapon 'who sensibly outdares his senseless sword,/And when it bows, stand'st up' (I.iv.53–4), or he becomes the sword itself: 'O me alone! Make you a sword of me!' (I.vi.76). His whole life becomes a kind of phallic exhibitionism, devoted to disproving the possibility that he is vulnerable.[6] In the transformation from oral neediness to phallic aggression, anger becomes his meat as well as his mother's; Volumnia's phrase suggests not only his mode of defending himself against vulnerability but also the source of his anger in the deprivation imposed by his mother. We see the quality of his hunger and its transformation into aggression when, after his expulsion from Rome, he tells Aufidius, 'I have ... /Drawn tuns of blood out of thy country's breast' (IV.v.99–100). Fighting here, as elsewhere in the play, is a poorly concealed substitute for feeding (see, for example, I.ix.10–11; IV.v.191–4, 222–4); and the unsatisfied ravenous attack of the infant on the breast provides the motive force for warfare. The image allows us to understand the ease with which Coriolanus turns his rage toward his own feeding mother, Rome.[7]

Thrust prematurely from dependence on his mother, forced to feed himself on his own anger, Coriolanus refuses to acknowledge any neediness or dependency: for his entire sense of himself depends on his being able to see himself as a self-sufficient creature. The desperation behind his claim to self-sufficiency is revealed by his horror of praise, even the praise of his general.[8] The dependence of his masculinity on warfare in fact makes praise (or flattery, as he must call it) particularly threatening to him on the battlefield: flattery there, where his independence has apparently been triumphant, would imply that he has acted partly to win praise, that he is not self-sufficient after all; it would ultimately imply the undoing of his triumphant masculinity, and the soldier's steel would grow 'soft as the parasite's silk' (I.ix.45). The juxtaposition of soldier's steel and parasite's soft silk suggests both Coriolanus's dilemma and his solution to it: in order to avoid being the soft, dependent, feeding parasite, he has to maintain his rigidity as soldier's steel; that rigidity would be threatened were he to be 'dieted/In praises sauc'd with lies' (I.ix.51–2). (The same fears that underlie Coriolanus's use of this image here are brought home to him by Aufidius's charges at the end of the play: that he broke 'his oath and resolution, like/A twist of rotten silk' [V.vi.95–6]; that he 'whin'd and roar'd away' the victory [V.vi.98]; that he is a 'boy of tears' [V.vi.101].)

The complex of ideas that determines Coriolanus's response to praise also determines the rigidity that makes him so disastrous as a political figure. As he contemptuously asks the people for their voices and later gives up his attempt to pacify them, the language in which he imagines his alternatives reveals the extent to which his unwillingness to ask for the people's approval, like his abhorrence of praise, depends on his attitude toward food: 'Better it is to die, better to starve,/Than crave the hire which first we do deserve' (II.iii.112–13); 'Pent to linger/But with a grain a day, I would not buy/Their mercy at the price of one fair word' (III.iii.89–91). Asking, craving, flattering with fair words are here not only preconditions but also equivalents of eating: to refuse to ask is to starve; but starvation is preferable to asking because asking, like eating, is an acknowledgement of one's weakness, one's dependence on the outside world. 'The price is, to ask it kindly' (II.iii.75), but that is the one price Coriolanus cannot pay. When he must face the prospect of revealing his dependence on the populace by asking for their favour, his whole delicately constructed masculine identity threatens to crumble. In order to ask, a harlot's spirit must possess him; his voice must become as small as that of a eunuch or a virgin minding babies; a beggar's tongue must make motion through his lips (III.ii.111–18). Asking, then, like susceptibility to praise, would undo the process by which he was transformed on the battlefield from boy or woman to man. That he imagines this undoing as a kind of reverse voice change suggests the extent to which his phallic aggressive pose is a defence against collapse into the dependent oral mode of the small boy. And in fact, Coriolanus's own use of language constantly reiterates this defence. Instead of using those linguistic modes that acknowledge dependence, Coriolanus spits out words, using them as weapons. His invective is in the mode of Hector's wound, aggressively spitting forth blood: it is an attempt to deny vulnerability by making the very area of vulnerability into the means of attack.[9]

Coriolanus's abhorrence of praise and flattery, his horror lest the people think that he got his wounds to please them (II.ii.147–50), his insistence that he be given the consulship as a sign of what he is, not as a reward (I.ix.26), his refusal to ask – all are attempts to claim that he is *sui generis*. This attitude finds its logical conclusion in his desperate cry as he sees his mother approaching him at the end:

> I'll never
> Be such a gosling to obey instinct, but stand
> As if a man were author of himself
> And knew no other kin.
> (V.iii.34–7)

The gosling obeys instinct and acknowledges his kinship with mankind;[10] but Coriolanus will attempt to stand alone. (Since his manhood depends exactly on this phallic standing alone, he is particularly susceptible to Aufidius's taunt of 'boy' after he has been such a gosling as to obey instinct.) The relationship between Coriolanus's aggressive pose and his attempts to claim that he is *sui generis* is most dramatically realised in the conquest of Corioli; it is

here that Coriolanus most nearly realises his fantasy of standing as
if a man were author of himself. For the scene at Corioli represents
a glorious transformation of the nightmare of oral vulnerability ('to
th'pot' [I.iv.47], one of his soldiers says as he is swallowed up by
the gates) into a phallic adventure that both assures and demonstrates his independence. Coriolanus's battlecry as he storms the
gates sexualises the scene: 'Come on;/ If you'll stand fast, we'll beat
them to their wives' (I.iv.40–1). But the dramatic action itself
presents the conquest of Corioli as an image not of rape but of
triumphant rebirth: after Coriolanus enters the gates of the city,
he is proclaimed dead; one of his comrades delivers a eulogy firmly
in the past tense ('Thou wast a soldier/Even to Cato's wish'
[I.iv.56–7]); then Coriolanus miraculously re-emerges, covered with
blood (I.vi.22), and is given a new name. For the assault on Corioli
is both a rape and a rebirth: the underlying fantasy is that
intercourse is a literal return to the womb, from which one is
reborn, one's own author.[11] The fantasy of self-authorship is complete when Coriolanus is given his new name, earned by his own
actions.[12]

But despite the boast implicit in his conquest of Corioli,
Coriolanus has not in fact succeeded in separating himself from
his mother; even the very role through which he claims independence was designed by her – as she never tires of pointing out
('My praises made thee first a soldier' [III.ii.108]; 'Thou art my
warrior: / I holp to frame thee' [V.iii.62–3]). In fact, Shakespeare
underlines Volumnia's point by the placement of two central
scenes. In Act I, scene iii, before we have seen Coriolanus himself
as a soldier, we see Volumnia first describe her image of her son
on the battlefield and then enact his role: 'Methinks I see him
stamp thus, and call thus: / "Come on you cowards, you were got
in fear / Though you were born in Rome"' (I.iii.32–4). This marvellous moment suggests not only the ways in which Volumnia
herself lives through her son, but also the extent to which his role
is her creation. For when we see him in the next scene, acting
exactly as his mother had predicted, we are left with the impression that he is merely enacting her enactment of the role that she
has imagined for him.

That Coriolanus is acting under Volumnia's direction even in the
role that seems to ensure his independence of her helps to explain
both his bafflement when she suddenly starts to disapprove of the
role she has created ('I muse my mother / Does not approve me

further' [III.ii.7–8]) and his eventual capitulation to her demand that he shift roles, here and at the end of the play. For his manhood is secure only when he can play the role that she has designed, and play it with her approval.[13] He asks her, 'Why did you wish me milder? Would you have me / False to my nature? Rather say I play / The man I am' (III.ii.14–16). But 'I play the man I am' cuts both ways: in his bafflement, Coriolanus would like to suggest that there is no distance between role and self, but he in fact suggests that he plays at being himself, that his manhood is merely a role. Given that Volumnia has created this dilemma, her answer is unnecessarily cruel, but telling: 'You might have been enough the man you are, / With striving less to be so' (III.ii.19–20). Volumnia is right: it is the intensity and rigidity of Coriolanus's commitment to his masculine role that makes us suspect the intensity of the fears that this role is designed to hide, especially from himself. For the rigidity of the role and the tenuousness of the self that it protects combine to make acknowledged play-acting of any kind terrifying for Coriolanus, as though he can maintain the identity of self and role, and hence his integrity, only by denying that he is able to assume a role. Because he cannot acknowledge the possibility of role playing, Coriolanus must respond to his mother's request that he act a new role as a request that he be someone other than Coriolanus. When he finally agrees to take on the role of humble supplicant, he is sure that he will act badly (III.ii.105–6), and that he will lose his manhood in the process (III.ii.111–23).

The fragility of the entire structure by which Coriolanus maintains his claim to self-sufficient manhood helps to account for the violence of his hatred of the plebeians. For Coriolanus uses the crowd to bolster his own identity: he accuses them of being exactly what he wishes not to be.[14] He does his best to distinguish himself from them by emphasising his aloneness and their status as multitude as the very grounds of their being.[15] Throughout, he associates his manhood with his isolation, so that 'Alone I did it' becomes a sufficient answer to Aufidius's charge that he is a boy. Hence the very status of the plebeians as crowd reassures him that they are not men but dependent and unmanly things, merely children – a point of view that Menenius seems to confirm when he tells the tribunes: 'Your abilities are too infant-like for doing much alone' (II.i.36–7). His most potent image of the crowd is as an appropriately infantile common mouth (III.i.22, 155) disgustingly willing to exhibit its neediness. Coriolanus enters the play identified by the plebeians as the person who is keeping them from eating (I.i.9–10); indeed, one of his main complaints about the plebeians is that they say they are hungry (I.i.204–7). Coriolanus himself has been deprived of food, and he seems to find it outrageous that others should not be. His position here is like that of the older brother who has fought his way into manhood and who is now confronted by an apparently endless group of siblings – 'my sworn brother the people' (II.iii.95), he calls them – who still insist on being fed by mother Rome, and whose insistence on their dependency threatens the pose of self-sufficiency by which his equilibrium is perilously maintained.[16] To disclaim his own hunger, Coriolanus must therefore disclaim his kinship with the crowd; 'I would they were barbarians – as they are, / ... not Romans – as they are not' (III.i.236–7). But the formulation of the disclaimer itself reveals the very tensions that it is designed to assuage. In so far as he wishes the people non-Roman, he acknowledges their Romanness; but this acknowledgement of kinship must immediately be denied by the assertion that they are in fact not Roman. The very insistence on difference reveals the fear of likeness.

But the multitudinous mouth of the crowd is horrifying to Coriolanus not only in so far as it threatens to reveal his own oral neediness to him but also in so far as it makes the nature of his vulnerability uncomfortably precise. In this hungry world, everyone seems in danger of being eaten. The crowd suspects the senators of cannibalistic intentions: 'If the wars eat us not up, they will; and there's all the love they bear us' (I.i.84–5). Since Coriolanus twice dismisses them as ignoble food ('quarry' [I.i.197]; 'fragments' [I.i.221]), their fears seem not entirely without basis. But Coriolanus thinks that, without the awe of the Senate, the crowd would 'feed on one another' (I.i.187). Given their choice, the tribunes would naturally enough prefer that the 'present wars devour' Coriolanus (I.i.257) instead of the populace. The people's belief that the death of Coriolanus would allow them to have corn at their own price (I.i.9) is eventually sustained by the plot, in so far as Coriolanus opposes the giving of corn gratis (III.i.113–17). But at the start of the play, we are not in a position to understand the logic behind their association between killing Coriolanus and an unlimited food supply; and in the context of all the cannibalistic images, the mysterious association seems to point toward a fantasy in which the people, rather than the wars, will devour Coriolanus.[17] Menenius explicates this fantasy:

Men. Pray you, who does the wolf love?
Sic. The lamb.
Men. Ay, to devour him, as the hungry plebeians would the noble
Martius.

(II.i.6–9)

And in the third act, as the people begin to find their teeth and rise
against Coriolanus, his images of them as mouths begin to reveal
not only his contempt for their hunger but also his fear of his own
oral vulnerability, fear of being bitten, digested, pecked at: 'You
being their mouths, why rule you not their teeth?' (III.i.35);
'How shall this bosom multiplied digest/The senate's courtesy?'
(III.i.130–1); 'Thus we debase / The nature of our seats, ... / ... and
bring in / The crows to peck the eagles' (III.i.134–8). The fear of
being eaten that lies just below the surface in these images is made
explicit when Coriolanus tells Aufidius that the people have
'devour'd' all of him but his name (IV.v.77).

The crowd, then, is both dependent, unmanly, contemptible –
and terrifyingly ready to rise up and devour Coriolanus. Through
his portrayal of the crowd, Coriolanus can manage to dismiss the
spectre of his own hunger and insist on his identity as an isolated
and inviolable thing ('a thing / Made by some other deity than
nature' [IV.vi.91–2], as Cominius says). But he cannot dismiss the
danger that exposure to their hunger would bring. His absolute
horror of the prospect of showing his wounds to win the consulship depends partly, I think, on the complex of ideas that stands
behind his characterisation of the crowd. In Plutarch, Coriolanus
shows his wounds; in Shakespeare, the thought is intolerable to
him and, despite many promises that he will, he never does. For
the display of his wounds would reveal his kinship with the plebeians in several ways: by revealing that he has worked for hire
(II.ii.149) as they have (that is, that he and his deeds are not *sui
generis* after all); by revealing that he is vulnerable, as they are;
and by revealing, through the persistent identification of wound
and mouth,[18] that he too has a mouth, that he is a dependent creature. Moreover, the exhibition of his wounds to the crowd is impossible for Coriolanus partly because his identity is sustained by
exhibitionism of another sort. Coriolanus is right in believing that
he must not 'stand naked' (II.ii.137) before the crowd, asking for
their approval; for this standing naked would reverse the sustain-
ing fantasy by which he hoped to 'stand / As if a man were author

of himself' (V.iii.35–6). For the phallic exhibitionism of Coriolanus's life as a soldier has been designed to deny the possibility of kinship with the crowd; it has served to reassure him of his potency and his aggressive independence, and therefore to sustain him against fears of collapse into the dependent mode of infancy. To exhibit the fruits of his soldiership as the emblems not of his self-sufficiency but of his vulnerability and dependence, and to exhibit them precisely to those whose kinship he would most like to deny, would transform his chief means of defence into a proclamation of his weakness: it would threaten to undo the very structure by which he lives. And finally, in so far as he would expose himself as vulnerable and dependent by displaying his wounds, he would invite the oral rage of the crowd to satisfy itself on him. 'If he show us his wounds and tell us his deeds, we are to put our tongues into those wounds and speak for them' (II.iii.5–8), the Third Citizen says; his grotesque image suggests that the sweet licked by the multitudinous tongue (III.i.155–6) would be 'sweet' Coriolanus himself (III.ii.107).[19]

During the first part of the play, Coriolanus uses his opposition to the crowd to define himself and to fend off his vulnerability. But after the exile from Rome, this source of definition fails, and Coriolanus turns toward his old enemy Aufidius to confirm himself. For if Coriolanus has throughout defined himself by opposition, he has defined himself by likeness as well; from the beginning, we have watched him create a mirror image of himself in Aufidius. As soon as he hears that the Volsces are in arms, Coriolanus announces the terms of his relationship with Aufidius: 'I sin in envying his nobility; / And were I anything but what I am, / I would wish me only he' (I.i.229–31). But the noble Aufidius is Coriolanus's own invention, a reflection of his own doubts about what he is, an expression of what he would wish himself to be. Shakespeare takes pains to emphasise the distance between the Aufidius we see and the Aufidius of Coriolanus's imagination. The Aufidius invented by Coriolanus seems designed to reassure Coriolanus of the reality of his own male grandeur by giving him the image of himself; his need to create a man who is his equal is in fact one of the most poignant elements in the play and helps to account for his tragic blindness to his rival's true nature as opportunist and schemer. Immediately after Coriolanus has imagined himself Aufidius, he allows us to see the extent to which he is dependent on Aufidius for his self-definition in a nearly prophetic confession: 'Were half to half the world by th' ears, and he / Upon my party, I'd revolt to make / Only my wars with him' (I.i.232–4). Later, the Coriolanus who shrinks violently from the praise of others eagerly solicits news of Aufidius's opinion of him; and his oddly touching 'Spoke he of me?' (III.i.12) reveals the extent to which he needs to see himself in Aufidius's eyes.[20] As he approaches Antium after the exile, he pauses to reflect on the strangeness of his actions but succeeds only in suggesting that the issue driving him from Rome and toward Aufidius is a 'trick not worth an egg' (IV.iv.21), as though for the moment the fact of his union with Aufidius is more important than the circumstances that drove him to it. His attempt to explain his actions begins and ends with the image of friends 'who twin, as 'twere, in love / Unseparable' (IV.iv.15–16), who 'interjoin their issues' (IV.iv.22). The movement of this soliloquy reveals the fantasy of twinship underlying his relationship with Aufidius both as foe and as friend.

The union with Aufidius is for Coriolanus a union with an alter ego; it represents a flight from the world of Rome and his mother toward a safe male world. Devoured in all but name by Rome (IV.v.77), Coriolanus enters Antium afraid of being eaten: he fears that the Volscian wives will slay him with spits (IV.iv.5) and tells the Third Servingman that he has dwelt 'i'th'city of kites and crows' (IV.v.43), a city of scavengers. (That this city is both the wilderness and Rome itself is suggested by Coriolanus's echo of his earlier peril, the crows who will peck the eagles [III.i.138].) Here, far from Rome, Coriolanus at last allows his hunger and his vulnerability to be felt, and he is given food. He presents himself to Aufidius during a great feast, from which he is initially excluded: 'The feast smells well, but I / Appear not like a guest' (IV.v.5–6). But here in Antium, the play moves toward a fantasy in which nourishment may be safely taken because it is given by a male, by a father-brother-twin rather than a mother. Coriolanus is finally taken into the feast. In the safe haven provided by his mirror image, he will not be devoured; instead, he will eat.[21] Aufidius's servants give us the final development of this fantasy:

> **First Serv.** ... Before Corioles he scotched him and notched him like a carbonado.
> **Second Serv.** And had he been cannibally given, he might have broiled and eaten him too.
>
> (IV.v.191–4)

The scene moves, then, from hunger and the fear of being eaten to an image of Coriolanus triumphantly eating Aufidius. Since his mother will not feed him, Coriolanus will find in Aufidius the only nourishment that can sustain him; and in so far as Aufidius is his alter ego, he, like his mother, will sup on himself.

When Coriolanus is banished from Rome, he responds with an infantile fantasy of omnipotent control: 'I banish you!' (III.iii.123). He then attempts to ensure the reality of his omnipotence by wishing on his enemies exactly what he already knows to be true of them: 'Let every feeble rumour shake your hearts! / ... Have the power still / To banish your defenders' (III.iii.125–8). Few curses have ever been so sure of instantaneous fulfilment. Having thus exercised his rage and assured himself of the magical power of his invective, Coriolanus finally makes his claim to true independence: 'There is a world elsewhere!' (III.iii.135). His encounter with Aufidius is an attempt to create this world, one in his own image; but even the union with Aufidius leads ultimately back to Rome and his mother. For Coriolanus's rage, like his hunger, is properly directed toward his mother; though it is deflected from her and toward the plebeians and Volscians for much of the play, it finally returns to its source. For Rome and his mother are finally one:[22] in exiling Coriolanus, Rome re-enacts the role of the mother who cast him out. Although in his loving farewell his family and friends are wholly distinguished from the beast with many heads, by the time he has returned to Rome they are no more than a poor grain or two that must be consumed in the general fire (V.i.27). (Even in his loving farewell we hear a note of resentment when he consoles his mother by telling her: 'My hazards still have been your solace' [IV.i.28].) As he approaches Rome, the devouring populace becomes indistinguishable from his loving mother. But Menenius has already pointed toward the fantasy that identifies them:

> Now the good gods forbid
> That our renowned Rome, whose gratitude
> Towards her deserved children is enroll'd
> In Jove's own book, like an unnatural dam
> Should now eat up her own!
> (III.i.287–91)

The cannibalistic mother who denies food and yet feeds on the victories of her sweet son stands at the darkest centre of the play, where Coriolanus's oral vulnerability is fully defined. Here, talion law reigns: the feeding infant himself will be devoured; the loving mother becomes the devourer. In this dark world, love itself is primitive and dangerous: both the First Citizen and Menenius suggest that here, to be loved is to be eaten (I.i.84–5; II.i.6–9).[23]

Coriolanus's return to Rome is not ultimately a return to his mother; it is rather a last attempt to escape her love and its consequences. If Coriolanus can make himself a new name, forged in the fires of burning Rome (V.i.14–15), he can construct a new identity independent of his mother: an identity that will demonstrate his indifference to her, his separation from her. For he can stand as author of himself only by destroying his mother. The return to Rome is an act of retaliation against the mother on whom he has been dependent, the mother who has cast him out. But it is at the same time an acting out of the child's fantasy of reversing the roles of parent and child, so that the life of the parent is in the hands of the omnipotent child. The child becomes a god, dispensing life and death (V.iv.24–5): becomes in effect the author of his mother, so that he can finally stand alone.

But Coriolanus can sustain neither his fantasy of self-authorship nor his attempt to realise a godlike omnipotent power. And the failure of both leaves him so unprotected, so utterly devoid of a sense of self that, for the first time in the play, he feels himself surrounded by dangers.[24] The capitulation of his independent selfhood before his mother's onslaught seems to him to require his death, and he embraces that death with a passivity thoroughly uncharacteristic of him:

> O my mother, mother! O!
> You have won a happy victory to Rome;
> But for your son, believe it, O, believe it,
> Most dangerously you have with him prevail'd,
> If not most mortal to him. But let it come.
> (V.iii.185–9)

Volumnia achieves this happy victory partly because she makes the dangers inherent in his defensive system as terrifying as those it is designed to keep at bay. Her last confrontation with her son is so appallingly effective because she invalidates his defences by threatening to enact his most central defensive fantasies, thereby making their consequences inescapable to him.

The very appearance of his mother, coming to beg him for the life of her city and hence for her own life, is an enactment of his attempt to become the author of his mother, his desire to have power over her. He has before found her begging intolerable (III.ii.124–34); when she kneels to him here, making the role reversal of mother and child explicit (V.iii.56), he reacts with an hysteria that suggests that the acting-out of this forbidden wish threatens to dissolve the very structures by which he orders his life:

> What's this?
> Your knees to me? to your corrected son?
> Then let the pebbles on the hungry beach
> Fillip the stars. Then let the mutinous winds
> Strike the proud cedars 'gainst the fiery sun,
> Murd'ring impossibility, to make
> What cannot be, slight work!
>   (V.iii.56–62)

At first sight, this speech seems simply to register Coriolanus's horror at the threat to hierarchy implied by the kneeling of parent to child. But if Coriolanus were responding only – or even mainly – to this threat, we would expect the threatened chaos to be imaged as high bowing to low; this is in fact the image we are given when Volumnia first bows to her son as if – as Coriolanus says – 'Olympus to a molehill should / In supplication nod' (V.iii.30–1). But Coriolanus does not respond to his mother's kneeling with an image of high bowing to low; instead, he responds with two images of low mutinously striking at high. The chaos imaged here is not so much a derivative of his mother's kneeling as of the potential mutiny that her kneeling seems to imply: for her kneeling releases the possibility of his mutiny against her, a mutiny that he has been suppressing all along by his exaggerated deference to her. His response here reveals again the defensive function of his hatred of the mutinous and levelling populace:[25] the violence of his images suggests that his mother's kneeling has forced him to acknowledge his return to Rome as a rising up of the hungry and mutinous forces within himself. With her usual acumen, Volumnia recognises the horror of potential mutiny in Coriolanus's response and chooses exactly this moment to assert, once again, his dependence on her: 'Thou art my warrior' (V.iii.62).

Coriolanus's forbidden wish to have power over his mother was safe as long as it seemed impossible. But now that protective impossibility itself seems murdered, and he is forced to confront the fact that his wish has become a reality. Nor are the hungry and mutinous forces within him content to murder only an abstract 'impossibility': the murderousness of the image is directed ultimately at his mother. And once again, Volumnia makes Coriolanus uncomfortably clear to himself: after she has enacted his terrifying fantasy by kneeling, she makes it impossible for him to believe that her death would be merely an incidental consequence of his plan to burn Rome.[26] For she reveals exactly the extent to which his assault is on both. Her long speech builds to its revelation with magnificent force and logic. She first forces him to see his attack on his country as an attack on a living body by accusing him of coming to tear 'his country's bowels out' (V.iii.103). Next, she identifies that body as their common source of nurture: 'the country, our dear nurse' (V.iii.110). Finally, as she announces her intention to commit suicide, she makes absolute the identification of the country with herself. After she has imagined him treading on his country's ruin (V.iii.116), she warns him:

> Thou shalt no sooner
> March to assault thy country than to tread –
> Trust to't, thou shalt not – on thy mother's womb
> That brought thee to this world.
> (V.iii.122–5)

The ruin on which Coriolanus will tread will be his mother's womb – a warning accompanied by yet another assertion of his dependence on her as she recalls to him the image of himself as a fetus within that womb.

If Coriolanus's mutinous fantasies are no longer impossible, if his mother will indeed die as a result of his actions, then he will have realised his fantasy of living omnipotently without kin, without dependency. In fact this fantasy, his defence throughout, is articulated only here, as he catches sight of his mother (V.iii.34–7), and its expression is the last stand of his claim to independence. Throughout this scene, Volumnia has simultaneously asserted his dependence on her and made the dangers inherent in his defence against that dependence horrifyingly clear; and in the end, it is the combination of her insistence on his dependency and her threat to disown him, to literalise his fantasy of standing alone, that cause him to capitulate. Finally, he cannot 'stand / As if a man were author of himself / And knew no other kin'; he must become a child again, a gosling, and admit his neediness. The presence of his own child, holding Volumnia's hand, strengthens her power over him. For Coriolanus seems to think of his child less as his son than as the embodiment of his own childhood and of the child that remains within him; even when we are first told about the son, he seems more a comment on Coriolanus's childhood than on his fatherhood. The identification of father and child is suggested by Coriolanus's response as he sees wife, mother, and child approaching: 'My wife comes foremost; then the honour'd mould / Wherein this trunk was fram'd, and in her hand / The grandchild to her blood' (V.iii.22–4). Here Coriolanus does not acknowledge the child as his and his wife's: he first imagines himself in his mother's womb and then imagines his child as an extension of his mother. Even Coriolanus's language to Menenius as he earlier denies his family reveals the same fusion of father and son: 'Wife, mother, child, I know not' (V.ii.80), he says, in a phrase that suggestively identifies his own mother as the mother of the child and the child he attempts to deny as himself. Volumnia had once before brought Coriolanus to submission by reminding him of himself as a suckling child (III.ii.129); now virtually her last words enforce his identification with the child that she holds by the hand: 'This fellow had a Volscian to his mother; / His wife is in Corioles, and his child / Like him by chance' (V.iii.178–80). But at the same time that she reminds him of his dependency, she disowns him by disclaiming her parenthood; she exacerbates his sense of himself as a child, and then threatens to leave him – as he thought he wished – alone. And as his fantasy of self-sufficiency threatens to become a reality, it becomes too frightening to sustain. Just as his child entered the scene holding Volumnia's hand, so Coriolanus again becomes a child, holding his mother's hand.

From Janet Adelman, *Suffocating Mothers: Fantasies of Maternal Origin in Shakespeare's Plays: 'Hamlet' to 'The Tempest'* (New York and London, 1992), pp. 131–64.

NOTES

[The original version of this classic psychoanalytical essay was published as '"Anger's My Meat": Feeding, Dependency, and Aggression in *Coriolanus*', in David Bevington and Jay L. Halio (eds), *Shakespeare: Pattern of Excelling Nature* (Cranbury, NJ, 1978). It was reprinted in a slightly revised version in Murray M. Schwartz and Coppélia Kahn (eds), *Representing Shakespeare: New Psychoanalytic Essays* (Baltimore, 1980).

The version reprinted here appears in Janet Adelman's book, although for reasons of space the introductory part of the essay on *Macbeth* has had to be cut. Ed.]

1. This chapter reproduces 'Anger's My Meat: Feeding, Dependency, and Aggression in *Coriolanus*' (in *Representing Shakespeare*, ed. Murray M. Schwartz and Coppélia Kahn [Baltimore, 1980]) unchanged, except for condensation of its opening paragraphs, some minor rearrangements of the notes and deletion of its closing paragraphs. That essay was largely written in 1975–76, when I was just beginning to become interested in feminism and object-relations psychoanalysis; since it was the founding essay for this book, it seemed to me appropriate to leave it unchanged. (Where I have not been able to tolerate the difference that fourteen years has made in my reading of the play, I have registered my objections in square brackets in the notes.) Since 1980, the usefulness of these perspectives for *Coriolanus* has been amply demonstrated in work by Coppélia Kahn (*Man's Estate* [Berkeley, CA 1981], pp. 151–72), Richard Wheeler (*Shakespeare's Development and the Problem Comedies* [Berkeley, CA, 1981], pp. 211–13), Richard P. Wheeler and C. L. Barber (*The Whole Journey: Shakespeare's Power of Development* [Berkeley, CA, 1986], pp. 303–5), Madelon Sprengnether ('Annihilating Intimacy in *Coriolanus*', in *Women in the Middle Ages and the Renaissance*, ed. Mary Beth Rose [Syracuse, NY, 1986], pp. 89–111), and Page Dubois ('A Disturbance of Syntax at the Gates of Rome', *Stanford Literature Review*, 2 [1985], 185–208). (But see also Lisa Lowe's important corrective to all readings that isolate Volumnia as the cause of Coriolanus's impossible position ['"Say I play the man I am": Gender and Politics in *Coriolanus*', *The Kenyon Review*, 8 (1986), 86–95]. In her view, these readings – like object-relations psychoanalysis itself – scapegoat the mother, blaming her for the broader social structures that make it impossible to achieve unambiguous masculine identity; I would answer only that the play, as well as the critics, performs this scapegoating, though I agree with her that it is important to notice its effects.)

2. John Stow, *Annales* (London, 1631), p. 890. See Sidney Shanker, 'Some Clues for *Coriolanus*', *Shakespeare Association Bulletin*, 24 (1949), 209–13; E. C. Pettet, '*Coriolanus* and the Midlands Insurrection of 1607', *Shakespeare Survey*, 3 (1950), 34–42; and Brents Stirling, *The Populace in Shakespeare* (New York, 1949), pp. 126–8, for discussions of this uprising and its political consequences in the play. See Edwin F. Gay, 'The Midland Revolt and the Inquisitions of Depopulation of 1607', *Transactions of the Royal Historical Society*, N. S. 18 (1904), 195–244, for valuable contemporary commentary on the uprising and an analysis of it in comparison with earlier riots of the sixteenth century.

3. Menenius's words point to the rigid and ferocious maleness so prized by Rome. Phyllis Rackin, in an unpublished paper entitled '*Coriolanus*: Shakespeare's Anatomy of *Virtus*' and delivered to the

special session on feminist criticism of Shakespeare at the 1976 meeting of the Modern Language Association, discusses the denial of female values in the play as a consequence of the Roman overvaluation of valour as the chiefest virtue. Rackin's analysis of the ways in which the traditionally female images of food, harvesting, and love are turned to destructive purposes throughout the play is particularly revealing. [This essay has since been published in *Modern Language Studies*, 13 (1983), 68–79.] The ideal Roman woman is in fact one who denies her womanhood, as we see not only in Volumnia but in Coriolanus's chilling and beautiful description of Valeria (V.iii.65–7). (Indeed, Valeria seems to have little place in the intimate gathering of Act V, scene iii; she seems to exist there largely to give Coriolanus an excuse to speak these lines.) The extent to which womanhood is shrunken in Roman values is apparent in the relative unimportance of Coriolanus's wife Virgilia; in her, the female values of kindly nurturing have become little more than a penchant for staying at home, keeping silent,. and weeping. (Given the extreme restrictions of Virgilia's role, one may begin to understand some of the pressures that force a woman to become a Volumnia and live through the creation of her exaggeratedly masculine son. In 'Authoritarian Patterns in Shakespeare's *Coriolanus*', *Literature and Psychology*, 9 [1959], 49, Gordon Ross Smith comments perceptively that, in an authoritarian society, women will either be passive and subservient or will attempt to live out their thwarted ambition via their men.)

4. The association of nobility with abstinence from food – and of the ignoble lower classes with excessive appetite for food, in connection with their traditional role as the embodiment of appetite – was first demonstrated to me by Maurice Charney's impressive catalogue of the food images in the play. See 'The Imagery of Food and Eating in *Coriolanus*', in *Essays in Literary History*, ed. Rudolf Kirk and C. F. Main (New Brunswick, NJ, 1960), pp. 37–54.

5. In fact, Coriolanus frequently imagines his death with a kind of glee, as the badge of his noble self-sufficiency. See, for example, III.ii.1–5, 103–4; V.vi.111–12.

6. [Here and elsewhere in this essay, I would now foreground the extent to which vulnerability and oral neediness are figured as female throughout the play: for Coriolanus, to be a boy is to be a woman, and eating is the sign of this femaleness. The battlefield, where he proves himself specifically not a woman by becoming his sword, is thus the ground of his separation from his mother; it is where he proves that he has no more milk in him than a male tiger and hence that he has not been contaminated by her femaleness. But if he were to feed on praise or on the people's favour, he would become a woman again (an effeminate parasite, a harlot, a virgin minding babies).] The extent to which Coriolanus becomes identified with his phallus is suggested by the

language in which both Menenius and Aufidius portray his death. For both, it represents a kind of castration: 'He's a limb that has but a disease: / Mortal, to cut it off; to cure it, easy' (III.i.293–4): 'You'll rejoice/That he is thus cut off' (V.vi.137–8). For discussions of Coriolanus's phallic identification and its consequences, see Robert J. Stoller, 'Shakespearean Tragedy: *Coriolanus*', *Psychoanalytic Quarterly*, 35 (1966), 263–74, and Emmett Wilson, Jr, 'Coriolanus: The Anxious Bridegroom', *American Imago*, 25 (1968), 224–41. In 'An Interpretation of Shakespeare's *Coriolanus*', *American Imago*, 14 (1957), 407–35, Charles K. Hofling sees Coriolanus as a virtual embodiment of Reich's phallic-narcissistic character. Each of these analysts finds Coriolanus's phallic stance to some extent a defence against passivity (Stoller, pp. 267, 269–70; Wilson, passim; Hofling, pp. 421, 424).

7. David B. Barron sees Coriolanus's oral frustration and his consequent rage as central to his character. See '*Coriolanus*: Portrait of the Artist As Infant', *American Imago*, 19 (1962), 171–93. This essay anticipates mine in some of its conclusions and many of its details of interpretation.

8. Most critics find Coriolanus's abhorrence of praise a symptom of his pride and of his desire to consider himself as self-defined and self-sufficient, hence free from the definitions that society would confer on him. See, for example, A. C. Bradley, 'Coriolanus', reprinted in *Studies in Shakespeare*, ed. Peter Alexander (London, 1964), p. 229; G. Wilson Knight, *The Imperial Theme* (London, 1965), p. 169; Irving Ribner, *Patterns in Shakespearean Tragedy* (London, 1960), p. 190; Norman Rabkin, *Shakespeare and the Common Understanding* (New York, 1967), p. 131; and James L. Calderwood, '*Coriolanus*: Wordless Meanings and Meaningless Words', *Studies in English Literature 1500–1900*, 6 (1966), 218–19.

9. In his discussion of Coriolanus's cathartic vituperation, Kenneth Burke suggests that invective is rooted in the helpless rage of the infant. See '*Coriolanus* – and the Delights of Faction', *Hudson Review*, 19 (1966), 200.

10. [Here again I would foreground gender. The 'mankind' Coriolanus wishes to deny kinship with is specifically female; like Macbeth, Coriolanus wants to imagine himself not born of woman, hence self-authored.]

11. To see Corioli as the mother's womb here may seem grotesque; the idea becomes less grotesque if we remember Volumnia's own identification of country with mother's womb just as Coriolanus is about to attack another city (see discussion elsewhere in this chapter). Wilson ('Coriolanus: The Anxious Bridegroom', pp. 228–9) suggests that the attack on Corioli represents defloration – specifically, that it expresses the equation of coitus with damaging assault and the resultant dread of a retaliatory castration.

12. The force of this new name is partly corroborated by Volumnia, who delights in reminding her son of his dependence on her: she has trouble learning his new name from the start (II.i.173) and eventually associates it with the pride that keeps him from pity for his family (V.iii.170–1). But several critics have argued convincingly that the self-sufficiency implicit in Coriolanus's acquisition of his new name is ironically undercut from the beginning by the fact that naming of any kind is a social act, so that Coriolanus's acceptance of the name conferred on him by Cominius reveals his dependence on external definition just at the moment that he seems most independent. See, for example, Norman Rabkin, *Shakespeare and the Common Understanding* (New York, 1967), pp. 130–2; Lawrence Danson, *Tragic Alphabet: Shakespeare's Drama of Language* (New Haven, CT, 1974), pp. 150–1; and Calderwood, '*Coriolanus*', pp. 219–23. [What Coriolanus wants, I think, is a name conferred on him specifically by men, and through masculine action: a name dissociated from his mother.]

13. Volumnia's place in the creation of her son's role, and the catastrophic results of her disavowal of it here, have been nearly universally recognised. For a particularly perceptive discussion of the consequences for Coriolanus of his mother's shift in attitude, see Derek Traversi, *Shakespeare: The Roman Plays* (Stanford, CA, 1963), pp. 247–54. In an interesting essay, D. W. Harding suggests Shakespeare's preoccupation during this period with the disastrous effects on men of their living out of women's fantasies of manhood. See 'Women's Fantasy of Manhood', *Shakespeare Quarterly*, 20 (1969), 252–3. Psychoanalytically oriented critics see Coriolanus as the embodiment of his mother's masculine strivings, or, more specifically, as her longed-for penis. See, for example, Ralph Berry, 'Sexual Imagery in *Coriolanus*', *Studies in English Literature*, 13 (1973), 302; Hofling, 'An Interpretation', pp. 415–16; Stoller, 'Shakespearean Tragedy', pp. 266–7, 271; and Wilson, '*Coriolanus*', p. 239. Several critics have noticed the importance of acting and the theatrical metaphor in the play. See, for example, William Rosen, *Shakespeare and the Craft of Tragedy* (Cambridge, MA, 1960), pp. 171–3, and Kenneth Muir, *Shakespeare's Tragic Sequence* (London, 1972), pp. 184–5. Harold C. Goddard in *The Meaning of Shakespeare* (Chicago, 1951), pp. 216–17, discusses acting specifically in relation to the role that Volumnia has cast for her son. Berry points to the acting metaphors as a measure of Coriolanus's inner uncertainty and his fear of losing his manhood if he shifts roles (pp. 303–6).

14. Goddard (*The Meaning of Shakespeare*, p. 238), Hofling ('An Interpretation', p. 420), and Smith ('Authoritarian Patterns', p. 46), among others, discuss Coriolanus's characterisation of the crowd as a projection of elements in himself that he wishes to deny, though they do not agree on the precise nature of these elements. Barron associates

Coriolanus's hatred specifically of the people's undisciplined hunger with his need to subdue his own impulses; here, as elsewhere, his argument is very close to my own ('Coriolanus', pp. 174, 180). The uprising of the crowd is in fact presented in terms that suggest the same transformation of hunger into phallic aggression that is central to the character of Coriolanus himself. In Menenius's belly fable, the people are 'th'discontented members, the mutinous parts', and 'the mutinous members' (I.i.110, 148); an audience for whom the mutiny of the specifically sexual member was traditionally one of the signs of the Fall would be prone to hear in Menenius's characterisation a reference to a part other than the great toe (I.i.154). When the first citizen tells Menenius, 'They say poor suitors have strong breaths: they shall know we have strong arms too' (I.i.58–60), his image of importunate mouths suddenly armed in rebellion suggests the source of Coriolanus's rebellion no less than his own.

15. And so does Shakespeare. In Plutarch, Coriolanus is accompanied by a few men both when he enters the gates of Corioli and when he is exiled from Rome. Shakespeare emphasises his isolation by giving him no companions on either occasion. Eugene Waith (*The Herculean Hero* [New York, 1962], p. 124) and Danson (*Tragic Alphabet*, p. 146) emphasise Coriolanus's position as a whole man among fragments.

16. Coriolanus himself is generationally ambiguous: though the populace considers him prime among the fathers who forbid access to food, we see him very much as a son, and he himself seems to regard the patricians as his fathers. His position midway between father and sons suggests the position of an older sibling who has made a protective alliance with the fathers and now fears the unruliness of his younger brothers: instead of fighting to take possession of the undernourishing mother, he will deny that he has any need for food. The likeness of the plebeians to younger siblings was first suggested to me by David Sundelson in conversation.

17. In his suggestive essay on the people's voices in *Coriolanus*, Leonard Tennenhouse notes that 'Coriolanus, the child denied love in the service of patrician ideals, is perceived by the mob as the one who denies. The mysterious source of the cannibalistic rage directed against him is the recognition by the plebeians that he would withhold from them what the patrician mother would withhold from her son – nurturance and thus life itself' ('*Coriolanus*: History and the Crisis of Semantic Order', *Comparative Drama*, 10 [1976], 335). I saw this essay only after the 1978 version of this essay was already published; it and the comments of Zan Marquis in an undergraduate class resulted in my exploration of cannibalism in this paragraph and the next in the 1980 version.

18. See, for example, I.iii.40–3 and II.iii.5–8. Exposed, Coriolanus's wounds would become begging mouths, as Julius Caesar's do (*Julius Caesar*, III.ii.225–6). [In the 1978 version of this essay, I associated

the wounds with castration and hence effeminisation – an association that I rejected in the 1980 version. I now think that rejection was premature: displayed wounds and mouths both seem to me to function as the sign of the female in this play. In constructing the plebeians as all mouth, Coriolanus constructs them as feminised; in displaying his wounds / mouths, he would display himself as similarly feminised.]

19. The Third Citizen's image points also toward the possibility that Coriolanus would be inviting homosexual rape by standing naked before the crowd. Dr Anne Hayman – to whom I am indebted for her many helpful comments on an early version of this essay – has suggested to me in conversation that Coriolanus's fear of his unconscious homosexual desires, especially of a passive feminine kind, is central to his character; she sees his fear of the wish for passive femininity as part of his identification with his mother, who shares the same fear. Her interpretation is to some extent borne out by Coriolanus's relationship with Aufidius, which is presented in decidedly homosexual terms (see, for example, IV.iv.12–16, 22; IV.v.110–19, 123–4); but ultimately – as I argue later in this chapter – that relationship seems to me more an expression of Coriolanus's need for a mirror image of himself than an expression of his homosexual desires.

20. That Coriolanus's identity is at issue in the turning toward Aufidius is made uncomfortably clear by the scene in which he comes to Antium. Despite the servingmen's comic and belated assertions that they had nearly pierced Coriolanus's disguise (IV.v.150–64), they clearly had no inkling of his stature before he revealed himself. Furthermore, Coriolanus's gradual unmasking before Aufidius suggests that he wants to be known as himself before he names himself (IV.v.55–66). The scene is in part a test of the power of Coriolanus's identity to make itself known without external definition; the results are at best ambiguous.

21. [Coriolanus in effect asks the male bond with Aufidius to do the work that should be done by the missing father: to reflect him back to himself whole, and male, and hence enable the process of separation from the mother. His creation of Aufidius as mirroring twin simultaneously protects him from and substitutes for merger with his mother, permitting a safer form of nurturance than any she would allow. I discuss this use of the male bond further in 'Male Bonding in Shakespeare's Comedies', in *Shakespeare's Rough Magic: Renaissance Essays in Honor of C. L. Barber*, ed. Peter Erickson and Coppélia Kahn (Newark, NJ, 1985), esp. pp. 94–5.]

22. Donald A. Stauffer, in *Shakespeare's World of Images* (New York, 1949), p. 252, points out that Rome is less *patria* than *matria* in this

play; he discusses Volumnia as a projection of Rome, particularly in V.iii.Virtually all psychoanalytic critics comment on the identification of Volumnia with Rome; Barron comments specifically that Coriolanus turns the rage of his frustration in nursing toward his own country at the end of the play ('Coriolanus', p. 175).

23. [See Stanley Cavell's powerful meditation on love, cannibalism, failed sacrifice, and theatre in *Coriolanus* (*Disowning Knowledge* [Cambridge, 1987], pp. 143–77.]

24. It is a mark of the extent to which external dangers are for Coriolanus merely a reflection of internal ones that he feels himself in no danger until the collapse of his defensive system. Unlike Coriolanus, we know that he is in danger before its collapse; Aufidius plans to kill him no matter what he does (IV.vii.24–6, 56–7).

25. Participants in the Midlands uprising were commonly called 'levellers', in startling anticipation of the 1640s (see, for example, Stow [*Annales*, p. 890] and Gay ['The Midland Revolt', p. 213, n. 2; p. 214, n. 1; p. 216, n. 3; and p. 242]); Shakespeare presents his uprising in relentlessly vertical terms and plays on fears of levelling when Cominius warns, 'That is the way to lay the city flat, / To bring the roof to the foundation, / And bury all which yet distinctly ranges / In heaps and piles of ruin' (III.i.202–5).

26. Rufus Putney, in 'Coriolanus and His Mother', *Psychoanalytic Quarterly*, 21 (1962), 368–9, 372, finds Coriolanus's inability to deal with his matricidal impulses central to his character; whenever Volumnia threatens him with her death, he capitulates at once.

2

The Name of the Rose in *Romeo and Juliet*

CATHERINE BELSEY

I

Is the human body inside or outside culture? Is it an organism, subject only to nature and independent of history? Or alternatively is it an effect of the signifier, no more than an ensemble of the meanings ascribed to it in different cultures, and thus historically discontinuous? Or, a third possibility, is this question itself reductive, a product of our wish to assign unambiguous causes and straightforward explanations?

When it comes to sexual desire, our culture is dominated by two distinct and largely contradictory models, both metaphysical in their assumption that we can identify what is fundamental in human nature. One metaphysic proposes that sex is a matter of the body, originating in the flesh and motivated by it, however people might deceive themselves with fantasies about romance. The other holds that love is a marriage of true minds, and that sex is (or ought to be) the bodily expression of this ideal relationship. Both models take for granted a dualist account of what it is to be a person, a mind on the one hand, and a body on the other, one of them privileged, the two either in harmony or in conflict. This dualism is associated with the Enlightenment and the moment of its crystallisation is the Cartesian *cogito*.[1]

But in practice desire deconstructs the opposition between mind and body. Evidently it exists at the level of the signifier, as it imagines, fantasises, idealises. Desire generates songs and poetry

46

and stories. Talking about it is pleasurable. At the same time, however, desire palpably inhabits the flesh, and seeks satisfaction there. Desire undoes the dualism common sense seems so often to take for granted.

The human body, we might want to argue in the light of our postmodernity, is subject to the imperatives of nature, but at the same time it does not exist outside culture. It owes to the differentiating symbol its existence as a single unit, with edges, limits. Psychoanalysis adds the presence of the symptom, evident on the body, the mark not of organic disease but of disorder at the level of the signifier, and psychoanalysis identifies the 'talking cure' as the disorder's remedy.[2] Desire, it urges, is an effect of difference, in excess of the reproductive drive. Furthermore, it knows itself as desire to the degree that it reads both the signifying practices of the body and the cultural forms in which desire *makes sense*. It is not possible to isolate the human body as natural organism, even methodologically: such a body would precisely not be human.

Romeo and Juliet is a play about desire. It is also a text poised on the brink of the Enlightenment, and it can be read as engaging with some of these issues, putting forward for examination in the process paradoxes that, for all the historical difference, a postmodern moment can find sympathetic. The bodies of the lovers are inscribed and, crucially, tragically, named. Their own account of love, while it displays a longing to escape the constraints of the symbolic order, reveals in practice precisely the degree to which it is culture that enables love to make sense. In *Romeo and Juliet* desire imagines a metaphysical body that cannot be realised.

II

Though there can be no doubt that Renaissance culture was profoundly and distinctively patriarchal, one sphere in which Shakespeare's women are perfectly equal to men is their capacity for experiencing sexual desire. Venus, Cleopatra, Portia in *The Merchant of Venice*,[3] and, of course, Juliet, are presented as sharing with their near-contemporaries, Alice Arden, the Duchess of Malfi, Beatrice-Joanna and Ford's Annabella, for example, an intensity of passion which is not evidently exceeded by that attributed to the men they love. These women are shown as subjects and agents of their own desire, able to speak of it and to act on the basis of it.

Meanwhile, Thomas Laqueur's *Making Sex* assembles persuasive documentation from the Greeks to the Renaissance of similar assumptions among European analysts of physiology and anatomy. Laqueur finds in this distinct sphere of knowledge, which is also, of course, a distinct discursive genre, what he calls the 'one-sex' model of the human body. The one-sex understanding of the body prevailed, he argues, until modern science redefined women and men as *opposite* and antithetical sexes. In the one-sex body the sexual organs are understood to be similarly distributed among men and women, though externally visible in men and internal in women. Thus the vagina commonly corresponds to the penis, the uterus to the scrotum, and so on. Laqueur is clear about the implications of this account for the understanding of erotic impulses themselves: both sexes were capable of intense sexual pleasure; both sexes experienced desire. Indeed, it was widely held that female pleasure was necessary to conception, and this was consequently seen as an important project of male sexual activity. Desire was not in any sense a masculine prerogative. [...]

In the medical treatises libido had no necessary moral implications: this was a knowledge which set out to record the world it found in the authorities and in experience. The drama, however, makes no attempt at value-free analysis. It cannot avoid showing the implications of the passions it depicts, and consequently it tends, whether incidentally or as its main project, to offer an assessment and evaluation of female desire. But the judgements it makes are by no means univocal or monolithic. As my examples suggest, desire may lead women into bad ways (*Arden of Faversham*, *The Changeling*); it may be radically misdirected (*'Tis Pity She's a Whore*), or innocent in itself but unfortunate in its consequences (*The Duchess of Malfi*); its moral status may be profoundly ambiguous (*Antony and Cleopatra*); it may be seen as lyrical but at the same time absurd (*Venus and Adonis*). But alternatively, desire reciprocated may be the foundation of conjugal marriage and (we are invited to assume) the nuclear family, as it is in Shakespeare's comedies. It was the Enlightenment, according to Laqueur, which insisted on the two-sex model of male and female bodies, the woman's lacking what defined the man's. And it was also the Enlightenment which tended to polarise male erotic activity and female passivity. Not until the nineteenth century was it established as a fact of nature that good women had no sexual feelings at all. The oppositional stereotypes of sexless virgin and voracious whore are not helpful in making sense of the work of Shakespeare and his contemporaries.

III

There was of course a convention, not that women should feel nothing, but that they should appear aloof in order to intensify male desire. This is the convention that Juliet unwittingly breaks when she declares her love at her window, only to be overheard by Romeo. It is quite late in their discussion, however, that she alludes, perhaps rather perfunctorily, to the proprieties of female behaviour: 'Fain would I dwell on form, fain, fain deny / What I have spoke, but farewell compliment!' (*Romeo and Juliet*, II.ii.88–9). The moment for observing the conventions has clearly passed, and propriety itself soon becomes matter for a teasing romantic overture on her part: 'If thou thinkest I am too quickly won, / I'll frown and be perverse, and say thee nay, / So thou wilt woo, but else not for the world' (II.ii.95–7).

At the heart of the play it is Juliet who speaks most eloquently and urgently to define, perhaps on behalf of both lovers, the desire experienced in the secret life of the body:

> Gallop apace, you fiery-footed steeds,
> Towards Phoebus' lodging; such a waggoner
> As Phaeton would whip you to the west,
> And bring in cloudy night immediately.
> (III.ii.1–4)

The opening imperative, in conjunction with the image of the pounding, burning hooves, suggests the speeding pulses and the impatient ardour of desire, as well as its barely controlled power, and the allusion to Phaeton which follows evokes the boy's failure to manage Apollo's unruly horses, and so implies a surrender of what remains of restraint. Juliet's speech is entirely explicit in its invocation of love performed, acted, possessed, and enjoyed. Their wedding night will be 'a winning match / Play'd' between a symmetrically and reciprocally desiring couple 'for a pair of stainless maidenhoods' (ll.12–13). This necessarily clandestine love – perhaps the more thrilling because it is clandestine, because the fear of discovery intensifies the danger and the excitement[4] – is to be enacted in secret, in total darkness, and in silence:

> Spread thy close curtain, love-performing night,
> That [th'] runaways's eyes may wink, and Romeo
> Leap to these arms untalk'd of and unseen!
> Lovers can see to do their amorous rites
> By their own beauties.
>
> (ll.5–9)

The (bed-) curtain of the dark is to exclude all outsiders, and the runaway god of love himself will close his eyes,[5] so that no one sees their union, not even the lovers. If 'see' is a metaphor (l.8), they are to be guided in the performance of their amorous rites by the beauty of each other's bodies. Love, the conceit implies, has no need of light, since its mode of 'seeing' is tactile, sensational. And the syntax here might lead us to suppose that if the lovers are 'unseen' by themselves as well as other people, so too, perhaps, the act is 'untalk'd of' by the lovers, since speech is also superfluous. Indeed, night is invited to obscure even the signifying practices of the virgin body: 'Hood my unmann'd blood, bating [fluttering] in my cheeks, / With thy black mantle' (ll.14–15). It is as if Juliet imagines the presence of the desiring bodies as pure sensation, sightless, speechless organisms in conjunction, flesh on flesh, independent of the signifier. A rose by any other name, she had earlier supposed, would smell as sweet (II.ii.43–4): the same gases, emanating from the same petals, striking the same nostrils, its physical being separable from the word that names it. The name, the signifier, and the symbolic order in its entirety are to be relegated to a secondary position, the place of the merely expressive and instrumental.

But these isolated, unnamed bodies (and roses) are only imaginary. The human body is already inscribed: it has no existence as pure organism, independent of the symbolic order in which desire makes sense. In the sixteenth-century text Juliet's imagined act of love is paradoxically defined in a densely metaphoric and tightly structured instance of signifying practice. The speech depends on invocations repeated with a difference ('Come civil night [...] Come night, come Romeo [...] Come gentle night [ll.10, 17, 20]), framing an elaborate conceit in which the love-performing darkness both is and is not synonymous with Romeo himself, the lover who is ultimately to be perpetuated in little stars (l.22). The text specifies a wish in a tissue of formally ordered allusions, comparisons and puns, which constitute a poem, the zenith of signification, both Ovidian and Petrarchan, self-conscious, artful, and witty. In order to bring before us its imagined bodies, the play here invokes a long poetic and rhetorical tradition, and in the process the lyricism which conjures up the act of love necessarily supplants it too. Moreover, this is a set piece, an epithalamion, though it is spoken, ironically, not by the assembled wedding guests, but by the bride herself, and in solitude.[6] What is enacted within it is desire imagining its fulfilment, and not the event itself, nor even any possible event. Love is inevitably performed within culture, within, indeed, a specific culture: bodies do not exist outside the cultural moment which defines them, and experience cannot be identified beyond the meanings a cultural tradition makes intelligible. What we call a rose might take any other name, but if it were name*less*, outside difference, who is to say that its smell would be 'sweet'? Here too a whole cultural tradition underlies the recognition (re-cognition) of this sweetness – and its association with love.[...] The letter invades the flesh, and the body necessarily inhabits the symbolic. This above all is the source of the tragedy of *Romeo and Juliet*.

Ovid, Petrarch, their names and the word of the Prince ('banished') are all decisive for the protagonists, but the symbolic order is not external to their identities: on the contrary, it is exactly the element in which they subsist. On the other hand, they exceed it too. The body which it defines is not contained by the symbol, and desire seeks to overflow the limits imposed by the differential signifier.

IV

In recognising that the name of the rose is arbitrary, Juliet shows herself a Saussurean *avant la lettre*, but in drawing the inference that Romeo can arbitrarily cease to be a Montague, she simply affirms what her own desire dictates.

> O Romeo, Romeo, wherefore art thou Romeo?
> Deny thy father and refuse thy name;
> Or, if thou wilt not, be but sworn my love,
> And I'll no longer be a Capulet [...]
> 'Tis but thy name that is my enemy;
> Thou art thyself, though not a Montague.
> What's Montague? It is nor hand nor foot,
> Nor arm nor face, [nor any other part]
> Belonging to a man. O, be some other name!
> What's in a name? That which we call a rose

By any other word would smell as sweet;
So Romeo would, were he not Romeo call'd.
Retain that dear perfection which he owes
Without that title. Romeo, doff thy name,
And for thy name, which is no part of thee,
Take all myself.

(II.ii.33–49)

Identity, the speech acknowledges, exists in the symbolic as the
Name of the Father. Juliet imagines a succession of (im)possibilities:
that Romeo should repudiate his father's name, or she hers; that he
should be named differently; and finally that he should simply
remove his name, as if it were extrinsic, separable from identity. In
place of Romeo's name Juliet offers her 'self', implying that beyond
their names, as beyond the name of the rose, the lovers could exist
as unnamed selves. This move to transcend the signifier, however,
the play at once makes clear, is precisely a contradiction. In offering
to take what she urges *literally*, Romeo can only propose punningly
to assume another *name*, to adopt a different location in the
symbolic:

I'll take thee at thy word
Call me but love, and I'll be new baptiz'd:
Henceforth I never will be Romeo.

(ll.49–51)

But the signifier, however arbitrary, is not at the disposal of the
subject. Romeo's name precedes him, makes him a subject, locates
him in the community of Verona. It is not optional. Later Romeo
will offer to excise his murderous name, but he cannot do so
without killing himself:

O, tell me, friar, tell me,
In what vile part of this anatomy
Doth my name lodge? Tell me, that I may sack
The hateful mansion.

(III.iii.105–8)

Unlike hand or foot, Romeo's name is not something that he can
lose and retain his identity, continuing to be the specific, differentiated Romeo that Juliet loves.

Jacques Derrida discusses the relationship between the lovers and
their names in his essay on *Romeo and Juliet*.[7] Lovers are prone to

perceive the imaginary essence of the object of desire, to identify a 'self', a presence which subsists beyond the symbolic order, the 'dear perfection' of the loved one independent of the public and external name. This is the evidence of their idealising passion. A lover who might be expected to know better, the author of Derrida's sequence of postcards, also affirms something of this kind:

> you will never be your name, you never have been, even when, and especially when you have answered to it. The name is made to do without the life of the bearer, and is therefore always somewhat the name of someone dead. One could not live, be there, except by protesting against one's name, by protesting one's non-identity with one's proper name.[8]

Here too, the letter kills, we are invited to suppose, but desire gives life. The name is a trapping, inessential, inherited or given, a reminder that the individual's autonomy is always imaginary, the effect of a place allotted by others, by the family, by a whole culture.

But Derrida's amorous-philosophical text is not naïve (of course!). The name is dead because it is ancestral; it is dead because in differentiating the person that it names, it constitutes a reminder of all the other possible objects of desire, and the arbitrariness that singles out *this* one; and it is dead finally because it stands in for the person it names, and thus supplants the being who elicits so much intensity, intervening between the lover and the loved one. But there is no suggestion that it is possible to do more than protest against the imposed identity, to insist on non-identity with *that*, to refuse the imposition. Though it imagines it in an oxymoron ('I am calling you [...] beyond your name, beyond all names',[9]) the text does not in the end suppose that the person could exist independently, a free-floating essence beyond nomenclature, which is to say beyond difference.

Nor, indeed, is Shakespeare's text naïve. The name of Montague, imposed, ancestral, *is* Juliet's enemy, the text as a whole makes clear. If Romeo's non-identity with his name legitimates their love, the repudiated name returns, nevertheless, to ensure their tragedy. Even though his name is no part of the man Juliet loves, the play at once draws attention to the impossibility of discarding the name which differentiates him. Hearing in the darkness a voice reply to her musings, the shocked Juliet demands, 'What man art thou?'

(l.52), and how else can Romeo indicate who he is but by reference to a name which precisely cannot be specified without identifying an opponent of all Capulets:

> By a name
> I know not how to tell thee who I am.
> My name, dear saint, is hateful to myself,
> Because it is an enemy to thee.
> (II.ii.53–6)

In the event, Juliet recognises his voice, a property of the lover like hand or foot, or any other part, and promptly puts her recognition to the test – by naming him:

> My ears have not yet drunk a hundred words
> Of thy tongue's uttering, yet I know the sound.
> Art thou not Romeo, and a Montague
> (ll.58–60)

The question of names recurs at intervals throughout Derrida's 'Envois' to *The Post Card*. The text is at least in part an engagement with the debate in Western philosophy concerning the question whether proper names have meaning. The answer to this question has implications for our understanding of the relationship between language and the world,[10] and this in turn is the problem Derrida has addressed throughout his work. Proper names imply that words may be no more than substitutes for things, labels for the objects they refer to, without meaning in themselves. What, after all, does 'Smith' mean? If names have no meaning, however, but only reference, what are we to say when the name is Medusa, and the referent does not exist? And is 'Homer' meaningless? Or does 'Homer' precisely *mean* the anonymous author(s) of the *Iliad* and the *Odyssey*, who must have existed, but probably not as Homer? If so, is meaning independent of what goes on in the world, a matter of shared, inherited knowledge, which may be false? Who does Homer's name belong to? To an individual? Or to a culture? What *gives* it its meaning?[11]

The 'Envois' to *The Post Card* consists of a series of love letters to an unnamed person, addressed poste restante 'because of all the families' (p. 45). The epistolary form throws into relief the problems of 'communication', and the story of a passionate clandestine love makes evident how much is at stake in the process of writing.

The secret love letter is a paradigm case of the urgency and the impossibility of meaning as immediate, transparent, individual, exclusive *presence*. All language is subject to what Derrida calls 'the Postal Principle as differential relay' (p. 54). The message is always differed and deferred (differantiated), since the intervals and the distance, the delays and relays, separate the people it was designed to unite. Much of Derrida's love story concerns a critical, definitive, 'true' letter which fails to arrive. Instead it is eventually returned unopened, and remains for ever unread by the addressee, unopened by the sender, though it goes on to haunt the relationship, since its existence cannot be forgotten. This 'dead letter' is at once outside the living love affair and formative for it. In response to Lacan's account of *The Purloined Letter*, Derrida's text insists that the letter never arrives at its destination.

At the same time, *The Post Card* proposes, the letter can never ensure its own secrecy. However cryptic it is, however coded, designed exclusively for the recipient, if the message is intelligible, it is always able to be intercepted, read, misread, reproduced. Since it is necessarily legible for another, who does the letter belong to? To the sender, the addressee, or an apparently irrelevant unspecified third party, representative of the symbolic order in all its (dead) otherness? Their secret love does not belong exclusively to Romeo and Juliet. To the degree that it inhabits the symbolic, to the extent that it is relayed in messages and letters, even when the messages in question are those of the signifying body itself, love is tragically not theirs to control.

Derrida's text refuses to name its object of desire, the secret addressee of the love letters, though it plays with a succession of possible names (Esther, Judith, Bettina [pp. 71–3, 231]). It names others, however, who feature in the itinerary of the lover (Neil Hertz, Hillis, Paul, Jonathan, and Cynthia, and a woman who seems tantalisingly, comically, to be called Metaphysics [p. 197]). It thus keeps the reader guessing, about the identity of the beloved, and about whether the named and apparently non-fictional figures can be ruled out (p. 223). It names the writer, but only (punningly?) as acquiescent, as *j'accepte* ('this will be my signature henceforth [...] it is my name, that *j'accepte*' [p. 26]), leaving in doubt whether the whole story is fictional, or in some disguised and elusive way referential, 'true', and problematising in the process those terms themselves. But though it withholds the name of the loved one, it substitutes a pronoun, 'you': a shifter, certainly, but no less differential for that. The amorous project is to locate the living object of desire beyond the inherited, dead signifier, to invest it with a transcendent existence outside mortality. At the same time, of course, *The Post Card* recognises this impulse as imaginary, 'metaphysical', and perhaps in the process offers another clue – or possibly a red herring – which might lead us to identify the object itself:

> You have always been 'my' metaphysics, the metaphysics of my life, the 'verso' of everything I write (my desire, speech, presence, proximity, law, my heart and soul, everything that I love and that you know before me).
>
> (p. 197)

The beloved is not named, but is not nameless either, for the lover or the world:

> I have not named you while showing you to others. I have never shown you to others with the name they know you by and that I consider only the homonym of the one that I give you, no, I have called you, yourself.
>
> (p. 219)

'Yourself' is not an unmediated self. It is not a name, but at the same time it is not independent of the signifier. And as a shifter, it patently does not belong to the unnamed object of desire.

Romeo and Juliet are not reducible to their proper names, but they are not beyond them either, though in their idealising, transfiguring imagery they repeatedly locate each other outside mortality, in the heavens, among the inauspicious stars, not at their mercy (II.ii.2; 15–22; III.ii.22–5). And their names are not their property: they do not belong to them in the same way as hand or foot, or any other part. As subjects, the lovers aspire both to love and to immortality only by virtue of the differentiating, inherited signifier, which subjects them, in the event, to death itself.

V

What is at issue in the *aubade* is the name of the lark.

> Wilt thou be gone? it is not yet near day.
> It was the nightingale, and not the lark,
> That pierc'd the fearful hollow of thine ear.
>
> (III.v.1–3)

The referential truth is available here, but it is not what matters. The debate is about the significance of the birdsong that the lovers hear, its meaning: not ornithology, but the time of day. The same bird known by any other name would make the same sound, but it would be of no interest unless a culture had already invested the song with the meaning of dawn. It is the lark: Romeo proves it on the evidence of other signifiers:

> Look, love, what envious streaks
> Do lace the severing clouds in yonder east.
> Night's candles are burnt out
> (ll.7–9)

The lark is already inscribed as 'the herald of the morn' (l.6), and while the time of day is also referential, a matter of fact, it too is in question here in its meaning, as the signifier of the moment when Romeo's banishment takes effect, separating, because of their names, the desiring bodies of the lovers. The world of nature, of birdsong and morning, is already invaded by culture, even though it also exceeds it, and the knowledge that it purveys is necessarily at the level of signification.

Juliet's epithalamion is uttered, ironically, in the direct shadow of the Prince's sentence, immediately after it is pronounced (III.i.186–97), but thanks to the Postal Principle she does not yet know it. When the message that Romeo is banished is finally delivered by the Nurse, her account initially obscures the truth, and Juliet believes that Romeo is dead (III.ii.36–70). Juliet's premature lament for Romeo here finds a parallel in the family's lamentations for her apparent death (IV.v). Both are displaced, inappropriate, and yet not wholly irrelevant, since they anticipate the events of the play, as if the signifier lived a life of its own, partly but not entirely independent of the referent. Meanwhile, Friar Lawrence's letter fails to reach its destination and Romeo, in possession of another narrative, the public account relayed by Balthasar, tragically returns to act on Juliet's supposed death.

The Prince speaks the sentence of banishment, but it is to be carried out on Romeo's body, causing either his absence or his death. Romeo's absence is a kind of death for Juliet too, she affirms:

> Some word there was, worser than Tybalt's death,
> That murder'd me; I would forget it fain,

> But O, it presses to my memory
> Like damned guilty deeds to sinners' minds:
> 'Tybalt is dead, and Romeo banished.'
>
> (III.ii.108)

The insistent signifier is determining for the bodies of the lovers, and yet at the same time it is not definitive, in the sense that its implications are not contained by its meaning. '"Romeo is banished": to speak that word, / Is father, mother, Tybalt, Romeo, Juliet, / All slain, all dead' (ll.122–4). The signifier, which differentiates, specifies limits and imposes boundaries, also evokes an unspeakable residue, boundless and unlimited: 'There is no end, no limit, measure, bound, / In that word's death, no words can that woe sound' (ll.125–6). The woe exceeds the word because no word can make it present. Supplanted by the signifier, it exists as an absence hollowed out within the utterance – just as it does within the corresponding signifying practice of the body, the weeping which is to follow (ll.130–1).

In the same way, the signifier cannot exhaust desire, since desire inhabits the residue that exceeds what can be said. Challenged to 'unfold' in speech the happiness of her marriage, Juliet replies:

> Conceit, more rich in matter than in words,
> Brags of his substance, not of ornament;
> They are but beggars that can count their worth,
> But my true love is grown to such excess
> I cannot sum up sum of half my wealth.
>
> (II.vi.30)

Love, Juliet claims, like the unnamed rose or the untalked of act, is more substantial than mere words. For this reason, she continues, its substance cannot be counted, cannot be summed up in words. And she makes the affirmation in an ornamental metaphor, an analogy between love and wealth familiar to us from the *Sonnets* and from Theseus's opening speech in *A Midsummer Night's Dream*. The comparison, which brings the intensity of the love before us, simultaneously has the effect of supplanting it, replacing it by the signifier, so that the speech demonstrates precisely the impossibility it affirms of putting love into words. This excess of love over the signifier is what invests desire with metaphysics, and at the same time, if Derrida is to be believed, the metaphysical with desire. As speaking subjects, we long for the unattainable verso of signifying practice – proximity, certainty, presence, the thing itself. Lovers long to make present the unspeakable residue which constitutes desire.

VI

Shakespeare's play ends with death, the golden statues – and names again. At the beginning of the final scene Paris decorously strews Juliet's tomb with flowers and sweet water, in a gesture appropriate to a man who would have been her bridegroom. He is interrupted by her actual bridegroom, whose intentions, in contrast, are excessive, in every sense of the word: 'savage-wild, / More fierce and more inexorable far / Than empty tigers or the roaring sea' (V.iii.37–9). Alan Dessen makes the point that modern productions commonly include a structure which represents the tomb. This, he argues persuasively, is not necessarily how the scene would have been staged in the 1590s. On the contrary, the tomb might well have been no more than a stage door or a trap door in the stage, and Juliet's body might have been thrust out on a bier at the point when the scene shifts to the inside of the tomb. Including the tomb, as they do, Dessen says, modern productions often leave out Romeo's mattock and crowbar. In consequence, they fail to do full justice to the emblematic contrast the scene sets up between Romeo and Paris, the one sprinkling scented water on the grave, and the other violating the tomb with an iron bar, forcing open what he himself calls this 'womb of death' (1.45).[12] When Romeo, who is beside himself with passion, offers to *strew* the churchyard with the interloper's limbs, the contrast is surely complete.

Explaining his purpose, Romeo 'lies' to Balthasar:

> Why I descend into this bed of death
> Is partly to behold my lady's face,
> But chiefly to take thence from her dead finger
> A precious ring ...
> (1.28)

The lie is also intelligible as a coded truth, a cryptic declaration of a real purpose, not intended to be legible to Balthasar, of re-enacting his clandestine marriage by a second exchange of rings. In the grotesque parody of the wedding night that follows, Romeo seeks a repetition in the tomb of the original darkness, silence, and secrecy invoked so eloquently in Juliet's epithalamion, though once again these amorous rites are to be lit by beauty, as Juliet, who once taught the torches to burn bright (I.v.44), now 'makes / This vault a feasting presence full of light' (V. iii.85–6).

This time, too, the body signifies. There is blood in Juliet's face once more, to the point where Romeo seems almost to read the message it puts out:

> O my love, my wife,
> Death, that hath suck'd the honey of thy breath,
> Hath had no power yet upon thy beauty:
> Thou art not conquer'd, beauty's ensign yet
> Is crimson in thy lips and in thy cheeks,
> And death's pale flag is not advanced there.
> (ll.91–6)

But because his understanding at this moment is constructed in accordance with another narrative, he cannot read the story of Juliet's living body. Again he turns to her, this time with a question: 'Ah, dear Juliet, / Why art thou yet so fair?' (ll.101–2). The audience could have told him the answer (and perhaps did in early productions?). But Romeo, in the light of what he thinks he knows, produces another hypothesis:

> Shall I believe
> That unsubstantial Death is amorous,
> And that the lean abhorred monster keeps
> Thee here in dark to be his paramour?
> (ll.102–5)

The re-enacting of the wedding night remains in consequence imaginary. They die, as Juliet performed their epithalamion, separately. 'These lovers of the night remain', as Kristeva puts it, 'solitary beings.'[13]

Their grave is not, however, a private place. On the contrary, it is the family vault of the Capulets, a memorial, precisely, to the name, which is all that remains of their ancestors, but which lives on to shadow the present so tragically. Moreover, no sooner has he established the close-curtained secrecy of this second wedding night, than Romeo interrupts his address to Juliet to recognise the dead body of Tybalt in its bloody sheet (l.97). Once again Tybalt, who insisted on the importance of Romeo's name and the 'stock and honour' of his own kin (I.v.54, 58, 61), and who for that reason fatally sustained the feud, intervenes between the lovers, as an emblematic third party, representative of the inherited symbolic order in all its dead – and deadly – otherness. Finally, the whole community crowds in, the community which is ultimately responsible for the arbitrary and pointless ancestral quarrel, and which is powerless to reverse the effects of a violence carried on in the names of Montague and Capulet, and enacted on the bodies of the new generation.

VII

Romeo and Juliet are immortalised as signifiers. The promised golden statues are, of course, a metamorphosis, effigies of their bodies, beautiful, precious, and lifeless. Metamorphosis enacts something of the project of desire, arresting, and stabilising the object, fixing it as possession – and supplanting it in the process. Like metaphor, metamorphosis offers an image in place of the thing itself, but the image is precisely *not the same*. Venus is able to hold the flower that Adonis becomes, but the flower is no longer Adonis.[14] The reconciling golden statues appear too late to interrupt the fatal invasion of the signifier into the living organism. Verona will recognise the effigies of Romeo and Juliet, but the effigies will signify concord, not desire.

And yet finally, as is to be expected of signifiers, the lovers are incorporated into a love story, foretold by the Prince, dramatised by Shakespeare. The play closes, appropriately, with their names, which are not synonymous with the lovers themselves, but which are not independent of them either. The play, and the legend of love that the play has become, have been astonishingly popular from the Restoration period on. Even in death, therefore, the record of the lovers' desiring, inscribed bodies is preserved in the archive, filed, appropriately enough, under their names:

> For never was a story of more woe
> Than this of Juliet and her Romeo.
> (V.iii.309–10)

Evidently it was possible, before the dualism of the Enlightenment separated us all neatly into minds and bodies, to identify another relationship between the organism and the culture in which it becomes a human being. *Romeo and Juliet* dramatises the sexual desire which is produced as an effect of the signifier and inscribes the body of the lover. The play also acknowledges the slippage between the signifier and the world it defines and differentiates. But above all, it puts on display the hopeless longing to escape the confines of the signifier, to encounter directly, immediately, the rose that exists beyond its name. And to this extent *Romeo and Juliet* suggests the degree to which the named, differentiated lover is always only a stand-in for something which cannot be embraced, a reminder, as Plato proposes, of 'an ideal that is out of sight, but present in the memory'.[15]

Does the continued popularity of the play, even in a predominantly Enlightenment culture, perhaps suggest a dissatisfaction with the neat Cartesian categories by which we have so diligently struggled to live?

From *The Yearbook of English Studies*, 23 (1993), 126–42.

NOTES

[This essay originally appeared in a slightly longer version in *The Yearbook of English Studies* and is representative of the Lacanian focus of Catherine Belsey's most recent work. See, for example, her *Desire: Love Stories in Western Culture* (Oxford, 1994), which includes an excellent introduction to Lacanian theory. Ed.]

I am grateful to Alan Dessen and Cynthia Dessen for their incisive comments on an earlier version of this essay.

1. The dualism of the Enlightenment differs from Plato's and Augustine's. Both Platonic and medieval souls are immortal and their affiliations are divine. But the Cartesian mind is predominantly secular and human. Nor is its relation to the body always one of superiority. Enlightenment science, paradoxically, had the eventual effect of reversing Descartes' hierarchy.

2. Charles Shepherdson, 'Biology and History: Some Psychoanalytic Aspects of the Writing of Luce Irigaray', *Textual Practice*, 6 (1992), 47–86. I owe to the clarity of that essay the theoretical framework of my argument here.

3. *The Merchant of Venice*, III.ii.108–14. Shakespeare references are to *The Riverside Shakespeare*, ed. G. Blakemore Evans and others (Boston, 1974).

4. Julia Kristeva, *Tales of Love*, trans. Leon S. Roudie (New York, 1987), p. 211.

5. Gary M. McCown, '"Runnawayes Eyes"' and Juliet's Epithalamium', *Shakespeare Quarterly*, 27 (1976), 150–70, pp. 156–65.

6. McCown, 'Runnawayes Eyes', p. 165.

7. 'Aphorism Countertime', *Acts of Literature*, ed. Derek Attridge (New York, 1992), pp. 414–33.

8. Jacques Derrida, *The Post Card: From Socrates to Freud and Beyond*, trans. Alan Bass (Chicago, 1987), p. 39.

9. Derrida, *The Post Card*, p. 130. Compare: 'But it is you I still love, the living one. Beyond everything, beyond your name, your name beyond your name' (p. 144).

10. See J. R. Searle, 'Proper Names and Descriptions', *The Encyclopaedia of Philosophy*, ed. Paul Edwards, 8 vols (London, 1967), VI, 487–91.

11. I am grateful to Andrew Belsey for a discussion of the problem of proper names.

12. Alan C. Dessen, 'Much Virtue in "As"', in *Shakespeare and the Sense of Performance: Essays in the Tradition of Performance Criticism in Honor of Bernard Beckerman*, ed. Marvin and Ruth Thompson (Newark, NJ, 1989), pp. 132–8.

13. Kristeva, *Tales of Love*, p. 216.

14. Catherine Belsey, 'Love as Trompe-l'oeil: Taxonomies of Desire in *Venus and Adonis*', *Shakespeare Quarterly*, 46 (1995), 257–76, p. 261.

15. Kristeva, *Tales of Love*, p. 269.

3

Spheres of Influence: Cartography and the Gaze in Shakespeare's Roman Plays

PHILIP ARMSTRONG

'GIVE ME THE MAP THERE'

From the fifteenth to the seventeenth centuries, a powerful carto-graphic paradigm emerges alongside early modern developments in linear perspective, mathematics and optics. The fundamental princi-ples of this cartography derive from Euclidean geometry and its Ptolemaic applications, as modified by practitioners such as Abraham Ortelius and Gerard Mercator in the Netherlands, and John Dee, John Davis, Richard Hakluyt and Edward Wright in Britain. It is possible to glimpse, inextricably caught up in the devel-opment of this visual and representational economy, one ancestor of that 'modern' subjectivity typified by and reliant upon its occu-pation of a single, fixed and centralised viewpoint.

Jacques Lacan insists that this subjectivity, as manifest in Europe and European-influenced cultures since Descartes and Pascal, constructs an ego which speaks, thinks or sees – these being its most characteristic functions – according to the displace-ments, elisions and distortions of precisely those principles at work in, and derived from, early modern experiments in perspec-tive painting: hence his lengthy discussion of the operation of linear perspective in Holbein's *Ambassadors*, or his repeated

64

exhortations to his listeners to study optics.[1] The subject, situated opposite and fixated upon the vanishing point of the painting (or, I will suggest, the map), functions as 'itself a sort of geometrical point, a point of perspective'.[2] I would argue that the same principles are at work, instituting the same ego according to the same operations, in the dissemination throughout Elizabethan culture of an innovative cartographic idiom, and that this idiom has a critical influence upon the rhetoric and dramaturgy of Shakespearean theatre.

King Lear offers the prime example, peremptorily demanding 'the map there' (*King Lear* I.i.37), and proceeding to reduce the political and phenomenal world to a cartographic representation.[3] Lear translates a land 'with shadowy forests and with champaigns riched, / With plenteous rivers and wide-skirted meads', into a set of geometrical divisions, 'these bounds even from this line to this' (I.i.63–5).[4] The mastery of his gaze over this realm appears explicit in Lear's imperious dissection of the map and, by extension, the kingdom itself. Such scenes actually occurred in Renaissance Europe with increasing frequency, as land was carved up and served out by politicians with no knowledge of the territory outside of its representation on maps and globes: one famous example being the arbitrary line of demarcation drawn by Pope Alexander VI in 1493 to divide Columbus' recently 'discovered' New World between Spain and Portugal.[5]

For Lear, however, it soon becomes apparent that his stable, potent and central symbolic position in this opening scene is illusory, dependent upon an imaginary correlation between his own unified image as king, and its reflection, the unified image of the kingdom. By dividing one, he inadvertently fragments both. Towards the middle of the play, this dehiscence of king and kingdom reaches its climactic expression in Lear's madness and the storm. Interestingly, however, although Lear seems to embrace this double disintegration, he does so in terms that seek to reconstitute the world precisely according to that device of cartographic representation which he employed to perform the initial division:

> thou all-shaking thunder,
> Strike flat the thick rotundity o'th' world,
> Crack nature's moulds, all germens spill at once
> That makes ingrateful man.
> (III.ii.6–9)

Lear demands that the three-dimensional world, with all its wealth of sensory and perceptual composition, be 'struck' flat, like an engraving, text, or map, like an image on a coin, an engraver's mould, or a printer's type. This translation from three dimensions into two would put the phenomenal world, in all its 'thick rotundity' once more under the sway of (his own) sovereign geometrical vision, as it was in the first scene when he unrolled, read, and redrew his map. The three-dimensional here acts as an unsettling irruption, into imaginary and symbolic space, of what Lacan would call the 'real', that which resists representation and disrupts the illusory correlation between ego and ideal image, king and map.

In another famous scene of map reading, Marlowe's Tamburlaine boasts that with his sword as a pen, he will 'reduce' those regions as yet unconquered, the New World, 'to a map', and remarks that 'here at Damascus will I make the point / That shall begin the perpendicular' (*Tamburlaine*, Part One, IV.iv.75–84).[6] The perpendicular or prime meridian, originating at the 'point' from which he surveys the area to be conquered, signifies both his own privileged viewing position and the central vanishing point around which he will reorganise the lines of perspective on the map of his empire. By the end of Part Two, Tamburlaine's imminent death reflects the disintegration of the world he has subjected. 'Give me a map, then let me see how much / Is left for me to conquer all the world' (Part Two, V.iii.123–4). With the same command used by Lear to signify his mastery over the realm and to inaugurate its dissection, the dying Tamburlaine enumerates his conquests, constructing a verbal map of an empire that disintegrates as he speaks. Again, 'symbolic' geography seeks to dom-inate the 'real': Tamburlaine's world map follows the contours of Ortelius' *Theatrum Orbis Terrarum* (1570), faithful even to its errors, inconsistencies and omissions.[7]

Such scenes, therefore, provide more than just powerful allegories of the way in which the phenomenological structures instituted by cartographic representation came to dominate the political perception and treatment of geographical terrain during this period. Maps did not simply influence political decisions or facilitate their coordination. Rather, in a very practical sense, countries, nations and empires – and, implicitly, their inhabitants – *became* maps, and were read and rewritten as such.

'CONSTANT AS THE NORTHERN STAR'

If a chart could be drawn showing the relationships between the various figures involved in the dissemination of maps and mapmaking technology in Shakespeare's England, a central place would be occupied by the work of Gerard Mercator as the most famous exponent of those cartographic innovations which were to revolutionise the shapes of world maps for the next few hundred years. Mercator relied upon and reformed the models and principles of Ptolemy's *Cosmographia*, which provided clear applications of Euclid's geometrical propositions to the drawing of map projections. Ptolemy's procedures involved the cartographer envisaging the globe from a single central viewing position, in which the eye was diametrically opposite to the chosen prime meridian, what Marlowe refers to as the 'point / That shall begin the perpendicular'. The 'thick rotundity' of the globe could then be 'struck flat', as the latitudes and longitudes were stretched out from this spot to produce a two-dimensional representation.

Mercator produced his projection by straightening the meridians – which, on a globe, would meet at either pole – until they extended parallel to one another. Because he was concerned to provide a projection usable by navigators, Mercator also needed to lengthen the meridians, in order to counteract the east–west stretching produced by straightening them. The resulting arrangement – which has been the dominant template for maps of the world until very recently – is remarkable for the increasing distortion of landmasses approaching the polar regions, while the Arctic 'circle' itself actually becomes a strip along the top edge. Mercator's map, moreover, required many further adjustments and calculations before it could be used by navigators. For although directions could now be accurately charted, distances – especially those further from the equator – were wildly inaccurate, so a series of mathematical scales needed to be provided to remedy this fault. The map was eventually modified by Edward Wright, a Cambridge mathematician, and John Davis, a mariner. Their version was published in 1599, along with an account of the latter's voyage to the New World, in Richard Hakluyt's *Principal Navigations ... of the English Nation*.[8] It is here, perhaps, that Shakespeare saw it.

In *Twelfth Night*, Maria remarks that, having fallen in love with Olivia, Malvolio 'does smile his face into more lines than is in the new map with the augmentation of the Indies' (III.ii.74–5). The three most obvious features of Wright's map are highlighted here: the novelty of the Mercator projection, the additions to the western coastline of the Americas, made during Drake's circumnavigation of 1577, and the peculiarly dense network of rhumblines drawn all over the map, fanning out from several compass roses placed at strategic positions around the world.

Rhumblines were drawn on a map in order to facilitate its use by mariners. The navigator, having drawn a line between the ship's position on the map and its intended destination, would find the rhumb parallel to this and, tracing this back to the appropriate compass rose, thereby discover the necessary direction to follow. Wright's 'new map', then, positions the gaze of the reader in several important ways. First, according to the principles of Ptolemy and Mercator, as outlined above, it demands the fixed viewing point characteristic of Renaissance linear perspective. From this spot, the map flattens the world, stretching it out along a grid of latitudes and longitudes reticulated from the central vanishing point located on the prime meridian. The actual central point of the map, the geometrical locus around which the parallels and perpendiculars are organised, remains a blank, located somewhere (or, in effect, nowhere) in the mid Atlantic, indicated on Wright's map only negatively, as the spot from which the middle star of compass rays fans out.

Faced by the nothingness of this vanishing point, the eye of the map reader is pushed inexorably outwards, along the rhumblines – radiating out from the central visual field like the crow's feet spreading out from Malvolio's eye – to the edges of the map. It is, of course, toward these areas – Northeast and Northwest, the West Coast of North America and the Far East, those parts of the map most extravagantly and anamorphically distorted – that the acquisitive eyes of Elizabethan merchants, explorers and colonists were mainly directed at this time, in the search for colonies and trading routes to Cathay and the Spice Islands. Moreover, in following the route taken by Sir Francis Drake – whose voyage of 1577 merits a special descriptive cartouche in the lower left hand corner – the calculating Elizabethan eye would be drawn back to these exaggerated extremities, down through the Straits of Magellan, and northwards to the invitingly unfinished western coastline of North America, culminating there in the suggestive name 'NOVA ALBION'. This point, in turn, becomes the origin for another set of rhumblines, inviting both eye and navigator to wander further still. The exaggerated landmasses produced at the edges of the known world create a centrifugal effect, for which the compass lines radiating out from the centre offer a striking diagram, which cannot but contribute to the desire to conquer, colonise and exploit the new worlds currently being drawn into European maps.

Unsurprisingly, this complicity between political and mercantile opportunism, navigation and cartography pervades many of the metaphors by which Shakespearean characters describe their nation and its relation with the rest of the world. In *King John*, Salisbury's speech performs just such a graphic redrafting of the map of Europe:

> O nation, that thou couldst remove;
> That Neptune's arms who clippeth thee about
> Would bear thee from the knowledge of thyself
> And gripple thee unto a pagan shore.
> (V.ii.33–6)

Salisbury's rhetoric wrestles his nation from its present shameful position and performs a drastic cartographic revision, imagining the British Isles manoeuvred into a new geographical alignment. The underlying nautical metaphor – 'grippled', as a variant of 'grappled' – recalls the expanding maritime activity which in Shakespeare's time was playing such an active role in redrawing political maps: Raleigh's voyage to Virginia, Drake's discoveries, the Spanish Armada. This 'tickling commodity', the 'smooth-faced gentleman' of political and commercial expediency, features earlier in the play in the Bastard's famous speech as 'the bias of the world':

> The world, who of itself is peised well,
> Made to run even upon even ground,
> Till this advantage, this vile-drawing bias,
> This sway of motion, this Commodity,
> Makes it take head from all indifferency,
> From all direction, purpose, course, intent:
> (II.i.574–9)

Two developments in Renaissance cosmography sustain this conceit. A Copernican universe displaces the Ptolemaic centrality of the earth, which can thus 'run' rather than standing still. But at the same time, the relationship between the personified Commodity and a world reduced to a globe the size of the bowling ball, on which 'all direction, purpose, course, intent' have been altered, also reflects the economy of the new cartographic relationship between the reader and the world map, as forged by the likes of Mercator modifying Ptolemy. Simultaneous with the displacement of the medieval religious cosmology, with 'man' at its centre under the gaze of God, comes the installation of the new subject, ruled by commodity, who takes 'his' bearings from an astronomical cosmos centred on the sun, and which places the earth under a powerful gaze of 'his' own.

In terms of the optical mechanics of this process, both the exploring mariner and the surveying cartographer employed the astrolabe (or one of its variants, the quadrant, sextant or octant) in order to fix the observer's position vis-à-vis these stars, according to the height of the sun or the Pole Star above the horizon at the place of observation.[9] An accurate point on the map could be plotted only when the eye was lined up, via the optical instrument, with the astronomical referent. Being hand-held, the accuracy of such measurements depended upon, and in turn consolidated, the fixed gaze of the cartographer or navigator, so that the practices of cartography once again effected the privileging of the monocentric viewpoint. The insistent invocation by Shakespearean figures of these astronomical bodies attests to the construction of a subject position guaranteed – by means of the infallibility of its optical geometry, its cartographic methods and its instruments – in diametric opposition to the constancy of the sun and the Pole Star. Richard II offers only one example of the many Shakespearean rulers who repeatedly designate their sovereignty through reference to the sun (*Richard II*, III.ii.32–49, III.iii.61–6), while Julius Caesar famously defines himself as being

> constant as the Northern Star,
> Of whose true fixed and resting quality
> There is no fellow in the firmament.
> The skies are painted with unnumbered sparks;
> They are all fire, and every one doth shine;
> But there's but one in all doth hold his place.
> So in the world;'tis furnished well with men,
> And men are flesh and blood, and apprehensive;
> Yet in the number I do know but one
> That unassailable holds on his rank,
> Unshaked of motion:
> (*Julius Caesar*, III.i.60–70)

'I am he', Caesar concludes, exemplifying an emergent subjectivity, almost invariably associated in Shakespearean drama with the 'great man', whose reference to the field of geometrical optical space both guarantees and represents his pre-eminent position in the symbolic realm, the world of politics, society, and knowledge.

This speech, of course, proves to be Caesar's last. It directly precedes and even provokes his assassination. Richard II, similarly, is deposed, melting away before 'the sun of Bolingbroke' (IV.i.251). In fact, wherever it appears in Shakespearean drama, this guaranteed stability granted by the privileged central viewing position in the scopic economy will prove to be both illusory and liable to dissolution.

Jacques Lacan has emphasised precisely this instability of the centralised mastery of the post-Renaissance subject in his discussion of the gaze. 'I see only from one point, but in my existence I am looked at from all sides' he remarks. The gaze 'is presented to us only in the form of a strange contingency, symbolic of what we find on the horizon'.[10] What the Elizabethan subject of cartography finds on the horizon, at the edges and the limits of its maps, threatens the organisation of that subject's own position. The distortion on the margins of what we might call this Elizabethan 'world picture' reveals the means of its construction and, implicitly, the 'strange contingency' of the centralised viewing position upon which it depends. This skewed perspective from the frame of the map thereby operates in the same way as Lacan's description of the anamorphosis in Holbein's *Ambassadors*, which decomposes the site of privileged vision by demanding from the spectator an ex-centric viewing position:

> All this shows that at the very heart of the period in which the subject emerged and geometral optics was an object of research, Holbein makes visible for us here something that is simply the subject as annihilated. ...
> For us, the geometral dimension enables us to glimpse how the subject who concerns us is caught, manipulated, captured, in the field of vision.[11]

Lacan identifies the emergence of anamorphoses in the development of the geometrical optical principles that produce both Albertian perspective painting and those maps based on Mercator's projection. These anamorphoses appear in pictorial art as grotesquely elongated shapes which only become legible from an oblique perspective, an alternative viewing position to that of the centralised spectator. They are thereby symptomatic of the limits of the optical economy being instituted, and of the inherent failure of that system to guarantee the place of the subject within it. Within the 'systematic establishment of the geometrical laws of perspective formulated at the end of the fifteenth and the beginning of the sixteenth centuries', Lacan remarks, the appearance of anamorphosis represents 'a sensitive spot, a lesion, a locus of pain, a point of reversal of the whole of history'.[12]

Elsewhere I have discussed the manifestation of this 'locus of pain' in the Dover cliff scene from *King Lear* (F IV.v).[13] In that scene, the displacement of the central viewing position emerges by means of the reversed line of sight which Edgar directs upwards from the foot of the cliff, once Gloucester has (supposedly) fallen through the vanishing point of the linear perspective Edgar had previously described from above. The imaginary Dover Cliff offers (as elsewhere in Shakespearean drama) a symbolic location to mark the farthest limit, the end of Lear's Britain. This representative function again links this scene to the role played by the distorted edges of the Elizabethan map, in which the enlargement of the Northern and Southern landmasses betrays the means employed in the construction of the map, and the political and commercial interests invested in it. In both cases, from the symbolic limits of a geographic entity (Lear's Britain, Wright's world), an anamorphic perspective returns to displace the pictorial or cartographic economy and the viewing subject's secure place within it.

'DEMI-ATLAS OF THE EARTH'

Two-dimensional maps were not the only product of the new cartography. The sixteenth and seventeenth centuries also saw modifications, and a widespread proliferation, in the creation and sale of spherical models of the earth, so that Hakluyt could draw a distinction in 1589 between 'the olde imperfectly composed, and the new lately reformed Mappes, Globes, Spheares, and other instruments of this Art ...'.[14]

Model globes, unlike two-dimensional maps, were of little practical use for the charting of exploratory or colonial ventures. Even more than the flat maps, however, they did possess a particular iconographic potency, as witnessed by the ubiquity of globes or orbs in contemporary royal portraiture. The 'Armada' portrait of Elizabeth I offers one famous example among many, in which 'a globe is tipped at an angle towards the viewer, and its meaning is derived from the central figure of the Queen, whose imperial hand extends to grasp the whole world'.[15] Not only monarchs, but politicians of all ranks and nationalities invested in the visual capital of the globe. Returning to Holbein's *Ambassadors*, painted in London in 1533, we might note that both terrestrial and celestial globes lie among the range of objects, symbolic of the Renaissance sciences and arts, furnishing the background to the figures of Jean de Dinteville and Georges de Selve.

However, the augmented emblematic power of the model globe contributes to the iconography of this incipient subjectivity in other ways as well. If the two-dimensional map – along with the astronomical, navigational and geometrical techniques required to produce and use it – situates its viewer in a centralised and exalted locus of optical mastery, a comparable metaphorical effect results from the visual contrast in any picture of the world reduced to the dimensions of a model globe alongside an enlarged human figure. The erect and frozen figures of Elizabeth or the Ambassadors ('stiffened in their showy adornments', as Lacan describes them) are granted, by these portraits, a representational and spatial dominance inversely proportional to their relationship with a shrunken world.[16] The globe thereby appears manipulable, within the reach and grasp of the human subject, reduced to the status of an object of learning, a commodity for possession, or a territory inviting political rule.

Shakespeare's Julius Caesar has already provided one instance of the exaltation of the subject within a geometrical and cartographic economy. He also exemplifies the appearance, in the metaphorical vocabulary of the plays, of this emblematic contrast between a diminished globe and an augmented human figure. Cassius, complaining to Brutus of the emergence of a new, imperial political idiom represented by the rise of Caesar, remarks,

> Why, man, he doth bestride the narrow world
> Like a colossus, and we petty men
> Walk under his huge legs and peep about
> To find ourselves dishonourable graves.
> (I.ii.136–9)

The attenuated gaze of the 'petty men' who 'peep about' also offers a contrast with the heightened omnivoyance of the giant, surveying a world contracted into a map or globe beneath his feet.[17] This shortsightedness, of course, will indeed bring Cassius to his 'dishonourable grave', for he kills himself after mistaking Titinius' victory for defeat. The text explicitly attributes this error to Cassius' myopia ('my sight was ever thick'), which he fails to redress by urging Pindarus to 'get higher on that hill', a vain attempt to approach the panoramic visual mastery of the colossus (V.iii.20–1). Increased stature, implementing a perspective from above, brings its own optical advantages, which – as Cassius' death proves – could prove strategically critical.

The contrast between a shrunken or 'narrow' world and the figure of the colossus astride it recurs throughout another of the Roman plays. *Antony and Cleopatra* repeatedly figures Caesar's protégé according to an identical conceit. At the beginning of the play Antony shares this exalted position with Octavius and Lepidus, as 'triple pillar of the world' (I.i.12). His first speech makes explicit the contrast between 'the dungy earth', in which 'Kingdoms are clay', and the dimensions of his own body or ego: 'Here is my space'. His self-aggrandisement, according to which he will 'stand up peerless', corresponds with his contraction of the world to a fragile construct: 'Let Rome in Tiber melt, and the wide arch / Of the ranged empire fall' (I.i.35–42). The gradual diminution of the status of Lepidus will reduce the triumvirate to a rivalry between the remaining two, so that a few scenes later Antony can be considered 'the demi-Atlas of the earth' (I.v.23).

This word 'Atlas' was, in Shakespeare's time, increasingly becoming associated with the cartographic representation of the earth. According to Lloyd Brown, the first widely distributed map collection to use the word in its title was Mercator's *Atlas sive Cosmographicae meditationes ...*, of which the first part was published in 1595.

> A genealogical tree in the introductory text gave the ancestry of Atlas, the mythological character who led the Titans in their war against the god Jupiter, and was therefore condemned to support the heavens on his shoulders.[18]

José Rabasa, however, offers an alternative explanation for the use of the name in connection with cartography, claiming that 'Mercator first coined the name Atlas after the mythical King of

Libya "who was supposed to have made the first celestial sphere"'.[19]
Both suggestions are consistent with our discussion so far of the
Shakespearean (and more widespread Renaissance) employment of
the emblematic relation between world and subject: that of a titan
whose vast dimensions enable him to hold the weight of the celestial dome, and that of a king who reduces the cosmos to a model.

Ultimately, Antony stands alone as a figure of colossal proportions, independent of his rival, in a metaphor which echoes and develops that used in the earlier play to describe his patron Julius
Caesar. Cleopatra describes her dream of 'an Emperor Antony':

> His face was as the heav'ns, and therein stuck
> A sun and moon, which kept their course and lighted
> The little O o'th'earth ...
> His legs bestrid the ocean; his reared arm
> Crested the world. His voice was propertied
> As all the tuned spheres, and that to friends;
> But when he meant to quail and shake the orb,
> He was as rattling thunder. For his bounty,
> There was no winter in't; an autumn'twas,
> That grew the more by reaping. His delights
> Were dolphin-like; they showed his back above
> The element they lived in. In his livery
> Walked crowns and crownets. Realms and islands were
> As plates dropped from his pocket.
>
> (V.ii.78–91)

This passage combines in one extended conceit the metaphorical
usages of all the cartographic optical structures discussed so far.
The world is reduced to a representation, either an orb which
shakes at the mere sound of Antony's voice, or the two-dimensional
map of a 'little O' drawn on paper. Antony, in contrast, has
attained the stature of a giant, straddling the ocean, with his
acquisitive grasp on the world signified by the reduction of its
component 'realms and islands' to 'plates', a word denoting both
appetite and silver coin. His gaze, like that of the cartographer
and the navigator, is fixed in reference to the celestial bodies, 'a
sun and moon' shining in the 'heavens' of his face. At such
moments, along with the cartographical shrinking and mastering
of the world, there emerges a corresponding increase in the stature
of 'man': the beginning, according to Lacan, of the ego's era,
which will facilitate and collude with the acceleration of imperialism and capitalism.

Yet in every case, along with the metaphors which elevate its protagonist to the stature of a colossus, Shakespeare's plays provide
accompanying images of that figure's deflation. Richard II, for instance, exchanges his 'large kingdom for a little grave' (*Richard II*,
III.iii.152); Hal remarks of Hotspur's death, 'ill-weaved ambition,
how much art thou shrunk!', adding that 'two paces of the vilest
earth / Is room enough' to contain the body of his defeated rival
(*1 Henry IV*, V.iv.87–91). Antony repeats this reaction as he stands
over Julius Caesar's corpse:

> O mighty Caesar! Dost thou lie so low?
> Are all thy conquests, glories, triumphs, spoils,
> Shrunk to this little measure?
> (*Julius Caesar*, III.i.149–51)

Antony's own fall from the political summit figures in more elaborate terms. His status, as 'The triple pillar of the world transformed
/ Into a strumpet's fool', appears ambiguous from the first few lines
of the play (*Antony and Cleopatra*, I.i.12–13). Not long after the
scene related by Octavius, in which Antony and Cleopatra publicly
map their empire by listing its dominions (III.vi.3–16), Antony's
defeats, rather than his achievements, begin to take on colossal proportions:

> The greater cantle of the world is lost
> With very ignorance; we have kissed away
> Kingdoms and provinces.
> (III.x.6–8)

At this point, his mastery of a submissive globe seems so uncertain
that 'the land bids me tread no more upon't, / It is ashamed to bear
me' (III.xi.1–2).

However, Antony expresses the evanescence of this egomorphic
gigantism most explicitly in his dialogue with Eros after the next
battle against Octavius, describing his dissolution into nothing from
a figure of gigantic visibility, a cynosure. Like a cloud in the shape
of 'A towered citadel, or blue promontory', Antony's imperial
image, which had seemed to loom over the earth, has evaporated,
becoming 'indistinct / As water is in water' (IV.xv.2–14). He de-
clines from an Atlas figure with the entire world in his grasp to one
who cannot even contain his own body: 'Here I am Antony, / Yet
cannot hold this visible shape' (ll.13–14). As he makes this speech,

in the BBC version of the play, Antony discards his armour, displaying to the audience the dramatic equivalent of a decomposing body, shedding its aspect of armed and statuesque potency.

The same contrast between the contained or self-sufficient ego, and its dissolution, structures the dominant idiom of another Roman play, *Coriolanus*. Caius Martius' political pre-eminence depends upon his capacity to integrate the civic collectivity into his own colossal stature, but his contempt for the public works against this process, nearly provoking the citizens into a dangerous realisation of their individuality, figured once more in explicitly cartographic terms:

> **Second Citizen** ... truly I think if all our wits were to issue out of one skull, they would fly east, west, north, south, and their consent of one direct way should be all at one to all the points o'th' compass.
>
> (II.iii.21–4)

Incapable of contracting this 'many-headed multitude' into a single frame, Coriolanus becomes the last of the figures from the Roman plays to attempt the assumption of colossal stature, and to suffer its subsequent disintegration. In his arrogance, he offers a particularly characteristic figure of one elevated (in his own eyes as well as others') to an exaggerated and tenuous mastery over a diminished world – 'The man is noble, and his fame folds in / This orb o'th' earth' (V.vi.124–5) – claiming the right to assert his supremacy over the people, even if they threaten to execute him:

> ... pile ten hills on the Tarpeian rock,
> That the precipitation might down stretch
> Below the beam of sight; yet will I still
> Be thus to them.
>
> (III.ii.1–6)

This passage participates in the same Albertian pictorial principles as Edgar's Dover cliff speech in *Lear*: a vertiginous perspectivism that proves liable to decomposition. Looking down upon the citizenry from his position of self-assured superiority, Coriolanus, like the other figures discussed so far, embodies the exorbitant stature and panoramic vision of the colossus. Here, the prospect of Coriolanus' fall from the extravagantly multiplied altitude of the Tarpeian Rock into a vanishing point 'below the beam of sight' represents the threat of collapse implicit within this structure.

'ACTS COMMENCED ON THIS BALL OF EARTH'

The anthropomorphic projections of the 'ego's era', therefore, result in what Lacan describes as the 'hominisation of the world, its perception in terms of images linked to the structuration of the body'.[20] Teresa Brennan points out that this perceptual and representational transaction takes as its ideal, specifically, the male body and its conventional association with activity. This ego produces, as its object, an inert, submissive body. In one sense, psychoanalysis can be read as the exploration of this dialectic, whereby masculinity and femininity respectively affiliate with one of the two poles of this activity–passivity opposition. Cartography collaborates in this version of gender in so far as it subjugates the geographical contours of the land under the rubrics of a two-dimensional projection or a spherical model, 'passifying' the world beneath the geometrical net cast from an erect and masterful gaze.[21] Lacan, moreover, describes this 'symbolic system' as a 'conquest, rape of nature, transformation of nature, hominisation of the planet', again implying the forcing of a passive femininity by an active masculinity.[22]

In another manifestation of this masculine gaze, *Antony and Cleopatra* provides, before the audience sees her for itself, a description of the heroine which superimposes her figure over the contours of the Egypt she rules, translating both into a text or a panorama, supine beneath the traversing eye of the male reader. 'Would I had never seen her!', remarks Antony, to which Enobarbus replies, 'O, sir, you had then left unseen a wonderful piece of work, which not to have been blessed withal would have discredited your travel' (I.ii.137–47).

The mention of 'travel' serves to contextualise the surveying gaze under discussion within a contemporary culture of sightseeing. References to Elizabethan and Jacobean travellers provide evidence that the emergence of the cartographic economy, and the subjectivity it heralds, although modelled upon the privileged view of the sovereign and the explorer, was not confined only to the monarchy and its immediate circle. A considerable number of Shakespeare's audience must have had some experience, if not of actual touring, then of maps or travellers' descriptions representing various parts of the known world. Shakespearean drama, with its ubiquity of geographical references, confirms its spectators in the positions prescribed for them by the cartographic economy: not only through

the rhetorical and theatrical representation of the spatial developments involved, but in the actual encounter that takes place
between audience and stage. It does so, however, in a thoroughly
conflicted way.

In the first place, the theatre itself offers a manifestation of the reduction of the world to a model for consumption by the spectator.
The emblematic figure of Rumour invokes this role of the stage in
the prologue to *II Henry IV*: 'I from the orient to the drooping
west, / ... still unfold / The acts commenced on this ball of earth'
(Induction, 3–5). The world and its histories can be folded and
unfolded like a map, diminished to the size of a ball, the object of
(a) play, while 'acts' of global significance become equivalent in
scope to those performed on the stage. It is hardly necessary, in this
connection, to recall the name of the theatre built by Shakespeare's
company in 1599. The titles of a number of contemporary atlases
and map collections may offer a less familiar correlation between
stage and cartography, from the *Theatrum Orbis Terrarum* of
Abraham Ortelius (1570 and later editions), to Speed's *Theatre of
the Empire of Great Britain* (1611).

However, the prologues of the plays often seem less than
confident in their ability to contain the world within the frame of
the stage. In the Prologue to *Henry V*, the Chorus expresses more
obvious reservations about the translation of world into theatre
when it wishes for

> A kingdom for a stage, princes to act,
> And monarchs to behold the swelling scene.
>   ... But pardon, gentles all,
> The flat unraised spirits that hath dared
> On this unworthy scaffold to bring forth
> So great an object. Can this cock-pit hold
> The vasty fields of France? Or may we cram
> Within this wooden O the very casques
> That did affright the air at Agincourt?
> O pardon: since a crooked figure may
> Attest in little place a million,
> So let us, ciphers to this great account,
> On your imaginary forces work.
> Suppose within the girdle of these walls
> Are now confined two mighty monarchies,
> Whose high upreared and abutting fronts
> The perilous narrow ocean parts asunder.
>   (ll.1–22)

This passage opens the play with an overt delineation of the geographical relationship between England and France, reliant – like the other Shakespearean charts of the nation discussed so far – on a correlation between the land and a 'girdled' female body, protected by inviolable boundaries, as exemplified by the habitual references to precipitous coastlines and an encircling sea. We can also recognise the precariousness of the demarcation between the nation and its others, sundered by an ocean both 'perilous' and 'narrow'.

The evocation of this familiar chorography, and its theatrical efficacy, depend upon the same 'imaginary forces' operating among the audience that contemporary writers describe at work in the 'closet travel' or vicarious sightseeing of Elizabethan readers poring over maps in their studies. But in drama, by contrast, the surveying eye produced by such a cartographic imagination operates communally, not in isolation. For the institution of a single spectatorial eye plainly conflicts with the actual conditions of Elizabethan and Jacobean public theatre, in which the relationship between audience and stage was dispersed, interactive, dialogic, and communal.[23] The 'wooden O' of the Shakespearean theatre could not actually play to a single, fixed or privileged spectatorial position. On the contrary, the round auditorium instituted a circular array of viewpoints which crossed and recrossed the stage, according to the conflicting perspectives elicited by the play. The Prologue hints at this conflict between a single privileged gaze and the multiple eyes of the public theatre when it expresses the desire for 'monarchs to behold the swelling scene'. In order to achieve the perfect illusion of three-dimensional cartographic perspective, so that a 'kingdom' may be equated with a 'stage' and 'princes' with actors, the drama needs to play to the monocentric viewpoint of the sovereign eye, as typified by the seat of the monarch watching a court masque.[24] In its failure to isolate in the audience such a privileged gaze, the stage degenerates into what the Prologue calls a 'flat unraised' representation, with the same two-dimensional limits and anamorphic distortions as a map or painting.

What, we might ask, would the successful establishment of this singular viewing position involve? For one thing, the repression of the vestigial medieval theatrical relationship between audience and stage, and the historical foreclosure of the gaze, in so far as it constitutes a multiplicity of perspectives, or a return of the line of sight upon the spectator from the stage. And how would the resulting theatre look? Precisely, I would say, like the 'realist' Shakespeare productions which dominated the nineteenth-century stage, in which a visually 'convincing' illusion could be produced on a vast stage behind the frame of the proscenium arch. At that time, furthermore, cartography was completing its long project of subjugating the entire British Empire beneath a single mapping gaze, culminating in the Ordnance Survey of Ireland, and the triangulation of the Indian subcontinent under the direction of Sir George Everest, after whom the highest point on the globe was subsequently named in implicit acknowledgement of the colonising role of the surveyor's omnivoyance. That these two movements coincided should not be surprising if, as my reading suggests, the space of the stage and that of cartography are conterminous, so that identical strategies and perceptual systems play from one to the other. It is the singular eye / I, as representative of an ascendant subjectivity instituted by this reconfigured space, which will find itself increasingly central to the theatre, the painting, the map, and the political sphere of post-sixteenth-century Europe.

From *Shakespeare Studies*, 23 (1995), 39–70.

NOTES

[A considerably longer version of this essay appeared under the title 'Spheres of Influence: Cartography and the Gaze in Shakespearean Tragedy and History' in *Shakespeare Studies*. Philip Armstrong has recently published another Lacanian analysis of Shakespeare: see 'Watching Hamlet watching: Lacan, Shakespeare and the mirror / stage' in Terence Hawkes (ed.), *Alternative Shakespeares, Vol. 2* (New York and London, 1996). Ed.]

1. See Jacques Lacan, *Ecrits: A Selection*, trans. Alan Sheridan (London, 1977), p. 71; *The Four Fundamental Concepts of Psychoanalysis*, trans. Alan Sheridan (London, 1979), pp. 79–119; *The Seminar of Jacques Lacan. Book I: Freud's Papers on Technique 1953–1954*, trans. John Forrester (Cambridge, 1988), pp. 74, 76.

2. Lacan, *The Four Fundamental Concepts*, p. 86.

3. All Shakespeare quotes are from the *Complete Works*, ed. Stanley Wells, Gary Taylor et al. (Oxford, 1988). In the case of *King Lear*, quotations are from the Folio text as given in that edition.

4. Terence Hawkes discusses Lear's division in terms of cartographic 'reduction' in *Meaning by Shakespeare* (London, 1992), pp. 121–40.

5. Samuel Edgerton, 'From Mental Matrix to Mappamundi to Christian

Empire: The Heritage of Ptolemaic Cartography in the Renaissance', in *Art and Cartography*, ed. David Woodward (Chicago, 1987), pp. 10–50, 46.

6. Christopher Marlowe, *Tamburlaine the Great*, ed. J. S. Cunningham (Manchester, 1981).

7. Ethel Seaton, 'Marlowe's Map', in *Marlowe: A Collection of Critical Essays*, ed. Clifford Leech (Englewood Cliffs, NJ, 1964), pp. 36–56.

8. Richard Hakluyt, *The Principal Navigations, Voyages, Traffiques and Discoveries of the English Nation*, Vol. 1 (London, 1903), p. 356. [The original version of Philip Armstrong's essay includes a copy of Wright and Davis's map of the world – Ed.]

9. Lloyd A. Brown, *The Story of Maps* (London, 1951), pp. 180–5.

10. Lacan, *The Four Fundamental Concepts*, p. 72.

11. Ibid., pp. 88–92.

12. Jacques Lacan, *The Seminar of Jacques Lacan, Book VII: The Ethics of Psychoanalysis 1959–1960*, trans. Dennis Porter (London and New York, 1992), p. 140.

13. Philip Armstrong, 'Uncanny Spectacles: Psychoanalysis and the Texts of *King Lear*', *Textual Practice*, 8:3 (Winter 1994), 414–34.

14. Hakluyt, Vol. 1, p. xviii.

15. J. B. Harley, 'Meaning and Ambiguity in Tudor Cartography', in *English Map-Making 1500–1650*, ed. Sarah Tyacke (London, 1983), pp. 22–45, 33.

16. Lacan, *The Four Fundamental Concepts*, p. 88.

17. Again, a famous portrait of Elizabeth offers a pictorial comparison, in this case, the 'Ditchley' portrait, in which the Queen 'towers over an England drawn after the Saxton model'; Richard Helgerson, *Forms of Nationhood: The Elizabethan Writing of England* (Chicago and London, 1992), p. 112.

18. Brown, *The Story of Maps*, p. 165.

19. José Rabasa, 'Allegories of the *Atlas*', in *Europe and Its Others: Proceedings of the Essex Conference on the Sociology of Literature July 1984*, Vol. 2, ed. Francis Barker et al. (Colchester, 1985), pp. 1–15, 1.

20. Lacan, *Seminar I*, p. 141.

21. Teresa Brennan, *History After Lacan* (London, 1993), pp. 7–8, 39–40 and passim. The pun is Lacan's, from *Ecrits*, p. 42.

22. Lacan, *Seminar I*, p. 265. A number of recent critics have discussed the feminisation of both Britain and the New World through the mapping

of the terrain by a specifically male gaze; see, for example Helgerson, *Forms of Nationhood*, pp. 118–20; Peter Hulme, 'Polytropic Man: Tropes of Sexuality and Mobility in Early Colonial Discourse', in Barker et al., *Europe and its Others* pp. 17–32; and Louis Montrose, 'The Work of Gender in the Discourse of Discovery', *Representations*, 33 (Winter), 1–41.

23. See Robert Weimann's *Shakespeare and the Popular Tradition in the Theatre: Studies in the Social Dimension of Dramatic Form and Function* (Baltimore, MD, 1978) for an unsurpassed discussion of the communal and dialogic nature of Shakespearean drama. Weimann does emphasise, however, that this medieval tradition of interactive theatre inherited by the Elizabethans was in transition. My discussion here might suggest some of the perceptual paradigms that influenced this evolution.

24. Stephen Orgel describes how, in the masque, 'Through the use of perspective the monarch, always the ethical centre of court productions, became in a physical and emblematic way the centre as well ... only the King's seat was perfect'. Stephen Orgel and Roy Strong, *Inigo Jones: The Theatre of the Stuart Court* (Berkeley, CA, 1973), Vol. 1, p. 7.

4

'Suche strange desygns': Madness, Subjectivity, and Treason in *Hamlet* and Elizabethan Culture

KARIN S. CODDON

'For, to define true madness, What is it but to be nothing else but mad?' reasons Polonius (II.ii.92–4). Whether Robert Devereux, second earl of Essex, was actually mad in any clinical sense of the word is not an issue for historicism.[1] But that his 'madness' was poor Robert's – and ultimately, the Tudor state's – enemy may be as illuminating for discussions of madness in Shakespearean tragedy as humoral psychology and the vogue of melancholy. Essex seems to have suffered from what Timothie Bright would have called a 'melancholie madnesse,' replete with bouts of near-stuporous despair and religious mania.[2] The possibility that the earl was punished with a 'sore distraction' is frequently viewed as a kind of colourful biographical sidelight to the rebellion of 1601: Essex, 'brilliant, melancholy and ill-fated', becomes the embodiment of the Elizabethan *mal du siècle*, his Icarian fall mirroring the fate of a generation of aspiring minds.[3] 'The flowre of chivalrie' who fell heir in his own lifetime to the heroic legacy of Sir Philip Sidney, Essex has been identified as the historical inspiration for Henry Bolingbroke, Hamlet, and Antony. But the affinities between Essex and the heroes of Shakespearean drama evoked in contemporary accounts of the earl's madness suggest a reciprocity more complex

84

than a mere one-to-one correspondence between history and fictions. Essex's madness, whatever its precise pathological nature, was profoundly engaged in his transgressions as subject, according to John Harington's diary entry of a few months prior to the insurrection:

> It restesthe wythe me in opynion, that ambition thwarted in its career, dothe speedilie leade on to madnesse; herein I am strengthened by what I learne in my Lord of Essex, who shyftethe from sorrowe and repentaunce to rage and rebellion so suddenlie, as well provethe him devoide of good reason or righte mynde; in my last discourse, he uttered suche strange desygns that made me hastene forthe, and leave his absence; thank heaven I am safe at home, and if I go in suche troubles againe, I deserve the gallowes for a meddlynge foole: His speeches of the Queene becomethe no man who hathe *mens sana in corpore sano*. He hathe ill advysors, and much evyll hathe sprunge from thys source. The Queene well knowethe how to humble the haughtie spirit, the haughtie spirit knowethe not how to yield, and the mans soule seemeth tossede to and fro, like the waves of a troubled sea.[4]

Harington attributes Essex's madness to 'ambition thwarted in its career', articulating a Tudor and Stuart commonplace: 'Ambition, madam, is a great man's madness'.[5] But in Harington's discourse the causal relation between overreaching and insanity is ambiguous; ambition may 'speedilie leade on to madnesse', but madness spurs the subjective overthrow of the pales and forts of reason that should constrain the 'haughtie spirit'. The discourse of madness becomes virtually indistinguishable from the discourse of treason: 'he uttered ... strange desygns'; 'His speeches of the Queene becomethe no man who hathe *mens sana in corpore sano*'; 'the haughtie spirit knowethe not how to yield'. Harington finds Essex's madness so alarming not because it is irrational but because it speaks 'strange desygns': reason, or treason, in madness. And yet he represents Essex nonetheless as a victim as well as violator subjected by his own disordered subjectivity: 'the mans soule seemeth tossede to and fro, like the waves of a troubled sea.' The mad Robert Devereux is, then, as radically self-divided a subject as Hamlet, though not because the fictive prince was 'inspired' by the historical earl. Madness is mighty opposite of the ideology of self-government, or what Mervyn James has called the 'internalisation of obedience'.[6] As such, madness dis-integrates the identity so precariously fashioned by notions of inward control and self-vigilance, notions whose contradictions become increasingly critical toward the end of Elizabeth's rule. Madness renders the subject not more but less himself; it becomes the internalisation of *dis*obedience, pre-requisite and portent of the external violation of order.[7]

Not all of Essex's transgressions against Elizabethan authority, of course, were merely internal. Yet even at the height of his polit-ical / erotic courtship of the queen, his potentially unruly disposi-tion is a topic of courtly conversation. William Camden recalls of Essex, 'Nor was he excusable in his deportment to the Queen herself, whom he treated with a sort of insolence, that seemed to proceed rather *from a mind that wanted ballast, than any real pride in him* ...'[8] That Camden casts the earl's 'insolence' as a psychologi-cal rather than spiritual defect is a telling qualification. Essex's sub-jectivity becomes the site of the displacement of sin by disorder; the Luciferean sin of pride has metamorphosed into a dangerous inward unfixity. This apparent displacement does not mitigate the earl's 'insolence' so much as it inscribes the inextricable – but here, disturbingly precarious – relation between subject and subjectivity; the instability of the latter is reciprocally engaged in the perform-ance of the former, as in Harington's description of the 'haughtie spirit'. This shift from soul to subjectivity is bound up in the cul-tural shift from medieval ecclesiastical authority to Renaissance secular authority; as the sinner was to the Church, now the disor-dered subjectivity is to the secular state. Subjectivity, 'a mind that want[s] ballast', is identified as the site of potential transgression and the object of authority and control.

The period between 1597 and 1601 saw the deterioration of Essex's favoured position with Elizabeth, a change that would cul-minate in the queen's fateful refusal to renew the lucrative sweet wines monopoly. But Essex's fall from grace was only partly due to the parsimony and caprice of the ageing queen. In 1598 occurred the notorious ear-boxing incident, in which Essex responded to Elizabeth's sharp cuff on the ear by reaching for his sword. The ap-parent if swiftly checked impulse toward regicide was compounded by Essex's self-justification questioning the infallibility of the sov-ereign will. 'What, cannot Princes err? cannot subjects receive wrong? Is an earthly power or authority infinite?' he wrote in a letter to Sir Thomas Egerton. 'Pardon me, pardon me, my good lord, I can never subscribe to such principles'.[9] But 'such princi-ples' were precisely those to which Tudor propaganda demanded subscription:

al subjectes are bounden to obey [Magistrates] as god's ministers: yea
although they be evil, not only for feare, but also for conscience's
sake ... let al marke diligently, that it is not lawful for inferiours and
subjectes, in any case to resist or stand against the superior powers:
for s. Paule's words be plain, that whosoever withstandeth the
ordinaunce of god. (*An Exhortation concerning good order and
obedience, to rulers and Magistrates)*[10]

Moreover, the writer of the *Exhortation* deems it 'an intolerable
ignoraunce, *madnes*, and wickednes, for subjectes to make any
murmuring, rebellion, resistance or withstanding, commocion, or
insurrection against there most dere and most dred soveraygne Lord
and king ...'.[11] Essex's outrage may have been as temperamental as
political, the effect of what Egerton diplomatically referred to as his
need 'to conquer [him]self', but the surly defiance of his letter
accords with the 'strange desygns' that perturbed Harington and
the sometimes flagrant insubordination that characterised the earl's
misadventures in Ireland in 1599. Openly disregarding the queen's
orders, Essex conferred knighthood upon over eighty members of
his company 'without even the justification of a military victory'.[12]
But when he chose to return to England against the queen's wishes,
and burst in upon a half-dressed Elizabeth in her private chamber,
his violation of the boundaries of subject took on yet more dangerous implications. If his making for his sword symbolically threatened the queen's body politic, his intrusion into her private room
also threatened the sacred, gendered body of the royal virgin.[13] Just
as the subject's identity was enabled by his inward and outward
adherence to the prescriptions of authority, the monarch's identity
depended upon the uniformity of obedience, as Elizabeth well
understood: 'I am no Queen. That man is above me', she raged to
her godson Harington.[14] Like Diana surprised by Actaeon,
Elizabeth exacted physical punishment upon the intruder, though
confinement, not dismemberment, was Essex's sentence. Essex spent
nearly six months in the custody of the Lord Keeper Egerton. A
letter from John Donne, then secretary to the Lord Keeper, to
Henry Wotton provides a window into the perception of the prisoner's condition:

> He withers still in his sicknes & plods on to his end in the same pace
> where you left us. the worst accidents of his sicknes are that he con-
> spires with it & that it is not here beleeved. that which was sayd of
> Cato that his age understood him not I feare may be averted of your

lord that he understood not his age: for it is a naturall weaknes of inno-
cency, that such men want lockes for themselves and keyse for others.[15]

While Essex was hardly suspected of putting on an antic disposition,
Donne's comments reveal the degree to which the physical and mental
anguish of the insubordinate earl was subjected to political scrutiny.
'Madness in great ones must not unwatched go' (III.i.89),
Claudius observes in *Hamlet*. With Essex's most erratic behaviour
explicitly bound up in gestures of disobedience, his inward distress
('he conspires with it') becomes as suspect as his public comport-
ment. Donne's conclusion 'that such men want lockes for themselves and keyse for others' is of a piece with Harington's comment
that 'the Queene well knowethe how to humble the haughtie spirit,
the haughtie spirit knowethe not how to yield', and with Camden's
reference to Essex's 'mind that wanted ballast'. All three observations imply an antagonism not only between the subject and power,
but between *subjectivity* and power, anticipating both the confrontation and the outcome. It is an agon in which the subject necessarily turns upon the 'self' as well as upon authority. For if, as
Foucault has suggested, power is realised and resisted in its effects,
i.e., in its 'government of individualisation', contestation disrupts
the 'form of power which makes individuals subjects' – subjects in
both senses of the word.[16] The problem of containment becomes
one of confinement. The disruption of the internalised relation
between authority and inwardness transforms the dialogue of 'sub-
jectification' into a problem of material subjugation: as authority
gives way to coercion, the body, not subjectivity, becomes its
object. Ultimately, 'a mind that want[s] ballast' can be disciplined
only by the exaction of punishment upon the body. In *Hamlet*, the
restoration of the 'mad' hero's wits is necessarily punctuated by the
death that swiftly follows his recovery of sanity. If the deployment
of physical punishment transforms as much as fulfils power relations,[17] the literal silencing of madness by confinement, constraint,
or extinction of the body is itself an unstable strategy of containment. For the division of inwardness and the body that enables
post-Reformation subjectivity situates madness nonetheless in the
equivocal space between interiority and exteriority. Neither wholly
confined to nor estranged from inwardness, madness in its semiotic
excess problematises the closure that is the object of rites of punishment, on both the stage and the scaffold.

Historian Lacey Baldwin Smith remarks that '[b]y the time Essex turned to treason, the deterioration in his character had passed beyond the point of hysteria: it was bordering on insanity which led him to confuse the fantasies of his own sick brain with reality'.[18] Smith's reference to the rebellion as 'an act of political madness' seems particularly resonant precisely because it may be tacitly redundant: was Essex's madness – or the madness of great ones, both onstage and at court – ever *not* 'political', that is, charged with implications *against* the inscription of order, obedience, and authority that fashioned and controlled identity in late Tudor and early Stuart England? When Essex's 'strange desygns' finally bodied forth action on February 8, 1601, the equivocal boundaries between representation and rebellion almost wholly collapse, though not quite in the way the earl had planned. If the playing of Shakespeare's *Richard II* '40 times in open streets and houses' failed to rouse the support of the citizens for the rebels, the consequences of the failed insurrection produced a spectacle of trial, repentance, and noble death that seemed to duplicate the form and effect of the tragic denouement. Although Essex repeatedly declared his innocence during the trial, once his fate was decided paranoiac self-justifications gave way to compliance with the art of dying. Entailing confession, repentance, and 'the return of the traitor to society and to himself', as Steven Mullaney puts it,[19] such performances were commonly described and, perhaps, implicitly *prescribed* in *ars moriendi* handbooks, published accounts of executions, and penultimate moments in contemporary tragedy.[20]

On February 25 Essex faced the executioner with a noble set speech in which he confessed his spiritual and political transgressions, forgave and prayed for forgiveness, and affirmed throughout the absolute justice of the authority that condemned him:

> Lord Jesus, forgive it us, and forgive it me, the most wretched of all; and I beseech her Majesty, the State, and Ministers thereof, to forgive it us. The Lord grant her Majesty a prosperous reign and a long one, if it be His will. O Lord, bless her and the nobles and ministers of the Church and State. And I beseech you and the world to have a charitable opinion of me for my intention toward her Majesty, whose death, upon my salvation and before God, I protest I never meant, nor violence to her person; yet I confess I have received an honourable trial, and am justly condemned. And I desire all the world to forgive me, even as I do freely and from my heart forgive the world.[21]

As J. A. Sharpe has discussed in a suggestive essay, the theatricality of 'last dying speeches' on the scaffold in sixteenth- and seventeenth-century England served a specific ideological function: noble traitors and common criminals alike became 'willing central participants in a theatre of punishment, which offered not merely a spectacle, but a reinforcement of certain values ... they were helping to assert the legitimacy of the power which had brought them to their sad end'.[22] And following James's analysis of Tudor and Stuart 'ideological controls' in the face of limited coercive power, Sharpe has suggested that this 'theatre of the gallows' demonstrated the condemned man's 'internalisation of obedience', the willing representation of inward acquiescence to good order.[23] The case of Essex, then, seems particularly stirring: not only the avowed traitor, but the disordered, self-divided subjectivity is restored, identity – as noble, Christian subject to her majesty and her ministers – recovered in the assertion of the righteousness and coherence of authority.[24] 'I am no Queen,' Elizabeth had complained upon Essex's violation of her royal imperatives; in dying, Essex effectively reaffirmed the monarch's identity as well as his own.

Yet there was enough uncertainty about semiotic containment in such spectacles of death that Essex's execution, like Mary Queen of Scots' beheading, was kept a semi-private affair, printed transcriptions of the event rather than the event itself entrusted with the dissemination of its ideological significance.[25] Hence the ideological efficiency of 'the theatre of the gallows' may be no less equivocal than the 'strange desygns' that prefaced the performance. As Foucault has remarked, 'there was ... on the part of the state power, a political fear of the effects of these ambiguous rituals'.[26] The willingness to spare Essex the humiliation of public execution may have stemmed in part from fear that the propaganda value of such a spectacle could backfire, especially given the popularity of the earl with the citizens.[27] Nor was the proliferation of official propaganda any insurance that the populace would be duly awed by the terrible enactment of power and punishment:

> The condemned man found himself transformed into a hero by the sheer extent of his widely advertised crimes, and sometimes the affirmation of his belated repentance. Against the law, against the rich, the powerful, the magistrates, the constabulary or the watch, against taxes and their collectors, he appeared to have waged

a struggle with which one all too easily identified. ... If the condemned man was shown to be repentant, accepting the verdict, asking both God and man for forgiveness for his crimes, it was as if he had come through some process of purification: he died, in his own way, like a saint.[28]

Indeed, three years after Essex's death one Robert Pricket published a tributory poem about the earl, 'Honor's Fame in Triumph Riding', in which the earl's downfall is attributed chiefly to the machinations of his enemies, just as he had claimed during his trial. The verses sent Pricket to prison.[29] For while the poem is not explicitly subversive, such lines as 'He died for treason; Yet no Traitor. Why?' stand in sharp contradiction with the official exegeses of the earl's demise.[30]

The ways in which that other great Elizabethan spectacle of death – tragedy – duplicates, appropriates, and, sometimes, questions the strategies of power informing productions of authority and punishment on the scaffold are thus ideologically as well as aesthetically significant. As Leonard Tennenhouse has commented, 'The strategies of theatre resembled those of the scaffold, as well as court performance ... in observing a common logic of figuration that both sustained and testified to the monarch's power ...'.[31] But the apparent exclusion of madness, of unreason, of disorder, from the final transcriptions of the actual traitor's death is consistently called into question, even subverted, in the punishment meted out by an ostensible tragic order. In the middle tragedies of Shakespeare, discrepanies between the spectacle and its discursive record bequeathed to the survivors undermine the closure apparently evoked in the hero's 'restoration to himself' in death; the words of Horatio, Edgar, and Macduff seem glaringly inadequate even as plot summaries. 'In Shakespeare ... madness still occupies an extreme place, in that it is beyond appeal. Nothing ever restores it either to truth or reason. It leads only to laceration and thence to death';[32] the highly stylised return to self before death is unsettled by the madness that outlives the individual subject in the gulf between tragic experience and its final retelling.[33] Madness does not deny authority so much as testify to a fissure in the structure of authority – and subjectivity, an excess that is not recuperated by the 'government of individualisation', to disrupt both subjection *and* subjectivity. As such, its discourse of 'wild and whirling words', of a 'soule ... tossede to and fro, like the waves of a troubled sea', is peculiarly resistant to strategies of containment.

Accordingly, among the most important mandates of Foucault's landmark if controversial work is that madness and its representations be investigated in terms of their functions within – and against – structures of power.[34] If the political drama of Essex's madness, rebellion, and noble death shares marked affinities with the tragedies contemporary to it, so does the theatre itself duplicate and reflect upon a more insidious crisis of authority swelling in late Elizabethan England. What will distinguish madness in such plays as *Hamlet* (1601) and *King Lear* (1605) from its depictions in the equally pathologically fixated tragedy of the late 1580s and early 1590s is the subordination to which it will subject other plot elements: madness does not serve narrative so much as narrative serves madness.[35] This narrative *non serviam* constructs a split not so much between 'plot' and 'character' as between agency and inwardness, a division clearly manifest in the so-called 'problem' of Hamlet but also informing tragedies as early as Marlowe's *Edward II* (1593) and as late as Webster's *Duchess of Malfi* (1613). The antagonism between subjectivity and the drama's 'syntygmatic axis',[36] between disorder and a linear mimesis, duplicates the position of power's subject in relation to the authority that, like the narrative, both constricts and constrains him. But the notion of tragic madness as overtly or even covertly 'subversive' is problematic.[37] In fact, madness displaces action, metaphorising it but also taking its place. If madness seems to privilege and enlarge the tragic hero's subjectivity, so does it also fragment, check, and defer it. As an inversion of internalised 'ideological controls' madness by definition precludes the realisation of a stable, coherent subjectivity in opposition to the disorder from without.

Foucault has discussed the historical liminality of the Renaissance madman positioned between the wandering lunatic of the Middle Ages and the construction of bourgeois individualist subjectivity, the rise of the modern 'anatomo-politics of the body' that banishes unreason.[38] Recent critical works by Francis Barker, Catherine Belsey, and Terry Eagleton have applied the Foucauldian notion of liminality to the Shakespearean subject, particularly in the paradigmatic case of Hamlet.[39] The absolute impenetrability of Hamlet's mystery, the absence of the full interiority apparently promised in the prince's claim that 'I have that within which passes show' (I.ii.85), leads Belsey to conclude that 'Hamlet is ... the most discontinuous of Shakespeare's heroes', riddled almost to the point of unintelligibility by the 'repressed discontinuities of the allegorical tradition'.[40] Barker and Eagleton go a step further; because humanist subjectivity has yet to fully emerge in the late sixteenth century, 'in the interior of [Hamlet's] mystery, there is, in short, nothing'.[41] But this nothing's more than matter; because the privatised subjectivity is incomplete, 'wild and whirling words' are never wholly opaque, much less transcendent. The discourse of madness, feigned, real, or a combination of both, remains in Shakespeare's plays as in Harington's diary a language of 'strange desygns', of matter and impertinency mixed. The break between subject and society is equivocal rather than absolute, and the idiom of unreason in Shakespeare retains resolutely social resonances.[42] The idealisation of madness as a transcendent world metaphysically autonomous of its material conditions is a romantic and post-romantic construct: 'Garde tes songes! Les sages n'en ont pas assez beaux que les fous!' concludes Baudelaire's 'La Voix'. But in Elizabethan and Jacobean theatre the mad hero is never an absolute exile; even when banished, like Lear, he is accompanied, if only by a parodic progress. His threat transgressive more than nihilistic, the mad tragic hero, unlike the fully demonised savage or 'ungovernable man', violates and recognises social boundaries simultaneously.[43] In his tragedy he lingers in the dangerous, equivocal space of 'reason in madness', but he is never completely marginalised. For he remains bound up in the social situation from which he is (subjectively) divided, linked to the spectre of a former self whose public form he reassumes in dying.[44]

Therefore, to consider the problem of madness in Hamlet – and in *Hamlet* – is to examine its manifestly political implications in the play. Political not in the sense of topical allusions to historical persons such as Essex, but rather in the sense that Hamlet's madness articulates and represents a historically specific division, by which inwardness, breaking down the pales and forts of reason, enacts the faltering of ideological prescriptions designed to define, order, and constrain subjectivity. The similarities between the madness of fictive Hamlet and that of historical Robert Devereux, the unreason that violates the sanctity of a virgin's private chamber or defies a monarch's command, derive from the transgression of ideological boundaries governing both treason and madness. That Shakespeare problematises Hamlet's 'antic disposition' at every turn is significant; the fact that Hamlet's madness cannot be pinned down, clarified, or debunked allows its consistent perception as a conduct of 'strange desygns' and a threat to the sovereign. The various attempts at diagnosing Hamlet's malaise ventured by Claudius, Polonius, and Gertrude are informed by a recognition that in the ambiguous space in which reason and madness intersect lies treason. As with Essex, it is not madness itself but the insidious presence of method in it that constitutes 'strange desygns'. This particular danger characterises no less the madness of Ophelia:[45]

> Her speech is nothing.
> Yet the unshaped use of it doth move
> The hearers to collection. They aim at it,
> And botch the words up to fit their own thoughts,
> Which, as her winks and nods and gestures yield them,
> Indeed would make one think there might be thought,
> Though nothing sure, yet much unhappily.
>
> (IV.v.7–13)

As Laertes quite rightly observes, 'This nothing's more than matter' (l.175); Ophelia's 'unshaped' speech no less than Hamlet's 'wild and whirling words' threatens to inscribe its disorder on the 'ill-breeding minds' of the body politic. In *Hamlet* it is not transcendent truth that unreason speaks, but 'dangerous conjectures' rooted in the subject's problematic relation to the authority against which his – or her – inwardness is constructed.

Madness in *Hamlet*, then, while engaging and even subjecting subjectivity, is not contained within it. As a particular mode of discourse it continually threatens to be construed – or misconstrued – into an incitement of social and political disorder. The metonymic markers for order – moderation, stoicism, obedience – are undermined throughout the play by the dangerous if impenetrable subjectivity of the hero. When Claudius urges Hamlet to give over his obdurate mourning, he invokes a series of maxims on authority and obedience to natural and divine order:

> But to persever
> In obstinate condolement is a course
> Of impious stubbornness. 'Tis unmanly grief,
> It shows a will most incorrect to heaven,
> A heart unfortified, a mind impatient,
> An understanding simple and unschooled.
> For what we know must be, and is as common
> As any the most vulgar thing to sense,
> Why should we in our peevish opposition
> Take it to heart? Fie, 'tis a fault to heaven,
> A fault against the dead, a fault to nature,
> To reason most absurd, whose common theme
> Is death of fathers.
>
> (I.ii.92–104)

Claudius may be 'a little more than kin, and less than kind', but his reasoning articulates views about mourning and self-government that were commonplaces of Elizabethan religious as well as psychological thought.[46] The Protestant emphasis on an all-encompassing providence identified the will of God in all human experience regardless of how apparently arbitrary or unpleasant, while the government of passions was particularly imperative in a culture with more than its share of life-threatening hazards.[47] Similarly, Claudius's insinuation that such mourning is effeminate tacitly genders melancholy; it is worth noting that Ophelia's madness, with its 'unshaped' content of sexual and political allusions, doubles and even parodies Hamlet's distraction.[48] That Claudius is so eager to attribute Ophelia's madness to 'the poison of deep grief' (IV.v.76), indeed, the filial grief for which he upbraids Hamlet in Act I, scene ii, suggests that the feminisation of madness in later periods has its seeds in the cultural construction of the rational, obedient male subject.[49]

But the claims of obedience upon inwardness are deflected by 'that within which passes show', by the implication that the wisdom of authority – divine, royal, filial – can neither order nor account for the subject's perception of his own experience. The moralisation of the inward space (''tis a fault to heaven'), designed to encourage the subject's self-surveillance against the possible disruption of 'unmanly' passion and madness, fails to dissuade Hamlet from his melancholy. But with the failure of inward constraints authority seeks to impose its will on the subject's body: Hamlet must stay in Denmark while Laertes is allowed to return to France. The inward refusal of covert ideological controls moves power to expose and flex its coercive underpinnings. As the play develops and Hamlet's melancholy intensifies into the more dangerous 'antic disposition', the question of his physical constraint becomes all the more literal and imperative. Denmark does become a prison: Rosencrantz warns Hamlet, 'You do surely bar the door upon your own liberty if you deny your griefs to your friend' (III.ii.345–6), while Claudius plots the ultimate physical curtailment: 'For we will put fetters about this fear, /Which now goes too free-footed' (III.iii.25–6).

But while madness addresses and reproduces the problematics of authority, the internalisation of disobedience precludes taking arms against a sea of troubles. The radical inutility of unreason divides subjectivity and agency, and hence the question of Hamlet's 'delay' should be considered in light of the more pervasive antagonism between inwardness and authority. The appearance of the ghost does not counter the vacuity of the preceding exercises in patriarchal authority but rather duplicates and even literalises it in the equivocal space of the supernatural.[50] Hamlet's initial address to the ghost identifies its ambivalence:

> Be thou a spirit of health or goblin damned,
> Bring with thee airs from heaven or blasts from hell,
> Be thy intents wicked or charitable,
> Thou comest in such a questionable shape
> That I will speak to thee.
>
> (I.iv.40–4)

As a figure of boundless semiotic ambiguity the ghost is aligned with madness and 'break[ing] down the pales and forts of reason' (I.iv.28).

Horatio, the paradigmatic reasonable man, is even more ineffectual than Claudius against unreason:

> What if it tempt you toward the flood, my lord,
> Or to the dread summit of the cliff
> That beetles o'er his base into the sea,
> And there assume some other, horrible form,
> Which might deprive your sovereignty of reason
> And draw you into madness?
>
> (I.iv.69–74)

The threat of madness or demonic possession, like Claudius's admonishment of unnatural grief bound up in the ideology of self-vigilance, holds no sway over the prince, who 'waxes desperate with imagination' (I.iv.87).

The uncertain origins of King Hamlet's ghost have been well documented. But its eschatological ambiguities may be less significant than the rhetoric of filial duty and natural bonds, the very idiom that Claudius employs in Act I, scene ii, in which the ghost couches its exhortations to revenge: 'If thou didst ever thy dear father love'; 'If thou hadst nature in thee, bear it not' (I.v.23, 81). But unlike the apparitions of *The Spanish Tragedy* and *Antonio's Revenge*, the spectre of King Hamlet is a figure of contamination as much as one of justice. 'Taint not thy mind' (I.v.85), it urges Hamlet, yet it is not revenge but its own sickly idiom that the ghost inscribes within the 'distracted globe' of Hamlet. The ghost claims in what is actually a mode of *occupatio*:

> But that I am forbid
> To tell the secrets of my prison house,
> I could a tale unfold whose lightest word
> Would harrow up thy soul, freeze thy young blood,
> Make thy two eyes like stars start from their spheres,
> Thy knotted and combined locks to part,
> And each particular hair to stand an end
> Like quills upon the fretful porpentine.
>
> (I.v.13–20)

But in reappearing to Hamlet in Gertrude's closet the ghost seem-ingly effects its own prophecy on Hamlet, whom Gertrude describes almost exactly as the ghost has hypothetically in Act I, scene v:

> Forth at your eye your spirits wildly peep,
> And, as the sleeping soldiers in th' alarm,
> Your bedded hair like life in excrements
> Start up and stand on end.
>
> (III.iv.120–3)

Although speaking from the conventional position of justice, the ghost shapes its claims on the government and direction of the subject through fragmentation, contamination, madness. It is worth noting that the so-called 'problems' of Hamlet's character – the ob-scurely motivated 'antic disposition', the delay, the swift transitions from brooding soliloquy to 'a kind of joy' – do not arise until the end of Act I, scene v, after the encounter with King Hamlet's ghost. The radically ambivalent nature of the ghost serves as an almost emblematic contradiction that subsumes the play's manifest at-tempts at narrative coherence. Intention and consequences will diverge wildly and overtly; wills and fates will so contrary run. Hamlet's subjectivity is riven by an exhortation to obedience under-mined by its own ontological and discursive equivocation.

That the dead king's exhortation to revenge and remembrance is neglected by the play as well as the prince demonstrates *Hamlet's* consistent reluctance to privilege wholeheartedly any generic or hierarchic discourse of authority, with the possible exception of playing itself.[51] 'The time is out of joint', Hamlet says at the end of Act I, scene v, words that are all but literalised in the act that follows. The elapse of fictive time between the first and second acts, during which Hamlet has apparently done nothing save 'put on' the ambiguous 'antic disposition', and the centring of the plot almost exclusively on his 'transformation' serve to turn the play away from the revenge plot commanded and authorised by the ghost. The discontinuities between Act I, scene v and Act II, scene i are as provocative as those informing Hamlet's 'too much changed' character, the only striking 'remembrance' of the precedent scene Ophelia's description of Hamlet surprising her in her closet. Because the strange encounter takes place offstage, the authenticity of Hamlet's demeanour remains, as is true of almost all of his 'mad' conduct, uncertain. But if Ophelia gives a typical enough picture of the conventional melancholy lover for Polonius to make an immediate, confident diagnosis, her reference to his 'look so piteous in purport / As if he had been loosed out of hell / To speak of horrors' (ll.82–4) contradicts the relative benignity of love-madness with an evocation of the supernatural, irrational incident of the prior scene. Again, it is significant to note that Ophelia speaks of Hamlet in terms markedly similar to those in which the ghost describes 'the secrets of my prison house'.

It is not until well over four hundred lines into Act II, scene ii that madness gives way to the subject of revenge, and even here it is a player's speech, 'a dream of passion', that recalls to Hamlet – and to *Hamlet* – the purpose exhorted by the ghost. But while playing is aligned neither with the specious aphorisms of the ideology of self-moderation nor with the radically disintegrating forces of unreason, *Hamlet's* play-within-a-play, unlike Hieronymo's in *The Spanish Tragedy*, speaks daggers but uses none. Its purpose falls upon the inventor's head, alerting Claudius not only to Hamlet's knowledge of the fratricide but also to an apparent threat to the king's own life. Far from a vehicle of revenge, the play-within-a-play comprises but another obstacle. Significantly, closure for 'The Mousetrap' is literally disrupted when the king, 'frighted with false fire', hastily departs. In 'The Mousetrap' as in *Hamlet*, in the place of closure there is madness; the ostensible revenger sings snatches of ballads, calls for music, and boasts to Horatio, 'Would not this, sir, and a forest of feathers – if the rest of my fortunes turn Turk with me – with two Provincial roses on my razed shoes, get me a fellowship with a cry of players, sir?' (III.ii.284–7). Hamlet's antic foolery and incongruous festivity counter and parody the sober purpose and implication of the preceding performance. Thus the authority of playing is problematised by the play's contradictory and ambiguous effects.

Hamlet's crisis of subjectivity, then, is *Hamlet's* crisis of authority; the ideological constructs that shape power and subjection as mutually constitutive, specifically, the ideology of inward obedience designed to bolster the pales and forts of reason, are scrutinised and exposed as ineffectual. The disintegration of subjective identity – madness – corresponds to the airy nothing of ghostly authority, to the 'king of shreds and patches', to the 'dream of passion' of the players. If his 'mousetrap' incites Hamlet to act, he nonetheless inverts the ghost's express command, bypassing the opportunity to kill Claudius and instead focusing on Gertrude, against whom he was told not to 'contrive'. First confronting the queen with words so 'wild and whirling' she fears for her life, then inadvertently stabbing the eavesdropping Polonius, Hamlet proceeds to deliver, ironically enough, a high-minded lecture on the queen's failure to govern her passions. But his argument for self-restraint swiftly gives way to a morbid explication of the particularly sexual nature of Gertrude's betrayal, the source of Hamlet's melancholy even before he learns of his father's murder.[52] As madness impedes narrativity, purpose degenerates into repetition, a motif Shakespeare manifestly explores in *King Lear*. In *Hamlet*, a play still marked by the absent linear form of revenge narrative, hollow gestures toward purpose are approached only to be reversed. The sudden appearance of the ghost functions not only to remind Hamlet of his 'almost blunted purpose', but also to rehearse the earlier encounter. Yet when it departs, Hamlet promptly reverts to another argument for sexual self-restraint ('Assume a virtue if you have it not'). As for Polonius, whose corpse has been almost comically forgotten for over a hundred lines, Hamlet asserts rather decorously that

> For this same lord,
> I do repent. But heaven hath pleased it so,
> To punish me with this, and this with me,
> That I must be their scourge and minister.
> I will bestow him and will answer well
> The death I gave him.
>
> (III.iv.173–8)

But identity – as noble revenger – is no sooner restored than overthrown by madness, which resists closure and subverts purpose. Hamlet requests 'One word more, good lady', then launches into an 'antic' tirade upon Gertrude's sexual relations with 'the bloat king'. And in overt contradiction of his lofty repentance of lines 173–8, Hamlet announces that 'I'll lug the guts into the neighbour room', and far from 'answering well' for Polonius's slaying, stashes the body in a cupboard.

The fragmentation displaced in the grotesque mutilations of earlier revenge tragedies has become in *Hamlet* the condition of the hero's subjectivity, the principle governing dramatic structure, the violence inscribed on the body of the play instead of on the body of the villain. Indeed, Hamlet's strange business with the body of Polonius replaces what is in the source stories the actual dismemberment of the spying minister. In the very brief Act IV, scene ii often cut from stage productions, and in the ensuing interrogation by the king ('Now, Hamlet, where's Polonius?' 'At supper.'), Hamlet's mysterious inwardness intersects with the contradiction of the body, the body that is at once absent and material, a thing and a thing of nothing. Madness, a discourse that collapses the ostensible distinction between the body and the 'self', speaking an idiom that conflates and confuses the political and the 'private', here posits as its referent the great leveller of differences, death. As Michael Bristol has commented, 'Hamlet's "extreame show of doltishness" reinterprets the basic distinctions of life: between food and corrupt, decaying flesh, between human and animal, between king and beggar. Temporal authority and indeed all political structures of difference are turned inside out.'[53]

> Your worm is your only emperor for diet. We fat all creatures else to fat us, and we fat ourselves for maggots. Your fat king and your lean beggar is but variable service – two dishes, but to one table. That's the end.
>
> (IV.iii.20–4)

Madness, then, is not so much metaphor as metonymy for death, a moment in which the materiality of the body overturns the authority of distinctions out of which coherent, unified subjectivity is constructed. For in *Hamlet* subjectivity is still engaged in materiality even as the autonomy of the 'self' ('is') from the body ('seems') is being asserted. By the graveyard scene the death-madness of Act IV, scenes ii and iii has become externalised, literalised in the representation of a gravedigger who 'sings in gravemaking' (V.i.66), in Hamlet's hypothetical histories of the skulls of courtiers, politicians, as 'Imperious Caesar' whose dust may stop a bung-hole. There is Yorick, too, the 'mad rogue' whose literal antic disposition was 'wont to set the table on a roar' (l.190).[54] The prince and the gravedigger discuss 'Young Hamlet, he that is mad and sent to England', in the third person, as though the radically fragmented hero of Acts II through IV has been banished across the imaginary sea. Madness, death, fragmentation, heretofore located in Hamlet's 'wild and whirling words', are in Act V, scene i presented as conditions of the play's world. Hamlet is again 'good as a chorus', pointing out, commenting upon and interpreting the old bones in the graveyard, the 'maimed rites' of Ophelia's funeral. At once justification and near-parodic literalisation of the stuff of Hamlet's privileged subjectivity, the gross materiality of the grave seems to claim an authority that subsumes inwardness and difference. If the scene owes a debt to the *memento mori* tradition, the skulls emblematise not so much the vanity of the world as the material necessity that implicates subject and authority alike.[55] Hamlet recognises the authority of death as absolute and inviolable, yet even as recognition of authority confers, accordingly, the unified identity ('This is I, Hamlet the Dane!') disrupted by the more problematic relations to power, Hamlet's 'towering passion' returns to destabilise the seemingly restored noble self. The scuffle with Laertes has an almost black comic aspect in contrast to the sober meditations on mortality that precede it, given the 'bravery' of Laertes's speech, reasonable Horatio's typically ineffectual 'Good my lord, be quiet', and Hamlet's somewhat incongruous question to the man whose father he has killed, 'What is the reason that you use me thus? I loved you ever' (ll.285–6). The containment apparently evoked in the dialogue with the gravediggers is contradicted as soundly as Hamlet's promise to 'answer well' for Polonius's death, madness once again violently usurping narrative order.

Yet Hamlet's outburst at Ophelia's grave exhausts his 'wild and whirling words'. In the final scene the hero at last becomes the 'courtier, soldier, scholar' of Ophelia's tribute, recounting to Horatio the rash but providentially sanctioned actions on the ship, bantering wittily with Osrick the waterfly, graciously agreeing to the king's request for the conciliatory game with Laertes. Hamlet's placid fatalism despite his premonition of death and his acquiescence to providential design transform 'distracted' subjectivity into noble subjection to the 'divinity that shapes our ends'. Hence Hamlet's apology to Laertes renounces madness, the unruly and disruptive force in the play as well as in his own 'distracted globe': 'His madness is poor Hamlet's enemy' (V.ii.233). In the past, critics have debated over the sincerity or lack thereof of Hamlet's apology, a consequence of overemphasis on Hamlet as a naturalistic character rather than as central feature of a play in which the ambiguities, the 'strange desygns', of madness are so foregrounded. Even when considered in a theatrical rather than purely textual context, wherein an actor is personating Hamlet, the tragic hero's last formal set speech, like that of Othello or even the premature 'Let's away to prison' speech of Lear, engages the public dimension informing rites of symbolic closure in Elizabethan England. In *Hamlet* as in the scaffold speech of Essex, an eloquent if stylised confession redeems the transgressing subject and affirms the order he has violated, disclaims 'a purposed evil' and restores the speaker to himself. Because the audience knows what Hamlet only presciently suspects, his death seems inevitable, in accord with the narrative logic so consistently violated before by the now-renounced madness.

But Shakespeare's decorous ritual of death, for all that it *seems* to observe a form of ideological closure, does not contain madness even by the hero's death and the extinction of his problematic subjectivity. 'Madness dissipated can be only the same thing as the imminence of the end. ... But death itself does not bring peace; madness will still triumph – a truth mockingly eternal, beyond the end of a life which yet had been delivered from madness by this very end.'[56] For Hamlet 'the rest is silence'; he bequeaths his 'story' to reasonable Horatio. But Horatio's recapitulation of the tragic events contradicts Hamlet's own providential interpretation of his tragedy:

> So shall you hear
> Of carnal, bloody, and unnatural acts,
> Of accidental judgements, casual slaughters,
> Of deaths put on by cunning and forced cause,
> And in this upshot, purposes mistook
> Fallen on th' inventors' heads.
> (V.ii.374–9)

Moreover, Horatio urges that the rather skeletal tale be recounted to ward off the semiotic slippage aligned with disruptive madness; his task must be performed 'Even while men's minds are wild, lest more mischance / On plots and errors happen' (ll.388–9). If Hamlet has retracted his madness, *Hamlet* stops short of following suit. The division that breeds 'dangerous conjectures' rests unreconciled; the condemned man's words enact a rite of obedience but affirm an order that is still estranged from the disorderly social reality of 'wild minds'. Shakespeare's tragedy, performed on the public stage, makes no attempt to contain the potentially dangerous play of signification that moved Tudor authority to make the executions of Mary and Essex semi-private affairs whose printed reports are as safely decontextualised as Horatio's account of what happens in *Hamlet*. Indeed, Shakespeare's investigation of the interplay of unreason's 'strange desygns' and the 'wild minds' of the body politic stands in reciprocal rather than imitative relation to the offstage drama of disobedience and melancholy, treason and madness, that led Robert Devereux to the scaffold. Whether Shakespeare's reflections were actually prompted by the ill-fated career of the queen's last favourite is ultimately less important than the pervasive crisis of inwardness and authority, enacted in *Hamlet*, acted upon by the earl of Essex. The ambiguous boundaries between treason and madness in Elizabethan England testify to the politicisation of subjectivity, the traces of which essentialist readings of Hamlet – and of the history of 'the self' – have repressed but not effaced.[57]

From *Renaissance Drama*, 20 (1989), 51–75.

NOTES

[Karin S. Coddon's essay, an excellent example of new historicist criticism in its interlacing of historical and textual detail, first appeared in the journal *Renaissance Drama*. It was reprinted in Suzanne L. Wofford (ed.), *Hamlet* (Boston and New York, 1994), pp. 380–402. Ed.]

1. Lacey Baldwin Smith has recently argued that the apparent madness of Essex, as well as a number of other Tudor traitors, was a manifestation of a more insidious 'cultural paranoia'. That is, 'the cause of irrationality need not lie exclusively in the tortured chambers of the mind; it can be external, and the self-destructive traitor can be a symptom of his society as well as a victim of his private insanity'. (*Treason in Tudor England: Politics and Paranoia* [Princeton, NJ, 1986], p. 12). For an acute commentary and critique, see Christopher Hill's review in *New York Review of Books*, 34:8 (7 May 1987), 36–8.

2. Timothie Bright, *A Treatise of Melancholie*, 1586 (New York, 1940), p. 2.

3. See J. Dover Wilson, *What Happens in Hamlet*, 1935 (Cambridge, 1982), and Anthony Esler, *The Aspiring Mind of the Elizabethan Younger Generation* (Durham, NC, 1966).

4. John Harington, *Nugae Antiquae*, Vol. 2, 1779 (Hildesheim, 1968), pp. 225–6.

5. *The Duchess of Malfi*, I.ii.125. For discussions of the relation of failed ambition to melancholy and madness, see Lawrence Babb, *The Elizabethan Malady: A Study of Melancholia in English Literature from 1580 to 1642* (East Lansing, MI, 1951), pp. 122–3; Esler, *The Aspiring Mind of the Elizabethan Younger Generation*, pp. 202–43; and L. C. Knights, *Drama and Society in the Age of Jonson* (New York, 1937), pp. 315–32.

6. Mervyn James, *English Politics and the Concept of Honour, 1485–1642, Past and Present*, Supp. 3 (London, 1978), p. 44.

7. Cf. Smith's characterisation of the Tudor traitor as 'so unbelievably bungling and self-defeating ... that it is difficult to believe [the traitors] were totally sane or that their treason, as perceived by the government, actually existed at all ...' (*Treason in Tudor England*, p. 2).

8. Quoted in Joseph Allen Matter, *My Lords and Lady of Essex: Their State Trials* (Chicago, 1969), p. 5 (emphasis mine).

9. Quoted in Robert Lacey, *Robert, Earl of Essex* (New York, 1970), p. 213.

10. Reprinted in Arthur F. Kinney (ed.), *Elizabethan Backgrounds: Historical Documents of the Age of Elizabeth I* (Hamden, CT, 1975), p. 63. For a valuable discussion of the inadequacy of 'the orthodox Elizabethan framework ... to absorb effectively the facts of heterodoxy and social flux' (p. 59), see Louis Adrian Montrose, 'The Purpose of Playing: Reflections on a Shakespearean Anthropology', *Helios*, ns. 7:2 (1980), 53–76.

11. Kinney, *Elizabethan Backgrounds*, p. 66 (emphasis mine).

12. Lawrence Stone, *The Crisis of the Aristocracy, 1558–1641*, abridged edn (New York, 1967), p. 401. Stone estimates that Essex was responsible for over 25 per cent of the total knighthoods conferred during Elizabeth's reign.

13. "Tis much wondered at here, that [Essex] went so boldly to her Majesty's presence, She not being ready, and he so full of dirt and mire that his very face was full of it', wrote Roland Whyte to Sir Robert Sidney about the incident (qtd in Matter, *My Lords*, p. 14).

14. Harington, *Nugae*, p. 134.

15. Quoted in R. C. Bald, *John Donne: A Life* (New York, 1970), p. 108. Bald holds that 'the writer shows the kind of knowledge of Essex's condition that one would expect from an inmate of York House, and more perhaps than the current gossip would furnish him with' (p. 108, n. 2).

16. Michel Foucault writes, 'This form of power applies itself to immediate everyday life which categorises the individual, marks him by his

own individuality, attaches him to his own identity, imposes a law of truth on him which he must recognise and which others must recognise in him. ... There are two meanings of the word "subject": subject to someone else by control and dependence; and tied to his own identity by a conscience or self-knowledge. Both meanings suggest a form of power which subjugates and makes subject to' ('The Subject and Power', *Critical Inquiry*, 8 [1982], 781).

17. Foucault, 'The Subject and Power', 794–5.

18. Lacey Baldwin Smith, *The Elizabethan World* (Boston, 1967), p. 266.

19. Steven Mullaney, 'Lying Like Truth: Riddle, Representation, and Treason in Renaissance England', *English Literary History*, 47 (1980), 33.

20. Beach Langston considers Essex's death as an embodiment of the *ars moriendi* tradition in 'Essex and the Art of Dying', *Huntington Library Quarterly*, 13 (1950), 109–29. Cf. Karin S. Coddon on *Macbeth*, 'Unreal Mockery: Unreason and the Problem of Spectacle in *Macbeth*', *English Literary History*, 56 (1989), 485–501.

21. Quoted in G. B. Harrison, *The Life and Death of Robert Devereux, Earl of Essex* (New York, 1937), p. 323.

22. J. A. Sharpe, 'Last Dying Speeches: Religion, Ideology, and Public Execution in Seventeenth-Century England', *Past and Present*, 107 (1985), 156.

23. Sharpe, 'Last Dying Speeches', 158–61. Cf. Mervyn James, *English Politics*, pp. 43–54. Other enlightening discussions of the stylistics and ideological implications of executions in early modern England are Foucault, *Discipline and Punish: The Birth of the Prison*, trans. Alan Sheridan (New York, 1977), pp. 3–69, and Samuel Y. Edgerton Jr, '*Maniera* and the *Mannaia*: Decorum and Decapitation in the Sixteenth Century', in *The Meaning of Mannerism*, ed. Franklin W. Robinson and Stephen G. Nichols, Jr (Hanover, 1972), pp. 67–103.

24. Mullaney has written suggestively on the condemned traitor's recovery of decorum in the ritual of execution: 'Confession, execution, and dismemberment, unsettling as they may seem, were not so much punishment as they were the demonstration that what had been a traitor was no longer, and that which had set him off from man and nature had been ... lifted from him. When the body bleeds, treason has been effaced; execution is treason's epilogue, spoken by the law' ('Lying like Truth', 33–4).

25. Langston's essay ('Unreal Mockery') considers a number of the printed accounts of Essex's 'beautiful death'. For a thorough overview of the *ars moriendi* in the English literary tradition, see Nancy Lee Beaty (ed.), *The Craft of Dying: A Study in the Literary Tradition of the Ars Moriendi in England* (New Haven, CT, 1970).

26. Foucault, *Discipline and Punish*, p. 65.

27. Foucault, *Discipline and Punish*, pp. 59–69.

28. Foucault, *Discipline and Punish*, p. 67.

29. Matter, *My Lords*, p. 78.

30. Quoted in ibid.

31. Leonard Tennenhouse, *Power on Display: The Politics of Shakespeare's Genres* (New York, 1986), p. 15.

32. Michel Foucault, *Madness and Civilization: A History of Insanity in the Age of Reason*, trans. Richard Howard (London, 1967), pp. 31–2.

33. Cf. Franco Moretti's commentary on Jacobean tragedy: 'Fully realised tragedy is the parable of the degeneration of the sovereign inserted in a context that *can no longer understand it*' (*Signs Taken for Wonders: Essays in the Sociology of Literary Forms*, trans. Susan Fisher et al. [London, 1983]), p. 55.

34. For critiques of *Madness and Civilization* and of Foucault's methodology, see H. C. Erik Midelfort, 'Madness and Civilization in Early Modern Europe: A Reappraisal of Michel Foucault', in *After the Reformation: Essays in Honor of J. H. Hexter*, ed. Barbara C. Malament (Philadelphia, 1980), pp. 247–65, and Lillian Feder, *Madness in Literature* (Princeton, NJ, 1980), pp. 29–34. Shoshana Felman offers a comparative critique of Foucault and Dérrida on madness in her *Writing and Madness* (Ithaca, NY, 1985), pp. 35–55.

35. What Robert Weimann observes of Hamlet's 'antic disposition' seems to me to be true of madness in much late Elizabethan and early Jacobean tragedy: 'Madness as a "method" of mimesis dissolves important links between the representer and the represented, and can only partially sustain a logical or psychological motivation. What, especially in the court scenes, the "antic dispostion" involves is another mode of release from representivity' ('Mimesis in *Hamlet*', in Patricia Parker and Geoffrey Hartman [eds], *Shakespeare and the Question of Theory* [New York, 1985], p. 204).

36. Franco Moretti, *Signs Taken for Wonders*, pp. 55–64.

37. The 'subversion / containment' debate has provoked lively and often constructive debate among the practitioners of 'new historicism' and 'cultural materialism'. These positions are perhaps most clearly exemplified by Stephen Greenblatt's *Renaissance Self-Fashioning: From More to Shakespeare* (Chicago, 1980), which argues that subversion is inevitably contained in Renaissance representations; and Jonathan Dollimore's *Radical Tragedy* (Chicago, 1984) which aligns representations with contestatory and revolutionary discourses in early modern England.

38. Foucault, *Madness and Civilization*, pp. 35–64; *History of Sexuality*, Vol. 1, trans. Robert Hurley (New York, 1978), pp. 139–45.

39. Francis Barker, *The Tremulous Private Body: Essays on Subjection* (London, 1984), pp. 25–41; Catherine Belsey, *The Subject of Tragedy: Identity and Difference in Renaissance Drama* (London, 1985), pp. 41–2; Terry Eagleton, *William Shakespeare* (Oxford, 1986), pp. 70–5.

40. Belsey, *Subject*, pp. 41–2.

41. Barker, *The Tremulous Private Body*, p. 37; Eagleton, *William Shakespeare*, concurs: Hamlet is a 'kind of nothing ... because he is never identical with himself' (p. 73).

42. Weimann offers an analysis of the popular culture and morality context of 'reason in madness' in *Shakespeare and the Popular Tradition in the Theater*, ed. Robert Schwartz (Baltimore, MD, 1978), pp. 120–33.

43. On the 'ungovernable man', see Greenblatt, *Renaissance Self-Fashioning*, pp. 147–8.

44. On the death of the tragic hero Barker comments, 'Tragic heroes have to die because in the spectacular kingdom death is in the body. There is no "merely" or metaphorically ethical death which does not at the same time entail the extinction of the body, and even its complete and austere destruction' (*Tremulous Private Body*, p. 40).

45. Elaine Showalter offers an enlightening commentary on critical representations of Ophelia's madness in 'Representing Ophelia: Women, Madness, and the Responsibilities of Feminist Criticism', in *Shakespeare and the Question of Theory*, ed. Patricia Parker and Geoffrey Hartman (New York, 1985), pp. 77–94.

46. See Michael MacDonald, *Mystical Bedlam: Madness, Anxiety, and Healing in Seventeenth-Century England* (Cambridge, 1981), pp. 72–85. Michael Neill considers the relation of tragedy to the post-Reformation problematising of death, with the Protestant rejection of 'the whole vast industry of intercession, and masses for the dead' (p. 180); see '"Exeunt with a Dead March": Funeral Pageantry on the Shakespearean Stage', in *Pageantry in the Shakespearean Theater*, ed. David M. Bergeron (Athens, GA, 1985). Clare Gittings also considers at length the social and psychological effects of the Reformation upon grieving and funeral practices in *Death, Burial, and the Individual in Early Modern England* (London, 1984).

47. See Keith Thomas, *Religion and the Decline of Magic* (New York, 1971), pp. 1–21.

48. Cf. Elaine Showalter, 'Representing Ophelia', pp. 80–3.

49. See Foucault, *History of Sexuality*, pp. 104, 121.

50. On the interplay of the equivocal, the irrational, and the supernatural (with particular reference to *Macbeth*) see Steven Mullaney, 'Lying Like Truth', 32–47; and Karin S. Coddon, 'Unreal Mockery: Unreason and the Problem of Spectacle in *Macbeth*', *English Literary History*, 56 (1989), 485–501.

51. On the theatre's construction of – and reflections on – its own authority see Louis Adrian Montrose, '"Shaping Fantasies": Figurations of Gender and Power in Elizabethan Culture', *Representations*, 44:2 (1983), 61–94.

52. Margaret Ferguson offers an interesting reading of the problematics of the closet scene in her fine essay '*Hamlet*: Letters and Spirits', in *Shakespeare and the Question of Theory*, ed. Patricia Parker and Geoffrey Hartman, pp. 292–309 (see esp. 296–7).

53. Michael D. Bristol, *Carnival and Theater: Plebeian Culture and the Structure of Authority in Renaissance England* (New York, 1985), p. 187.

54. Insightful comments on the 'antic' qualities of the graveyard scene may be found in Robert Weimann, *Shakespeare and the Popular Tradition*, pp. 239–40; Barker, *The Tremulous Private Body*, pp. 39–40.

55. Ferguson's essay ('*Hamlet*: Letters and Spirits') considers the complex function of the *memento mori* in *Hamlet* (302–5). For a reading of *Hamlet* as a '*memento mori* poem', see Harry Morris, *Last Things in Shakespeare* (Tallahassee, FL, 1985), pp. 311–41.

56. Foucault, *Madness*, p. 32.

57. In each of its many metamorphoses, this essay has benefited from the criticism, guidance, and encouragement I have received from Louis A. Montrose; to him I extend my gratitude.

5

Shakespeare Bewitched

STEPHEN GREENBLATT

For the great witchmongers of the late Middle Ages and early Renaissance, those who wrote that there should be more fear, more denunciations of women, more confessions extorted under torture, and above all more executions, the initial task was to reverse a dangerous current of literate disbelief. They saw themselves as beginning, that is, less with a confused mass of folk practices that they had to sift through and organise into a coherent demonology, than with well-established and socially acceptable doubt. Indeed the doubt was not only socially acceptable but had for centuries been theologically sanctioned, for in a series of important medieval texts church authorities had attacked those people – for the most part, as the church conceived it, women – who had been seduced by what Reginone of Prüm in the tenth century called 'the phantasms and illusions of demons' (*daemonum illusionibus et phantasmatibus seductae*).[1]

Reginone's phrase leaves unclear the exact status of the seductive fantasies: they could refer to a mistaken belief in the existence of certain demons who do not exist or to illusions caused by demons who do in fact exist or to a belief in non-existent demons caused by Satan. His work, *De Ecclesiasticis Disciplinis*, is not, it needs hardly be said, a thoroughgoing sceptical critique of supernatural agency, but it vigorously encourages scepticism about a whole series of claims associated with the witch cult:

> Wicked women who have given themselves back to Satan and been seduced by the phantasms and illusions of demons believe and declare that they can ride with Diana the pagan goddess and a huge

throng of women on chosen beasts in the hours of night. They say that in the silence of the night they can traverse great stretches of territory, that they obey Diana as though she were their mistress and that on certain nights she calls them to her special service.[2]

For Reginone, the world of the ancient gods is not a solid, undeniable reality that must be proven demonic rather than divine but a mirage, a set of vain, seductive dreams behind which lurks the Father of Lies. Reality is leached out, as it were, from the old beliefs and concentrated in the figure of Satan.[3]

This project was furthered in the early eleventh century by Burchard, bishop of Worms. In his influential penitential canon, known as the *Canon episcopi*, Burchard wrote that belief in witchcraft was itself a sin, a heretical relapse into paganism. He is, like Reginone, particularly contemptuous of dreams of night-flying with Diana, Hecate, or the German Holde, and his scepticism extends to tales of horrific acts:

> Do you believe this, in common with many women who are followers of Satan? Namely that, in the silence of the night, when you are stretched out upon your bed with your husband's head upon your breast you have the power, flesh as you are, to go out of the closed door and traverse great stretches of space with other women in a similar state of self-deception? And do you believe that you can kill, though without visible arms, people baptized and redeemed by the blood of Christ, and can cook and eat their flesh, after putting some straw or a piece of wood or something in the place of the heart? And then that you can resuscitate them after you have eaten them and make them live again? If yes, then you must do forty days of penance, that is, a Lent, on bread and water for seven consecutive years.[4]

It is important to note the relative leniency of the penalties Burchard assigns here and elsewhere. These penalties, ranging from forty days to two years,[5] reflect a conviction that witches have no real malevolent powers but rather have succumbed to illusions of diabolic agency, vain dreams of night-flying and animal metamorphosis, and impotent fantasies of murderous potency. The fact that such fantasies are widespread does not, for Burchard, testify to their reality but rather suggests that they are the stuff of nightmare: 'Who is there who has not been taken out of himself in dreams and nightmares and seen in his sleep things he would never see when awake? Who is imbecile enough to imagine that such things, seen only in the mind, have a bodily reality?'[6]

By the later fourteenth century, in the wake of the Black Death, intellectual convictions and institutional alignments had shifted, scepticism was no longer officially encouraged, and nightmares began to assume once again a bodily reality. But the *Canon episcopi* remained on the books and there must have been a considerable reservoir of doubt, for in the famous *Malleus maleficarum* of 1484, the Dominican inquisitors, Heinrich Kramer and James Sprenger evidently believe that they can swing their hammer at witches only by swinging it simultaneously at sceptics. The *Canon episcopi*, they argue, has been completely misunderstood; it condemned a narrow range of heretical beliefs but was never intended to deny the actual existence of witchcraft practices attested to in the Holy Scriptures and credited by a wide range of unimpeachable authorities. Indeed, write Kramer and Sprenger, it would be heretical to deny the real menace of witchcraft (p. 4); hence 'all Bishops and Rulers who do not essay their utmost to suppress crimes of this sort ... are themselves to be judged as evident abettors of the crime, and are manifestly to be punished'.[7]

The *Malleus maleficarum* then sets as its task the transfer of a set of concepts, images, and fears from the zone of the imaginary to the zone of the real. What is the zone of the imaginary? In the late sixteenth century Spenser imagined it as a chamber of the mind filled with 'leasings, tales, and lies', a jumble of images that sober reason or common sense or those in positions of power deem misshapen, confused, forged, incredible, or simply false.[8] Churchmen like Reginone and Burchard had painstakingly crated up and moved into such a chamber the whole vast furniture of pagan belief, and with it the nightmare images of witch cults. Now Kramer and Sprenger take it upon themselves to unpack those images and officially confer upon them once again the unfeigned solidity of embodied reality. But the task is not uncomplicated.

Dogmatic assertion is, of course, the inquisitor's stock-in-trade – as Empson put it, 'heads I win, tails I burn you at the stake' – but to confer the air of truth on practices that had been earlier condemned by the church itself as pernicious fantasies called for a supplement to threats of 'terrible penalties, censures, and punishment ... without any right to appeal' (p. xlv). Such threats by themselves were more likely to bully people into grudging, silent compliance than to inspire them to robust belief. Hence Kramer and Sprenger are drawn to supplement their affirmations with something like evidence, the evidence of narrative. 'There was in the diocese of Basel', a typical passage begins, 'in a town called Oberweiler situated on the Rhine, an honest parish priest, who fondly held the opinion, or rather error, that there was no witchcraft in the world, but that it existed in the imagination of men who attributed such things to witches.' This sentence characteristically introduces not simply a theory (in this case, the rationalising theory of imaginative projection that Kramer and Sprenger oppose) but an anecdote, an instructive tale in which the misguided doubter is brought to a correct view of the matter: 'And God wished so to purge him of this error that ...' (p. 103).

We don't need to rehearse the nasty little story that follows, but the point is that they did. They evidently felt that scholastic arguments and belligerent appeals to authority were not enough to establish witchcraft doctrines on a stable footing; Kramer and Sprenger needed to confer on what their own church had labelled fantasies the solidity of palpable truth, to give invisible agents, secret compacts, obscene rites, spectacular transformations both a compelling general theory and a convincing local habitation. After all, they wanted men and women not merely to assent formally to a set of abstract theoretical propositions about the operation of evil but to denounce and kill their neighbours. Faced with the necessity of producing the effect of the real out of the materials of fantasy, the inquisitors turned to narrative. The *Malleus maleficarum* rehearses dozens of tales crafted to redraw the boundary between the imaginary and the real, or rather to siphon off the darkest contents of the imagination and pour them, like a poison, into the ear of the world.

Why shouldn't we say the same thing about Shakespeare's *Macbeth*? Why shouldn't we say that the play, with immeasurably greater literary force, undertakes to re-enchant the world, to shape misogyny to political ends, to counteract the corrosive scepticism that had called into question both the existence of witches and the sacredness of royal authority? Recent criticism has come close to saying this: *Macbeth*, writes Peter Stallybrass, 'mobilises the patriarchal fear of unsubordinated woman, the unstable element to which Kramer and Sprenger attributed the overthrow of "nearly all the kingdoms of the world"'.[9] And in a compelling analysis of the play's fantasies of masculine vulnerability to women, Janet Adelman has suggested that 'the final solution, both for Macbeth and for the play itself, though in differing ways, is ... [a] radical excision of the female'. 'The play that begins by unleashing the terrible threat of maternal power and demonstrates the helplessness of its central male figure before that power', Adelman argues, 'ends by consolidating male power, in effect solving the problem of masculinity by eliminating the female.'[10] Why shouldn't we say then that *Macbeth*, with its staging of witches and its final solution, probably contributed, in an indirect but powerful way, to the popular fear of demonic agency and the official persecution and killing of women? Why shouldn't we say that this play about evil is evil?[11]

There are important and cogent reasons why we should not say anything like this. First, though it gestures toward history, *Macbeth* is a self-conscious work of theatrical fiction, an entertainment in which nothing need be taken as real, in which everything can be understood, as Shakespeare suggested elsewhere, to be 'shadow' or 'dream'. Second, no one in the period, least of all the players themselves, understood the designation 'King's Men' to imply an official, prescriptive function, the equivalent of the papal bull that was printed with the *Malleus maleficarum*. Neither Shakespeare nor his company was speaking dogmatically or even indirectly on behalf of any institution except the marginal, somewhat disreputable institution of the theatre, disreputable precisely because it was the acknowledged house of fantasies. Third, there is no attempt in the play to give counsel to anyone about how to behave toward the witches and no apparent sanctioning – as in Dekker's *Witch of Edmonton*, for example, or in Shakespeare's own *I Henry VI* – of legal prosecution or execution. It would have been simple enough to have the victorious Malcolm declare his determination to rid his kingdom of witches, but he does no such thing. Instead, with none of the questions their existence poses answered, they simply disappear: 'The Witches Dance, and vanish.' Fourth, within *Macbeth*'s representation of the witches, there is profound ambiguity about the actual significance and power of their malevolent intervention. If the strange prophecies of the Weird Sisters had been ignored, the play seems to imply, the same set of events might have occurred anyway, impelled entirely by the pressure of Macbeth's violent ambition and his wife's psychological manipulation. (Macbeth, Hecate complains to her followers, is a 'wayward son' who 'loves for his own ends, not for you' [III.v.13]).[12] And fifth, even if we could demonstrate that witch prosecutions in England were somehow prolonged or intensified by *Macbeth* – and, of course, the actual proof of such horrible consequences is almost impossible to establish – in the absence of evidence of malign authorial intention, we would not, I think, deem Shakespeare's play evil, any more than we have held Salmon Rushdie's *Satanic Verses* to be evil because of the deaths that occurred in the riots caused by its publication.[13]

It is possible to identify evil texts – the *Malleus maleficarum* is one, I believe – and these in principle may include works of art. Such a judgement would involve, at a minimum, the demonstration of a calculated attempt to produce by means of discourse effects that are morally reprehensible – for example, to incite racial hatred and murder.[14] But it is notoriously hazardous to submit works of art to political or moral judgement or to calculate their practical consequences. If it is perilous to try to gauge the political valence of works of art written in our own time, how much more implausible is it to apply a test of progressive politics to works written almost four hundred years ago? I should add that I think it important, in the interest of preserving the small breathing space of the imagination, to resist the recent tendency to conflate, or even to collapse into one another, aesthetics, ethics, and politics.

And yet, and yet. What is the point of speaking at all about the historical situation of works of art if ideological entailments and practical consequences are somehow off-limits, and if they are not off-limits, how can we avoid moral judgements? What is the point of interrogating the status of literature – of challenging the cult of autonomy, undermining the illusion of aesthetic aloofness, questioning the very existence in the Renaissance of an independent aesthetic sphere – if we are not to insist that the power of a work like *Macbeth* must be a power *in* the world, a power *for* something? We may tell ourselves that its power is to produce a specific form of pleasure and that a distinction between the production of pleasure and other purposes such as exchange or functional utility is quite important.[15] But a radical distinction between pleasure and use is difficult to maintain, especially for a Renaissance text. The period's defences of the stage routinely include accounts of the social power of drama, accounts echoed in Hamlet's deployment of *The Murder of Gonzago*, and if the claims seem extravagant to the point of absurdity, there is ample evidence of a significant, if less spectacular, cultural and political power. More important, perhaps, the specific pleasure produced by *Macbeth* is bound up with the representation of witches, and that representation was only possible in and through a particularly fraught cultural negotiation with theological and political discourses that had a direct effect on the lives of men and women. The play may not be reducible to its political and ethical consequences, but it cannot escape having consequences, even if those consequences are difficult to trace and to evaluate.

In the early seventeenth century, it was impossible to contain a depiction of witches strictly within the boundaries of art, for the status of witches – the efficacy of their charms, their ability to harm, the reality of their claims or of the charges brought against them, their very existence – was not a fixed feature in the cultural landscape but a subject of contestation.[16] The contestation was not, of course, due to any censoring power possessed by those who were called or who called themselves witches – one of the central paradoxes of the discourse of witchcraft, widely recognised in the period, is that the women identified as wielding immense metaphysical power were for the most part socially marginal.[17] In their own local communities some of them may well have exercised power both to harm and to heal, but they had no control over their representations (let alone access to the means of self-representation in print), so that a playwright, for example, could figure them as he wished without calculating any conceivable objections from them. It was principally among the educated elite, among those who had it in their power to punish, to pardon, and to represent, that there was serious disagreement about how witches should be conceived or even whether they should be said to exist at all.[18] To represent witches on the public stage was inevitably to participate in some way or other in the contestation.

Let us recall the anonymous parish priest who claimed that 'there was no witchcraft in the world, but that it existed in the imagination of men who attributed such things to witches'. The sceptics against whom Kramer and Sprenger write had withdrawn witchcraft from the real world and relocated it in the 'imagination', the place haunted by what Reginone and others had called demonic illusions and phantasms. 'It is useless', the *Malleus maleficarum* replies, 'to argue that any result of witchcraft may be a phantasy and unreal, because such a phantasy cannot be procured without resort to the power of the devil, and it is necessary that there should be made a contract with the devil, by which contract the witch truly and actually binds herself to be the servant of the devil and devotes herself to the devil, and this is not done in any dream or under any illusion, but she herself bodily and truly cooperates with, and conjoins herself to, the devil' (p. 7). The reality of witchcraft here is secured by the reality of the demonic contract – a contract insisted upon dogmatically, we may suggest, precisely because it is the one thing (unlike withered arms, dead cattle, or male impotence) that is *never* actually witnessed. That founding reality, theoretically necessary and secured by inquisitorial authority, then licenses a sophisticated blurring of the boundaries between reality and illusion: Kramer and Sprenger concede that allegedly demonic harms may at times be fantasies, because they claim that such fantasies are themselves consequences (and hence evidence) of the demonic contract.[19]

According to the scholastic psychology of the *Malleus maleficarum*, devils provoke and shape fantasies by direct corporeal intervention in the mind: demonic spirits can incite what Kramer and Sprenger call a 'local motion' in the minds of those awake as well as asleep, stirring up and exciting the inner perceptions, 'so that ideas retained in the repositories of their minds are drawn out and made apparent to the faculties of fancy and imagination, so that such men imagine these things to be true'. This process of making a stir in the mind and moving images from one part of the brain to another is, they write, called 'interior temptation' (p. 50).[20] It can lead men to see objects before their eyes – daggers, for example – that are not in fact there; conversely, it can lead men *not* to see other objects – their own penises, for example – that are still there, though concealed from view by what Kramer and Sprenger call a 'glamour' (p. 58). Hence, they write, 'a certain man tells that, when he had lost his member, he approached a known witch to ask her to restore it to him. She told the afflicted man to climb a certain tree, and that he might take which he liked out of a nest in which there were several members. And when he tried to take a big one, the witch said: You must not take that one; adding because it belonged to a parish priest.' 'All these things', they soberly add, attaching the ribald anticlerical folktale to their humourless explanatory apparatus, 'are caused by devils through an illusion or glamour ... by confusing the organ of vision by transmuting the mental images in the imaginative faculty' (p. 121).[21]

One hundred years after the publication of the *Malleus maleficarum*, an English country gentleman, Reginald Scot, was tempted to regard much of the work as a 'bawdie discourse', a kind of obscene joke book. But he checked the impulse: 'These are no jestes', he writes, 'for they be written by them that were and are judges upon the lives and deaths of those persons' (p. 45). Scot's response to Kramer and Sprenger and Bodin and the whole persecutorial apparatus is *The Discoverie of Witchcraft*, the greatest English contribution to the sceptical critique of witchcraft. The *Discoverie* attacks witchcraft beliefs across a broad front, but at its centre is an attempt to locate those beliefs not *in* but *as* the imagination. That is, Scot's principal concern is with the boundary between the imaginary and the real, and where Kramer and Sprenger had viewed that boundary as porous, Scot views it as properly closed. The sickness of his own times is precisely its inability to distinguish the projections of troubled fantasy from the solid truths of the material world. The principal cause of this sickness – spiritual weakness – turns out to be one of its principal consequences as well: 'The fables of Witchcraft have taken so fast hold and deepe root in the heart of man', the book begins, 'that fewe or none can (nowadaies) with patience indure the hand and correction of God.'

It is, Scot's language suggests here, fables rather than devils that have taken possession, invading the body and fixing themselves in the heart: the world, he writes, is 'bewitched and over-run with this fond error' (p. 3). This shift from demonic agency to the vicious power of human fictions is the crucial perception of the *Discoverie*.[22] Hence Scot's obsession with the exact operation of sleights of hand, his tireless description of what from this distance seem to us jejune parlour tricks, his careful exposition of the hidden mechanisms by means of which certain theatrical illusions, such as decapitation, are achieved. For these tricks, in Scot's view, have fuelled the spiritual impatience and shaped the anxious fantasies of men, until maddened crowds, deluded by fraudulent spectacles, call for the death of witches, and magistrates hang unloved, vulnerable, and innocent old women.

Scot's project is disenchantment in the interest of restoring proper religious faith: he must take away from the witches themselves and from the culture that has credited (and, as Scot perfectly understands, largely created) their claims and confessions their air of wonder. Accordingly, his witches are blear-eyed, toothless village misfits or contemptible swindlers. Scot would have dismissed as pernicious nonsense the notion, recently revived by certain anthropologists and historians, that the 'wise women' and 'cunning men' of this period represented half-suppressed currents of ancient ecstatic religion or articulated a deep popular protest against the social order or exercised significant power to threaten and to cure.[23] Women accused of witchcraft, he strenuously argues, are for the most part harmless melancholiacs and hysterics incapable of distinguishing between reality and fantasy.[24] Scot is willing to concede a small measure of initiative to a few self-described witches, but only the initiative of unscrupulous 'jugglers', itinerant tricksters willing to profit from the gullibility and foolishness of country folk. Even a juggler of modest talent can convince people that they have seen with their own eyes what does not in fact exist; hence the eyewitness testimony so often advanced to prove the existence of witchcraft only proves the unreliability of the sense and what Marx called the idiocy of rural life.

To succeed in his project it is not enough to challenge the authority of the eyewitness. Scot must not only demystify vision, but also expose the extent to which the experience of wonder – the thrilled recognition of the presence of supernatural power in the material world – depends upon language. 'Natural magic', Scot remarks, 'consisteth as well in the deceit of words, as in the sleight of hand' (p. 250). Hence he writes portentously of two 'most miraculous matters'. Of one of these, he says, he has himself been '*Testis oculatus*', of the other he has been 'crediblie and certeinelie informed'; that is, one comes to him via sight, the other via words. The extended descriptions of the exotic objects – a 'peece of earth' from Russia that shrinks from heated steel but pursues gold and silver; an Indian stone that contains within it a substance of 'marvellous brightnes, puritie, and shining' – are an anthology of the verbal cues for wonder, but the wonder lasts only as long as the reader fails to realise that Scot is describing man and fire. Once the reader understands what is going on, admiration vanishes, leaving a sense of irony that borders on contempt: these are, after all, deliberately bad jokes. In both of them, it is the language of description that confers upon the objects their supernatural strangeness,[25] and, Scot observes, the 'deceipt of words' here need not involve any outright falsehood: 'Lieng is avoided with a figurative speech, in the which either the words themselves, or their interpretation have a double or doubtfull meaning' (p. 176).

It is figurative speech then, supported by visual illusion, that for Scot lies at the heart not only of the discourse of witchcraft but of the practices and persecutions that are linked with this discourse. Men cannot stand the experience of certain powerful emotions – uncertainty, for example, or fear – that are not attached to *figures*, and they are consequently vulnerable to anyone who offers them the satisfaction of figuration: 'Men in all ages have beene so desirous to know the effect of their purposes, the sequele of things to come, and to see the end of their feare and hope; that a seelie witch, which had learned anie thing in the art of cousenage, may make a great manie jollie fooles' (p. 197). And what makes men vulnerable also makes them murderous. In their impatience or their terror or their desire, men compulsively cross what we may call the threshold of figuration; they have fashioned metaphors and then killed the crazed women who have been unprotected or foolish enough to incarnate their appalling fantasies. Hence the force of the wordplay, ironically re-enchanting what he most wishes to disenchant, to which Scot is repeatedly drawn: 'The world is now so bewitched ... with this fond error' (p. 3) or again, the whore's 'eie infecteth, entiseth, and (if I maie so saie) bewitcheth' (p. 172) or again, 'illusions are right inchantments' (p. 9). For it is this figurative capacity of language that has led men to take witchcraft literally and even to find support for their fatal mistake by misreading the Scriptures.

The Scriptures are driven by the grossness of human understanding to express spiritual truths in figurative expressions that men characteristically misinterpret; many men are 'so carnallie minded', observes Scot, 'that a spirit is no sooner spoken of, but immediatlie they thinke of a black man with cloven feet, a paire of hornes, a taile, clawes, and eies as broad as a bason' (p. 507). To be 'carnally minded' is to have a mind that is flesh, a mind inextricably linked to the material world, a mind that resists the saving, bodiless abstractions of the spirit. Such a mind cannot pass, as it properly should, from the Bible's figures to immaterial, other-worldly truths but moves instead in the opposite direction: from imaginary figures to literal bodies. And the key to this fatal error is the dangerous power of human language, its capacity to figure what is not there, its ability to be worked into 'double or doubtfull meaning', its proneness to deceit and illusion. Witches are the immaterial figures of the mind made flesh; behind the twisted belief and fear and killing lurks a misplaced faith in metaphor.

The problem then, to adapt a phrase of Wittgenstein's, is 'the bewitchment of our intelligence by means of language'.[26] And, predictably, it is the masters of language, the poets, who have been the principal sources of the false figures. '*Ovid* affirmeth', writes Scot, that witches

> can raise and suppresse lightening and thunder, raine and haile, clouds and winds, tempests and earthquakes. Others do write, that they can pull downe the moone and the starres. Some write that with wishing they can send needles into the livers of their enimies. Some that they can transferre corne in the blade from one place to another.

> Some, that they can cure diseases supernaturallie, flie in the aire, and dance with divels. ... They can raise spirits (as others affirme) drie up springs, turne the course of running waters, inhibit the sunne, and staie both day and night, changing the one into the other. They can go in and out at awger holes, & saile in an egge shell, a cockle or muscle shell, through and under the tempestuous seas. They can go invisible, and deprive men of their privities, and otherwise of the act and use of venerie. They can bring soules out of the graves. ... But in this case a man may saie, that *Miranda canunt / sed non credenda Poetae.*
>
> (1.4.8)

The poet's wonders must not be believed. 'All this stuffe', Scot writes, 'is vaine and fabulous' (p. 260). Human language, as opposed to the word of God, does not possess authentic creative power, only the ability to counterfeit that power; 'for by the sound of the words nothing commeth, nothing goeth, otherwise than God in nature hath ordeined to be doone by ordinary speech' (p. 124). Against bewitching metaphors the *Discoverie* marshals the sceptical, aphoristic wisdom – empirical, political, and aesthetic – of the everyday:

> If all the divels in hell were dead, and all the witches in *England* burnt or hanged, I warrant you we should not faile to have raine, haile, and tempests.
>
> (p. 3)
>
> They can also bring to passe, that chearne as long as you list, your butter will not come; especially ... if the maids have eaten up the cream.
>
> (p. 6)
>
> The pope maketh rich witches, saints; and burneth the poore witches.
>
> (p. 179)
>
> I for my part have read a number of their conjurations, but never could see anie divels of theirs, except it were in a plaie.
>
> (p. 258)

'Except it were in a plaie.' I do not know what plays Scot who published the *Discoverie* in 1584 had in mind. (He had been a student at Oxford and may have seen or acted in plays there.) The great English Renaissance drama – including, of course, *Doctor Faustus* and *Macbeth* – lies ahead. What, if anything, does it mean for this drama to come after Scot? Scot's book had no official or

semi-official standing. We are not dealing with a situation comparable to exorcism in the 1590s, where the state and the church
decided to stop a controversial charismatic practice, a practice consequently branded by institutional spokesmen as a kind of illicit
theatre. In that case, as I have argued elsewhere, Shakespeare could
appropriate for the stage the intense social energies that were under
attack as theatrical; he could at once confirm the theatricality of exorcism and recreate its suspect power, now dutifully marked out as
fraudulent, for his own purposes. But this model of mutually
profitable circulation does not apply to witchcraft. We are dealing
instead with a contestation in which a straightforward appropriation or exchange is not possible. For while the Elizabethan ruling
elite shared very little of the Continental enthusiasm for witchcraft
prosecutions, they were in general unwilling to adopt Scot's wholly
sceptical position and had no ideological interest in handing over
the representation of witches to the theatre.

Even before James (whose *Daemonologie* includes an attack on
Scot) brought his own complex interest in witchcraft to the throne,
English intellectuals were struggling to work out ways of answering
Scot – often by adopting certain aspects of his scepticism and at the
same time containing them within a continued persecutorial structure. Hence George Gifford's spokesman, Daniel, in *A Dialogue
Concerning Witches and Witchcraftes* (1593), grants that witches
can harm no one through supernatural intervention – they are only
miserable and deluded old women – but argues that they should be
'rooted out and destroyed' (H1v) because of their evil intentions and
their threat to the faith. The threat is a serious one because if the
witches' compact with the devil gives them no power beyond
nature, it does give them access to extraordinarily acute knowledge
of nature. The devil has, after all, been around for millennia; he has
become a brilliant pathologist and can see long before any human
observer when a child or a valuable animal is about to become ill
through entirely natural causes. He then hurries to his follower the
witch and incites her to claim credit for the incipient illness, whereupon a natural cause is read by everyone as a supernatural cause
and a tribute to the devil's power. Similarly, King James (who had
Scot's book burned) concedes that much of what passes for
manifestation of the demonic is mere trickery, but then he reminds
his reader that the devil is notoriously agile. Hence it stands to
reason that Satan will teach his followers 'many juglarie trickes at
Cardes, dice, & such like, to deceiue mennes senses thereby'

(*Daemonologie*, p. 22) – and hence too what is for Scot a sign of the fraudulence and emptiness of the discourse of witchcraft becomes for James a further proof of the demonic compact.

There is textual evidence – especially in *Midsummer Night's Dream* and *Macbeth* – that Shakespeare had read the *Discoverie*, but even if he had not, he could not have escaped an awareness of the contestation. [...]

Scot had argued that any credible representation of a witch was an illegitimate attempt to give form to an inchoate emotion; to discredit witchcraft beliefs was to return the individual to a proper acceptance of God's judgements. But giving visible form to inchoate emotions is exactly the task of the dramatist. His whole project is the imaginative manipulation of the verbal and visual illusions that Scot tirelessly sought to expose as empty. What is at stake here is a divergence between the ethical and theatrical conditions of figurability.[27] For Scot the passage from inchoate emotion to figuration – from fear or impatience or desire to an identifiable, luminously visible figure – is the source of evil; for Shakespeare it is the source of the dramatist's art.

Witchcraft provided Shakespeare with a rich source of imaginative energy, a collective disturbance upon which he could draw to achieve powerful theatrical effects. But a dramatist could only achieve these effects, as both classical and Renaissance literary theorists argued, if this energy were conjoined with what Aristotle called *enargeia*, the liveliness that comes when metaphors are set in action, when things are put vividly before the mind's eye, when language achieves visibility.[28] The most important classical account of *enargeia* is by the great first-century rhetorician Quintilian for whom it is an essential technique in arguing cases before a court of law. How do you make your legal arguments persuasive? That is, how do you impress your account of what really happened, your version of the truth, upon your auditors and, for that matter, upon yourself? By drawing on the power of fantasies or visions, 'images by which the representations of absent objects are so distinctly represented to the mind, that we seem to see them with our eyes, and to have them before us' (*Institutes*, 6.2.29). The person who best conceives such images, who can 'vividly represent to himself things, voices, actions, with the exactness of reality [*verum optime finget*]', will have the greatest power in moving the feelings. We all produce such images readily, Quintilian observes, whenever we idly indulge in chimerical dreams, disposing of wealth or power that is not our own; and shall we not, he asks, 'turn this lawless power of our minds to our advantage?'

For Quintilian then the orator's task is to make something out of the imagination's capacity to fashion illusions – specifically, to bring forth the strong emotions that accompany the conviction of reality. 'I make a complaint that a man has been murdered; shall I not bring before my eyes everything that is likely to have happened when the murder occurred? Shall not the assassin suddenly sally forth? Shall not the other tremble, cry out, supplicate, or flee? Shall I not behold the one striking, the other falling? Shall not the blood, and paleness, and last gasp of the expiring victim, present itself fully to my mental view? Hence will result that *enargeia* which is called by Cicero *illustration* and *evidentness*, which seems not so much to narrate as to exhibit; and our feelings will be moved not less strongly than if we were actually present at the affairs of which we are speaking.'

It is this imaginative capacity to make what is absent present, to give invisible things the emotional force of embodied realities, that Reginald Scot fears and despises, for it has led in his view to a massive collective delusion and to the persecution of thousands of innocent victims. And Quintilian's account enables us to see why Scot is so deeply critical of poets: poets are particularly dangerous because they are the masters of *enargeia*. Scot seeks in effect to block the fusion of emotional disturbance and illusory embodiment in the discourse of witchcraft, for if inward anxieties are given no visible outlet, if they fail to achieve credible representation, if they are not enacted, witches will no longer be either believed or persecuted. We have no way of knowing if Shakespeare took Scot's position seriously, though *The Comedy of Errors* may suggest that on at least one occasion he did;[29] we do know from *I Henry VI* and from *Macbeth* that Shakespeare was willing to present witchcraft as a visible, credible practice.

But there is a crucial difference – beyond the quantum leap in theatrical power – between the representation of witchcraft in *I Henry VI* and *Macbeth*. The demonic in Shakespeare's early history play makes history happen: it accounts for the uncanny success of the French peasant girl, for her power to fascinate and to inspire, and it accounts too for her failure. The witches in *Macbeth* by contrast account for nothing. They are given many of the conventional attributes of both Continental and English witch lore, the signs and wonders that Scot traces back to the poets: they are associated with tempests, and particularly with thunder and lightning; they are shown calling to their familiars and conjuring spirits; they recount killing livestock, raising winds, sailing in a sieve; their hideous broth links them to birth-strangled babes and blaspheming Jews; above all, they traffic in prognostication and prophecy.[30] And yet though the witches are given a vital theatrical *enargeia*, though their malevolent energy is apparently put in act – 'I'll do, I'll do, and I'll do' – it is in fact extremely difficult to specify what, if anything, they do or even what, if anything, they are.[31]

'What are these', Banquo asks when he and Macbeth first encounter them,

> So wither'd and so wild in their attire,
> That look not like th'inhabitants o'th'earth,
> And yet are on't?
> (I.iii.39–42)

Macbeth echoes the question, 'Speak, if you can: – what are you?' to which he receives in reply his own name: 'All hail, Macbeth!' Macbeth is evidently too startled to respond, and Banquo resumes the interrogation:

> I'th' name of truth,
> Are ye fantastical, or that indeed
> Which outwardly ye show?
> (I.iii.52–4)

The question is slightly odd, since Banquo has already marvelled at an outward show that would itself seem entirely fantastical: 'You should be women, / And yet your beards forbid me to interpret / That you are so.' But 'fantastical' here refers not to the witches' equivocal appearance but to a deeper doubt, a doubt not about their gender but about their existence. They had at first seemed to be the ultimate figures of the alien – Banquo initially remarked that they did not look like earthlings – but now their very 'outwardness', their existence outside the mind and its fantasies, is called into question.[32]

What is happening here is that Shakespeare is staging the epistemological and ontological dilemmas that in the deeply contradictory ideological situation of his time haunted virtually all attempts to determine the status of witchcraft beliefs and practices.[33] And he is at the same time and by the same means staging the insistent, unresolved questions that haunt the practice of the theatre. For *Macbeth* manifests a deep, intuitive recognition that the theatre and witchcraft are both constructed on the boundary between fantasy and reality, the border or membrane where the imagination and the corporeal world, figure and actuality, psychic disturbance and objective truth meet. The means normally used to secure that border are speech and sight, but it is exactly these that are uncertain; the witches, as Macbeth exclaims, are 'imperfect speakers', and at the moment he insists that they account for themselves, they vanish.

The startled Banquo proposes a theory that would keep the apparition within the compass of nature: 'The earth hath bubbles, as the water has, / And these are of them.' The theory, whose seriousness is difficult to gauge, has the virtue of at once acknowledging the witches' material existence – they are 'of the earth' – and accounting for the possibility of their natural disappearance. If witches are earth bubbles, they would consist of air around which the earth takes form; hence they could, as Macbeth observes, vanish 'into the air'. But Banquo's theory cannot dispel the sense of a loss of moorings, for the hags' disappearance intensifies the sense of the blurring of boundaries that the entire scene has generated: 'What seem'd corporal', Macbeth observes, 'Melted as breath into the wind' (I.iii.81–2).[34]

Virtually everything that follows in the play transpires on the border between fantasy and reality, a sickening betwixt-and-between where a mental 'image' has the uncanny power to produce bodily effects 'against the use of nature', where Macbeth's 'thought, whose murther yet is but fantastical' can so shake his being that 'function is smother'd in surmise, / And nothing is, but what is not' (I.iii.141–2), where one mind is present to the innermost fantasies of another, where manhood threatens to vanish and murdered men walk, and blood cannot be washed off.[35] If these effects could be securely attributed to the agency of the witches, we would at least have the security of a defined and focused fear. Alternatively, if the witches could be definitively dismissed as fantasy or fraud, we would at least have the clear-eyed certainty of grappling with human causes in an altogether secular world. But instead Shakespeare achieves the remarkable effect of a nebulous infection, a bleeding of the demonic into the secular and the secular into the demonic.

The most famous instance of this effect is Lady Macbeth's great invocation of the 'spirits / That tend on mortal thoughts' to unsex her, fill her with cruelty, make thick her blood, and exchange her milk with gall. The speech appears to be a conjuration of demonic powers, an act of witchcraft in which the 'murdering ministers' are directed to bring about a set of changes in her body. She calls these ministers 'sightless substances'; though invisible, they are – as she conceives them – not figures of speech or projections of her mind, but objective, substantial beings.[36] But the fact that the spirits she invokes are 'sightless' already moves this passage away from the earth-bubble corporeality of the Weird Sisters and toward the metaphorical use of 'spirits' in Lady Macbeth's words, a few moments earlier, 'Hie thee hither, / That I may pour my spirits in thine ear' (I.v.24–5). The 'spirits' she speaks of here are manifestly figurative – they refer to the bold words, the undaunted mettle, and the sexual taunts with which she intends to incite Macbeth to murder Duncan – but, like all of her expressions of will and passion, they strain toward bodily realisation, even as they convey a psychic and hence invisible inwardness. That is, there is something uncannily literal about Lady Macbeth's influence on her husband, as if she had contrived to inhabit his mind – as if, in other words, she had literally poured her spirits in his ear. Conversely, there is something uncannily figurative about the 'sightless substances' she invokes, as if the spirit world, the realm of 'Fate and metaphysical aid', were only a metaphor for her blind and murderous desires, as if the Weird Sisters were condensations of her own breath.[37]

We can glimpse the means by which Shakespeare achieves what I have called 'bleeding' – the mutual contamination of the secular and the demonic – if we recall the long passage from Scot about the fraudulent wonders that Ovid and the other poets attribute to witches: raising thunder and lightning, causing unnatural darkness, going in and out at auger holes, and so forth. We happen to know that Shakespeare read this passage: his eye was caught by the phrase 'auger hole'. But he did not use it to characterise his witches; instead it surfaces after the murder of Duncan when the justifiably terrified Donalbain whispers to Malcolm that they should flee:

> What should be spoken here,
> Where our fate, hid in an auger hole,
> May rush and seize us?
> (II.iii.117–19)

The auger hole has ceased to be an actual passageway, uncannily small and hence virtually invisible, for witches to pass through and has become a figure for the fear that lurks everywhere in Macbeth's castle. And the Weird Sisters, of whose existence Malcolm and Donalbain are entirely unaware, have been translated into the abstraction to which their name is etymologically linked – fate. The phantasmagorical horror of witchcraft, ridiculed by Scot, is redistributed by Shakespeare across the field of the play, shaping the representation of the state, of marriage, and, above all, of the psyche. When Lady Macbeth calls upon the 'spirits / That tend on mortal thoughts' to unsex her, when she directs the 'murdering ministers' to take her milk for gall, the terrifying intensity of her psychological malignity depends upon Shakespeare's deployment or – to borrow a term from Puttenham's *Arte of English Poesie* (1589) – his 'translacing' of the ragged, filthy materials of inquisitorial credulity.[38]

Translacing is a mode of rhetorical redistribution in which the initial verbal elements remain partially visible even as they are woven into something new. Hence Lady Macbeth is not revealed to be a witch, yet the witches subsist as a tenebrous filament to which Lady Macbeth is obscurely but palpably linked.[39] This redistribution does not, let us note, enable the playwright to transcend what we have identified as the ethical problem inherent in staging witches in early seventeeth-century England. If I were a woman on trial for witchcraft, I would call upon Reginald Scot, misogynistic, narrow-minded, suspicious of the imagination, to testify on my behalf, not upon Shakespeare. *Macbeth* leaves the Weird Sisters unpunished, but manages to implicate them in a monstrous threat to the fabric of civilised life. The genius of the play is bound up with this power of implication by means of which we can never be done with them, for they are most suggestively present when we cannot see them, when they are absorbed in the putatively ordinary relations of everyday life. That is what translacing means: if you are worried about losing your manhood, it is not enough to look to the bearded hags on the heath, look to your wife. 'When you durst do it, then you were a man' (I.vii. 49). If you are worried about 'interior temptation', fear your own dreams: 'Merciful powers, / Restrain in me the cursèd thoughts that nature / Gives way to in repose' (II.i.7–9). If you are anxious about your future, scrutinise your best friends: 'He was a gentleman on whom I built / An absolute trust' (I.iv.14–15). And if you fear spiritual desolation, turn your eyes on the contents not only of the hideous cauldron but of your skull: 'O, full of scorpions is my mind, dear wife' (III.ii.39).

The whole point of the discourse of witchcraft was to achieve clarity, to make distinctions, to escape from the terror of the inexplicable, the unforeseen, the aimlessly malignant. Whatever other satisfactions it gave the magistrates, the torture to which accused witches were subjected was intended to secure this clarity by extracting full confessions, gratifying confirmations of the theoretical truths. The fact that these confirmations were produced by torture did not compromise their usefulness; indeed for King James, *voluntary* confessions were suspect, since they suggested an unhinged mind neurotically bent on self-incrimination: 'Experience daylie proues how loath they are to confesse without torture, which witnesseth their guiltines, where by the contrary, the Melancholicques neuer spare to bewray themselues. ...'[40] In *Macbeth* the audience is given something better than confession, for it can see visible proof of the demonic in action, but this visibility, this powerful *enargeia*, turns out to be maddeningly equivocal. The 'wayward' witches appear and disappear, and the language of the play subverts the illusory certainties of sight. The ambiguities of demonic agency are never resolved, and its horror spreads like a mist through a murky landscape.[41] 'What is't you do?' Macbeth asks the Weird Sisters; 'A deed without a name' (IV.i.49–50).[42]

For Reginald Scot, to relocate witchcraft as theatrical illusion was to move it decisively into the zone of the imaginary and to end the equivocation: 'I for my part have read a number of their conjurations, but never could see anie divels of theirs, except it were in a plaie' (p. 258). Scot does not rail against the theatre; it is imposture he hates, fictions pretending to be realities. He confidently expects that anything self-consciously marked out as fiction, any play recognised as a play, will have no force. The playhouse, for Scot, is the house of unbelief. Show people how the juggling tricks are done; show them how their desire to know 'the sequele of things to come, and to see the end of their feare and hope' is manipulated; show them how they are deceived by the 'double or doubtfull' sense of language, and they will henceforth be free – free, that is, to submit themselves to the Almighty. *Macbeth* rehearses many of the same disillusioning revelations, including even a demonstration of the bad jokes by which, as Scot puts it, 'plaine lieng is avoided with a figurative speech'. Birnam Wood come to Dunsinane and the man 'of no woman born' are close relations to the piece of earth from

Russia and the marvellous substance in the Indian stone with which Scot sought to work his disenchantment. And when Macbeth understands the equivocations by which he has been deceived, he takes a step toward unbelief:

> And be these juggling fiends no more believed
> That palter with us in a double sense,
> That keep the word of promise to our ear
> And break it to our hope.
>
> (V.vii.49–52)

Not believing the juggling fiends, of course, is different from not believing in their existence, but that sceptical doubt too, as we have seen, has been articulated in the course of the play. Moreover, Shakespeare's play does not attempt to conceal the theatricality of witchcraft,[43] on the contrary, a self-conscious theatricality tinges all of the witches' appearances, becoming explicit in the scene, possibly part of Middleton's contribution to the play, in which Hecate complains that she was 'never called to bear my part / Or show the glory of our art'.[44] But in *Macbeth* the acknowledgement of theatrical artifice is a sign not of polemical scepticism but of the tragedy's appropriate power, an effect not of ethical redemption but of irresistible histrionic life.

In the last analysis – if there ever is a last analysis – Shakespeare's theatre, like most of the art we value, is on the side of a liberating, tolerant doubt, but on the way to that doubt there is the pleasure and the profit of mystification, collusion, imaginary enchantment. Shakespeare was part of a profession that made its money manipulating images and playing with the double and doubtful senses of words. If the life of the player comes to seem an empty illusion, it does so in the light not of Scot's faith but of Macbeth's despair:

> Life's but a walking shadow, a poor player
> That struts and frets his hour upon the stage,
> And then is heard no more. It is a tale
> Told by an idiot, full of sound and fury
> Signifying nothing.
>
> (V.v.24–8)

The closing moments of the play invite us to recoil from this black hole just as they invite us to recoil from too confident and simple a celebration of the triumph of grace. For Shakespeare the presence of the theatrical in the demonic, as in every other realm of life, only intensifies the sense of an equivocal betwixt-and-between, for his theatre is the space where the fantastic and the bodily, *energia* and *enargeia* touch.[45] To conjure up such a theatre places Shakespeare in the position neither of the witchmonger nor the sceptic. It places him in the position of the witch.

From *New Historical Literary Studies: Essays on Reproducing Texts, Representing History*, ed. Jeffrey N. Cox and Larry Reynolds (Princeton, NJ, 1993), pp. 108–35.

NOTES

[Stephen Greenblatt's essay on *Macbeth* appears here in a slightly short-ened version of the original. It is illustrative of Greenblatt's critical method-ology (as seen, for example. in his ground-breaking *Shakespearean Negotiations: The Circulation of Social Energy in Renaissance England* [Oxford, 1988]), which explores the mutually generative intersections of social discourse and theatrical representation. Ed.]

1. Quoted in Carlo Ginzburg, *Storia natturna: Una decifrazione del sabba* (Torino, 1989), p. 65.

2. Quoted in Valerie I. J. Flint, *The Rise of Magic in Early Medieval Europe* (Princeton, NJ, 1991), p. 122. I have changed 'phantasms' to a plural, in keeping with the Latin.

3. Reginone's project is not, like that of Eusebius in the fourth century, to persuade his readers that the ancient gods and goddesses were actually demons. Eusebius begins with the assumption that the apparitions of the pagan deities were real enough; that is, they did not simply occur in the minds of the credulous believers. Demons, he suggests, cun-ningly play the parts of pagan deities in order to shore up superstitious beliefs. See Eusebius, *Evangelicae praeparationis (The Preparation for the Gospel)*, ed. and trans. E. H. Gifford (Oxford, 1903): 'The minis-trants of the oracles we must in plain truth declare to be evil daemons, playing both parts to deceive mankind, and at once time agreeing with the more fabulous suppositions concerning themselves, to deceive the common people, and at another time confirming the statements of the philosophers' jugglery in order to instigate them also and puff them up: so that in every way it is proved that they speak no truth at all' (p. 139).

   Eusebius argues that the fact that spirits can be compelled to appear by magical charms is proof in itself that they are not good spirits. (He cites Porphyry on the fact of the compulsion.) 'For if the deity is not subject to force or to compulsion, but is in nature superior to all things, being free and incapable of suffering, how can they be gods who are beguiled by juggling tricks managed by means of such dresses, and lines, and images? – beguiled, I say, by wreaths also and flowers of the earth, and withal by certain unintelligible and barbarous cries and voices, and subdued by ordinary men, and, as it were, enslaved by bonds so that they cannot even keep safe in their own control the power of independence and free will' (p. 214). Presumably, then, the fact that Christian angels will not necessarily come when they are called is a sign of their reality.

4. Quoted in Flint, *The Rise of Magic*, p. 123.

5. See Julio Carlo Baroja, *The World of Witches*, trans. Nigel Glendinning (Chicago, 1968). Burchard argued that those who believed in witchcraft were participating in a revival of paganism and were crediting what were only satanic delusions.

6. Quoted in Flint, *The Rise of Magic*, p. 123.

7. P. 155. A similar hard-line toward authorities unwilling to prosecute witches is taken by Bodin. Here, as elsewhere, the issue of witchcraft is linked to an intensification of the claims of sovereignty. Such a link would seem to be present – though only in an oblique way – in *Macbeth*, where the 'existence' of the witches is part of a strategy whereby Macbeth is not simply a ruthless political opportunist but a metaphysical nightmare and Duncan, Malcolm, Banquo (and Fleance), and ultimately James VI/I are not simply admired rulers but agents of the divine will.

8. Edmund Spenser, *The Faerie Queene*, ed. Thomas P. Roche, Jr (Harmondsworth, 1978), book 2, canto 9, stanza 51. The chamber of *Phantastes* swarming with such things 'as in idle fantasies do flit', includes 'Infernall Hags'.

9. Peter Stallybrass, '*Macbeth* and Witchcraft,' *Focus on 'Macbeth'*, ed. J. K. Brain (London, 1982), p. 205.

10. Janet Adelman, '"Born of Woman": Fantasies of Maternal Power in *Macbeth*', in *Cannibals, Witches, and Divorce: Estranging the Renaissance* (English Institute Essays), ed. Marjorie Garber (Baltimore, MD, 1987), pp. 103, 111. I should make it quite clear that Janet Adelman is not concerned to condemn the play as evil. Indeed it is one of the strengths of psychoanalytic criticism that it can accept, even celebrate, the expression of dangerous fantasies.

11. The question of the play's evil would involve at least three distinct or distinguishable questions: (1) was it morally responsible for Shakespeare to represent women as witches? (2) did the representation have bad consequences in its own time? (3) does the representation have bad consequences in our own time?

12. The sense that the witches are marginal is explicitly thematised in Hecate's complaint to the hags that she was 'never called to bear my part / Or show the glory of our art'. Though these words seem initially to refer only to the fact that the 'saucy and overbold' hags had trafficked with Macbeth without involving Hecate, they imply that the art of witchcraft has somehow been displaced on the stage by something else. Within the psychological and moral world of the play, the displacement seems to be focused on Macbeth's motivation. He is not a worshipper of the dark powers whom the witches serve; hence Hecate's complaint that he is a 'wayward son'. In the metatheatrical sense that I am pursuing in this paper, the 'glory' of the witches' art is displaced by the glory of Shakespeare's.

13. That is, our belief system requires evidence of a more direct and premeditated malice in a text we would judge to be evil. By 'our belief system' I refer to the secular humanism – the heritage of what Pocock calls 'the Machiavellian moment' – that has largely dominated Western conceptions of culture, and particularly of literary culture, since the eighteenth century. I am well aware that this belief system is neither timeless nor universal – a bitter controversy about belief is, after all, the historical situation addressed in this paper – and I understand, of course, that the little word 'our' is contestable.

14. Of course, what one culture or generation or ideological faction regards as repellent or criminal, another may regard as an exalted necessity, but this possibility of conflicting evaluation is the condition of all moral judgements and does not place art beyond good and evil. Nor can art be exempted from judgement on the principle that it is a kind of dream – and hence, as even Plato said of dreams, outside the canons of morality. For even if we all agree that art functions as a kind of culturally-sanctioned dream work, art is *intended* dreaming and hence morally accountable.

    We might, however, want to separate an aesthetic judgement of art works from a moral judgement: that is, it would be possible to find a work evil and at the same time to acknowledge its aesthetic power. Moreover, it is possible to imagine a response that would find the intention behind a particular work of art to be evil, while at the same time finding a moral value in that very work of art on the grounds that it allows a kind of imaginative freedom or that the revulsion it inspires awakens a moral response. (One could, conversely, find that a particular work was moral in intention but immoral in action.)

15. Cf. Thomas Greene, 'Magic and Festivity at the Renaissance Court', in *Renaissance Quarterly*, 40 (1987), 641.

16. The possibility of prosecuting anyone for witchcraft depended on the prior public recognition that witchcraft 'actually' existed – that it was not a brainsick fantasy or a fraud but a malevolent reality – and this recognition is precisely what is in question in this period. As Christina

Larner writes, 'If the relatively simple crimes of adultery and murder were ambiguous without social indentification, witchcraft was non-existent. Witchcraft is the labelling theorist's dream' (*Witchcraft and Religion: The Politics of Popular Belief* [Oxford, 1984], p. 29).

17. In disputing the claim the witches are melancholiacs, James VI's spokesman in the *Daemonologie*, Epistemon, claims that they are 'rich and worldly-wise, some of them fatte or corpulent in their bodies, and most part of them altogether given over to the pleasure of the flesh, continual haunting of companie, and all kind of merrines'. (*Daemonology*, pp. 28–30, quoted in Stuart Clark, 'King James's *Daemonologie*: Witchcraft and Kingship', in Sydney Anglo, *The Damned Art* [Boston, 1977], p. 171.) This view, which is apparently linked to James's response to the principal North Berwick defendants, is wildly at variance with the marginality, poverty, and hence vulnerability of witches amply documented elsewhere, and not only by those who were challenging the persecution. The most powerful theatrical acknowledgement of the vulnerability of witches is in Dekker's *Witch of Edmonton*, a play that nonetheless stages without protest the witch's execution.

18. It will not do to exaggerate the extent of this contestation; in England, unlike Germany, France, or Scotland, witchcraft prosecutions were relatively infrequent, and while there is a substantial discourse, there is no sign of a cultural obsession. But even before James came to the English throne and greatly intensified the official interest in witchcraft, its ramifications were broad, and there is a constant recourse to witchcraft (as metaphor or image, for example) in a wide range of discourses.

19. The contract also licenses the violent persecution (rather than medical treatment or exorcism) of witches, for it is the sign of their 'absolute liberty' (p. 16) and hence their full responsibility for their actions.

20. 'Again, although to enter the soul is possible only to God Who created it, yet devils can, with God's permission, enter our bodies; and they can then make impressions on the inner faculties corresponding to the bodily organs. And by those impressions the organs are affected in proportion as the inner perceptions are affected in the way which has been shown: that the devil can draw out some image retained in a faculty corresponding to one of the senses; as he draws from the memory, which is in the back part of the head, an image of a horse, and locally moves that phantasm to the middle part of the head, where are the cells of imaginative power; and finally to the sense of reason, which is in the front of the head. And he causes such a sudden change and confusion, that such objects are necessarily thought to be actual things seen with the eyes' (p. 125).

21. What is going on here? Kramer and Sprenger may tell this tale less to address a particular hysterical symptom that they claim is widespread

than to represent the sense that the penis is independent of one's control. Hence they remark that witches 'sometimes collect male organs in great numbers, as many as twenty or thirty members together, and put them in a bird's nest, or shut them up in a box, where they move themselves like living members, and eat oats and corn, as has been seen by many and is a matter of common report' (p. 121). In its grotesque way, the story registers an Augustinian anxiety that the stirrings and appetites of sexuality are not under the control of the rational will.

22. It is also the source of its originality in relation to the Continental sources on whom Scot greatly depends. For, as Michel de Certeau has observed, in the Continental debates over witchcraft, the issue is the relation between the supernatural and the natural: Wier and Bodin grant the same facts and then disagree bitterly about the cause of those facts. But there is another response to phenomena that apparently escape the ordinary and observable norms of the natural, a response that consists in suspecting the presence of illusion. And, as de Certeau remarks, while this perspective seems less theoretical, it is in fact the more radical, for it challenges perception itself: visual testimony which was the principle of verification ('I would have doubted it, if I hadn't seen it for myself') is now called into question. See Michel de Certeau, *L'Absent de l'histoire* (Paris, 1973), p. 30. Similarly, Michel Foucault points out that neither Molitor at the end of the fifteenth century nor Wier or Erastus in the sixteenth century actually abandons the idea of the demonic. Their argument against Sprenger, Bodin and others, Foucault remarks, does not contest the existence of the devil or his presence among men but centres on his mode of manifesting himself, on the way he conceals himself beneath appearances. See Michel Foucault, 'Les déviations religieuses et le savoir médical', in *Heresies et sociétés dans l'Europe pre-industrielle 11e–18e siècles*, Communications et debats du Colloque de Royaumont, ed. Jacques Le Goff (Paris, 1968).

23. See, above all, Jules Michelet's visionary *Satanism and Witchcraft: A Study in Medieval Superstition [La sorcière]*, trans. A. R. Allinson (Secaucus, NJ, n.d.). Michelet's views, long dismissed as romantic claptrap, were revived for feminism by Hélène Cixous and Catherine Clément, *The Newly Born Woman*, trans. Betsy Wing (Minneapolis, 1975). It would be possible too to see a connection between Michelet's attempt to reconstruct a secret history of ecstatic experience among medieval peasants and Carlo Ginzburg's remarkable *Ecstasies: Deciphering the Witches' Sabbath*, trans. Raymond Rosenthal (London, 1989). The crucial point, for our purposes, is that Scot cannot concede any authentic heterodox religious experience to witches, any more than he can concede to them the possession of any actual power. To do so would be both to compromise his own religious convictions and to endorse the arguments of the witchmongers. One peculiar consequence is that Clément and Ginzburg seem far closer in

their views to the inquisitors than to those who, like Scot, worked to stop the persecution.

24. Scot participates then in the process described by Juliana Schiesari in *The Gendering of Melancholia: Feminism, Psychoanalysis, and the Symbolics of Loss in Renaissance Literature* (Ithaca, NY, 1992). The melancholy that functions as a sign of genius in the elite male Hamlet is in these village women a mark of impotence and confusion. But it is important to recognise that the misogynistic diagnosis, like the insanity defence, plays a role at this time in mitigating judicial punishment.

Scot's position is very close to that articulated, again in a juridical context, by his contemporary Montaigne:

> A few years ago I passed through the territory of a sovereign prince, who, as a favour to me and to beat down my incredulity, did me the kindness of letting me see, in his own presence and in a private place, ten or twelve prisoners of this nature, and among others one old woman, indeed a real witch in ugliness or deformity, long very famous in that profession. I saw both proofs and free confessions, and some barely perceptible mark or other on this wretched old woman, and I talked and asked questions all I wanted, bringing to the matter the soundest attention I could; and I am not the man to let my judgement be throttled much by preconceptions. In the end, and in all conscience, I would have prescribed rather hellebore than hemlock. *It seemed to me a matter rather of madness than of crime* [Livy] ['Of Cripples', in *The Complete Essays of Montaigne*, trans. Donald M. Frame (Stanford, CA, 1948), p. 790].

25. Alternatively, it is our banalisation of the marvellous aspects of the familiar world that has made these authentic wonders seem ordinary and has led to the invention of false miracles.

26. Ludwig Wittgenstein, *Philosophical Investigations*, 3d edn, trans. G. E. M. Anscombe (London, 1958), p. 47 (#109).

27. In 'The Index of the Absent Wound (Monograph on a Stain)', *October*, 29 (1984), Georges Didi-Huberman speaks of 'a sense of *figurability*, understood as a *means of staging* – a translation suggested by Lacan for what is generally called the consideration of representability, which Freud refers to as *Rücksicht auf Darstellbarkeit*. This is where the field I referred to as *figurative Aufhebung* has its fantasmatic extension, in thoughts expressed as images or, as Freud says, as pseudo-thoughts; in substituting for logic pure relationships of formal contiguity; in the play of displacements of plastic intensity, in their ability to focus and fascinate' (p. 73).

28. Aristotle counselled the dramatist to 'put the actual scenes as far as possible before his eyes. In this way, seeing everything with the vividness of an eyewitness as it were, he will devise what is appropriate' (*Poetics* 455ᵃ in *The Complete Works of Aristotle*, ed. Jonathan

Barnes, 2 vols [Princeton, NJ, 1984], 2:2328–9). Florio translates *energia* as 'efficacie, or effectuall operation'; *enargeia* as 'evidence, perspicuitie, evident representing of a thing', *A Worlde of Wordes, Or a Most copious, and exact Dictionarie in Italian and English*, collected by John Florio (London, 1598).

29. In *The Comedy of Errors* the ethical and theatrical conditions of figurability converge, as they do whenever Shakespeare uses the discourse of witchcraft solely to designate the confusion and projection of a troubled consciousness.

30. Their prognostications, to be sure, turn out to depend upon equivocations, the 'double or doubtfull words' that Scot saw as sources of credulity. But the bitter disillusionment that follows – 'And be these juggling fiends no more believed / That palter with us in a double sense' (V.vii.48–9) – is not at all what Scot had in mind, for it does not signal a recognition that witchcraft is itself fraud and delusion.

31. On the insistent thematising of vision in *Macbeth*, see Huston Diehl, 'Horrid Image, Sorry Sight, Fatal Vision: The Visual Rhetoric of *Macbeth*', in *Shakespeare Studies*, 16 (1983), 191–203. 'The play itself', Diehl argues, 'is centrally concerned with the problematics of vision. It examines the act of seeing and interpreting an uncertain visible world' (p. 191). Diehl suggests that the audience is led to realise what Macbeth, Lady Macbeth, and Duncan all fail to grasp: 'that sight is both objective and ethical' (p. 191). But I have tried to show throughout this paper that, in the context of the witchcraft contestation, there is something ethically problematical in sight.

32. 'What matters here is not hunting down an answer to the question "What are the witches?" All the critical and theatrical efforts to answer that question demonstrate that the question cannot be answered. What those frantic answers also demonstrate – and what matters – is the fact of the question.' Stephen Booth, *'King Lear', 'Macbeth', Indefinition, and Tragedy* (New Haven and London, 1983), p. 102.

33. The questions were almost impossible to resolve, even for Scot, because virtually everyone who had access to print (and presumably most of the population as well) was committed to maintaining traditional Christian beliefs in the supernatural. Those beliefs were so closely bound up with fantasies of the demonic that it was extremely difficult to dismantle the latter without irreparably damaging the former. In a fuller account of the play, we would have to explore not only the problematic character of these traditional Christian beliefs but the extent to which sovereignty too is bound up with the queasy and ambiguous status of the witches.

34. 'Were such things here, as we do speak about', Banquo asks, 'Or have we eaten on the insane root, / That takes the reason prisoner?' (I.iii.83–5).

35. Paul Alpers has pointed out to me that the English repeatedly psychologised enargeia, by confusing it with energia.

36. From this Walter Curry concluded that Lady Macbeth must actually have been possessed: 'Without doubt these ministers of evil do actually take possession of her body even in accordance with her desire' (in *Shakespeare's Philosophical Patterns* [Baton Rouge, LA, 1937], p. 87).

37. Lady Macbeth's two invocations of spirits are conjoined by a brief scene in which a nameless messenger brings her the startling news, 'The King comes here tonight.' When she expresses her incredulity that Macbeth himself has not brought word in person, the messenger answers,

> One of my fellows had the speed of him,
> Who almost dead for breath, had scarcely more
> Than would make up his message.
>   (I.v.33–5)

The lines have the odd effect of insisting on the literal meaning of a phrase like 'breathless haste', and in doing so they provide a clue to the connection between the literal and figurative uses of the term spirit: both rest on the breath.

The relation between breath, spirit, and inspiration was well-known in the early seventeenth century. Hobbes remarks,

> On the signification of the word *Spirit* dependeth that of the word INSPIRATION; which must either be taken properly; and then it is nothing but the blowing into a man some thin and subtile aire, or wind in such manner as a man filleth a bladder with his breath; or if Spirits be not corporeall, but have their existence only in the fancy, it is nothing but the blowing in of a Phantasme; which is improper to say, and impossible; for Phantasmes are not, but only seem to be somewhat. (*Leviathan*, p. 440)

38. Puttenham introduces the term in an account of the rhetorical figure of '*Traductio*, or the Translacer', 'which is when ye turne and tranlace [sic] a word into many sundry shapes as the Tailor doth his garment, & after that sort do play with him in your dittie', *Arte of English Poesie* (Menston, 1968), p. 170.

39. As Jonathan Crewe has observed (in a response to this paper), Lady Macbeth in consequence comes to seem evil in excess of anything that she actually *does*; the history of *Macbeth* criticism is a history of incrimination, a long bill of indictment brought less against the murderous hero than against his wife. For example, there are children murdered in the play, but their murder is ordered by Macbeth who does so without consulting his 'dearest chuck'. And yet critics return compulsively to the horrible inward intensity of Lady Macbeth's fantasy of infanticide:

I would, while it was smiling in my face,
Have plucked my nipple from his boneless gums
And dashed the brains out, had I so sworn
As you have done to this.

(I.vii.56–9)

Lady Macbeth's evil has been so obsessively discussed by criticism, Crewe suggests, because she has made an effort to repossess her body, to empower herself (by identifying with what she perceives as masculine strength, even as she intuitively understands that she herself has created masculine strength), to be something other than the figure of reproduction in the nuclear family. In fact her power comes from a literacy – her ability to read Macbeth's letter, to read his character – virtually uncanny in a woman. She is, Crewe suggests, the place of greatest ideological resistance in a play that implies that the proper role of a woman should be that of a sleepwalker.

40. *Daemonologie*, p. 30.

41. For an alternative view, see Ninian Mellamphy, 'Macbeth's Visionary Dagger: Hallucination or Revelation?' in *English Studies in Canada*, 4 (1978), 379–92. Mellamphy argues that the play's ambiguities are sorted out if one keeps in mind 'the Renaissance distinction between distorting fantasy (the fantastic imagination) and good fantasy (the icastic imagination)' (p. 385). But it is just this distinction that continually breaks down in *Macbeth*.

42. The witches, Dennis Biggins observes, 'occupy a kind of twilight territory between human and supernatural evildoing', 'Sexuality, Witchcraft, and Violence in *Macbeth*', in *Shakespeare Studies*, 8 (1968), 256.

43. Shakespeare in effect endorsed Scot's association of witchcraft with illusion-mongering, but of course Scot's fury is at those who do not admit that they are the purveyors of illusion, who allow people to believe that their powers are supernatural. Shakespeare, however, seems less persuaded than Scot that a frank acknowledgement of theatricality substantially reduces the power of the representation.

44. In an astonishing moment, Hecate and the witches actually sing a song from another play, Middleton's *The Witch*. The scene has been much lamented by scholars: 'It is to be hoped that this song was altered for *Macbeth*, as some lines are relevant only to the plot of Middleton's play. But the 1673 edition of *Macbeth* prints them without alteration. No exit is marked for Hecate and the spurious witches; but the sooner they depart the better' (Kenneth Muir, Arden *Macbeth* [New York, 1962], note to IV.i.43). But the moment seems to me not a regrettable 'non-Shakespearean interpolation' but rather a deliberate quotation, a marking of the demonic as the theatrical.

45. Touch but not fuse: their relation remains itself equivocal. 'Equivocation is not so much a major theme in the play, as a number of critics have observed, but the very condition of the play', in Lucy Gent, 'The Self-Cozening Eye', *Review of English Studies*, 34 (1983), 419. Gent argues that 'the work of art's equivocation is innocuous; that of the world of Macbeth is mortal' (p. 424). I'm not sure that this consoling distinction can hold up; for Reginald Scot, the equivocation of the work of art is a key to the whole sickness.

For Shakespeare to identify the theatrical with witchcraft was to invent the fantasmatic as the site of the psychological – that is, to invent the staged discourse of interiority – and to do so out of the odds and ends of Continental witchcraft. (Adelman thinks that Continental beliefs are 'transferred away from the witches and recur as the psychological' – but I would argue that these beliefs are the materials out of which the psychological is constructed.)

6

'Fashion it thus': *Julius Caesar* and the Politics of Theatrical Representation

JOHN DRAKAKIS

In David Zucker's 1988 film of *The Naked Gun*, a hapless Los Angeles Chief of Police, Lieutenant Frank Drebin, is warned by his relatively pacifist Mayoress employer to curb his propensity for violence. Drebin, himself an exaggerated post-modernist collocation of easily recognisable film texts, counters with a policy statement of his own sufficient to rival any pronouncement of Clint Eastwood's Dirty Harry:

> Yes, well when I see five weirdos dressed in togas stabbing a guy in the middle of the park in full view of a hundred people, I shoot the bastards. That's my policy.

The response of his outraged employer is the embarrassed revelation that: 'That was a Shakespeare in the park production of *Julius Caesar* you moron. You killed five actors: good ones.' The choice of the assassination scene from *Julius Caesar* to illustrate the violence necessary to redress an alleged crime echoes parodically one of two familiar critical readings of this Shakespearian text. In Zucker's film the comic extolling of Caesarism through the wholly inept efficiency of a law enforcement officer unaware of his own representational status and also, at the same time, unable to distinguish other forms of representation, is reinforced by the reactionary nature of his task: the protection of a visiting English queen against the threat of assassination. The latter, ironically republican critical perspective is exemplified in Alex Cox's film *Walker* (1988) which utilises a scene from *Julius Caesar* to explore, in the thinly veiled allegorical setting of nineteenth-century Nicaragua, the ironies and contradictions inherent in an imperialist project.[1]

The case of Lieutenant Drebin is not unlike that of Julius Caesar himself, who, according to Thomas Heywood, was so accomplished an 'actor' that on at least one occasion he was involuntarily taken in by the veracity of representation itself. In *An Apology for Actors* (1612), in an argument designed, astonishingly, to advance the cause of acting, Heywood relates the following incident:

> *Julius Caesar* himselfe for his pleasure became an Actor, being in shape, state, voyce, judgement, and all other occurrents, exterior and interior excellent. Amongst many other parts acted by him in person, it is recorded of him, that with generall applause in his owne Theater he played *Hercules Furens*, and amongst many other arguments of his compleatenesse, excellence, and extraordinary care in his action, it is thus reported of him: Being in the depth of a passion, one of his seruants (as his part then fell out) presenting *Lychas*, who before had from *Deianeira* brought him the poysoned shirt, dipt in the bloud of the Centaure, *Nessus*: he in the middest of his torture and fury, finding this *Lychas* hid in a remote corner (appoynted him to creep into of purpose), although he was, as our Tragedians vse, but seemingly to kill him by some false imagined wound, yet was *Caesar* so extremely carried away with the violence of his practised fury, and by the perfect shape of the madnesse of *Hercules*, to which he fashioned all his actiue spirits, that he slew him dead at his foot, & after swoong him *terq; quaterqu*; (as the Poet sayes) about his head.[2]

This incident is not recorded, unfortunately, in North's translation of *Plutarch's Lives*, and it has all the hallmarks of an apocryphal story. Indeed, apart from Caesar's allegedly acting in a Senecan play, at least some forty years before the birth of Seneca, it is likely that Heywood confused two stories from Philemon Holland's translation of Suetonius' *The Historie of Twelve Caesars* (1606), conflating episodes from the lives of Julius Caesar and Nero.[3] For Heywood Julius Caesar forsakes his status as an historical personage and becomes an actor himself, a focus for a range of narratives invested with sufficient authority to underwrite the activities of other 'actors'. In short, Caesar is adapted for a particular purpose, endowed with what Roland Barthes might call 'a type of social *usage*',[4] accorded the status of a 'myth' which is then used to legitimise an institution whose preoccupation is the business of representation itself. As a mythical entity, the figure of Caesar consisted of material that, as Barthes would say, had *already* been worked on so as to make it suitable for communication.[5]

Some twelve years before the appearance of Heywood's *An Apology for Actors*, and in the newly built Globe Theatre, on 21 September 1599, the Lord Chamberlain's Men mounted a production of *The Tragedie of Julius Caesar*. A Swiss visitor, Dr Thomas Platter, saw the performance, and recorded that 'at the end of the play they danced together admirably and exceedingly gracefully, according to their custom, two in each group dressed in men's and two in women's apparel'.[6] *Julius Caesar* is hardly a play to set the feet tapping, and if, indeed, this was the play that was written, as Dover Wilson conjectured, 'expressly for the opening' of the Globe[7] then the dance about which Dr Platter enthused may have had more to recommend it than mere 'custom'. Indeed, in the light of a persistent outpouring of anti-theatrical sentiments throughout this period, combined with what Jonas Barish identified as 'a deep suspicion toward theatricality as a form of behaviour in the world',[8] such a gesture, in a newly opened theatre, may be interpreted as an act of flagrant political defiance.[9] This view receives some general reinforcement from Steven Mullaney's persuasive argument that the suburbs where the public theatres were situated constituted 'a geo-political domain that was crucial to the symbolic and material economy of the city ... traditionally reserved for cultural phenomena that could not be contained within the strict or proper bounds of the community'.[10] Moreover, the potential for resistance derived from this contextualisation of the theatre is reinforced by his suggestion that dramatic performance may be defined as 'a performance *of* the threshold, by which the horizon of community was made visible, the limits of definition, containment and control made manifest'.[11] In other words, the liminal position of the theatre, which it shared with other forms of festivity, far from simply ventriloquising the discourses of political domination, engaged in forms of representation through which other, potentially subversive voices could be heard.

A useful model for this complex process might be Volosinov's reformulation of the Freudian opposition between the 'conscious' and the 'unconscious', as a conflict between 'behavioural ideology', which, he argues, is, in certain respects, 'more sensitive, more responsive, more excitable and livelier' and 'an ideology that has undergone formulation and become "official"'.[12] In an attempt to recuperate the Freudian unconscious for a political account of the relationship between the individual and society, Volosinov insists that what is repressed or censored represents a *conscious* expression of 'behavioural ideology' in so far as it expresses 'the most steadfast and the governing factors of class consciousness'.[13] More recently, Antony Easthope has challenged the notion of a 'political unconscious' as it emerges in the work of Pierre Macherey and Fredric Jameson, on the grounds that while the notion of 'class' as a means of positioning the individual 'is involuntary and acts against the individual's will ... it is not *unconscious* or *repressed* in the psychoanalytic sense of these terms'.[14] For Volosinov, where forms of human behaviour which are not divorced from what he calls 'verbal ideological formulation', but which remain 'in contradiction with the official ideology', it is manifestly not the case that they 'must degenerate into indistinct inner speech and then die out', but rather that they 'might well engage in a struggle with the official ideology'.[15] It is the resultant maintenance of contact both with society and with communication that gives to certain forms of behavioural ideology their revolutionary potential. Volosinov grounds the motive for such a struggle on '*the economic being of the whole group*', but he goes on to suggest that such motives develop within 'a small social milieu' before being driven into 'the underground – not the psychological underground of repressed complexes, but the salutary political underground'.[16] This is not to suggest that the Elizabethan public theatre was a fully conscious proponent of 'revolutionary ideology', but it does go some way to ascribing intention of a sort within a very complex social formation, while at the same time designating this emergent institution as responsive, excitable, and lively. Indeed, when we consider the timing of performances, the constraints of official censorship, the social heterogeneity and consequent volatility of public theatre audiences,[17] along with the desire for respectability amongst practitioners, and the attempts to secure influential patronage, it becomes clear that the liminal status of a theatre such as the Globe effectively guaranteed its relative 'openness' to the production of contradictory cultural meanings. In addition, Volosinov goes on to suggest that where there is discontinuity between behavioural and official ideologies, then the result is a radical decentring of the individual human subject; he argues:

Motives under these conditions begin to fail, to lose their verbal countenance, and little by little really do turn into a 'foreign body' in the psyche. Whole sets of organic manifestations come, in this way, to be excluded from the zone of verbalised behaviour and may become *asocial*. Thereby the sphere of the 'animalian' in man enlarges.[18]

We see some evidence of this decentring, and of the crisis of representation which results from it, in Shakespeare's second tetralogy, and especially in *Henry V*, a play very close temporally and thematically to *Julius Caesar*, where theatrical production itself is something for which a choric apology is required as the precondition of a larger revisionary justification for authority.[19] For Henry V, like his father before him, authority resides primarily in those ritual representations through which class interests and force are articulated: the 'idol ceremony' which is defined, somewhat defensively, in terms of a rhetorical question which discloses the operations of ideology: 'Art thou aught else but place, degree, and form, / Creating awe and fear in other men?' (*Henry V*, IV.i.243–4). As Jonathan Dollimore and Alan Sinfield have cogently argued, at this point the king 'claims to be an effect of the structure which he seemed to guarantee',[20] but he also manipulates those symbols from which he seeks some temporary disengagement in order to elicit sympathy for what we might call, with the benefit of hindsight, 'the management interest'. Of course, the figure of the king is what Derrida, in another context, identifies as a 'central presence',[21] responsible for the ordering, extending, and multiplying of a range of signifiers. And it is precisely this presence, 'which has never been itself, has always already been exiled from itself into its own substitute',[22] which the decline and death of Richard II reinforces as what we might call an '*imaginary* signification'.[23] The difficulty for *Henry V* arises directly from the confrontation which takes place in the play between a central organising signification charged with the task of reconstituting its authority, and the behavioural ideology which challenges, on the terrain of history itself, its efficacy as an instrument for restricting meaning. The relocation – which is also to some extent a dislocation – of this process in the setting of the beginnings of Imperial Rome, and the invocation of a narrative *differentially* constructed along the axis of an opposition between 'popular' and 'humanist' readings of the Caesarian myth, makes *The Tragedie of Julius Caesar* an exemplary text whose own 'ambivalence' is brought into constitutive alignment with the openness and instability of the theatre itself. Indeed, as I shall try to show, the play's concern is not with the *subject* of representation: that is, of rendering a hitherto inaccessible reality present whose ontological status is not in question; but rather with what Robert Weimann has identified as the 'difference within the act of representation' through which a struggle for 'material interests' is articulated.[24] Indeed, if the theatre deals in representations and metaphors it also has the capability to disclose the power that authority *invests* in them, sometimes in the very act of denying their efficacy.

As a number of commentators have shrewdly observed, *Julius Caesar* contains no king; that is, absent from the play is what Derrida calls 'a re-assuring certitude which is itself beyond the reach of play'.[25] Caesar's appropriation of the feast of Lupercal, historically and mythically a festival of origins, clearly has the effect of suppressing *difference*, although this ceremonial affirmation of presence is rendered ambivalent by the anti-theatrical puritanism of Flavius and Marullus who challenge this specific *use* of 'holiday'.[26] In his instruction to Marullus to 'Disrobe the images / If you do find them decked with ceremonies' (I.i.64–5), Flavius initiates a deconstruction of the very representations which are a constitutive element of Caesar's success. They are the signifying practices which position Caesar 'above the view of men' at the same time as they reinforce the social hierarchy by keeping 'us all in servile fearfulness' (I.i.74–5). The following scene firmly inscribes Caesar in the process of 'ceremony' both as a producer and an actor, of whom Antony can say: 'When Caesar says "Do this", it is perform'd' (I.ii.12), and who insists upon a complete performance: 'Set on, and leave no ceremony out' (I.ii.13). By contrast, Brutus admits, 'I am not gamesom' (I.ii.30), although this anti-festive expression is quickly belied by a tacit admission of consummate acting: 'If I have veiled my look, / I turn the trouble of my countenance / Merely upon myself' (I.ii.39–41); and similarly, the Cassius who eschews ritual but articulates his political desires through its language is later affirmed by Caesar as an enemy of theatrical performance: 'He loves no plays' (I.ii.204). But it is ironical that while one performance is taking place elsewhere, to which the audience is denied full access, Cassius proposes to Brutus a performance of another kind, deeply dependent upon the mechanics of representation. In an attempt to disclose his 'hidden worthiness' (I.ii.59), Cassius constructs a 'self' for Brutus which the latter identifies as both dangerous and alien, and it is one which involves the exposure of the means through which the allegedly tyrannical image of Caesar is sustained. Ironically, the demythologising of Caesar, which involves divesting his name of political resonance, is itself dependent upon a representation: 'I, your glass, / Will modestly discover to yourself / That of yourself which you yet know not of' (I.ii.70–2). Here the 'self' is not that ontologically stable '*Center* of my circling thought' of Sir John Davies's *Nosce Teipsum*,[27] but a fabrication that can be persuaded that it is fully the subject of its own actions:

> Men at some time were masters of their fates.
> The fault, dear Brutus, is not in our stars,
> But in ourselves, that we are underlings.
>   (I.ii.140–2)[28]

Indeed, it is characteristic of all the conspirators that they oppose 'truth' to a distinctly theatrical falsity, as evidenced in the opposition Casca sets up between Caesar the theatrical performer and himself as a 'true man': 'If the tag-rag people did not clap him and hiss him, according as he pleased and displeased them, as they use to do the players in the theatre, I am no true man' (I.ii.258–61). Also, it is not entirely inappropriate that Messala's eulogy over the body of Cassius at the end of the play should focus upon the ambivalence of representation itself: 'Why dost thou show to the apt thoughts of men / The things that are not?' (V.iii.67–8). Indeed, in the play as a whole, one man's truth is another man's theatre. If, as Ernest Schanzer speculated, 'perhaps there is no real Caesar, that he merely exists as a set of images in other men's minds and his own',[29] then the same is doubly true of Brutus, a self fashioned in accordance with the demands of an ambivalent narrative which elicits, to use Schanzer's phrase, 'divided responses'.[30]

Cassius, the stage machiavel, whose metaphorical location in the play, despite protestations in principle to the contrary, is 'Pompey's Theatre' (I.iii.152) – significantly, also, the place where Caesar's own death will be staged in accordance with the generic demands of *de casibus* tragedy – initiates here a theatrical process which resonates through the remainder of the play. Casca, plucked by the sleeve, will, like a metropolitan drama critic, 'after his sour fashion, tell you / What hath proceeded worthy note today' (I.ii.181–2). Cassius himself will script the representations of an alternative theatre where language itself is an irreducibly material phenomenon, and where signifiers such as 'offence', 'virtue' and 'worthiness' will depend for their meanings upon the alchemical process produced by an appearance: 'that which would appear offence in us / His countenance, like richest alchemy, / Will change to virtue and to worthiness' (I.iii.158–60). As a subject of this discourse, where the stakes are political supremacy, Brutus, to use Althusser's phrase, works by himself. Indeed, in a speech which, in part, echoes Marlowe's Machevil,[31] he fabricates a narrative which radically opposes personal obligation – the friendship and 'love' through which imperial politics articulate their hierarchical interests – against a republican view which justifies human intervention in the social order:

> But 'tis a common proof
> That lowliness is young ambition's ladder,
> Whereto the climber-upward turns his face;
> But when he once attains the upmost round,
> He then unto the ladder turns his back,
> Looks in the clouds, scorning the base degrees
> By which he did ascend. So Caesar may.
> Then lest he may, prevent. And since the quarrel
> Will bear no colour for the thing he is,
> Fashion it thus:
>
> (II.i.21–30)

Brutus, like Cassius before him, conjures here a representation of a Caesar that the play never allows us to observe as anything other than a wholly fabricated identity, and as a consequence the action is pushed further into that liminal realm already occupied by the theatre itself.

Cassius and Casca's 'fashioning' of Brutus is an indispensable precondition for the success of the conspiracy, and Brutus's soliloquy at the beginning of Act II moves the action deeper into that liminal area where ideology and subjectivity intertwine. It is also the area where strategies for the controlling and contesting of meaning are formulated. There is very little in the play as a whole that does not generate alternative readings, whether it be public display, ritual sacrifice, or psychic phenomenon, and it is this hermeneutic instability, the consequence of the existence of two radically opposed forms of authority in Rome, that returns the analysis of motive and action to the space occupied by the theatre which can now claim both to produce *and* to interrogate ideologies. The theatre itself achieves this complex objective, to use Michael Holquist's formulation, through bending language 'to represent by representing languages';[32] and we can see precisely what

is involved here in Brutus's response to Cassius's suggestion that
Antony and Caesar should 'fall together' (II.i.161). In this debate, as
elsewhere in the play, critics of the most liberal of persuasions have
sided with Cassius,[33] but it is Brutus more than Cassius who grasps
the importance of mediating the conspiracy through existing rituals
and institutions.[34] Here representation accumulates a level of irony
which discloses it as misrepresentation:

> Let's be sacrificers, but not butchers, Caius.
> We all stand up against the spirit of Caesar,
> And in the spirit of men there is no blood.
> O, that we then could come by Caesar's spirit,
> And not dismember Caesar! But, alas,
> Caesar must bleed for it.
>
> (II.i.166–71)

Clearly, liberation from alleged tyranny cannot be permitted to result
in absolute freedom for all. If so, authority and power are not worth
having. Resistant though the conspirators are to the Caesarian
control of institutions and meanings, they formulate a strategy of
temporary release and restraint which parallels the *ideological* usage
of festivity, extending the potential for containment to the affective
power of tragic form itself. These concerns are concentrated with remarkable economy in Brutus's appeal to his fellow conspirators:
'And let our hearts, as subtle masters do, / Stir up their servants to an
act of rage, / And after seem to chide 'em' (II.i.175–7). From this
point on the talk is of 'fashioning', of manufacturing, and hence of
historicising, truth, and, inevitably, of theatrical representation. The
fully fashioned Brutus will now undertake to 'fashion' Caius Ligarius
(II.i.219), an assertion that may well have received an added irony in
the original performance where it is thought that the parts of Cassius
and Caius Ligarius may have been doubled.[35] Such a suggestion
would give added ironical point to Cassius's own speculation in his
soliloquy at I.ii.314–15: 'If I were Brutus now, and he were Cassius, /
He should not humour me.' Also Cassius's bid to revive Roman self-
presence with his exhortation to the conspirators to 'Show yourselves
true Romans' (II.i.222) is expanded by the one character whose
'countenance' is endowed with transformative power: 'Let not our
looks put on our purposes; / But bear it as our Roman actors do, /
With untired spirits and formal constancy' (II.i.224–6). Here theatrical representation is neither illusion nor self-delusion, rather it is the
ground upon which the symbols of authority are contested. It is no

accident that Thomas Beard could refer to the conspirators as those who 'were actors in this tragedy',[36] or that William Fulbecke could refer to Brutus as 'chiefe actor in Caesars tragedie'.[37]

If the conspirators are exhorted to sustain a 'formal constancy', then the Caesar which the first two acts of the play reveals is as consummate a Roman actor as his adversaries. To recuperate the assassination as the *origin* of a theatrical tradition in which the tragic protagonist is the unwitting participant, as Cassius later does, is simultaneously to expose the discursive mechanisms, at the moment that it seeks to reinforce, the historical and material determinants, of political power: 'How many ages hence / Shall this our lofty scene be acted over / In states unborn and accents yet unknown!' (III.i.112–14). In an augmentation of the practice of scripting, Brutus urges his accomplices to: 'Let's all cry "Peace, freedom, and liberty"!' (III.i.111), but this is followed almost immediately by the entry of a 'servant' who produces, not the voice of a free subject, but that of his 'master' Antony which he proceeds to ventriloquise. In the following scene it is the plebeian voice, emanating from an onstage audience credited with a dutiful quiescence which the actual Globe audience was unlikely to have reflected, which, ironically, through a replication of conspiratorial locutions, confirms the continuity of the rhetoric and symbols of political power: 'Let him be Caesar', 'Caesar's better parts / Shall be crowned in Brutus.' (III.ii.51–3). As in the later play *Coriolanus* the 'audience' is simultaneously empowered and disempowered, allotted a role from which it cannot escape. In the later play, where the Roman populace is given a more substantial critical voice, the *irony* of this position is laid open to question as the Citizens are obligated to support a patrician in whom they have little confidence:

> We have power in ourselves to do it, but it is a power that we have no power to do. For if he show us his wounds and tell us his deeds, we are to put our tongues into those wounds and speak for them; so if he tell us his noble deeds we must also tell him our noble acceptance of them. Ingratitude is monstrous, and for the multitude to be ungrateful were to make a monster of the multitude, of the which we, being members, should bring ourselves to be monstrous members.
>
> (*Coriolanus* (II.iii.4–13)[38]

If this is so, then it is extremely doubtful whether such self-consciously theatrical allusions serve, as Anne Righter has argued, 'preeminently to glorify the stage'.[39] This representation of the workings of political power, irrespective of intention, discloses an unstable institution proceeding gingerly into a terrain fraught with considerable political danger. Cast in a subversive role, confronted with the demands of official censorship, but nevertheless seeking legitimation, the actual choice of dramatic material would have been crucial. In *Julius Caesar* the Chamberlain's Men could displace their own professional anxieties onto a narrative which, by virtue of its very ambivalence, offered a space for the exploration of the ideology which governs the exchange of representations which take place between society and theatre, centre and margins.

In a culture in which those who would oppose theatrical representation continued to insist upon the power that inheres in the theatrical image itself, *Julius Caesar* is not so much a celebration of theatre as an unmasking of the politics of representation per se. The play does not *express* meaning; rather, in its readings of Roman history it *produces* meanings. Moreover, in its shuttling between the generic requirements of *de casibus* tragedy, and the Senecan tragedy of revenge, historical possibilities are simultaneously disclosed and withdrawn, in such a way as to propose an alignment of enjoyment with danger and with resistance. In its vacillation between 'fate' and human agency as the origins of action, and hence of history itself, *Julius Caesar* enacts the precarious position of the Globe itself. This is not the Shakespeare that we have been encouraged to regard as 'profoundly moving, or spiritually restoring, or simply strangely enjoyable', as recently proposed by Professor Boris Ford;[40] this carefully tailored brand of anti-intellectual prophylactic consumerism demands a kind of passivity that refuses to contemplate, among other things, the popular significance of that unsettling carnivalesque dance that closed the Globe performance of *Julius Caesar*. It subscribes tacitly to a teleological conception of Art not too far removed from the advice proffered by the Arts Minister, Richard Luce, as part of an argument in support of the suppression of modern 'popular' theatre: 'You should accept the political and economic climate in which we now live and make the most of it. Such an attitude could bring surprisingly good results.'[41] Of course, as we know from our own media representations of a crisis which is much nearer to us than Renaissance readings of the origins of Imperial Rome, no gun is ever naked.

From *Shakespeare Survey*, 44 (1992), 65–72.

NOTES

[John Drakakis' essay first appeared in the journal *Shakespeare Survey* and was reprinted in Ivo Kamps (ed.), *Materialist Shakespeare* (London and New York, 1995), pp. 280–91. It is representative of Drakakis' interest in the relationship between ideology and identity, and in the cultural appropriation of theatre in the formation of ideology, both in Shakespeare's time and our own. See his introduction to *Alternative Shakespeares* (London and New York, 1990), pp. 1–25. Ed.]

1. See Geoffrey Bullough, *Narrative and Dramatic Sources of Shakespeare*, 8 vols (London and New York, 1977), Vol. 5, pp. 58–211, for the full range of source material for *Julius Caesar*.

2. Thomas Heywood, *An Apology for Actors*, I.G., *A Refutation of The Apology for Actors, The English Stage: Attack and Defense 1577–1730* (New York and London, 1973), sig. E3V.

3. C. Suetonius Tranquillius, *The Historie of Twelve Caesars, Emperors of Rome*, trans. Philemon Holland (London, 1606), sigs. C2v-3, and sigs. R4–v4. See also Suetonuis, *The Twelve Caesars*, trans. Robert Graves (Harmondsworth, 1957), pp. 26ff. and pp. 219ff.

4. Roland Barthes, *Mythologies*, trans. Annette Lavers (St Albans, Herts, 1973), p. 109.

5. Ibid., p. 110.

6. William Shakespeare, *Julius Caesar*, ed. A. R. Humphreys (Oxford and New York, 1984), p. i.

7. William Shakespeare, *Julius Caesar*, ed. J. Dover Wilson (Cambridge, 1941), p. ix.

8. Jonas A. Barish, *The Antitheatrical Prejudice* (Berkeley, Los Angeles, and London, 1981), p. 133.

9. See John Drakakis, *The Plays of Shackerley Marmion (1603–39): A Critical Old-spelling Edition*, 2 vols, unpublished PhD thesis, University of Leeds (1988), Vol. I, pp. 494ff, for a full account of the controversial position of dancing during the late sixteenth and early seventeenth centuries.

10. Steven Mullaney, *The Place of the Stage: License, Play and Power in Renaissance England* (Chicago and London, 1988), p. 9.

11. Ibid., p. 31.

12. V. N. Volosinov, *Freudianism: A Marxist Critique*, trans. I. R. Titunik (New York, San Francisco and London, 1976), p. 88.

13. Ibid., p. 88.

14. Antony Easthope, *Poetry and Phantasy* (Cambridge and New York, 1989), pp. 36–7. For a fuller articulation of the debate to which Easthope responds, see Pierre Macherey, *A Theory of Literary Production*, trans. Geoffrey Wall (London, 1978), pp. 85ff., and Fredric Jameson, *The Political Unconscious: Narrative as a Socially Symbolic Act* (London, 1981), pp. 17–103.

15. Volosinov, *Freudianism*, pp. 89–90.

16. Ibid., p. 90.

17. Cf. Andrew Gurr, *Playgoing in Shakespeare's London* (Cambridge, 1987), pp. 51–7.

18. Volosinov, *Freudianism*, p. 89.

19. See John Drakakis, 'The Representations of Power in Shakespeare's Second Tetralogy', *Cosmos: The Yearbook of the Traditional Cosmology Society*, Vol. 2 (1986), ed. Emily Lyle, pp. 111–35.

20. Jonathan Dollimore and Alan Sinfield, 'History and Ideology: the instance of *Henry V*', in John Drakakis (ed.), *Alternative Shakespeares* (London, 1985), pp. 222–3.

21. Jacques Derrida, *Writing and Difference*, trans. Alan Bass (London, 1978), p. 280.

22. Ibid.

23. See Cornelius Castoriadis, *The Imaginary Institution of Society*, trans. Kathleen Blamey (Cambridge, 1987), pp. 146–56.

24. Robert Weimann, 'Towards a Literary Theory of Ideology: Mimesis, Representation, Authority', in Jean E. Howard and Marion O'Connor (eds), *Shakespeare Reproduced: The Text in History and Ideology* (New York and London, 1987), p. 271.

25. Derrida, *Writing and Difference*, p. 279.

26. Cf. Richard Wilson, '"Is This a Holiday?": Shakespeare's Roman Carnival', *English Literary History*, 54: 1 (Spring, 1987), 31–44. See also Mark Rose, 'Conjuring Caesar: Ceremony, History, and Authority in 1599', *English Literary Renaissance*, 19: 3 (Autumn, 1989), 291–304. For a more general discussion of the anti-authoritarian notion of festivity, see also Mikhail Bakhtin, *Rabelais and His World*, trans. Helene Iswolsky (Cambridge, MA, and London, 1968), pp. 21ff., and Peter Burke, *Popular Culture in Early Modern Europe* (London, 1979), pp. 182ff.

27. Sir John Davies, *The Poems of Sir John Davies*, ed. Robert Kreuger (Oxford, 1975), pp. 182ff.

28. I have followed the reading of l.140 in *William Shakespeare: The Complete Works*, ed. Stanley Wells, Gary Taylor, John Jowett, and

William Montgomery (Oxford, 1986). However, the Folio reading of the line is: 'Men at sometime, are Masters of their Fates', and this is followed in A. R. Humphreys (ed.), *Julius Caesar* (Oxford and New York, 1984), and T. S. Dorsch (ed.), *Julius Caesar* (London, 1965). The use of the present tense of the verb lends greater immediacy to Cassius's machiavellian proposition to Brutus.

29. Ernest Schanzer, *The Problem Plays of Shakespeare* (London, 1963), p. 32.

30. Ibid., p. 6.

31. Cf. Christopher Marlowe, *The Jew of Malta*, ed. N. W. Bawcutt (Manchester, 1978), p. 63:

> Though some speak openly against my books,
> Yet will they read me, and thereby attain
> To Peter's chair; and when they cast me off
> Are poisoned by my climbing followers.
> (Prologue, ll.10–13)

32. Michael Holquist, 'The Politics of Representation', in *Allegory and Representation*, ed. Stephen Greenblatt (Baltimore and London, 1981), p. 169.

33. Cf. Irving Ribner, *Patterns in Shakespearian Tragedy* (London, 1969), p. 60. See also Ernst Honigmann, *Shakespeare: Seven Tragedies: The Dramatist's Manipulation of Response* (London, 1976), p. 50; Alexander Leggatt, *Shakespeare's Political Drama: The History Plays and the Roman Plays* (London, 1988), p. 144; and Vivian Thomas, *Shakespeare's Roman Worlds* (London, 1989), p. 76.

34. For a more negative view, see Robert S. Miola, *Shakespeare's Rome* (Cambridge, 1983), p. 93, where it is suggested that 'Brutus's words reveal the savagery of the impending Roman ritual; in addition they expose the self-delusion of the conspirators'.

35. A. R. Humphreys (ed.), *Julius Caesar*, pp. 80–1. I am also grateful to Professor Gunther Walch for having drawn this possibility to my attention in his unpublished paper '"Caesar did never wrong, but with just cause": Interrogative Dramatic Structure in *Julius Caesar*'.

36. Thomas Beard, *The Theatre of God's Judgements* (London, 1597), p. 249, *STC* 1659.

37. William Fulbecke, *An Historicall Collection of the Continuall Factions, Tumults and Massacres of the Romans and Italians* (London, 1601), p. 170, *STC* 11412.

38. See John Drakakis, 'Writing the Body Politic: Subject, Discourse, and History in Shakespeare's *Coriolanus*', in *Shakespearean Discourses* (forthcoming).

39. Anne Righter, *Shakespeare and The Idea of The Play* (Harmondsworth, 1967), p. 141.

40. Boris Ford, 'Bardbiz', *Letters: The London Review of Books*, 12: 14 (2 August 1990).

41. John McGrath, *The Bone Won't Break: On Theatre and Hope in Hard Times* (London, 1990), p. 161.

7

Perspectives: Dover Cliff and the Conditions of Representation

JONATHAN GOLDBERG

THE WAY TO DOVER

Act III of *King Lear* opens with a description that a nameless gentleman makes to the disguised Kent, a description of Lear blasted 'with eyeless rage' (III.i.8).[1] Before we are offered the horrific spectacle of the king raging on the heath, we have this image of the king whom the storm would 'make nothing of' (l.9). And virtually simultaneously, before the full force of Lear's expulsion from Gloucester's home becomes apparent, the possibility that the movement of the play contains within it a counterforce is voiced by Kent. It crystallises around Dover. Kent responds to the gentleman's annihilative vision; of his nothing he would make something, offering the hope of secrets to be revealed – the restorative forces of France, the return of Cordelia, the regaining of identity. Kent sends the gentleman, fortified with these hopeful words, with tokens 'to Dover' (l.36); as if to answer the blinding storm and its 'eyeless rage', he assures him of the possibility that he will 'see Cordelia' (l.46) there. A compensatory pattern, initiated in this interchange and focused on the word *Dover*, continues in the scenes that follow.

Thus, just as we are offered *Dover* as the possibility of a happy ending before Lear's agony on the heath, the word appears again after Lear has endured the storm. Gloucester directs Kent to 'drive toward

Dover ... where thou shalt meet / Both welcome and protection'
(III.vi.89–90). The king is borne sleeping to the place where he can
escape the plots of death that threaten him. That direction and the re-
iteration of *Dover*, however, are even more forceful in the scene that
follows, Gloucester's blinding at the hands of Regan and Cornwall.
Shatteringly, the path of escape from 'eyeless rage' becomes the path
to its realisation. It is because Gloucester has sent the king to Dover
that he suffers the inquisition of Cornwall and Regan:

> **Cornwall**   Where has thou sent the king?
> **Gloucester**   To Dover.
> **Regan**   Wherefore to Dover? Wast thou not charged at peril –
> **Cornwall**   Wherefore to Dover? Let him answer that.
> **Gloucester**   I am tied to th' stake, and I must stand the course.
> **Regan**   Wherefore to Dover?
> **Gloucester**   Because I would not see thy cruel nails
>   Pluck out his poor old eyes
>
> (III.vii.5–57)

The pathos of the escape to Dover emerges in the repeated question,
'wherefore to Dover?' Wherefore, indeed.

When Gloucester has endured what he would not see, Regan
sends him to 'smell / His way to Dover' (III.vii.93–4). Gloucester's
path, doubling Lear's, collapses the antinomy of 'eyeless rage' and
the hope of recovery. Gloucester emblematises, literalises, and
makes fully horrific a path of fulfilled desire – the desire not to see.
The desire and hope constellated around Dover sickens. In the next
scene, Edgar, disguised as poor Tom, meets his father with his
bleeding eyes, and Gloucester asks him to lead 'i' th' way to Dover'
(IV.i.43). 'Know'st thou the way to Dover?' (l.55), he asks, and
asks again, 'Dost thou know Dover?' (l.71). To Edgar's affirmative
response, the old man describes the cliff that is his utmost desire, a
verge from whose dizzying height he expects no return.

Either way – as the place where Lear will see Cordelia, or the place
where Gloucester will have the satisfaction of suicide – in these reiterations of *Dover*, the word names a site of desire, the hope for recovery or, at least, repose, restoratives to answer 'eyeless rage', or the
final closing of the eyes in a sleep without end. Lear will awaken in
Cordelia's sight, perceiving himself deprived that ultimate rest: 'You
do me wrong to take me out o' th' grave' (IV.vii.45). Before that,
Edgar will have fulfilled Gloucester's request in a way that as
strongly undercuts any hope that Dover might embody. For, after

Gloucester's reiterated questions to Edgar, the word *Dover* never recurs in *King Lear*. Instead of the place, we arrive at Dover Cliff only in the lines that Edgar speaks to his father in Act IV, scene vi. In 'Shakespeare Imagines a Theatre',[2] Stephen Orgel argues persuasively for the imaginative weight and force of these lines, and I will not repeat his observations here. It suffices to say that Dover Cliff exists only in Edgar's lines and nowhere else in the play. The refusal to allow the word *Dover* to arrive at the place it (apparently) names, the failure, in other words, for signifier to reach signified – the failure of the sign – establishes the place that *Dover* occupies in the text. It is the place of illusion – the illusion of the desire voiced by Kent or Gloucester, the illusion of recovery *and* the illusion of respite and end. Yet, to come to the central point that I wish to make here, Edgar's lines describing Dover Cliff establish themselves as illusion by illusionistic rhetoric. His description answers to a particular mode of seeing, and the limits that *Dover* represents in the text are the limits of representation themselves. Paradoxically, a speech that represents space in a realistic mode points to the incapacity of the stage – and of language – to realise what the lines represent.

PERSPECTIVES

Here are Edgar's lines:

> Come on, sir; here's the place. Stand still. How fearful
> And dizzy 'tis to cast one's eyes so low!
> The crows and choughs that wing the midway air
> Show scarce so gross as beetles. Halfway down
> Hangs one that gathers samphire – dreadful trade;
> Methinks he seems no bigger than his head.
> The fishermen that walk upon the beach
> Appear like mice; and yond tall anchoring bark,
> Diminished to her cock; her cock, a buoy
> Almost too small for sight. The murmuring surge
> That on th' unnumb'red idle pebble chafes
> Cannot be heard so high. I'll look no more,
> Lest my brain turn, and the deficient sight
> Topple down headlong.
>
> (IV.vi.11–24)

The lines come ten lines into a scene in which the information given is, at best, ambiguous, Gloucester insisting that the ground he treads is flat, and that he can hear no sea roaring. There is no evidence to his imperfect senses that he approaches the verge that suddenly looms in Edgar's lines; as Orgel argues, the evidence of the audience's eyes and ears would confirm Gloucester's denials. Still, an audience would also know that were we to witness a scene at Dover Cliff, Shakespeare's stage would have no way of representing that event save in the language of those on stage who could testify to such an arrival; in this scene, only Edgar could report the evidence of sight. The stage would be, whether we were at Dover Cliff or not, flat; language would tell us to see it otherwise.

Such had been Shakespeare's practice elsewhere. Thus, the Chorus before *Henry V* directly addressed the audience on the question of what the stage might represent and the possible transformation that the 'wooden O' (Prologue, l.12) could undergo, bringing something out of nothing. The limits of representation is the theme of the prologue to the play. Although he desires to show a 'swelling scene' (l.4), all the Chorus can give is the 'great accompt' (l.17), 'flat unraised spirits' (l.9) in 'little place' (l.16) offering themselves and their words to the multiplying capacity of the audience: 'Piece out our imperfections with your thoughts: / Into a thousand parts divide one man / And make imaginary puissance' (ll.23–5). The Chorus describes here a Shakespearean transaction regularly enacted: to allow the force of imagination to go beyond the limits possible on the stage, and to take what the mind makes as the goal at which representation aims. Representation strives to be presentation; the audience credits the illusion as real event.[3]

Allowing words to become events on stage through the transformative capacity of images is the crucial Shakespearean metamorphosis to which the Chorus alludes. Banquo outside Inverness stops to observe birds building nests in the castle walls:

> This guest of summer,
> The temple-haunting martlet, does approve
> By his loved mansionry that the heaven's breath
> Smells wooingly here. No jutty, frieze,
> Buttress, nor coign of vantage, but this bird
> Hath made his pendant bed and procreant cradle.
> Where they most breed and haunt, I have observed
> The air is delicate.
>
> (I.vi.3–10)

Like Gloucester, the audience can neither hear nor see Banquo's birds, but we credit his description and supply the sight he offers. When Edgar describes Dover Cliff, we might suppose that the lines work on similar principles. The reiterations of *Dover* seem to have been leading to the place as surely as the gentleman's lines in Act III, scene i describing the almost unimaginable scene of Lear in the raging storm, cursing and screaming as the storm unleashes its parallel rage, becomes the staged fact in Act III, scene ii. Kent exits in Act III, scene i to seek his master, and the empty stage then discovers Lear enacting what the words before had done. This transformation realises the words; but, on the other hand, the scene works in part because it has first been imagined and verbalised. What is staged has already been supplemented beforehand by the gentleman's lines. Language has been there before the act, and the scene is all the more potent because of what has come before it. *Dover* tantalises us with these expectations only to deny them.

The arrival at Dover in *King Lear* may be less overtly self-conscious about staging than the opening lines of the Chorus in *Henry V*; it is nonetheless much more incisive about the problems that such a moment represents. For in *King Lear*, the possibility of the creation of the illusion of place through language is entangled in the significance of that illusory place in the text.[4] To reach Dover means something crucial in the careers of Gloucester and Lear, and the testing of the limitations of representation collapses at one time both the questions about the stage's capacity to represent as well as the hopes and desires that have constelled around the cliffs of Dover. For unlike the imagined scenes that the Chorus of *Henry V* offers, the scene that Edgar paints is couched in a language of illusionistic rendering that is virtually unprecedented in Shakespeare. The representation of the real, the realisation of representation, is in question. Edgar's description of Dover recasts a version of illusionistic representation upon which Renaissance painting depends. The lines offer a perspective on perspective.[5]

The theory of (Italian) Renaissance painting as presented in a treatise like Alberti's *Della pittura* depends on a few elements.[6] The viewer is imagined as stationary. The surface of the painting is considered as a framed window, and the distance of the viewer's eye from the surface of the painting determines the distance into space of the painting, which is organised around a vanishing point that represents the horizon of vision, and which is placed exactly correspondent to the fixed eye viewing the scene. All elements beyond the frame diminish proportionally until they reach the limit of vision which organises the pictorial space.

Blind Gloucester is positioned to have this illusionistic experience. Edgar roots him to 'the place' and insists that he 'stand still' (IV.vi.11). Between the spot where they are supposed to stand and the dizzying prospect, a series of midpoints is marked, dividing the space into mathematical segments. Birds appear the size of beetles; a man at this distance 'seems no bigger than his head' (l.16). Further down, they are even smaller; men become mice. The last objects seen are described in a kind of algebra that expresses a verbal version of a formula of proportion, a:b::b:c, 'yond anchoring bark, / Diminished to her cock; her cock, a buoy, / Almost too small for sight' (ll.18–20). The diminution in scale is insistent. Equally important is the illusionism of this carefully constructed view, the truth of what is apparent: *show, seem, appear* are the operative terms in Edgar's account.

The exactitude of visual placement in Edgar's scene is remarkable. When Banquo draws our eyes to see his nesting birds, he fills every 'jutty, frieze, / Buttress ... [and] coign of vantage' (I.vi.5–6) with scenes of procreation. These reflect his mind and his host's, and the moral and rhetorical pointing is telling.[7] But the audience to these lines is not asked to imagine an exact scene, but to countenance the meanings read into it. We grant Banquo his sight because we measure his imagination by it. We need not see where the architectural elements are in relation to each other, or where precisely each bird builds. Similarly, the Chorus of *Henry V* instructs: 'Think, when we talk of horses, that you see them / Printing their proud hoofs i' th' receiving earth' (Prologue, ll.26–7). The scene he asks to be seen derives its realisation from a graphic art, the translation of words heard into the imprinting of an impression. The words stamp themselves on the mind so that what is seen as a picture is something like words as they come to be on a page. The Chorus focuses on a particular action here, just as Banquo does. But unlike Edgar's vision, the emphasis is verbal, on the power of words to work on the imagination. By respecting the limits of representation and not insisting that the stage can go beyond itself, Banquo's birds or the horses of the Chorus can make their imaginary mark. But in Edgar's lines, 'imaginary puissance', as the Chorus called it (l.25), the power of images, is pushed to its limits. Dover is to be realised, not simply to be imagined.

The moral meanings to be read in Edgar's description derive precisely from the attempt at passing from representation to actual presentation. Like Banquo's, his lines measure the mind of the beholder, too. The lines comment, in their visual form, on the limits of possibility in the real and on the impossibility of the realisation of language and desire. The real rests on an insubstantial basis. One sign of this is that Edgar's vision is fearfully reductive, not only in its mathematics, but also in valuation: the birds metamorphosed into beetles or the fishermen turned mice are diminished on the scale of being; the 'dreadful' trade of the herbgatherer is further horrific in his dismemberment – he has become nothing but a head. Intimated, then, in Edgar's lines is the notion that the creation of illusionistic space and a belief in it depend upon acts of annihilation. To make the scene plausible, it must draw towards the limits of visibility. Illusionistic representation depends upon reductions. The illusion of continuous space rests upon what cannot be seen, on exhausting the limits of sight and arriving at what is 'too small for sight' (l.20). Vision depends upon both blindness and invisibility; it rests upon a vanishing point.

These lines, spoken for the benefit of a blind man, establish him as the best audience for a mode of vision. Similarly, this diminishing scene is, like a painting, utterly silent: 'The murmuring surge / That on th' unnumbered idle pebble chafes / Cannot be heard so high' (ll.20–2). And, seeing this way, Edgar feels that he will go blind and be drawn into the scene, and be destroyed by it: 'I'll look no more / Lest my brain turn, and the deficient sight / Topple down headlong' (ll.22–4). Albertian notions of the continuity between the viewer's space and the space of the painting become a prospect of madness in which the conviction of illusion produces the annihilation of the viewer. Gloucester embraces this illusion and plunges into it. He has been convinced by the *trompe l'oeil* of representation and his fall shows that he is the perfect audience for it.

Yet the effect of the scene, at least in retrospect, is to call representation into question. If the lines demonstrate that pictorial space is an illusion, they also show that words succeed only in perpetrating illusion. If they show that our eyes cannot be trusted, they do not, therefore, give us confidence that what we see subsequently can be believed. Nor do they restore faith in blindness, for they make blindness and sight coincident. When we return to Gloucester's initial perspective – the stage is flat, there is no roaring sea to be heard – we come back to a bare stage stripped of the possibilities that Edgar's language invoked. Gloucester's life is no 'miracle' (1.55), but a cheat. And all miracles that we might have supposed to lie at Dover will be equally guilty of the charge of illusion. The scene, employing the language by which a convincing real space is created, shows up the power of the stage.

The perspective from the imagined cliffs of Dover is so unusual in Shakespeare that there is barely the linguistic evidence that such a scene lay within his knowledge.[8] Only in sonnet 24 is the word *perspective* used with some possibility that it means what Alberti meant by it: 'perspective it is best painter's art' (l.4). The sonnet describes how the beloved's picture has been inscribed in the lover's heart; it is a matter of the exchange of eyeglances that transfers what is seen to what is within, this picture displaying the art of the painter and framed by the body of the seer:

> Mine eye hath played the painter and hath stelled
> Thy beauty's form in table of my heart;
> My body is the frame wherein 'tis held,
> And perspective it is best painter's art.
>
> (ll.1–4)

The more usual use of *perspective* can be found in *Richard II*. There, attempting to talk the queen out of her grief, Bushy offers this description of misprision: 'sorrow's eye, glazed with blinding tears, / Divides one thing entire to many objects, / Like perspectives, which rightly gazed upon, / Show nothing but confusion – eyed awry, / Distinguish form' (II.ii.16–20). Bushy's perspective is anamorphosis, the art of placing an object in a picture, which, to be seen correctly, must not be seen head on.[9] In anamorphic art, the spectator must be in two places at once to take in the picture. Only in the mind can the double act of seeing be reconciled. There is some possibility that the 'painter's art' of sonnet 24 is an optical illusion of this sort rather than the illusion of actuality since it is about seeing through others' eyes and the discrepancy between what is seen without and within. 'Now see what good turns eyes for eyes have done' (1.9), the final quatrain opens, and the 'turns' may well be anamorphic metamorphoses. At any rate, the conclusion of the sonnet opens a distance between 'painter's art' and knowing: 'Yet eyes this cunning want to grace their art; / They draw but what they see, know not the heart' (ll.13–14).

It is striking to note that Bushy's version of misprision anticipates the Chorus of *Henry V* asking for what is seen to serve as the basis for multiplication; by not seeing what is on stage and taking single things as signs of more, the viewer can provide the false perspective necessary to the truth of theatrical illusion. The Chorus to *Henry V* thus implies that Shakespeare's is, regularly, a theatre of perspective, but of the sort that Bushy describes, a stage where what is seen and heard invites one to go beyond the evidence of the senses. In this respect, a quintessential moment occurs at the end of *Twelfth Night* when the twins Viola and Sebastian are finally on stage together and in the Duke's sight. Orsino comments, 'A natural perspective that is and is not' (V.i.209). The stage has made itself at that moment a multiplying glass; the opposing tendencies in the language and desires of the characters have been realised – as if naturally – when the twins face each other. This 'natural perspective', however, is not Albertian. Rather, it issues in an art of multiplicity and not an order determined by a vanishing point. The Chorus of *Henry V* is intent upon a mathematics in which a 'wooden O', the theatre-as-nothing, can contain all. In *King Lear*, nothing comes of nothing, and the very language which would seem (to us) solidly to locate the world slides into an abyss, an uncreating, annihilative nothingness.

In the scene that Edgar presents, two perspectives are in question, the one that can be associated with the optical illusion of anamorphosis – the theatre, that is, as illusion and multiplicity, and another perspective, associated with representation (or illusionism), theatrical reality, and one-point mathematics. Ironically, the latter system, which we might be inclined to say shows the capacities of the mind and the reality of the material world, seems wanting. And it undermines even the first perspective, which is embedded in the notion that Edgar's *lines will give us a scene*. What is of further interest here is the fact that these two modes of perspective are crucial in understanding the history of the stage in Shakespeare's time; theatrical representation offers another perspective on Edgar's lines.

Two or three years before *King Lear*, English audiences, at least those privileged to attend court theatricals, had first seen illusionistic scenery. We know, from some contemporary eyewitness accounts, that these proved baffling, unconvincing. The distortions that Edgar enumerates as the enabling conditions of perspective, birds become beetles, men become heads, were all that Sir Dudley Carleton saw at a performance of Ben Jonson's *The Masque of Blackness*. Rather than seeing the representational necessity in what

Inigo Jones had designed, here is what Carleton saw: an 'Engine …
which had Motion … in it the Images of Sea-Horses …', and, he
concludes, 'The Indecorum was, that there was all Fish and no
water'. Carleton saw the elements, but not the design.[10] Unlike
Edgar, he was in no danger of being absorbed in the illusion. He
didn't see it. Edgar's lines present the new convention of staging
that was to challenge and ultimately supplant representation at the
Globe. Gloucester's initial affirmation of the flat stage in which representation depends almost entirely on language is challenged by
Edgar's pictorialism. Shakespeare in the scene is not only enacting a
version of the familiar trope analogising the arts, *ut pictura poesis*,
he is posing one kind of stage against another. And, of course, he
was implicated in both. From 1603 on, Shakespeare's company had
worn the royal livery, and by the time of *King Lear* they did not
only continue to perform at the Globe, but were performing at
court as well, where the King's Men took part in the masques that
Jones was designing for the royal eye.

Those scenes, in fact, are the best evidence for Shakespeare's
knowledge of Albertian perspective. Certainly, English painting
until the 1620s conceived of the surface of a painting in terms more
akin to anamorphic than to illusionistic perspective. Summarising
the qualities of the Elizabethan image, Roy Strong comments on the
'schematic and episodic view of a picture's surface', and concludes:
'Inscriptions, emblems, symbolic objects and whole inset scenes are
meant to be read separately as well as together; they are not governed by the single perspective viewpoint as re-created by the artists
of Renaissance Italy.'[11] It was Inigo Jones's importation of Italian
scene design that changed the conception of the surface of English
painting, replacing an organisation of two-dimensional surface co-
ordinates with a three-dimensional hierarchy that invited the translation of surface positions into perceptions of depth. Subordination
replaced co-ordination.

Edgar's lines cross and recross these pictorial paths. Hearing
them, Gloucester kneels, addressing the 'mighty gods', renouncing
the world 'in your sights' (ll.34–5). What is *our* sight at that
moment? What is our perspective on the scene? Edgar has presented
an illusion one must be blind to see, has disabled *at once*
Gloucester's stage that depends on language and the stage that
depends on pictorial illusion. The scene, summoning up the powers
of representation, shows the limits of representation. Gloucester
makes something of Edgar's nothing, and Edgar's imagined Dover

is a working out of illusion that rests on nothing: silence, invisibility, blindness. Pictorial space is founded on the meeting of the eye and the vanishing point. Acceding to this representation, Gloucester passes through the vanishing point and topples down headlong into double blindness, for he has agreed to see what cannot be seen – as we do when we refer to Act IV, scene vi as the Dover Cliff scene, or credit it with working miracles. The scene, however, insists that it is an illusion, and what it offers is a anatomy of the techniques of illusion – verbal and pictorial – upon which Shakespearean theatre depends. The 'eyeless rage' (III.i.8) that beats upon King Lear's head and that would 'make nothing of' him is visited upon Gloucester and upon the audience to the scene. 'Nothing will come of nothing' (I.i.90), Lear had told Cordelia, and the anatomy of representation in Act IV, scene vi is spaced between the nothing of the vanishing point and Gloucester's assumption of Lear's 'poor old eyes' (III.vii.57). This is the space of representation. By invoking these nothings as the condition of representation, Act IV, scene vi shows just what we accede to in seeing *King Lear*, and implicates the audience in its annihilative vision.

From *Poetics Today*, 5 (1984), 537–47.

NOTES

[The original version of this classic example of deconstruction, entitled 'Dover Cliff and the Conditions of Representation: *King Lear* IV.vi in Perspective', was published in the journal *Poetics Today*, and reprinted in a slightly revised version (with its current title) in G. Douglas Atkins and David Bergeron (eds), *Shakespeare and Deconstruction* (New York, 1988), pp. 245–65. A shortened version of the Atkins–Bergeron revision was reprinted under the same title in Kiernan Ryan (ed.), *King Lear: Contemporary Critical Essays* (London, 1993), pp. 145–57; it is the version in Ryan's collection which is reprinted here. Ed.]

1. All citations are from *The Complete Pelican Shakespeare*, ed. Alfred Harbage (Baltimore, MD, 1969).

2. Stephen Orgel, 'Shakespeare Imagines a Theatre', *Poetics Today*, 5 (1984), 549–61, esp. pp. 556–7.

3. For a discussion of Shakespearian representation that shares many of the concerns of this essay, see David Marshall, 'Exchanging Visions: Reading *A Midsummer Night's Dream*', *English Literary History*, 49 (1982), 543–75.

4. On linguistic places (*topoi*), see Marion Trousdale, *Shakespeare and the Rhetoricians* (Chapel Hill, NC, 1982).

5. Edgar's lines have been seen in the context of perspective by Marshall McLuhan in *The Gutenberg Galaxy* (Toronto, 1962), pp. 15–17, and again in McLuhan and Harley Parker, *Through the Vanishing Point* (New York, 1968), pp. 14, 74–5; the emphasis in both treatments is on the fragmentation of the visual.

6. See Leon Battista Alberti, *On Painting*, trans. John R. Spencer (New Haven, CT, 1956), pp. 45–8, 56, for the summary I offer. For a particularly stimulating discussion, see Harry Berger, Jr, 'L. B. Alberti: Art and Actuality in Humanist Perspective', *Centennial Review*, 10 (1966), 237–77. On the subject in general, see John White, *The Birth and Rebirth of Pictorial Space* (Boston, 1967), and the review essay by Robert Klein, 'Studies on Perspective in the Renaissance', in *Form and Meaning* (New York, 1979). Svetlana Alpers, *The Art of Describing* (Chicago, 1983) might point to a non-Italian tradition of representation (linking graphic representation, writing, and description) which provides an alternative to Albertian perspective within Edgar's speech.

7. For a provocative reading of these lines, see Harry Berger, Jr, 'The Early Scenes of *Macbeth*: Preface to a New Interpretation', *English Literary History*, 47 (1980), 1–31, esp. pp. 28–30.

8. On the knowledge of Italian theories in England, and the terminology of sixteenth-century Englishmen, see Lucy Gent, *Picture and Poetry: 1560–1620* (Leamington Spa, 1981), esp. pp. 23–5 on perspective. For a reading of sonnet 24 that takes up many of the issues pursued here and places them within the broader context of ideas of vision in the sequence, see Joel Fineman, *Shakespeare's Perjured Eye* (Berkeley, CA, 1986), pp. 135–40. See also Jonathan Goldberg, *Voice Terminal Echo* (New York, 1986), pp. 92–8.

9. On anamorphosis, especially in its literary use, see Claudio Guillén, 'On the Concept and Metaphor of Perspective', in *Comparatists at Work*, ed. Stephen G. Nichols, Jr and Richard B. Vowles (Waltham, MA, 1968), and Ernest B. Gilman, *The Curious Frame* (New Haven, CT, 1978). For the broader cultural implications, see Stephen Greenblatt, *Renaissance Self-Fashioning: From More to Shakespeare* (Chicago, 1980).

10. My comments depend upon Stephen Orgel and Roy Strong, *Inigo Jones: The Theatre of the Stuart Court*, 2 vols (London and Berkeley, 1973), I, 6–8, 11–12, 89.

11. Roy Strong, *The Cult of Elizabeth* (London, 1977), p. 111.

8

Fantasies of 'Race' and 'Gender': Africa, *Othello* and Bringing to Light

PATRICIA PARKER

I

the lap or privity dilated or laide open ...
(Helkiah Crooke)
... descried and set forth the secretes and privities of women.
(Eucharius Roesslin)

In the 1573 edition of *Des monstres et prodiges* – in a passage so controversial that it was finally moved to his less accessible technical treatise on anatomy – the influential French surgeon Ambroise Paré included a section on the secret parts of women which 'grow erect like the male rod', making it possible for them to 'disport themselves with them, with other women', and hence necessary 'with such women' that 'one must tie them and cut what is superfluous because they can abuse them'.[1] Paré's text pauses at this point to defend his mention of such practices, however incredible they may seem ('Now that these women, who by means of these caruncles or nimphes, abuse one another is a thing as true as it is *monstrous and difficult to believe*'). He does so, in a passage added to the 1575 edition, by appealing to the testimony of Leo Africanus, the converted Moor whose *Geographical Historie of Africa*, written in Arabic and Italian in 1526, had been widely translated and reprinted in Europe after its publication by Gian Battista Ramusio in Venice in 1550.[2] This confirming testimony is found in a story Africanus tells of some women of Fez in Mauretania who, claiming familiarity with demons, 'rub one another for pleasure, and in truth ... are afflicted of that wicked vice of using one another carnally'. Sometimes, the interpolated story reports, women of the town who wished to join these female traffickers with 'demons' in 'carnal copulations' would use their husbands as unknowing accomplices in their own cuckoldry, as go-betweens to fetch or to prepare feasts for a 'venerable band' of such women, leaving the wife free to go where, and with whom, she wished (though some husbands, it notes, would 'get the spirit driven out of their wives' bodies with a good hard clubbing'). Paré's text then links this story out of Africa with another part of the *Geographical Historie*, on clitoral excision:

> That is what Leo Africanus writes about it, assuring us in another place that in Africa, there are people who go through the city like our castrators ... and make a trade of cutting off such caruncles, as we have shown elsewhere under *Surgical operations*.

Paré's *On Monsters and Prodigies* was a popular and much-cited text, part of the burgeoning 'monster' literature of the European sixteenth century and its vogue for quasi-pornographic display. In this sense it was a phenomenon parallel to the growing European appetite for travel narratives at the threshold of the early modern period – filled by texts like the repeatedly translated one of this converted Moor.[3] Janis Pallister, in her recent translation of Paré, notes the derivation of 'monsters' both from the root of warnings or 'signs' (*monere* + *-strum*) and from a sense of bringing forth to 'show' (*monstrare*). But what is being 'warned' about here – and then 'shown' more graphically through illustration from Africanus's *Historie* – are not foreign 'monsters' but civic or domestic ones, the dangerous practices of women close to home made paradoxically more credible by reference to women of 'the principall citie of all Barbarie'.[4] When in 1579 Paré suppressed the story taken from Africanus's *Historie* – the only concession made to his censors – he replaced it by mention of the case of two French women, Françoise de l'Estage and Catherine de la Manière,[5] accused of being 'so abominable that they hotly pursue other women, as much or more than a man does a woman' ('femmes tant abominables qu'elles suyvent de chaleur autres femmes, tout ainsi, ou plus, que l'homme la femme') and who narrowly escaped being put to death. In the textual history of this

African anecdote, the crossings multiply between civil and barbarous, exotic and domestic: a forbidden (and threatening) female sexuality at home is projected on – and verified by – a story of the women of 'Barbarie'; and the story then returns home, to local instances.

Paré's text of monsters – supplemented by the anecdote from Africanus incorporated into the text of his *Anatomy* – offers a glimpse into the secret sexual lives of European women, with validating reference to the women of 'Barbarie'. (This link, of course, would not disappear from medical and scientific writing: Freud speaks of the 'dark continent' of female sexuality and Marie Bonaparte, at a signal moment of psychoanalytic history, tells of his having given her Felix Bryk's *Neger Eros* to read concerning clitorectomy or the 'ritual sexual mutilations imposed on African women since time immemorial', as confirmation of the psychoanalytic dogma of orgasmic transfer from the 'infantile' clitoridal zone to the more 'mature' vagina.)[6] The history of the anecdote in Paré is finally also a history of repression: by the time the French surgeon's anatomical writings were translated into English by Thomas Johnson in 1634, both the larger discussion of this hidden and secret female part and the anecdote from Africanus had been relegated to a footnote on this 'obscene part' that only the more curious, or determined, reader might pursue.[7]

This early modern linking of fascination with the secrets of female sexuality to a story out of 'Barbarie' provided by the travel narrative of a converted Moor does not, however, appear only in the work of Ambroise Paré. It also figures in Helkiah Crooke's English anatomy – *Microcosmographia: A Description of the Body of Man* (London, 1615) – largely a translation of the medical authorities of the continent. Treating of 'the Lap or Privities' of woman, Crooke writes of the 'clitoris' or 'the womans yard' that

> although for the most part it hath but a small production hidden under the *Nymphes* and hard to be felt but with curiosity, yet sometimes it groweth to such a length that it hangeth without the cleft like a mans member, especially when it is fretted with the touch of the cloaths, and so strutteth and groweth to a rigiditie as doth the yarde of a man. And this part it is which those wicked women doe abuse called *Tribades* (often mentioned by many authours, and in some states worthily punished) to their mutuall and unnaturall lustes.

In the margin appears in Latin 'Tribades odiosae feminae'. Beside it 'Leo Africanus'.[8]

Crooke goes on in this text to note that by the 'motion and attrition' of this female member, though for this 'business it was not necessary it should be large', the 'imagination' of women

> is wrought to call that out that lyeth *deeply hidden in the body*, and hence it is called aestrum Veneris & dulcedo amoris; for in it with the ligaments inserted into it is, the especial seate of delight in their veneral imbracements, *as Columbus imagineth he first discovered.*

The 'Columbus' cited here along with his 'discovery' is not Christopher but Renaldus, who in 1559 claimed to have brought this previously unknown territory to light.[9] Some clear link exists, then, in these European treatises of anatomy – Paré's in French, Crooke's in English, and the Latin treatise of another Columbus – between the anatomist's opening and exposing to the eye the secrets or 'privities' of women and the 'discovery' or bringing to light of what were from a Eurocentric perspective previously hidden worlds. Crooke's discussion of the female 'Lap or Privities' draws on the early modern sense of 'lap' as something 'folded' which the anatomist's description, like his diagrams, then unfolds, displays, or opens to the eye. And indeed, it furnishes illustration of this 'cleft' of the lap or privity *'dilated or laide open'* to the reader's view.[10]

II

> ... regions of the material globe ... have been in our times laid widely open and revealed.
>
> (Francis Bacon, *The New Organon*)
>
> Africa, which for a thousand yeeres before had lien buried ... is now plainely discovered and laide open to the view of all beholders.
>
> (Jean Bodin, in praise of Leo Africanus)

What is striking in these early modern texts – of 'monsters' shown to the eye of the curious or the 'privities' of women opened simultaneously to scientific 'discovery' and the pornographic gaze – is thus not only the crossings they negotiate between domestic and exotic or, in the references to Africanus, between Europe and 'Barbarie', but the shared language of opening, uncovering or bringing to light something at the same time characterised as 'monstrous' or 'obscene'.[11] Such a language of 'opening' to the eye's inspection what had been secret, closed, or hid characterises European discovery narratives from the beginning. The Epistle to Charles V reproduced in the English translation of Peter Martyr's *Decades* in 1577 includes in its praise of the Emperor that

> the divine providence, from the time that he fyrst created the worlde, hath reserved unto this day the knowledge of the great and large Ocean sea. In the which tyme he hath *opened the same*, chiefly unto you (most mightie Prince)

– a passage which involves both opening and ownership. Its wider context is the emphasis on 'ocularly recognising' that links accounts of the uncovering of previously unknown worlds to the language of early modern science and anatomy.[12]

Crooke's provision of a diagram of the hidden place of woman 'dilated or laide open' to the view is part of the ocular impulse of anatomy more generally – its preoccupation with what William Harvey called 'ocular inspection', an impulse that has led several recent commentators to align it with the specularity and scopophilia of theatre. Francis Bacon – principal theorist of the emergent epistemology – routinely used Columbus, Magellan, and the 'distant voyages and travels' through which 'many things in nature have been *laid open and discovered*' as emblems of the potential development of science itself as a 'masculine birth of time', opening and laying bare 'the remoter and more hidden parts' of a feminised 'nature'. European and English curiosity about Africa or 'Barbarie' is, then, in this respect part of a characteristic early modern preoccupation with the ocular, an appetite which, as with the appeal of prodigy and 'monster' literature, involved the hunger to 'know' as a desire to 'see'.[13]

The presentation of Leo Africanus to an English audience is also marked throughout by this emphasis on the ocular, and its substitutes. The text of John Pory's translation, in 1600, of *A Geographical Historie of Africa Written in Arabicke and Italian by Iohn Leo a More* literally enacts the experience of unfolding and exposing to the eye, including as it does in its prefatory materials a map of Africa folded and closed upon itself, which, when opened up, brings before the reader's gaze the land of monsters, of Amazons, of prodigious sexuality and of peoples who expose those parts which should be hid.[14] Its frontal material evokes the desire to see and know 'the secrets and particularities of this African part of the world' – which it promises to disclose 'at large' – through Africanus's narrative 'now *plainely discovered and laide open to the view of all beholders'*. To the text of this African *Historie* – the first to open the interior of Africa to European inspection – is affixed an 'approbation of the historie ensuing' by none other than Richard Hakluyt, the veteran of New World 'discovery' who persuaded Pory to undertake the translation of Africanus into English. It affirms this traveller's narrative to be 'the verie best, the most particular, and methodocall, that ever was written, or at least hath *come to light* concerning the countries, peoples, and affaires of Africa'. It is joined in this same preface by reference to the account of 'John Baptista Ramusius, Secretarie to the State of Venice', treating of the manifold difficulties he had earlier undergone in order 'to bring the important discourses therein *to light'*.[15]

The 'secrets and particularities' of unknown parts of the world were visually displayed not just by the opening of pages or unfolding of maps but by the early modern textual innovation of an 'index' – still in this period heavy with its etymological meaning of 'informer' – an indicator or pointer that made the contents of these massive volumes even more accessible to ready survey by the eye. One text promises, for example, to bring before its reader

> the most famous and memorable laws, customes, and manners of all nations ... collected, abridged, digested, and compacted together in this short and compendious Breviary; wherein you may easily finde whatever you have occasion to looke for ... *lying open before thine eyes.*[16]

Travellers and 'discoverers' were themselves informers to a European audience, bringing reports of matters otherwise hidden and unseen – an ocular emphasis that frequently makes the activity of reporting on the foreign or exotic one of 'informing' in the sense of espial or spying out. Hakluyt calls upon this complex when he urges English voyagers to Virginia (simultaneously named after a Virgin Queen and suggestive of yet unopened virgin territory) to strive 'with *Argus eies* to see' what this new territory might be made to 'yield' – a visual language of espial reminiscent of the sexualised currency of other contemporary discourses.[17]

It is this shared language of 'discovery' as informing or spying on something hid that gives to so many of these exotic histories their affinities with the ocular preoccupations of the growing network of *domestic* informers and spies charged with ferreting out secret or hidden crimes, those least accessible to 'ocular proof'.[18] Historians of early modern England speak of the 'dilations' or 'delations' ('secret accusations') that were a crucial part of this new domestic apparatus of 'discovery' in this other sense of bringing something hid to light. (The 'close dilations' of the informer Iago in *Othello* depend, as we shall see, both on the meaning of 'close' as 'secret' and on this contemporary network of 'informing', evoking not just a dilating or opening up – in ways simultaneously visual and sexual – but the whole domestic world of 'delators' and spies.)[19] One text from the 1590s reports on the omnipresence of 'secret spies' who 'do insinuate themselves into our company and familiarity' with such pretence of 'zeal, sincerity, and friendship' that they are able to 'give intelligence' of the most 'secret intents'. Francis Walsingham, the Elizabethan secretary of state who extended this nascent network into the first national secret service, was described as 'a most diligent searcher of *hidden secrets*'.[20] Once again, the similarity in language charts a crossing of foreign and 'domestic', exotic secrets and ones closer to home.

There was, moreover, an even more important link between this domestic preoccupation with informing and the testimony provided by travellers' histories. Pory reproduces from 'Ramusius' an account which speaks of the delight of the European audience of Africanus's *Historie* to have unfolded through it a report 'Concerning which part of the world, even till these our daies, we have had no knowledge in a manner out of any other author, or at leastwise never any *information so large*' (in the early modern sense of 'dilated' or set out 'at large') or '*of so undoubted truth*'.[21] Pory's promise to unfold 'at large' and hence bring to light formerly unknown regions of Africa is a promise to bring what had been hid, or revealed only in part, before his readers' eyes. But the gaze is a vicarious gaze, a substitution of narrative or report for what a later such text would call the eye-witness or 'occular ... view'.[22] The principal criterion for such substitutes for the directly ocular therefore became their reliability as testimony. Not only did they need to provide lifelike description, bringing the unseen as if before the eye through verbal *enargeia* or the rhetorical creation of convincing pictures (the root of seeing or 'illustration' that links *enargeia* – or *evidentia* – to the '*Argus*' of the many eyes); they also needed to be trustworthy messengers. Yet it is precisely the reliability of their testimony which was repeatedly questioned. Proliferating accounts of the monsters and prodigies of foreign lands circulated in the early modern period in an environment prey to the danger, and constant accusation, of counterfeit report, of substitutes for ocular proof that put the reader in 'false gaze', as it is said at the beginning of *Othello* of the report of 'Signior Angelo' that ominously anticipates the falsified informing of Iago, the figure whose name evokes not Venice but England's Iberian rivals in the African trade.[23] What the English translator of one travel text calls the 'multitude of Mandivels' that 'wander abroad in this pampletting age in the habite of sincere Historiographers', relating 'meere probabilities for true', casts doubt on all reported 'ceremonies & customes used in certaine countries, which seeme so *absurde, monstrous* and *prodigious*, as they appear utterly voide of credit'.[24]

Leo Africanus was one of these informing messengers, bearing tales from territories formerly off the stage of European history. Pory's presentation of his report thus raises more than once what appear to be needed 'vouches' or warrants of his reliability, in a climate it too notes is populated by 'mountebanks and Mandevilles'. His prefatory 'To the Reader' presents this African narrator as worthy 'to be regarded' because, though 'by birth a More, and by religion for many yeeres a Mahumetan', his 'conversion to Christianie', along with 'his busie and dangerous travels', render him a reliable informer on matters that before 'were either *utterly concealed, or unperfectly and fabulously reported*'.[25] Africanus's own narrative, in Pory's translation, repeatedly invokes the language of the eye-witness, or where 'ocular proof' was unavailable, the informer whose information bears the stamp of truth. Its 'vouches' are filled with the sense of bringing vicariously but reliably before the gaze, as a credible substitute for the directly ocular:

> These are the things memorable and woorthie of knowledge seene and observed by me John Leo, throughout al Africa, which countrey I have in all places travelled quite over: wherein whatsoever I sawe woorthy the observation, I presently committed to writing: and *those things which I sawe not*, I procured to be at *large declared unto me by most credible and substantiall persons*, which were themselves *eie-witnesses* of the same.
>
> (p. 358)

As Pory's presentation of Africanus to his English audience makes clear, that which is narratively declared 'at large' becomes a substitute for what the eye has not seen, as well as testimony whose reliability must be vouched for.

III

This would not be believ'd in Venice,
Though I should swear I saw't.
                                            (*Othello*)

Othello has long been linked both with Mandeville's 'fabulous' reports and with this converted Moor's African *Historie* through the 'travellours historie' (as the Folio text has it) provided by Othello, the Moor of Venice, in answer to charges of 'witch-craft' in the wooing of a white Venetian bride.[26] It is this tale of 'Cannibals that each other eat, / The Anthropophagi, and men whose heads / Do grow beneath their shoulders' (I.iii.143–5) that Othello provides first to Brabantio, a prominent Venetian citizen eager to hear his story, then in response to Desdemona's prayer 'That I would all my pilgrimage dilate, / Whereof by parcels she had something heard' (ll. 153–4), and finally (in its staging simulta-neously) to a Venetian and English audience ignorant of events in a double sense by them unseen – the monsters and adventures of these exotic worlds and the offstage wedding (and in Iago's vivid *enargeia*, the imagined bedding) of a Venetian virgin by a 'lascivi-ous' Moor, an 'extravagant and wheeling stranger / Of here and every where' (I.i.136–7). As a 'travellours historie', its presentation evokes all the familiar contemporary associations of such trav-ellers' tales – the European appetite or hunger for report (synec-dochally by its reference to the 'greedy ear' of Desdemona that did 'devour up' this stranger's discourse, subtly and chiastically linking this form of domestic consumption with the figures of the 'Cannibals' in these same lines); the converted Moor whose narra-tive is accepted as a reliable 'vouch' (I.iii.106) of events to which his European audience has no direct eye-witness or 'ocular' access; and, later, the questioning of its credibility as report, when Iago (the figure who will soon become a 'domestic' informer in every sense) charges that this Moor's tales are mere 'bragging and telling ... fantastical lies' (II.i.223).[27]

The links between Othello's exotic 'travellours historie' – its verbal pictures bringing offstage events vicariously before the eye – and Iago's manipulation of *evidentia* (vicarious substitute for ocular 'evidence') when attention turns to the domestic secrets of a Venetian woman, become part of this play's own extra-ordinary emphasis on bringing to 'light', on the hunger to 'know' as the desire to 'see', and its obsession with offstage events, domestic and exotic, related both to the sexualised 'chamber' of a woman and to the origins of an outsider Moor. The two combine in the vivid fantasies of miscegenation exploited in the opening scene, in Iago and Roderigo's verbal evocations of 'an old black ram ... tupping your white ewe'. They continue in Othello's 'dilation' of his 'travellours historie', and finally in his hunger to see and know through the medium of *his* native informant, to spy out the secrets of a woman whose 'honor' is an 'essence that's *not seen*' (IV.i.16).

The play itself suggests – in one unmistakable and striking verbal echo – this central chiastic crossing of foreign and domestic, exotic and sexual. The 'travellours historie' provided by the Moor of Venice in answer to Desdemona's entreaty that he might 'all [his] pilgrimage dilate' (I.iii.153) has its clear echo in the sexualised object of the 'close dilations' of the Temptation Scene (III.iii.123), where Iago, Venetian informer on these more domestic secrets, begins to 'unfold' not hidden exotic worlds but the 'close' or 'secret' place of Desdemona's sexuality which his informing promises to bring to 'light' (I.iii.404). It is these 'close dilations' (with their pun on the 'delations' or secret accusations of the informer and their beginning, like Othello's dilated narrative, from what is first glimpsed only in 'parcels' or in part) that lead to the Moor's conviction that this informer 'sees and knows more, much more, than he *unfolds*' (III.iii.242–3). The language of dilating, opening, or unfolding (enacted in Pory's presentation of Africanus's exotic *Historie*, with its enfolded map and promise to dilate 'at large' what is hidden from the eye) begins, as *Othello* narrows to domestic secrets, to mark this new hunger to bring before the eye something unseen, offstage, hid – a movement that leads first to the 'napkin' or handkerchief which both substitutes for 'ocular proof' and increases the appetite for it, and finally to Desdemona's hidden 'chamber', only in the final Act brought forth to 'show'.

To 'dilate' in early modern usage came not only with a sense of opening or enlarging something 'too much closed', but with this sense of opening up to 'show' – 'displaying some object ... first of all through a lattice or inside a wrapping, and then unwrapping it and opening it out and displaying it *more fully to the gaze*'. This is the double sense invoked in the scene of Othello's exotic 'travellours historie'. At the same time, however, it carried with it resonances of a specifically sexual opening, and, combined with the visual, of a voyeuristic, even prurient desire to 'know', not just a way to open or 'spread abroad' something closed or hid but a means through which 'to open the bosom of nature and to *shew* her branches, to that end they may be *viewed and looked upon, discerned and knowen*'.[28] It is this simultaneously eroticised and epistemological impulse to open up to show that thus enables the easy movement between rhetorical and sexual opening exploited in the link between *Othello*'s evocation of tales of African or New World discovery and the simultaneously visual and sexual 'close dilations' of Iago's domestic informing, pruriently, even pornographically exposing a hidden 'chamber' to the eye.

Within the almost unbearably protracted Temptation Scene, the 'close dilations' which lead to this demand for 'show' are echoed in a passage whose terms are strikingly both epistemological and sexual:

> Iago My lord, I would I might entreat your honor
> To *scan this thing no farther*; leave it to time.
> Although 'tis fit that Cassio have his place –
> For sure he fills it up with great ability ...
> (III.iii.244–7)

Hidden within the visual language of this informer's advice to 'scan this thing no farther' is the 'thing' which elsewhere is the 'common thing' (III.iii.301–2) Emilia offers to her husband, the female privity or *res* that Iago vulgarly sexualises when she intrudes to offer him what he terms a 'trifle' (l.322). Advice that appears to speak only to an epistemological hunger to 'see' and 'know' introduces into the lines that follow the double meanings of a 'place' Cassio 'fills up' with 'great ability', a 'place' whose sexual inference is joined by the threat to Othello's 'occupation' (III.iii.357) through the obscener sense of 'occupy'. What is secret or unseen here is the ambiguous sexual 'place' of all the double-meaning references to the place Cassio might occupy as Othello's place-holder or 'lieu-tenant'.[29]

From the beginning, the protracted process of 'unfolding' in *Othello* involves not only fascination with what is hidden from the eye, but, as Karen Newman and Michael Neill have differently remarked, a sense of bringing forth to 'show' some 'monster' too 'hideous' to be 'shown', a link made in the lines that lead into this

informer's 'close dilations' as a glimpse of something to be brought
to light:

> By heaven, thou echo'st me,
> As if there were some *monster* in thy thought
> Too *hideous* to be *shown*...
> If thou dost love me,
> *Show* me thy thought.
>
> (III.iii.106–16)

The passage plays on the link between 'monstrous' and 'shown'
already exploited in a 'monster' literature that displays vicariously
to the eye the otherwise 'monstrous and difficult to believe' (as
Paré had put it in citing Africanus's 'Barbarie' as verification
of 'monstrous' domestic female sexual practices). And it links
the dilating, unfolding, or opening to the eye made possible
through Othello's 'travellours historie' – with its monstrous
'Anthropophagi' and 'Cannibals' – to Iago's 'close dilations' of a
hidden female place which, as in Crooke, is both 'dilated and laide
open' to the gaze and 'too obscoene to look upon'. 'Hideous', as
Neill suggests, is in this complex pun 'virtually an Anglo-Saxon
equivalent for the Latinate "obscene"' that which according to a
powerful if false etymology should be kept 'offstage', linking the
scaenum or stage to the obscene as what should be hidden, unseen,
not 'shown'.[30]

Othello itself, however, provokes a constant, even lurid, fascination with the offstage or in this sense ob-scene, starting from the
vividly racialised rhetoric of Iago and Roderigo at its opening,
focused on an unseen sexual coupling, or imagined coupling, involving the 'monstrous' opening of a Venetian virgin by a 'lasciv-
ous Moor'. The fact that these and other secrets of this imagined
'chamber' are offstage and hence barred from vision prompts what
mounts in the play both as hunger for more narrative or report –
Othello's entreaty that *his* informer might '*all* [his narrative] *dilate*'
– and as desire that what is 'hid' be brought forth to 'show'. The
desire to show or bring this 'monstrous' place on stage also involves, however, a pornographic doubleness that simultaneously
panders to the eye and averts the gaze,[31] a movement that leads,
after the final bringing of this hidden 'chamber' to 'light', to the
opposing desire to 'Put out the light' (V.ii.7), to reclose what has
been unfolded and disclosed ('The object poisons sight, / Let it be
hid').

IV

My mother had a maid call'd Barbary.
(*Othello*)

… this thing of darkness I / Acknowledge mine.
(*The Tempest*)

Othello's 'dilated' traveller's tale, opening to Venetian (and English) eyes exotic worlds beyond the direct reach of vision, combined with the 'close dilations' of a Venetian informer on the secrets of Desdemona's 'chamber', chart the crossing in this play of domestic and exotic, 'civil' and 'barbarian', explicitly within the register of fascination and the vicariously visual. The evocation of a female *res* or 'thing' available to be 'dilated and laide open' to the eye in Iago's 'scan this thing no farther', links it to the language applied to Othello the Moor ('the sooty bosom / Of such a *thing* as thou,' I.ii.70–1), a language that returns in the description of Caliban – possible anagram of 'Cannibal' – as the 'thing of darkness' Prospero will later call his own. Both sexualised and racialised 'thing' converge in *Othello* in the trifling 'thing' Emilia offers to her husband – the handkerchief or 'napkin' which becomes the sign at once of Desdemona's unseen 'honor' (IV.i.16) and of Othello's exotic history, linked with Africa and with Egypt ('that handkerchief / Did an Egyptian to my mother give'; 'there's magic in the web of it', III.iv.55–8; 69ff.). Embroidered 'alla moresca' in the play's Italian source, 'spotted with strawberries' (III.iii.435) in Shakespeare's addition, it evokes, as Lynda Boose has argued, a specific form of bringing forth to 'show' the hidden sexual place of woman as a token of 'opened' or lost virginity, the 'bloody napkin' that figures not just in exotic or African narratives but as a resonance within domestic European anxieties surrounding the secrets of female sexuality and its control.[32]

Paré's text, in its English version, cites the 'bloody linnen cloth' described by 'Leo the Affrican' in the midst of a discussion not just of virginity but of the 'deceit of bauds and harlots' who, 'having learned the most filthy and infamous arts of bawdry', seek to make men 'to beleeve that they are pure virgins' – a passage which resonates against the language of another converted Moor ('I took you for that cunning whore of Venice / That married with Othello', IV.ii.88–9).[33] In *Othello*, the evidence of the spotted 'napkin' presented as substitute for direct or 'ocular proof' conjures in one powerfully economical

image the token of opened virginity and hence of a chamber potentially kept by a 'bawd', and the exoticised origins of the stranger
Moor, split between that history and the perspective of a Venetian
husband informed of secrets that in Venice are not only 'monstrous'
but withheld from 'show' ('In Venice they do let God see the pranks /
They dare not *show* their husbands', III.iii.202–3).

What links, then, what might be termed the 'fantasies' of 'race'
and 'gender' exploited within this play of dilating, uncovering, and
bringing to light is something like the crossing of exotic and domestic already traced in several early modern contexts, but also the
extraordinary series of exchanges and divisions in which
Desdemona and Othello cross and occupy each side of that divide.
The play produces a series of powerful chiastic splittings.
Desdemona the white Venetian daughter becomes, as it proceeds,
the sexually tainted woman traditionally condemned as 'black', part
of the representational schema that gives ironic resonance to the
choice of the name 'Bianca' ('white') for the character most explicitly linked to that taint and that releases the 'demon' within her
own name. 'Desdemon' (as she is called by Othello in V.ii.25) sings
toward the end the song of a 'Maid call'd Barbary' (IV.iii.26) while
Othello the Moor, the 'Barbary horse' (I.i.111) and 'erring barbarian' (I.iii.355) of the opening Act, comes to occupy the perspective
of a wronged Venetian husband, executing judgement on a 'blackened' or erring wife (III.iii.387–8: 'now begrim'd and black / As
mine own face').[34]

It is not insignificant in relation to these crossings in both directions that the loci of this play are Venice and Cyprus. Venice, on
Europe's margins, was the port of entry or opening to Africa (it is
through 'Ramusius, Secretarie to the State of Venice', that
Africanus's *Historie* was first introduced). Homophone of 'Venus',
it was paradoxically both open and closed, impregnable 'Virgin
Citie' and a place notorious for its courtesans. Cyprus was both the
classical refuge of Venus and the contemporary colonial outpost
most vulnerable to invasion from the 'barbarian' Turk. (The link
between the sexual invasion of Desdemona by an 'erring barbarian'
and the vulnerability of Cyprus – threatened by Turkish invasion
throughout the sixteenth century and in Turkish possession by the
time of the play – is underlined by the defeated Brabantio's
response to the Duke: 'So let the Turk of Cyprus us beguile, / We
lose it not, so long as we can smile', I.iii.210–11.) Venus was denounced by Stephen Gosson as 'a notorious strumpet' who 'made

her self as common as a Barbars chayre' and 'taught the women of Cyprus to set up a Stewes'. Desdemona is associated with 'Barbary' through suspicion of her 'common' sexuality (IV.ii.72–3).[35] In the paranomastic play on 'Moor' and 'more' made easier by the variable orthography of early modern English, Othello, the Moor of Venice already contains within it the corresponding suggestion of the 'More' of 'Venus', chiastically linking the 'Moor' so often spelled 'More' with a potentially uncontrollable female excess.[36]

This crossing of exotic and domestic, 'Moor' and female 'more', within Othello, is rendered even more complexly layered by the resonances within this play of another eliding of an imperial encounter with a domestic one. Othello's 'travellours historie', reminiscent of travel narratives both ancient and contemporary, possesses the power to 'detaine' that Bodin ascribed to Leo Africanus's exotic and extended Historie.[37] But both in its opening and in this power to 'detaine', the story 'dilated' by the Moor and unfolded to Venetian Desdemona's 'greedy ear' also recalls an earlier precedent for the encounter of Europe and Africa, female and male, itself a locus classicus for the dilation of all such visually evocative narratives. This is the tale of Aeneas to African Dido, a 'Moore among the Moores', told by another 'extravagant and wheeling stranger' to the ear of a woman of 'Barbarie'.[38] The tale of Othello the converted Moor is thus strangely put in the place of the traveller Aeneas – Trojan and ultimately Roman standard-bearer of a triumphant Western and European history – a figure who abandons a woman and 'Barbarie' at once.

An echo of Aeneas and African Dido in a tale already overlaid with echoes of contemporary narratives of 'discovery' should not come as a surprise in the work of the playwright whose Antony and Cleopatra and The Tempest similarly conflate different moments in the history of empire, or for that matter in a century of imperial rivalry that gave to one Spanish New World outpost the name of 'Carthago'. It might even be expected in a play that turns, as Othello does, between the poles of war and love, the competing calls of duty and the domestic. In relation to the play's repeated references to Desdemona as 'our great captain's captain' (II.i.74) and commanding 'general' ('Our general's wife is now the general', II.iii.315) – as well as its broader evocation of pavor feminae – it needs also, however, to be remembered that Aeneas's sojourn with Dido was in this period a powerful monitory emblem (both domestic and imperial) of domination by a woman. Antony and Cleopatra draws on the familiar Virgilian opposition of the virility of imperial Rome to the effeminating influence of this African queen, in that confluence of misogyny and orientalism that linked Cleopatra's Egypt with Dido's Carthage as exotic kingdoms ruled by women. Closer to home, the outlines of this imperial history hovered in complex ways around the rule of an *English* kingdom by a queen linked in name with Dido or 'Elissa' as well as with Aeneas her putative Roman male ancestor, a queen associated with what John Knox denounced as the 'monstrous regiment' of female rule. This other Dido / Elissa, both patron of English imperial ventures and the Virgin whose virginity figured the inviolability of England's borders, was a queen whose realm was not only highly vulnerable to invasion but sailed upon by self-styled Aeneases. To add to this complexity, however, she was also the monarch who ordered the expulsion of 'Negroes and blackamoors' from that realm, on the grounds that the incursion of these particular outsiders had become excessive.

Othello's dilated narrative in Act I – with its effect on a woman whose 'greedy ear' did 'devour up his discourse' – casts the pair of outsider Moor and white Venetian daughter from the beginning, then, as an Aeneas and Dido, the pair echoed in *Antony and Cleopatra's* more explicit version of this imperial history. In so doing, it crosses gender and racial identities, (mis)placing Othello in the position of Aeneas the 'European' male and Desdemona in that of a dominating (and abandoned) female 'Moor', a woman of 'Barbarie' whose chastity in this tradition was suspect and open to question.[39] The crossing of female and black, Europe and 'Barbarie', is thus adumbrated in the play even before Desdemona, 'blackened', sings the song of an abandoned 'Maid call'd Barbary' – the song which turns out to be the Willow Song already linked with Dido, the African Queen.[40] The associations of Moorish Dido – a woman of 'Barbarie' who dominates a man, is tainted with an adulterous sexuality and is finally rendered passive and abandoned, in striking contrast to her earlier command – hover around the representations of Venetian Desdemona, the woman who is both 'half the wooer' and forthright in her speech, but who becomes, as the play proceeds, the increasingly passive figure for whom hearing a stranger's tale also involves a disastrous consequence.

If, then, in this evocation of an ancient imperial history of male and female, Africa and Rome, Othello evokes Aeneas, male and 'European', Desdemona the figure of Dido, female and Moor, the splitting of Desdemona into 'white' and 'black' in relation to her 'fidelity' is mirrored by the splitting of Othello into faithful Venetian general and Turkish 'infidel'. The echo of African Dido and Roman Aeneas early in the play invokes the history of imperial conquest in the context of the tragedy that is Shakespeare's most intimately domestic, focusing as it does on bringing to light the 'chamber' of a wife suspected of infidelity, as well as on the adulterating union of 'white' and 'black' at a time when the meaning of 'adultery' included the taint of miscegenating mixtures. Othello's 'dilated' traveller's tale recalls Africanus, Mandeville, Pliny, and the rest as well as the domestic English hunger for such narratives, in the context of a plot which turns on the reliability of an act of informing or report. But it does so by also summoning an echo of the 'greedy ear' of a woman of 'Barbary', and hence not just the history of imperial rivalries but the complex and crucially *asymmetrical* crossings of 'gender' and 'race' at work in the period – a period which could figure Desdemona as becoming 'black' while retaining, in another register, her class and insider position or celebrate the imperial Roman heritage of English Elizabeth even as it linked her with the threatening female rule of a Moorish queen.

Othello as a whole is filled with such split chiastic exchanges and divisions: in the case of Othello himself, one crossing maps the apparent move from outsider to insider, from the perspective of 'stranger' Moor to that of Venetian husband suspicious of the purity or 'whiteness' of his wife. Othello, the converted Moor and enemy of the 'Infidel', is explicitly split between insider and outsider in the scene of the night brawl on Cyprus, the island anxiously guarded from invasion by the Turkish fleet ('Are we *turn'd Turks*, and to ourselves do that / Which heaven hath forbid the Ottomites? / For *Christian* shame, put by this *barbarous* brawl', II.iii.170–2). By the play's end, in the speech that leads to the self-division of his suicide, these split identities are embodied in yet another travel narrative, one of which he now is simultaneously both object and subject ('And say besides, that in Aleppo once, / Where a malignant and a turban'd Turk / Beat a Venetian and traduc'd the state, / I took by th' throat the circumcised dog / And smote him – thus', V.ii.352–6). And in their notorious textual confusion, the final lines suggest a proliferating series of exoticised others – 'base Indian' (Q1) or 'Judean' (F1), 'Arabian', and perhaps obscure allusion to the Jews and Edomites from the story of Mariam and Herod, another husband who in a fit of jealousy had his wife killed.[41]

V

> Friends all, but now, even now,
> In quarter, and in terms like bride and groom
> Devesting them for bed. ...
> (*Othello* II.iii.179–81)

The pervasive echoes in *Othello* of European Aeneas and a queen of 'Barbarie' chart the complexly and asymmetrically interrelated issues of race and gender in this play, in a context that also summons the role of dilation as both engrossing narrative and bringing to 'light'. But even this account of the play's complex exchanges of 'barbarous' and domestic is not complete without reference to one other of its crossings, and asymmetrical splits. Othello comes in one respect to 'occupy' the place of a Venetian husband, in a play that insistently calls attention to the occupying or changing of 'place'. But in the process he also becomes the more passive receiver of another's informing, his ear 'pierced' (I.iii.219), 'abused' (l.395), or – in a different metaphorics – 'colonised' by that informer, his 'occupation' gone as he himself is 'occupied', in a process described as bringing a 'monstrous birth' to light (l.404). This other coupling complicates the heterosexual erotics of the play with all of its insistent homoerotic imagery, climaxing in the parody-marriage of Iago and Othello in Act III and adding to the already multiple senses of 'informing' that of the 'monstrous' shaping or giving form that comes of this displaced insemination and conception. It thereby adds to the play's fantasies of heterosexual miscegenation (the coupling of white Desdemona and 'lascivious' Moor) the complications of a monstrous union of Iago and the Moor – a relation in which this Moor is by implication sexually 'fallowed' ('as asses are', I.iii.402) rather than loyally 'followed' by his Venetian subordinate (I.i.58), a reversal of their hierarchical relationship into a form of 'service' frequently associated with such racialised others in the period of the play.[42]

We started with women 'abusing themselves with women' – a phrase loaded with all the early modern freighting of *abusio* as a term for 'unnatural' sexuality and linked in Paré's account with the practices of 'Barbarie'. We need to complete this picture – again, chiastically but asymmetrically – by bringing into this play's (and its culture's) projections, crossings, and splittings a sense of all that was involved in the designation of the 'barbarous', including this other 'abusive' and 'monstrous' practice projected onto the other and outside, as the opposite to the 'civil' or 'civilised'. In the example from Paré, the projection of 'monstrous' female sexuality from cases close to hand onto an otherness called 'Barbarie' appears to link certain European and African women as 'monstrous' others in an exchange of alien and domestic reflected in the common currency of 'bringing to light', while still retaining the ethnographic separation of the exotically different. In *Othello*, Iago 'abuses' the ear of a Moor of 'Barbary',[43] a form of penetration that leads (with Desdemona excluded) to the 'monstrous birth' that becomes the only progeny of the fantasies of miscegenation that haunt this play from its beginning, starting with Iago's vivid imagining of all that is to ensue from the adulterating of 'kind' ('your daughter cover'd with a Barbary horse, you'll have your nephews neigh to you ... coursers for cousins, and gennets for germans', I.i.111–13).

The 'monstrous' in this play – as in its culture – includes the *abusio* of homoerotic practices as yet another barbarous form of 'sin against kinde', the coupling that in the equally charged *enargeia* or vivid description of Cassio embracing Iago in bed (III.iii.413–26) produces Othello's 'O monstrous! monstrous!' (l.427), glancing as it passes at the term for the 'monstrous' abuses of an English theatre in which the 'secret' of Desdemona included the fact that she was acted by a boy. The domestic 'open secret' of male sexual relationships (both private and prominent, as in the cases of Francis Bacon or James I, the monarch before whom *Othello* was performed) coexisted in complex and contradictory ways with denunciations of this other 'monstrous' sexual practice, projected onto non-European or non-English others (including Iberians and inhabitants of 'Barbary') as yet another familiar staple of 'travellours histories'.[44]

I put this pressure, finally, on more of what was included within the early modern designation of the 'monstrous' because we have to do, both in this play and in its culture, with the violence of projection itself, propelled by the uneasy sense of 'occupation' that comes from the blurring of boundaries between alien and civil, outside and an inside already occupied by 'adulterating' mixtures.[45] *Othello* provides us not only with this violence, and its chiastic splittings, displayed and summoned forth to 'show', but with the charged oxymoron of the '*civil* monster' (IV.i.64), a phrase which, detached from its immediate context, might be applied to the Venetian / Iberian figure of Iago, producer of the 'monstrous' sight that 'poisons sight', but which in more general, pervasive, and unsettling ways exposes the contradications at the heart of the civilised or 'civil'. It is this only apparent oxymoron from *Othello* that perhaps best conveys the sense in the play, or more largely within early modern culture, of the projected other as both mirror and split chiastic counterpart of the 'monstrous' at home, a home already 'occupied' and hence unsettingly incapable of fortification against 'invasion'. Within the realm of the visual, it might also name that particular form of crossing and othering in which what is brought to 'light' is at the same time that which cannot – or *must* not – be 'seen'.

From *Women, 'Race', and Writing in the Early Modern Period*, ed. Margo Hendricks and Patricia Parker (London and New York, 1994), pp. 84–100.

NOTES

[Patricia Parker's distinctive scholarly style combines linguistic analysis, theory, and history, and often focuses on issues of gender, race, and sexuality. See also her *Literary Fat Ladies: Rhetoric, Gender, Property* (New York and London, 1987), and *Shakespeare from the Margins: Language, Culture, Context* (Chicago, 1996). Ed.]

1. See Janis L. Pallister (trans.), *On Monsters and Marvels* (Chicago 1982), pp. 188–9, and the text removed to Paré's *De l'anatomie de tout le corps humain* (1585), in Ambroise Paré, *Oeuvres complètes*, ed. J. F. Malgaigne (Paris, 1840; Geneva, 1970), I: 168–9.

2. See Jean Céard (ed.), *Des monstres et prodiges* (Geneva, 1971), pp. 26–7, on the reference to Africanus added to *Les Oeuvres de M. Ambroise Paré* (Paris, 1575), and Thomas W. Laqueur, 'Amor Veneris, vel Dulcedo Appeletur', *Fragments for a History of the Human Body*, ed. Michel Feher et al., Part 3 (New York, 1989), pp. 116–17, who cites the anecdote in the context of a different argument. On Africanus (baptised Giovanni Leone or 'Leo' by Pope Leo X), see among others Eldred Jones, *Othello's Countrymen* (London, 1965), pp. 21–5, 27; and Christopher Miller, *Blank Darkness: Africanist Discourse in French* (Chicago, 1985), esp. pp. 12–13.

3. On the titillating appeal of this 'monster' literature, see Katharine Park and Lorraine J. Daston, 'Unnatural Conceptions: The Study of Monsters in Sixteenth-Century France and England', *Past and Present*, 92 (August 1981), 20–54. On European hunger for travel narratives, see Jones, *Countrymen*, ch. 1, and Winthrop D. Jordan, *White over Black* (Chapel Hill, NC, 1968), pp. 1–63.

4. John Pory (trans.), *A Geographical Historie of Africa* (London, 1600; rpt. Amsterdam, 1969), Book III, p. 122. The story of the 'abominable vice' of the 'Fricatrices' appears on pp. 148–9 here.

5. See Céard (ed.) *Des monstres et prodiges*, p. 163.

6. See Marie Bonaparte, *Female Sexuality* (New York, 1953), p. 203, with Laqueur, 'Amor veneris', p. 121.

7. See Book 3, ch. xxxiv, 'Of the Wombe', in *The Workes of that Famous Chirurgion Ambrose Parey*, trans. Thomas Johnson (London, 1634, p. 130): '*Cleitoris*, whence proceeds that infamous word *Cleitorizein* (which signifies impudently to handle that part). But because it is an obscene part, let those which desire to know more of it, reade the Authors which I cited.'

8. *Microcosmographia*, Book 4, ch. 16, 'Of the Lap or Privities', p. 238.

9. On this Columbus, author of the *De re anatomica* (Venice, 1559), see Laqueur, *Making Sex* (Cambridge, MA, 1990), p. 64.

10. See *Microcosmographia*, Book 4, ch. xiii, p. 220; and, *inter alia*, John Minsheu's *Ductor in linguas* (London, 1617), 'to Lappe, or fould up'.

11. See Crooke, *Microcosmographia* (p. 239) on the female 'privitie' as 'too obscoene to look upon'; John Banister's *Historie of Man* (London, 1578), ch. 6, as to 'Why the partes of women are here not spoken of'; and on Crooke's frontispiece, modestly shielding these female parts from view, Karen Newman, *Fashioning Femininity and English Renaissance Drama* (Chicago and London, 1991), p. 3.

12. See *The History of Travayle*, trans. Richard Eden, augmented by Richard Willes (London, 1577), p. 6, a passage which depends on the figure of the 'Eye' of God; and P. Ashton's translation of Joannes Boemus's *Omnium gentium mores* (1520), as *The Manners, Lawes and Customes of all Nations* (London, 1611), p. 470, on 'God … to whom nothing is hidden'. The phrase 'ocularly recognising' is applied to Marc Lescarbot's *Histoire de la Nouvelle France* (1609) in Alphonse Dupront, 'Espace et humanisme', *Bibliothèque d'Humanisme et Renaissance*, 8 (1946), 7–104.

13. See Luke Wilson, 'William Harvey's *Prelectiones*: The Performance of the Body in the Renaissance Theater of Anatomy', *Representations*, 17 (Winter 1987), 69–95, with *The Anatomical Lectures of William Harvey*, trans. G. Whitteridge (Edinburgh, 1966), 4[lv]. On science and the feminisation of nature, see *inter alia* Evelyn Fox Keller, *Gender and Science* (New Haven, CT, 1985), pp. 33–65 and Carolyn Merchant, *The Death of Nature* (San Francisco, 1980), and on Baconian science and New World 'discovery', Patricia Parker, *Literary Fat Ladies* (London, 1987), p. 142. The quotation from Bacon is from

The New Organon and Related Writings, ed. Fulton H. Anderson (Indianapolis, 1960), pp. 13, 91, 89.

14. On 'prodigies' and monsters linked with Africa (as in Massinger's 'prodigy / Which Afric never equalled' and 'Some monster, though in a more ugly form / Than Nile or Afric ever bred'), see Jones, *Countrymen*, pp. 126–7; Anthony Barthelemy, *Black Face, Maligned Race: The Representation of Blacks in English Drama from Shakespeare to Southerne* (Baton Rouge, LA, 1987); and Newman, *Femininity*, ch. 5.

15. See pp. 57–8 of Pory's prefatory addition to Africanus's text.

16. 'The Authors Preface to the Reader', *The Manners, Lawes and Customes of all Nations*.

17. *The Original Writings and Correspondence of the Two Richard Hakluyts*, ed. E. G. R. Taylor, Hakluyt Society, 2nd series, nos. 76–7 (London, 1935), vol. II, p. 333.

18. See Alison Plowden, *Danger to Elizabeth* (New York, 1973), p. 226; and *The Elizabethan Secret Service* (New York, 1991), with R. A. Haldane, *The Hidden World* (New York, 1976), pp. 59–65, and Lowell Gallagher's *Medusa's Gaze: Casuistry and Conscience in the Renaissance* (Stanford, CA, 1991).

19. See G. R. Elton, *Policy and Police* (Cambridge, 1972), p. 329, on 'delations and informations' in judicial 'discovery', with Patricia Parker, '"Dilation" and "Delation" in *Othello*', in Patricia Parker and Geoffrey Hartman (eds), *Shakespeare and the Question of Theory* (London, 1985), pp. 54–74, and '*Othello* and *Hamlet*: Dilation, Spying, and the "Secret Place" of Woman', *Representations*, 44 (Fall 1993).

20. See, respectively, 'Father Richard Holtby on Persecution in the North' (1593), in John Morris (ed.), *The Troubles of Our Catholic Forefathers* (London, 1877), vol. 3, p. 121; and Neville Williams, *Elizabeth I, Queen of England* (London, 1971), p. 261.

21. Pory (trans.), *Geographical Historie*, p. 58 of the prefatory material to Africanus's *Description*.

22. See, respectively, George Alsop, *A Character of the Province of Mary-Land* (London, 1666 edn), with *Literary Fat Ladies*, pp. 144–6; on the problem of testimony and evidence generally, Barbara J. Shapiro, *Probability and Certainty in Seventeenth-Century England* (Princeton, NJ, 1983); and on the Greek *arg* ('luster', as in 'illustration') in *enargeia* and the Latin *vid-* as the root of 'seeing' in *evidentia*, Terence Cave, *The Cornucopian Text* (Oxford, 1979), pp. 27–32, with *Literary Fat Ladies*, pp. 138–40.

23. On the Iberian resonances of Iago's name in relation to the 'Portugals' named in Africanus as 'the destroyers of Africa and her peoples', see Newman, *Femininity*, p. 164 n.31.

24. See Ashton's 'To the Friendly Reader', in *The Manners, Lawes, and Customes of all Nations.*

25. See Pory's 'To the Reader', and its defensive assurances that St Augustine and Tertullian were also 'writers of Africa', with Emily C. Bartels, 'Making More of the Moor: Aaron, Othello, and Renaissance Refashionings of Race', *Shakespeare Quarterly*, 41: 4 (Winter 1990), 433–54, esp. pp. 437–8.

26. See Stephen Greenblatt, *Renaissance Self-Fashioning* (Chicago, 1980), p. 237; Jones, *Countrymen*, pp. 21ff.; and Rosalind Johnson, 'African Presence in Shakespearean Drama: Parallels between Othello and the Historical Leo Africanus', *Journal of African Civilization*, 7 (1985), 276–87, with the critique of her emphases in Bartels, 'Making More of the Moor', pp. 435–8.

27. On Desdemona's hunger for Othello's narrative, see Ruth Cowhig, 'Blacks in English Renaissance Drama and the Role of Shakespeare's *Othello*', in David Dabydeen (ed.), *The Black Presence in English Literature* (Manchester, 1985), pp. 1–25, esp. p. 8, with the addition that for her it would provide escape from a 'claustrophobic patriarchal confine' in Ania Loomba's landmark discussion in *Gender, Race, Renaissance Drama* (Manchester, 1989), p. 55.

28. See, respectively, Erasmus, *De copia* Book II, in *The Collected Works*, ed. C. R. Thompson (Toronto, 1978), vol. 24, p. 572; Henry Peacham, *The Garden of Eloquence* (1593), ed. William G. Crane (Gainesville, GA, 1954), pp. 123–4. Italics mine. Crooke not only displays the female 'lap' or privity 'dilated or laide open' to the eye but marks this 'close' or secret place – 'like the letter, o, small and wondrous narrow' – as capable of being 'more open' or more contracted 'according to a woman's appetite'; Columbus in the *De re anatomica* (p. 445) describes this female 'opening' as 'dilated with extreme pleasure in intercourse'; Crooke observes that in the sexual 'opening' of virgins 'the Membranes are dilated'. But the possibility that a virgin could be sexually 'opened' in this sense also introduced the possibility of a female sexuality out of control – that, as Othello puts it, 'we can call these delicate creatures ours, / And not their *appetites*' (III.iii.269–70).

29. See Erik S. Ryding, 'Scanning This Thing Further: Iago's Ambiguous Advice', *Shakespeare Quarterly*, 40: 2 (Summer 1989), 195; on 'occupy', *Literary Fat Ladies*, p. 132, with Marlowe's *The Massacre at Paris* ('whereas he is your landlord, you will take upon you to be his, and till the ground which he himself should occupy'), and Peter Stallybrass, 'Patriarchal Territories: The Body Enclosed', in Margaret W. Ferguson et al. (eds), *Rewriting the Renaissance* (Chicago, 1986), p. 128. On place-holding see Michael Neill, 'Changing Places in *Othello*', *Shakespeare Survey*, 37 (1984), 115–31, esp. p. 119; and

Julia Genster, 'Lieutenancy, Standing In, and *Othello*', *English Literary History*, 57 (1990), 785–809.

30. See Michael Neill, 'Unproper Beds: Race, Adultery, and the Hideous in *Othello*', *Shakespeare Quarterly* (Winter 1989), p. 394; Newman, *Femininity*, pp. 91–2. 'Show', as in *Hamlet* (III.ii.139–46), or the pun on the 'shoe with the hole in it' in *Two Gentlemen of Verona* (II.iii.14–18) resonates with overtones of female sexuality; see *Literary Fat Ladies*, p. 129. On the 'act of shame', see Edward Snow's 'Sexual Anxiety and the Male Order of Things in *Othello*', *English Literary Renaissance*, 10 (1980), 384–412.

31. On this play in relation to the rise of pornography in the period, see Lynda E. Boose, '"Let it be hid": Renaissance Pornography, Iago, and Audience Response', in *Autour d'Othello*. Proceedings of conference sponsored by the University of Amiens and the University of Paris VII (Paris, 1987), 138–46.

32. 'Othello's Handkerchief: "The Recognizance and Pledge of Love"', *English Literary Renaissance*, 5 (1975), 360–74.

33. See Book 24, ch. xlii of Johnson's English translation of Paré.

34. See Newman, *Femininity*, pp. 151–3; Stallybrass, 'Patiarchal Territories', pp. 135ff.; and Bartels, 'Making More of the Moor', pp. 450–1. Ania Loomba's revisionary account is particularly acute here. See n. 42, below.

35. For the complex of 'Barber / Barbary' linked to a 'common' female sexuality see *All's Well*, II.ii.17 and Richard Burton's *Anatomy of Melancholy*, III.iv.l.iii (1651 edn), p. 665; with *Antony and Cleopatra*, II.ii.224 ('Our courteous Anthony ... Being *barber'd* ten times o'er'), lines which link a 'barbarous' nation, a 'common' woman (though a queen), and implications of effeminacy.

36. See Ann Rosalind Jones, 'Italians and Others: Venice and the Irish in *Coryat's Crudities* and *The White Devil*', *Renaissance Drama*, NS 18 (1987) (Evanston, IL, 1988), pp. 101–19, esp. pp. 101–10 on Venice; on Cyprus, Neill, 'Changing Places', p. 115, with Emrys Jones, '"Othello", "Lepanto" and the Cyprus Wars', *Shakespeare Survey*, 21 (Cambridge, 1968), 47–52; S. Gosson, *A Shorte Apologie of the Schoole of Abuse* (London, 1579), p. 83; on 'Moor / More', Helge Kökeritz, *Shakespeare's Pronunciation* (New Haven, CT, 1953), p. 130. On the perceived excess of 'Mores' in England as well as the image of the 'lascivious Moor', see Jones, *Countrymen*, pp. 8, 12, with Ania Loomba, *Gender, Race, Renaissance Drama*, p. 43, who stresses the economic motive of controlling or reducing their 'populous' numbers in challenging G. K. Hunter's argument that Elizabethans had 'no continuous contact' with black people and 'no sense of economic threat from them', in his *Dramatic Identities and Cultural Tradition* (Liverpool, 1978), p. 32.

37. See the text from Jean Bodin included in the frontal material to the Pory trans., p. 60.

38. See John M. Major, 'Desdemona and Dido', *Shakespeare Quarterly*, 10 (1954), 123–5; and *The 'Aeneid' of Thomas Phaer and Thomas Twyne* (1573), ed. Steven Lally (New York, 1987), p. 82, which describes Dido as the Moorish Queen of 'Moores, that have of dooble toong the name' (p. 24) and Carthaginians both as 'Moors' and, in the Preface, 'white Moors in Affrike' (p. 5). The overriding distinction throughout remains 'Trojan / Roman' as opposed to 'Moor' and 'Affrike'. Sidonian-Carthaginian Dido is clearly identified with the 'Affrika' (p. 72) Aeneas is commanded to 'forsake' in Book IV; and Carthage is part of 'Barbarie' as described at the opening of 'Iohn Leo his First Booke' (Pory trans., p. 2). On the 'Moor / white Moor' distinction in commentary on *Othello*, see especially Loomba, *Gender, Race, Renaissance Drama*, ch. 2, who also provides a critical overview of criticism linking 'gender' and 'race' in the play; on Carthage, Elizabeth, and Dido, see Stephen Orgel, 'Shakespeare and the Cannibals', in Marjorie Garber (ed.), *Cannibals, Witches, and Divorce: Estranging the Renaissance* (Baltimore, MD, 1987), pp. 58–66. For the proclamation citing 'the great number of Negroes and blackamours', *ca.* January 1601 (43 Elizabeth I), four years before the performance of *Othello* at the court of her successor, see Eldred Jones, *Countrymen*, plate 5, and Loomba, *Gender, Race, Renaissance Drama*, p. 43. According to *Thomas Clarkson's History of the Rise, Progress, and Accomplishment of the Abolition of the African Slave Trade* (1816), p. 30, Sir John Hawkins imported the first slaves into England from Africa in 1562. Contact with Africa, in other words, preceded the period of major English contact with the 'New World'. On Dido's effeminating effect, see William Caxton (trans.), *Eneydos* (1490), sig. E$_4$ ('effemynate, wythout honour, rauysshed in to dileectacion femynyne'); Henry Howard, Earl of Surrey (trans.), *Certain Bokes of Virgiles Aenaeis* (London, 1557), sig. E$_4$ ('wife-bound'). Phaer (sig. I$_3$v) translates Virgil's 'uxorious' with 'doting … To pleas thy lusty spouse', and describes the effeminated Aeneas as made Moor-like through the 'roabe of Moorishe purple' hanging from his shoulders in 'Morisco gise', a 'web' wrought by this Moorish queen. See also, on Dido and Cleopatra (linked with Africanus), Janet Adelman, *The Common Liar* (New Haven and London, 1973), esp. pp. 71ff.; on Dido and Aeneas echoes surrounding Tamora and Aaron the Moor in *Titus Andronicus*, Bartels, 'Making More of the Moor', p. 445; on the 'monstrous' rule of women, John Knox, *The First Blast of the Trumpet Against the Monstruous regiment of women* (Geneva, 1558); for one self-styled Aeneas sailing upon England as the realm of a new Dido, Gallagher, *Medusa's Gaze*, p. 79; on the complexities of English / Spanish as well as Roman / Carthaginian relations in respect of the racial and gender stereotypes activated by Marlowe's Dido, see Margo Hendricks, 'Managing the Barbarian: *The Tragedie of Dido Queene of Carthage*' (*Renaissance Drama* forthcoming). The 'liberal' reception of a stranger that opens this queen of

'Barbarie' to the *double entendres* surrounding 'widow Dido' in *The Tempest* (II.i.77–82) makes her an even more ambiguous parallel for the Venetian daughter who welcomes another 'extravagant … stranger' and then appears to become a uxorious 'general's general'.

39. I stress the importance of asymmetry and of misplacement / displacement within this apparent chiasmus for the reasons that Loomba's reading of these crossings and splits elicits (p. 54) in applying to *Othello* Homi Bhabha's gloss on Frantz Fanon's split subject, in his Introduction to *Black Skin, White Masks*, trans, Charles Lam Markmann (London and Sydney 1986), p. xvi: 'black skins, white masks is not … a neat division; it is a doubling, dissembling image of being in at least two places at once which makes it impossible for the devalued … to accept the coloniser's invitation to identity.' As Loomba points out, it is not simply that 'Othello's colour and gender make him occupy contradictory positions in relation to power' (p. 41) but that his shift to the position of Venetian husband also involves his increasing racial isolation and differentiation (pp. 48, 50, 54, 60). Desdemona, condemned as 'black' when sexuality is figured by colour, both appears to occupy the place of a woman of 'Barbary' and yet retains the position of white insider that Iago can use to unsettle the confidence of the Moor. It is crucial to recognise the coexistence in *Othello* of separate narratives which cannot be conflated or symmetrically analogised and of different kinds of oppression, objectification, and projection.

40. See *The Merchant of Venice* V.i.9–12 ('In such a night / Stood Dido with a willow in her hand / Upon the wild sea-banks, and waft her love / To come again to Carthage'). Though there is no space to develop this here, it is crucial to note that the phrase 'My mother had a maid call'd Barbary' (IV.iii.26) suggests not just an association with Desdemona but the class and racial overtones of a servant to a Venetian matron, either literally a woman of 'Barbarie' or bearing a name evocative of it.

41. See Dympna Callaghan, pp. 163–77, and *The Tragedy of Mariam Fair Queene of Jewry* by Elizabeth Cary, Lady Falkland, with *The Lady Falkland: Her Life*, ed. Barry Weller and Margaret Ferguson (Berkeley and Los Angeles, 1993).

42. See Guido Ruggiero, *The Boundaries of Eros: Sex Crime and Sexuality in Renaissance Venice* (Oxford, 1988), ch. 6 ('Sodom and Venice'); and the entries for 'Barber', 'Buggery', 'Servant, Serving-man', and 'Turk', in Frankie Rubinstein, *A Dictionary of Shakespeare's Sexual Puns and Their Significance* (London, 1984). 'Bugger' is of course a contraction of 'Bulgarian'. On 'fallow / follow' see Herbert A. Ellis, *Shakespeare's Lusty Punning in Love's Labour's Lost* (The Hague, 1973), pp. 132–5.

43. On Iago's penetration / insemination of Othello through the 'ear', see, *inter alia*, John N. Wall, 'Shakespeare's Aural Art: The Metaphor of the Ear in *Othello*', *Shakespeare Quarterly*, 30:3 (Summer 1979), 358–66, esp. p. 361.

44. The King James (1611) version of 1 Corinthians 6 speaks of 'abusers of themselves with mankind'. See, on 'monster' in this sense, Alan Bray, *Homosexuality in Renaissance England* (London, 1982), pp. 13ff., with his discussion (pp. 71–6) of the cultural othering of sodomitical practices, including the English case of Domingo Cassedon Drago (a 'negar' accused of 'buggery'); on transvestite theatre, Laura Levine, 'Men in Women's Clothing: Anti-theatricality and Effeminisation from 1579 to 1642', *Criticism*, 28: 2 (Spring 1986), 121–43, and Stephen Orgel, 'Nobody's Perfect: Or Why Did the English Renaissance Stage Take Boys for Women?' in Ronald R. Butters et al. (eds), *Displacing Homophobia* (Durham, NC, 1989), pp. 7–30; on the 'open secret', Jonathan Goldberg's *Sodomitries: Renaissance Texts, Modern Sexualities* (Stanford, CA, 1992), ch. 3; on the contradictions between denunciation of sodomy among unforgivable 'crimes' (James I, *Basilicon Doron*) and the practices of figures as prominent as Francis Bacon and the king himself, see Bruce R. Smith, *Homosexual Desire in Shakespeare's England* (Chicago, 1991), esp. pp. 14, 26, 176; on visibility in relation as well to sexual acts between women and on the differences between England and the continent, see Valerie Traub's important discussion in *Desire and Anxiety* (London, 1992), esp. pp. 106–13.

45. For readings of *Othello* in relation to fears of invasion and 'the enemy within', see Richard Marienstras, *New Perspectives on the Shakespearean World*, trans. Janet Lloyd (Cambridge, 1985), chs 5 and 6, and Jonathan Dollimore, 'The Cultural Politics of Perversion: Augustine, Shakespeare, Freud, Foucault', *Genders*, 8 (July 1990), 1–16; on the 'Turk' as uncomfortably close double of the European, see Timothy J. Hampton, 'Turkish Dogs: Rabelais, Erasmus, and the Rhetoric of Alterity', *Representations*, 41 (Winter 1993), 58–62.

9

Transvestism and the 'body beneath': Speculating on the Boy Actor

PETER STALLYBRASS

My paper starts from a puzzle:[1] what did a Renaissance audience *see* when boy actors undressed on stage? The puzzle could, of course, be resolved by a simple (and, for my argument, damaging) move. The boy actor doesn't undress, or, at least, doesn't undress to the point of disturbing the illusion; the audience *sees* nothing. Against such a move, I want on the one hand to think quite bluntly about the prosthetic devices through which gender is rendered visible upon the stage. In that sense, the visible is an empirical question (although a question to which we seem to have surprisingly few answers). But, on the other hand, I want to suggest the degree to which the Renaissance spectator is required to *speculate* upon a boy actor who undresses, and thus to speculate upon the relation between the boy actor and the woman he plays. This speculation depends upon a cultural fantasy of sight, but a fantasy, I shall argue, that plays back and forth between sexual difference as a site of indeterminacy (the undoing of any stable or given difference) and sexual difference (and sexuality itself) as the production of contradictory fixations (fixations articulated through a fetishistic attention to particular items of clothing, particular parts of the body of an imagined woman, particular parts of an actual boy actor). I want to suggest that on the Renaissance stage the demand that the spectator *sees* is at its most intense in the undressing of the boy actor, at the very moment when *what* is seen is most vexed, being the point of intersection between spectatorship, the specular, and the speculative.

THE PROSTHETIC BODY

Perhaps the most substantial theatrical property of many Renaissance companies was a bed. It is a property which is called for in play after play, mainly in tragedy, but also in history and comedy. *Volpone* revolves around the bed in which Volpone simulates death, the bed from which he rises in his attempted rape of Celia; *Cymbeline* hinges upon Iachimo spying upon Imogen while she lies asleep in bed; in *The Maid's Tragedy*, Evadne ties the king to the bed in which they have made love before she kills him; in *Othello*, the bed bears the bodies of Desdemona, Emilia and Othello in the final scene. One becomes accustomed to stage directions like: 'King a bed'; 'Enter Othello, and Desdemona in her bed'; 'Enter Imogen in her Bed, and a Lady'.[2] The bed becomes a focal point of scenes of sleep, of sex, of death. But bed scenes also focus upon facts so obvious that they resist interpretation as we hasten on to find out what these scenes are *about:* they draw attention to undressing or being undressed, to the process of shedding those garments through which class and gender were made visible and staged. They stage clothes as signs which can be put on and off, outward signs which can be assumed or shed.

At the same time, bed scenes foreground the body: the body which is either literally or symbolically about to be exposed. And here we come to a peculiar problem. The consensus of recent scholars on Renaissance transvestism has been that it is self-consciously staged mainly, or only, in comedy. Lisa Jardine, in her important work on the boy actor to which I am deeply indebted, states what has now become a commonplace:[3]

> the eroticism of the boy player is invoked in the drama whenever it is openly alluded to: on the whole this means in comedy, where role-playing and disguise is part of the genre. In tragedy, the willing suspension of disbelief does customarily extend, I think, to the taking of the female parts by boy players; taken for granted, it is not alluded to.[4]

But in bed scene after bed scene in Renaissance tragedy, we begin to witness an undressing or we are asked to see or to imagine an undressed (or partially undressed) body within the bed. What is it we are being asked to see?

If we take *Othello* as our starting point, we may reach some puzzling conclusions. As Lynda Boose has finely argued, the 'ocular proof' that Othello demands is reworked in the play as the audience's voyeuristic desire to *see*, to grossly gape.[5] But what are we to gape *at*? From the beginning of the eighteenth century, as Michael Neill has shown, illustrators of *Othello* were obsessively concerned with the depiction of the final bed scene. Even as Desdemona's 'Will you come to bed, my Lord?' (V.ii.24) was cut from theatrical productions, illustrators focused upon the dead Desdemona lying in bed.[6] And what the illustrators above all reveal (requiring that the spectator grossly gape) are the bedclothes and clothing pulled back to show a single exposed breast.[7] The bed scene, then, is taken by the illustrators as an opportunity for the display of the female body, and in particular of a woman's breast.

Although we cannot take such illustrations as reflecting eighteenth-century stage productions, we do, in fact, find the exposure of the female breast recurrently called for by stage directions after the introduction of women actors to the stage in the previous century. On the Renaissance stage, actual boys played seeming 'boys' who were 'revealed' to be women – Ganymede as Rosalind, Cesario as Viola.[8] But on the Restoration stage, women played boys who were revealed to be women. And they were often revealed as women by the exposure of their breasts.

In fact, the commonest technique for the revelation of the 'woman beneath' after the Restoration was the removal of a wig, whereupon the female actor's 'true' hair would be seen. In Boyle's *Guzman* (1669), for instance, a woman disguised as a priest is exposed when 'Francisco pulls off her Peruque, and her Womans Hair falls about her ears'.[9] Now this, of course, can depend upon the interplay of prostheses, an interplay which would have been perfectly possible on the Renaissance stage. The audience would have no means of knowing (any more than we do today) whether the hair beneath the wig was the hair of the actor or another wig. The play of difference (male wig / female hair) had no necessary relation to the anatomical specificities of the actor's body. If, then, the distinction of the sexes is staged as a distinction of hair (and above all of hair length), it will be constantly transformed by changes in hair styles. Sexual difference may, in this case, seem essentially prosthetic: the addition (or subtraction) of detachable (or growable / cuttable) parts.

It is precisely such a prosthetic view which William Prynne had denounced in *The Unlovelinesse of Lovelockes* (1628). There, he elaborates at length on St Paul: 'Doth not even nature itself teach you, that, if a man have long hair, it is a shame unto him? But if a woman have long hair it is a glory to her' (I Corinthians, 11.14–15). From Prynne's perspective, the problem is precisely that 'nature' doesn't seem to have taught its lesson thoroughly enough. Cavalier men flaunt their long hair (and, from 1641, were to ridicule their opponents as 'Roundheads', in reference to their close-cropped hair). Prynne asserts that gender is defined by 'the outward Culture of [our] Heads, and Bodies',[10] and that the long hair of men and the short hair of women erase sexual difference. We live, he claims, in 'Unnaturall, and Unmanly times: wherein ... sundry of our Mannish, Impudent, and inconstant Female sexe, are Hermaphrodited, and transformed into men' because they 'unnaturally clip, and cut their Haire'.[11] Asserting hair as a sign of *natural* difference, Prynne is particularly fierce in his denunciation of wigs: 'the wearing of counterfeite, false, and suppositious Haire, is *utterly unlawfull*'.[12] In using the putting on and the taking off of wigs as the mark of gender difference, the Restoration stage turned Prynne on his head. 'Natural' signs became the artifices of malleable gender. [...]

There can be little doubt that Restoration stagings of the female actor's breasts were usually constituted for the arousal of the heterosexual male spectator. (A more extended discussion of this point would look at the significant position of the Restoration theatre in the *construction* of the 'heterosexual male spectator'.) According to Colley Cibber, the very presence of female actors upon the stage helped to constitute a new audience (or rather new spectators): 'The additional Objects then of real, beautiful Women, could not but draw a portion of new Admirers to the Theatre'.[13] In the Epilogue to Nathaniel Lee's *The Rival Queens* (1677), the actors protest that if their male spectators continue to lure female actors away from the stage, they will return to using boy actors:

> For we have vow'd to find a sort of Toys
> Known to black Fryars, a Tribe of choopping Boys.
> If once they come, they'l quickly spoil your sport;
> There's not one Lady will receive your Court:
> But for the Youth in Petticoats run wild,
> With oh the archest Wagg, the sweetest Child.
> The panting Breasts, white Hands and little Feet

No more shall your pall'd thoughts with pleasure meet.
The Woman in Boys Cloaths, all Boy shall be,
And never raise your thoughts above the Knee.[14]

There are several interesting features about this epilogue: first, the threat to replace women with boy actors is not imagined as a *general* loss but as a loss to the male spectator alone. The female spectator, on the contrary, is imagined as running wild after the 'Youth in Petticoats'. The boy actor is thus depicted as particularly alluring to women, a possibility that has been addressed by Stephen Orgel.[15]

But the grammar of the Epilogue is strangely playful about the crucial question: the difference between a boy actor and a female actor. 'The panting Breasts, white Hands and little Feet' seem at first to follow directly on from, and thus to be the attributes of, the archest wags, the sweetest children, but this possibility is retracted in the next line: 'No more' shall such breasts, hands and feet be seen when boy actors return. Yet the *feet* of the boy actor would seem to be adequate enough for his female role, if we are to take literally that he will 'never raise your thoughts above the Knee'. The crucial point of that latter line, of course, is what the boy actor does *not* have: implicitly a vagina; explicitly breasts.

It is that explicit absence upon which I want to dwell here. For recent criticism has been particularly concerned with the 'part' that the boy actor has which is not in his part. (I would want to suggest, incidentally, that that part has been peculiarly distorted [and enlarged] by being thought of as a 'phallus', as if a boy's small parts weren't peculiarly – and interestingly – at variance with the symbolic weight of THE phallus.) Criticism has thus been concerned with what Shakespeare calls the 'addition' which the boy actor brings to a female role. But in bed scene after bed scene, what is staged is a tableau in which we are about to witness the female body (and most particularly the female breast), even as it is a boy who is undressing. Indeed, there seems to be something so odd about this fact that it has simply been overlooked.[16]

So let me declare first of all what the puzzles are to which I have no solution. Did boy actors wear false breasts? There seem to be no records of such a practice, but the female fury at the beginning of *Salmacida Spolia* was presumably played by a professional actor and his / her '*breasts hung bagging down to her waist*'.[17] Or did boys use tight lacing to gather up their flesh so as to create a cleavage, or were they simply flat-chested, or ...? While John Rainolds denounces Achilles' transvestism, which William Gager had used in defence of the academic stage, he notes that Achilles had learned from Deidamia 'howe *he must hold his naked brest'*.[18] A further question: in undressing scenes, how far did the boy actor go in actually removing his clothes or, if he was in bed, how much of his flesh was revealed? These are the questions I shall *not* be attempting to resolve.

Indeed, I want less to suggest a resolution than to express the dimensions of the problem. Lisa Jardine, whom I quoted above, assumes that the significance of the boy actor is virtually erased in tragedy (although her argument as a whole finely attends to the crucial importance of the cross-dressed boy). And Kathleen McLuskie (in what I take to be an implicit critique of Jardine) pushes for a *generally* conventional view of the boy actor.[19] [...]

But what I want to emphasise here is the extent to which the subsumptions of the physical body of the boy by the conventions of femininity signified by costume and gesture were also played with to the point of their undoing. That they *could* be played with has something to do with systematic dislocations between visual and linguistic systems of representation in the Renaissance. I noted above the extent to which visual representations of women in play quartos move between representations which depend upon costume / hair / gesture and those which also depend upon a display of the naked body, and in particular of the naked breast. The displayed breast is a metonymy for woman. Since for us, both 'breast' and 'bosom' are always already gendered, this comes as little surprise. But in the Renaissance, both 'breast' and 'bosom' are used interchangeably for men and women. ('Pap', on the other hand, was usually applied only to women.) 'Bosom', indeed, seems to be more frequently gendered as *masculine*. For instance, after the 1611 translation of the Bible which introduced the Hebraic 'wife of thy bosome' and 'husband of her bosome', it was only the *former* expression which became current, thus re-emphasising the bosom as male (see *OED*). In Ford's *'Tis Pity She's a Whore*, Giovanni offers his dagger to his sister, Annabella, and says: 'And here's my breast; strike home! / Rip up my bosom'.[20] The language of breasts and bosoms tended to be either ungendered or absorbed into the power of the patriarch. To 'toy' with breasts verbally, then, had no obvious implications for the relation of the boy actor to his female role.

But this indeterminacy of gender at the verbal level (an indeterminacy which, I would argue, was determined by a motivated absorption of the female body) was opposed by the visual codes in which the breast was insistently gendered as female. What remains extraordinary is the extent to which this female-gendered breast is staged by the boy actor. In Jonson's *The Devil is an Ass*, for instance, as Wittipol approaches '[t]hese sister-swelling brests' of Frances Fitz-Dottrell, the stage direction reads: '*he growes more familiar in his Courtship, plays with her paps, kisseth her hands, &*'.[21] But the boy actor's 'female body' is most commonly the object of attention in tragedy and tragi-comedy. There, we are asked not to *imagine* the boy actor as he is dressed *up*, but literally to *gaze* at him whilst he *un*dresses.

This staging of the undressing boy is particularly striking in death scenes and bed scenes which draw attention to the boy actor's 'breast'. In Ford's *Love's Sacrifice*, the Duke says to Bianca 'Prepare to die', and she responds:

> I do; and to the point
> Of thy sharp sword with open breast I'll run
> Half way thus naked.[22]

But even more striking is the way in which Shakespeare in both *Antony and Cleopatra* and *Cymbeline* changes his sources so as to stage the boy's breast. In Plutarch, Cleopatra attaches an asp to her *arm*. Shakespeare retains this, but only after she has already placed an asp upon her *breast*. And Cleopatra / the boy actor, who has already imagined seeing '[s]ome squeaking *Cleopatra* Boy my greatnesse', focuses upon the contradictory vision of Cleopatra's nursing breast / the boy actor's breast: 'Dost thou not see my Baby at my breast, / That suckes the Nurse asleepe'.[23] An audience seems to be required to observe the splitting apart of what later critics assumed to be a stable 'convention'. More than that, critics have appealed to the presence of the boy actor to 'explain' that certain stagings would have been 'impossible'. Enobarbus's description of Cleopatra is thus taken as a technique of avoidance, by which the audience is spared the embarrassment of gazing at a transvestite boy. But what becomes of such explanations when, again and again, we find Renaissance dramatists going beyond their sources to demand that we witness the boy actor at the very point which a later audience has ruled unimaginable?

In *Cymbeline*, for instance, as Iachimo observes Imogen asleep in bed, he fetishises both the chamber, the bracelet which will represent her lost honour, and a 'mole Cinque-spotted' upon 'her left brest'.[24] This last detail, like the asp on Cleopatra's breast, is truly remarkable. It has been argued that Shakespeare used *Frederyke of Jennen* as a source for *Cymbeline*, and in that pamphlet John of Florence notes *not* a mole on the *breast*, but a wart on the *arm* of Ambrose's wife: 'it fortuned that her lefte arme lay on the bed; and on that arme she had a blacke warte'.[25] But Shakespeare replaces the wart with a mole (thus following Boccaccio's version of the story), a mole which is given a *precise* but *imaginary* location upon the body of the boy actor. To make the left breast the object of this voyeuristic scene is to focus our attention on one of the sites of the cultural differentiation of gender. But that site produces antithetical readings: Imogen's swelling breast; the breast of a boy actor. It is as if within the dramatic fiction, the fetishistic signs of presence are forced to confront the absences which mark the actor's body. Or perhaps we might rather say that two contradictory realities are forced to peer into each other's faces. In *Cymbeline*, at the very moment where a later audience would expect a discrete effacement of the theatrical means by which gender is produced, those means are verbally and visually staged. [...]

To be aware of the fetishistic staging of the boy actor, of the insistence that we see what is not there to see, is to conceptualise the erotics of Renaissance drama in totally unfamiliar ways. Think, for instance, of the end of *Othello*.[26] 'Prithee, tonight / Lay on my bed our wedding-sheets', Desdemona says to Emilia. But interpolated between the command and the on-stage arrival of the bed itself, we are asked to witness the boy actor prepare for bed. In one sense, the scene suggests that this preparation is itself a kind of transvestism – a crossing from day to night, from the clothes of a Venetian noble to a shift. And it is curious to note how such 'closet' scenes are frequently – and strangely – marked by an explicit movement from formal to informal dress. Even ghosts obey this convention, if we are to believe the first quarto of *Hamlet*, where Hamlet Senior, appearing to his son in Gertrude's closet, has put off his armour and put on his nightgown. Both in *Othello* and *Hamlet*, the body seems to be simultaneously sexualised and made vulnerable. But in *Othello*, the movement from one set of clothes to another is curiously truncated. Desdemona's command to Emilia, 'Give me my nightly wearing', is followed some twenty lines later by Emilia's

enquiry, 'Shall I go fetch your nightgown?' to which Desdemona
answers 'No'. In fact, the absence of the nightgown makes all the
more insistent the fact that we are witnessing Desdemona / a boy
actor undress. The undressing is the more *present* as a strip-tease
for the *absence* of any substitute clothing. 'Prithee unpin me',
Desdemona says, and later, rejecting the nightgown, 'No, unpin me
here'.[27]

Before I return to this moment of voyeuristic suspense where the
staged body prepares to split into the unpinned clothes and the
'body beneath', I want to note how the scene as a whole stages a
series of splittings or – to put it another way – a series of radical
crossings of perspective. First, there is the presentation to the audience of Emilia's impressively relativistic view of sexual morality, a
view which threatens to re-present the whole play as grotesque
farce, the absurd magnification of 'a *small* vice'. Curiously, and to
the disturbance of many critics, the 'sport' which Emilia commends
seems to migrate into the language of Desdemona:

> **Desdemona**   unpin me here;
>   This Lodovico is a proper man.
> **Emilia**   A very handsome man.
> **Desdemona**   He speaks well.
> **Emilia**   I know a lady in Venice would have walk'd
>   barefoot to Palestine for a touch of his nether lip.
>
> (IV.iii. 34–9)

As Desdemona is unpinned, Othello is displaced by that 'proper
man', Lodovico. At the same time, Desdemona herself takes on the
voice of a maidservant called Barbary. (I am here indebted to
Raima Evans's work on this scene.) The willow song is the song of
that maid, whose name is itself a curious transposing of Iago's slur
against Othello as he goads Brabantio: 'you'll have your daughter
cover'd with a Barbary horse; you'll have your nephews neigh to
you'. Barbary: the name for bestial male sexuality; the name for a
maid betrayed in love – 'poor Barbary'. A single signifier slides
between male and female, animal and human, betrayer and betrayed, and at the same time between opposed notions of the 'barbarian' as oppressor and as victim. And it is the song of a poor
maid which the Venetian noble will reiterate.

I want to draw attention to these slippages within the signifier
because they provide one possible model through which we could
read the undressing of Desdemona. On such a reading, the closure of

the play would be unsettled by a startling moment of indeterminacy when we are held in suspension between cultural antitheses and, at the same time, between the fiction of Desdemona and the staging of the boy actor. But I do not believe that 'indeterminacy' is an adequate way of thinking about these moments. Rather, we are forced into contradictory attitudes about both sexuality and gender: on the one hand, gender as a set of prosthetic devices (in which case, the *object* of sexual attention is absorbed into the play of those devices); on the other, gender as the 'given' marks of the body (the breast, the vagina, the penis) which (however analogous in Galenic medicine) are read as the signs of an absolute difference (in which case, sexuality, whether between man and woman, woman and woman, or man and man, tends to be organised through a fixation upon the supposedly 'essential' features of gender). But on the Renaissance stage, even those 'essential' features are located – whether prosthetically or at the level of the imaginary – upon *another body*. [...]

In other words, if Renaissance theatre constructs an eroticism that depends upon a play of differences (the boy's breast / the woman's breast), it also equally conjures up an eroticism which depends upon the total absorption of male into female, female into male. In the printed text of Shakespeare's *The Shrew* in 1623, the boy is named as 'Bartholomew my Page' (Ind. I. 103) and yet, in changing into the clothes of a woman, he is entirely subsumed into her role. When in *A Shrew*, a stage direction reads '*Enter the boy in Woman's attire*', in *The Shrew* it reads: '*Enter Lady with Attendants*' (Ind. 2. 99). Moreover, the speech prefixes are all for '*Lady*' or '*La*'. The text thus accomplishes what John Rainolds warns against in *Th' Overthrow of Stage-Plays*: 'beware the beautifull boyes *transformed into women* by putting on their raiment, their feature, lookes and facions'.[28] This transformation is carefully erased by a modern editor like Brian Morris, who emends the stage direction to read '*Enter [*PAGE *as a] lady*' and changes the speech prefixes to read '*Page*'.[29] In the Folio *The Shrew*, we are thus presented with a wild oscillation between contradictory positions: the plot of the induction demands that we remain aware of Bartholomew *as* Bartholomew, while the language of the text simply cuts Bartholomew, replacing him with 'Lady'. [...]

The power of clothes, like language, to *do* things to the body is suggested in both dramatic and non-dramatic texts, and it is this power of clothes which is so insistently asserted by anti-theatricalists. Calvin, in his sermons on Deuteronomy, if he sometimes thinks of clothes as *manifesting* sexual difference, equally thinks of them as *creating* difference: 'God intended to shew us that every bodies attyring of themselves ought to be such, *as there may be difference betweene men and women*'.[30] Similarly, Prynne thinks of women who 'mimic' masculinity as 'hermaphrodited and transformed into men'[31] and of male actors 'metamorphosed into women on the Stage'.[32] And he follows Calvin in arguing that 'a mans attyring himselfe in womans array ... perverts one principall use of garments, *to difference men from women*'.[33]

The anti-theatricalists thus feared the power of clothes to *produce* new subjects, to metamorphose boy into woman, commoner into aristocrat. John Rainolds' powerful attack upon the academic stage (and, by extension, upon all theatrical activity) was provoked in the first instance by the almost magical properties of transvestism.[34] Rainolds, one of the greatest scholars of his day, had himself cross-dressed in his youth[35] and in *Th' Overthrow of Stage-Playes* he admits that 'he did play a womans part upon the same stage, the part of Hippolyta'.[36] But what exactly *is* the danger of transvestism? Here, Rainolds' citations are frequently opaque, as, for instance, the following from Dionysius Carthusianus:

> *the apparell of wemen* (saith he) *is a great provocation of men to lust and leacherie: because a womans garment being put on a man doeth vehemently touch and move him with the remembrance and imagination of a woman: and the imagination of a thing desirable doth stir up the desire.*[37]

What does Rainolds' translation imply? That the woman's body is imprinted upon or within the clothes? That women's clothes, when they touch and move the male wearer, will awaken the desire *for* women (whom he will remember and imagine) or the desire *to be* a woman? Will the desire be homo- or heteroerotic and will it be directed towards another or towards the self?

The Renaissance theatre was thus the site for the prosthetic production of the sexualised body through the clothing of the body and the mimed gestures of love. But it was also the site where the prosthetic production was dramatically staged and speculated upon, as the boy actor undressed, as the fixations of spectators were drawn back and forth between the clothes which embodied and determined a particular sexual identity and contradictory fantasies of the 'body beneath' – the body of a woman, the body of a boy; a body with and without breasts.

THE TRANSVESTITE BODY[38]

The interplay between clothing and undressing on the Renaissance stage organised gender around a process of fetishising, which is conceived *both* as a process of fixation *and* as indeterminable. If the Renaissance stage demands that we *'see'* particular body parts (the breast, the penis, the naked body), it also reveals that such fixations are inevitably unstable. The actor is both boy and woman, and he / she embodies the fact that sexual fixations are not the product of any categorical fixity of gender. Indeed, all attempts to fix gender are necessarily *prosthetic:* that is, they suggest the attempt to supply an imagined deficiency by the exchange of male clothes for female clothes or of female clothes for male clothes; by displacement from male to female space or from female to male space; by the replacement of male with female tasks or of female with male tasks. But all elaborations of the prosthesis which will supply the 'deficiency' can secure no essence. On the contrary, they suggest that gender itself is a fetish, the production of an identity through the fixation upon specific 'parts'. The imagined 'truth' of gender which a post-Renaissance culture would later construct is dependent upon the disavowal of the fetishism of gender, the dis-avowal of gender as fetish. In its place, it would put a fantasised biology of the 'real'.

But it is this notion of the 'real' which seems to be dramatically undone in undressing scenes, as in *Othello* when Desdemona / the boy actor is unpinned. Lynda Boose has demonstrated how the play itself demands both concealment (of the sexual scene, of the bed and its burden which 'poisons sight') and exposure (the stimulated desire that we should *see,* should 'grossly gape'). But, as I have argued, *what* we should see is radically uncertain. It is not so much a moment of indeterminacy as of contradictory fixations. On the one hand, the clothes themselves – the marks of Desdemona's gender and status – are held up to our attention; on the other, we teeter on the brink of seeing the boy's breastless but 'pinned' body revealed. It is as if, at the moments of greatest dramatic tension, the Renaissance theatre stages its own transvestism.

Contradictory fixations, though, are precisely what mobilise *Othello.* Think, for instance, of how Iago constructs the narrative of Desdemona's betrayal so that Othello can approach the 'grossly gaping' of her being 'topp'd'. He does it by casting *himself* in the role of Desdemona:

> I lay with *Cassio* lately ...
> In sleepe I heard him say, sweet *Desdemona*,
> Let us be wary, let us hide our Loves,
> And then (Sir) would he gripe, and wring my hand:
> Cry, oh sweet Creature: then kisse me hard,
> As if he pluckt up kisses by the rootes,
> That grew upon my lippes, laid his Leg ore my Thigh,
> And sigh, and kisse...
>
> (III.iii.419–31)

It is these contradictory fixations (Desdemona and / as the boy actor, Desdemona and / as Iago) which a later theatre would attempt to erase, precisely because the *site* of the audience's sexual fixation is so uncertain.

This uncertainty is, paradoxically, most powerfully felt by anti-theatrical writers. They oscillate between seeing the boy actor as woman, as neither woman nor man, as alluring boy, as male prostitute (or 'dogge', to use Rainolds' term). Prynne, for instance, incorporates Cyprian's account of how the theatre taught 'how a man might be effeminated into a female, how their sex might be changed by Art'.[39] But he can also think of actors as those who, 'by unchaste infections of their members, effeminate their manly nature, being both effeminate men and women, yea, being neither men nor women'.[40] Yet the uncertainty of *what* anti-theatricalists saw in no way inhibited the fascinated fixity of their (imaginary) gaze. What they gazed at was a theatre imagined *as a bedroom*, a bedroom which spills off the stage and into the lives of players and audience alike:

> O ... that thou couldest in that sublime watch-tower insinuate thine eyes into these Players secrets; or set open the closed dores of their bed-chambers, and bring all their innermost hidden Cels unto the conscience of thine eyes ... [M]en rush on men with outragious lusts.[41]

So writes Prynne, translating Cyprian. And Phillip Stubbes sees the actors as contaminating the spectators so that, 'these goodly pageants being done, every mate sorts to his mate ... and in their secret conclaves (covertly) they play *the Sodomits*, or worse'.[42] But *what* antitheatricalists saw in the 'secret conclaves' of the theatrical bedroom constantly shifted, thus mimicking the shifting perspectives of the Renaissance stage itself.

For the bed scenes and undressing scenes with which I have been concerned produce moments of dizzying indeterminacy. It was such moments that Freud attempted to describe in his essay on 'Fetishism', where the fetish stands in for and mediates between the marks of sexual difference.[43] Freud writes:

> In very subtle instances both the disavowal and the affirmation of the castration (of woman) have found their way into the construction of the fetish itself. This was so in the case of a man whose fetish was an athletic support-belt which could also be worn as bathing drawers. This piece of clothing covered up the genitals entirely and concealed the distinction between them. Analysis showed that it signified that women were castrated *and* that they were not castrated; and it also allowed of the hypothesis that men were castrated, for all these possibilities could equally well be concealed under the belt ...

The athletic support-belt, through its concealments, supports contradictory hypotheses. But for Freud, all those hypotheses must be grounded in the fantasy of castration. Why? Because Freud needs to find a fixed point (and a *male* point) outside the play of fetishism, a point to which all other fetishes will teleologically point. The fetishist is, Freud suggests, someone whose interest *'comes to a halt half-way, as it were'* (my emphasis). 'Thus the foot or shoe owes its preference as a fetish – or a part of it – to the circumstance that the inquisitive boy peered at the woman's genitals from below, from her legs up.' The fetish is, for Freud, but part of the larger category of perversions. 'Perversions', he writes in the 'Three essays on the theory of sexuality':

> are sexual activities which either a) *extend*, in an anatomical sense, beyond the regions of the body that are designed for sexual union, or b) *linger*, over the intermediate relations to the sexual object which should normally be traversed rapidly on the path towards the sexual aim.[44]

The very notion of the perverse, like that of the fetish, can only emerge in relation to a) the parts of the body which are 'naturally' sexual and b) a teleological path towards the genitals. The transvestite theatre of the Renaissance, though, does not allow for any such distinction between the 'perverse' and the normal teleological path.

From a Freudian perspective, it 'comes to a halt half-way, as it were'. It does so because it resists the sexual and narrative teleologies which would be developed in the eighteenth and nineteenth centuries. But that resistance is, I believe, less a matter of indeterminacy than of the production of contradictory fixations: the imagined body of a woman, the staged body of a boy actor, the material presence of clothes. Freud's brilliant insight was to see that the 'real person' was itself a displacement of fetishism:

> The progressive concealment of the body which goes along with civilisation keeps sexual curiosity awake. This curiosity seeks to complete the sexual object by revealing its hidden parts. It can, however, be diverted ('sublimated') in the direction of art, if its interest can be shifted away from the genitals on to the shape of the body as a whole.[45]

'The body as a whole', then, is itself a fantasy, a sublimation. But for Freud, the real tends to reappear *behind* or *beneath* that fantasy, a real which always tends towards the formation of sexual difference. In the 'mingle-mangle', the 'hodge-podge', the 'gallimaufry' of Renaissance tragedy, though, contradictory fetishisms (body parts, costumes, handkerchiefs, sheets) are staged not in the play of pure difference but in the play between indeterminacy and fixation.

From *Erotic Politics: Desire on the Renaissance Stage,* ed. Susan Zimmerman (Routledge, 1992), pp. 64–83.

NOTES

[This essay represents a shortened version of its original. Peter Stallybrass' studies of early modern culture frequently focus on the construction of gender and sexuality. His essay on 'Patriarchal Territories: The Body Enclosed' (in Margaret W. Ferguson, Maureen Quilligan, and Nancy J. Vickers [eds], *Rewriting the Renaissance: The Discourses of Sexual Difference in Early Modern England* [Chicago, 1986], pp. 123–42) has become a *locus classicus* in gender studies. Ed.]

1. I am deeply indebted for ideas, references and challenges to Lynda Boose, Greg Bredbeck, Linda Charnes, Lisa Jardine, David Kastan, Michael Shapiro, and Valerie Traub; and I couldn't even have begun without the stimulus of Jonathan Dollimore, Marjorie Garber, Ann Rosalind Jones, Stephen Orgel, Phyllis Rackin and Susan Zimmerman.

2. Beaumont, F. and Fletcher, J., *The Maid's Tragedy,* ed. A. Gurr (Berkeley, CA, 1969), V.i.12; *Othello,* V.xii; *Cymbeline,* II.ii. All references to Shakespeare's plays are to *The First Folio of Shakespeare: The Norton Facsimile,* ed. C. Hinman (New York, 1968).

3. For important revisions to Lisa Jardine's earlier work, see her 'Twins and Travesties' essay in *Erotic Politics: Desire on the Renaissance Stage*, ed. Susan Zimmerman (London, 1992).

4. Lisa Jardine, *Still Harping on Daughters: Women and Drama in the Age of Shakespeare* (Brighton, 1983), p. 23.

5. Linda Boose, '"Let it be Hid": Iago, Renaissance pornography, and *Othello's* "grossly gaping" audience' (unpublished MS, 1987).

6. M. Neill, 'Unproper beds: Race, adultery, and the hideous in *Othello*', *Shakespeare Quarterly*, 40:4 (1989), 383–412, 35 fn.

7. See the illustrations by Boitard (1709), Loutherbourg (1785), Metz (1789), and Leney (1799) in Neill, 'Unproper beds', 386–9.

8. On the occasional presence of women on English stages prior to the Restoration, see for instance J. Stokes, 'The Wells Cordwainers show: New evidence concerning guild entertainments in Somerset', *Comparative Drama*, 19: 4 (1985–6), 332–46; G. E. Bentley, *The Jacobean and Caroline Stage*, Vol. 1 (Oxford, 1941), p. 25; and S. Gossett, '"Man-maid, begone!": Women in masques', *English Literary Renaissance*, 18 (1988), 96–113.

9. Quoted in J. H. Wilson, *All the King's Ladies: Actresses of the Restoration* (Chicago, 1958), p. 84.

10. W. Prynne, *The Unlovelinesse of Lovelockes* (London, 1628), A3v.

11. Ibid., A3, G2.

12. Ibid., C4v, original emphasis.

13. C. Cibber, *An Apology for the Life of Colley Cibber*, ed. B. R. S. Fone (Ann Arbor, 1968), p. 55.

14. Nathaniel Lee, *The Rival Queens*, in T. B. Stroup and A. L. Cooke (eds), *The Works of Nathaniel Lee* (New Brunswick, NJ, 1954), p. 282.

15. Stephen Orgel, 'The boys in the back room: Shakespeare's apprentices and the economics of theatre', paper given at the Modern Languages Association, New Orleans (1989), p. 8.

16. An important exception, to which I am deeply indebted, is Michael Shapiro, 'Crossgender casting, crossgender disguise, and anxieties of intimacy in *Twelfth Night* and other plays', paper given at the Shakespeare Association of America, Philadelphia (1990); for an earlier attempt to touch on this subject, see M. Rosenburg, *The Masks of Othello* (Berkeley, CA, 1971), pp. 17, 19.

17. Quoted in Gosset, '"Man-maid begone!"', 112.

18. J. Rainolds, *Th' Overthrow of Stage-Plays* (London, 1599), p. 17.

19. K. McLuskie, 'The act, the role, and the actor: Boy actresses on the Elizabethan stage', *New Theatre Quarterly*, 3: 10 (1987), 120–30.

20. J. Ford, *'Tis Pity She's a Whore*, in H. Ellis (ed.), *John Ford* (New York, 1957), I. iii.

21. *The Devil is an Ass*, in C. H. H. Percy and E. Simpson (eds), *Ben Jonson*, Vol. 6 (Oxford, 1938), II.vi.71. Michael Shapiro, 'Crossgender casting', 1–2, gives other striking examples.

22. J. Ford, *Love's Sacrifice* in H. Ellis (ed.), *John Ford*, V.i.

23. *Antony and Cleopatra*, V.ii.218, 308–9. For other accounts of Cleopatra and the boy actor, see Phyllis Rackin, 'Shakespeare's boy Cleopatra, the decorum of nature, and the golden world of poetry', *PMLA*, 87 (1972), 201–12; Michael Shapiro, 'Boying her greatness: Shakespeare's use of coterie drama in *Antony and Cleopatra*', *Modern Language Review*, 77: 1 (1982), 1–15; and W. Gruber, 'The actor in the script: affective strategies in Shakespeare's *Antony and Cleopatra*', *Comparative Drama*, 19:1 (1985), 30–48.

24. *Cymbeline*, II.ii.37–8.

25. Anon, *Frederyke of Jennen*, in J. M. Nosworthy (ed.), *Cymbeline*, the Arden Shakespeare (London and New York, 1955), p. 197.

26. *Othello*, IV.iii.

27. John Russell Brown has pointed out to me that, in the dominant theatrical tradition, the 'unpinning' refers to Desdemona's *hair*. That there is no Renaissance warrant for this is suggested by the OED, which actually quotes Desdemona's lines as referring to the unpinning of *clothes*, and also gives further examples.

28. Rainolds, *Th' Overthrow*, p. 34, my emphasis.

29. Brian Morris (ed.), *The Taming of the Shrew*, the Arden Shakespeare (London and New York, 1981), p. 168.

30. J. Calvin, *The Sermons of M. John Calvin Upon ... Deuteronomie*, trans. A. Golding (London, 1583), p. 773, my emphasis.

31. W. Prynne, *The Unlovelinesse of Lovelockes* (London, 1628), A3.

32. W. Prynne, *Histrio-Mastix* (London, 1633), p. 171.

33. Ibid., p. 207, original emphasis.

34. See F. S. Boas, *University Drama in the Tudor Age* (Oxford, 1914), pp. 231–4; K. Young, 'William Gager's defence of the academic stage', *Transactions of the Wisconsin Academy of Sciences, Arts, and Letters*, 18 (1916), 593–604; J. W. Binns, 'Women or transvestites on the Elizabethan stage? an Oxford controversy', *Sixteenth Century Journal*,

5:2 (1974), 95–101; Lisa Jardine, *Still Harping on Daughters: Women and Drama in the Age of Shakespeare* (Brighton, 1983), pp. 14–17.

35. Boas, *University Drama*, pp. 105–6.

36. Rainolds, *Th' Overthrow*, p. 45.

37. Ibid., p. 96.

38. My account of transvestism, and of the boy actor in general, is deeply indebted to Jonathan Dollimore's brilliant essay on 'Subjectivity, sexuality and transgression: the Jacobean connection', *Renaissance Drama*, n. s. 17 (1986), 53–81.

39. Prynne, *Histrio-Mastix*, p. 169.

40. Ibid.

41. Ibid., p. 135.

42. Phillip Stubbes, *The Anatomie of Abuses*, ed. F. J. Furnivall, New Shakespeare Society (London, 1877–9), pp. 144–5.

43. My account of fetishism is deeply indebted to Marjorie Garber, 'Fetish envy', paper given at the Modern Language Association, New Orleans (1989). See also her fine, wide-ranging study, *Vested Interests: Cross-Dressing and Cultural Anxiety* (New York and London, 1991).

44. Sigmund Freud, 'Three essays on the theory of sexuality', in James Strachey and Angela Richards (eds), *On Sexuality*, trans. James Strachey (Harmondsworth, 1977), p. 62.

45. Ibid., p. 69.

10

'The swallowing womb': Consumed and Consuming Women in *Titus Andronicus*

MARION WYNNE-DAVIES

I

Christine de Pisan, one of the first female authors to write in defence of women, devoted three chapters of *The Book of the City of Ladies* (1404) to rape:

> Then I, Christine, spoke as follows, 'My lady [Rectitude], I truly believe what you are saying, and I am certain that there are plenty of beautiful women who are virtuous and chaste and who know how to protect themselves well from the entrapments of deceitful men. I am therefore troubled and grieved when men argue that many women want to be raped and that it does not bother them at all to be raped by men even when they verbally protest. It would be hard to believe that such great villainy is actually pleasant for them.'[1]

Her comments remain valid today; for example, they could have been usefully addressed to Judge David Wild, who said, in his summing up of a 1986 rape trial:

> Women who say no do not always mean no. It is not just a question of saying no. It is a question of how she says it, how she shows it and makes it clear. If she doesn't want it, she only has to keep her legs shut and there would be marks of force being used.[2]

Not surprisingly, the man was acquitted. While in no way suggesting an essentialist reading, it becomes impossible to ignore the fact that the issue of rape is founded upon certain premises about women's sexuality that have remained unchanged for five centuries. This male intransigence, then as now, provokes virulent debate from both sides, cutting across different areas of cultural production and allowing an insidious concoction of social and moral value judgements to infiltrate the supposed 'impartiality' of the law. [...]

The early history on the law of rape is minimal, since there are very few acts of Parliament to cover, but one of the most significant changes occurred in 1597, about four years after the staging of *Titus Andronicus*, a play which has at its heart one of the most horrific rape scenes in English drama.[3] The 1597 act legislates that:

> Whereas of late times divers women, as well maidens as widows and wives, having substance, some in goods moveable, and some in lands and tenements, and some being heirs apparent to their ancestors, for the lucre of such substance been oftentimes taken by misdoers contrary to their will, and afterward married to such misdoers, or to others by their assent, or defiled, to the great displeasure of God, and contrary to Your Highness laws, and disparagement of the said women, and great heaviness and discomfort of their friends, and ill example of others; which offences, albeit the same made felony by a certain Act of Parliament made in the third year of King Henry the seventh, yet for as much as Clergy hath been heretofore allowed to such offenders, divers persons have attempted and committed the said offences, in hope of life by the Benefit of Clergy. Be it therefore enacted ... that all and every such person and persons, as at any time after the end of the present session of Parliament ... shall in every case lose his and their Benefit of Clergy, and shall suffer pains of death.[4]

The act is primarily concerned with the 'benefit of clergy', which meant that a man who could claim certain clerical skills had the right to be tried by an ecclesiastical rather than a civil court. Although this had originally functioned with a degree of probity, it became open to vast abuse and particularly favoured the nobility, who were more likely to be literate. By 1576, the only penalty incurred by a rape conviction was imprisonment for a year or less.[5] When the 1597 act withdrew the benefit of clergy it gave the state authority to punish, or legally enact vengeance upon, the perpetrator of the crime, a power hitherto denied. Apart from this strengthening of retributive powers, the act tacitly accepts that the crime committed is one against the corporal person of the woman, rather than one of theft against her family.[6]

In medieval Europe a woman was often abducted and sexually penetrated in order to force an unwanted or unsuitable marriage, thereby enabling her abductor to take possession of her lands and inheritance. Legally this was seen as the theft of property by one man from another, and once wedlock occurred very little redress was obtainable; indeed, the marriage redeemed the offender from any punishment. Henry VII's act of 1486 had removed this matrimonial protection, thereby allowing the family to reclaim its possessions, but the criminal went unpunished through benefit of clergy.[7] Elizabeth I's act of 1597 makes the crime against the woman's person more important, and punishable regardless of the property element. The simple presence of rape legislation after a century's inactivity reveals a peak of interest in, and concern about, sexual assault, but the change enacted suggests a greater signification for the female identity as a whole in late sixteenth-century England. From this point on a woman's body in its sexual sense was seen legally to be her own possession and not that of her nearest male relative. Although this legal gesture towards female self-determination was hardly adhered to in practice, its very existence suggests that by the 1590s the idea of women as independent subjects was sufficiently substantial to be encoded within a legal text. It is hardly surprising, then, that the fissure which had opened up between property and independent female subject should be seen on the public stage as well as in the civil courts of Elizabeth I.

Rape is a crime primarily enacted by men against women, but in all circumstances it is used to assert the absolute authority of one being over another.[8] In one of the most influential and pioneering cultural analyses of rape, *Against Our Will: Men, Women and Rape*, Susan Brownmiller suggests that 'Rape became not only a male prerogative, but man's basic weapon of force against woman, the principal agent of his will and her fear',[9] and she explicitly associates rape with social control, property and the domination of women. Moreover, as sexual identity in the early modern period was inextricably bound to personal identity, the violation of the body became an invasion and domination of the inner subject, an absolute depersonalising. There can hardly be a dramatic scene more redolent of feminine repression and the annulment of the subject than when Lavinia staggers onto the stage, her body violated by rape, her tongue cut out so that she cannot speak and her hands severed so that she may not write. The Empress's sons proceed to taunt their victim:

> **Demetrius** So now go tell, an if thy tongue can speak,
> Who 'twas that cut thy tongue and ravished thee.
> **Chiron** Write down thy mind, bewray thy meaning so,
> An if thy stumps will let thee play the scribe ...
> An 'twere my cause, I should go hang myself.
> **Demetrius** If thou hadst hands to help thee knit the cord.
> (II.iv.1–4, 9–10)[10]

Not only is Lavinia denied the means of self-expression, but her ability to claim death and the absence it creates, with all its purport of deconstructive power, is eliminated. Her function as a meaningful entity appears to end, although her role is immediately metamorphosed in Marcus's subsequent speech. The denial of individual identity is clearly part of the assault on Lavinia, but it is important to bear in mind that the play never once lets us forget the physical horror of rape, even through the grotesque inversion of Ovidian rhetoric.[11]

While provoking our repugnance, however, the play gradually appears to offer the audience a satisfying (only in that it is just) conclusion: when Lavinia participates in the revenge against Chiron and Demetrius. This would have had greater impact on an Elizabethan audience, steeped as it was in the conventions of revenge tragedy. More usually the revenger was a man, and the violated woman, as in the stories of Christine de Pisan, would kill herself for the sake of 'honour'. But by the end of the play Lavinia is no longer 'Rome's rich ornament' (I.i.52), the idealised feminine beauty possessed by a patriarchal Rome; instead she becomes an active participant in the revenge, who, while her father cuts the throats of Demetrius and Chiron

> ...'tween her stumps doth hold
> The basin that receives [their] guilty blood.
> (V.ii.182–3)

By accessing the convention of revenge tragedy, normally assigned to male characters, Lavinia seems to evade containment within the sign of property and lays claim to an independent self, unrestricted by gender conventions.[12] Whether this device can successfully undermine the dominant ideological circumscription of female sexuality remains a moot point, but what is clear is that the play briefly offers up this subversive possibility as an acceptable, indeed desirable, alternative.

That rape is an essential theme in *Titus Andronicus* cannot be questioned: the word is mentioned fifteen times in the play compared to five times in all of Shakespeare's other works, including *The Rape of Lucrece*.[13] Still, the associations between this latter poem and the play are numerous: their composition dates are, at the most, two years apart; both deal with a threat to civic order through the political allegory of a Roman setting; they link rape to revenge; poetically both employ an exaggerated rhetoric to describe brutal violence; and, most strikingly, the history of Lucrece is specifically referred to in the play (II.i.109, and III.i.297). Coppélia Kahn, in her intelligent and forthright article 'The rape in Shakespeare's *Lucrece*', asserts that

> the poem's insistent concern [is] with the relationship between sex and power. That relationship is established by the terms of marriage in a patriarchal society. The rape is ultimately a means by which Shakespeare can explore the nature of marriage in such a society and the role of women in marriage.[14]

Whereas in *Lucrece* female identity is centred exclusively upon marriage, in *Titus* it is seen in a broader familial context; women are mothers and daughters first, wives second. The political import of an emphasis on lineage, rather than matrimony, foregrounds the importance of women in genealogical terms and raises questions about the validity of inheritance and descent. When rape occurs it inevitably threatens the values of the patrilineal society and necessitates a breakdown of its value systems and laws. Both texts engage in the problem of rape, *Lucrece* within the more intimate confines of marriage and *Titus* in the glare of lineage and political accountability.

Titus Andronicus and *The Rape of Lucrece* are not the only works written in the early 1590s which carry overtones of sexual assault: *Venus and Adonis* inverts the traditional gender roles and makes Venus the attacker: 'Her lips are conquerors, his lips obey' and 'her blood doth boil, / And careless lust stirs up a desperate courage' (ll.549, 555–6).[15] Like the paradigmatic rapist, Venus uses force to overcome her victim, while her powerful sexuality carries a covert threat of castration. Whatever the metaphor, however, Venus cannot rape Adonis biologically, and the poem continually sidles into the comic absurdity that this realisation must provoke. What seems to me intriguing is that the idea of rape is related to a powerful, mature woman in an analogous fashion to the rape in *Titus*, which is condoned and encouraged by Tamora, herself a character of independent political power and forceful sexuality. Indeed, in Thomas Nashe's *The Unfortunate Traveller* (1594), which has clear linguistic parallels with *Titus*, the rape victim is Roman and 'a noble and chaste matron' with grey hair.[16] It almost seems as if we are being offered the well-worn dichotomy of virgin and whore, the abused and depersonalised maidens – Lavinia and Lucrece – and the threatening sexuality of a puissant woman – Tamora and Venus.

The importance of strong, but older, female characters in late sixteenth-century texts is further evinced by a unique and contemporary representational response to *Titus* by Henry Peacham. The Longleat manuscript consists of a drawing which illustrates Tamora begging for the lives of her sons, and several lines from the play. These extracts include the Empress's plea (I.i.104–20) and Aaron's catalogue of his crimes (V.i.125–44).[17] The two central figures in the cartoon are not dressed in contemporary costume; Titus wears Roman garb, while Tamora appears in stately robes and wearing a crown, as befits her role as queen of the Goths. The figure of Aaron is set to the side, and he is outstanding in that Peacham has chosen to colour his face and limbs a matt black. The two prominent speeches recorded are by Tamora and Aaron. Peacham's choice of the Moor is understandable, partly because of the artistic novelty of representing an archetypically villainous negro, and partly because he provides an archetypically villainous counterpart to Titus on the page. Tamora, however, poses a more intriguing response. She is dressed as a queen and the lines quoted are both touching and pure; this is not the woman who rejects Lavinia's claims for pity, or the incarnation of revenge who tries to drive Titus mad. Why, then, did Peacham choose to depict Tamora as royal and sympathetic?

It is now a critical commonplace that Rome often stands as a mirror of the Elizabethan world for Shakespeare and his contemporaries, and on these grounds we can well imagine Tamora as a distantly refracted image of Elizabeth I.[18] *Titus*, however, is too awkward a play to settle exclusively into close political allegory. This movement towards complexity rather than neat identifications recurs in the play's rejection of the common stereotyping of women into virgins and whores. Instead, it appears both to enact and to confuse these treatments of women: feminine power and female sexuality are inextricably linked, simultaneously provoking and repressed. *Titus* is about the limits of these identifications and the point at which woman as subject is confronted with a destructive depersonalisation. The rape of Lavinia is the physical enactment of a more pervasive assault in the play on that which is feminine, and on the manifold metaphors drawn from the female body.

II

Since rape is a central theme of *Titus Andronicus*, it seems darkly appropriate that one of the corporal symbols of the play should be the womb. While Act I is set in the imperial city, Act II offers the alternative world of a wooded valley, at the heart of which lies a 'detested, dark, blood-drinking pit', an 'unhallowed and bloodstained hole' 'whose mouth is covered with rude-growing briers, / Upon whose leaves are drops of new shed blood' (II.iii.224, 210 and 199–200). The imagery is blatant, the cave being the vagina, the all-consuming sexual mouth of the feminine earth, which remains outside the patriarchal order of Rome. This is the 'swallowing womb' (l.239) that links female sexuality to death and damnation. The association is not unique in Shakespeare, the most famous example being Lear's condemnation of women and his description of their wombs:

> There's hell, there's darkness, there is the sulphurous pit –
> Burning, scalding, stench, consumption.
>
> (*King Lear*, IV.vi.128–9)

An analogous description occurs in *Romeo and Juliet*, when the tomb is described as 'detestable maw' and a 'womb of death' (V.iii. 45).[19] The association of hell, death and consumption with the womb clearly evokes a concept of woman's sexuality that is both dangerous and corrupting. The identification was not a purely artistic one: the physiological suppositions concerning the uterus in the medieval and Renaissance periods saw it as something alien. For example, Plato's description of the womb as an animal in its own right was often cited, and the organ was thought to be dominated exclusively by external forces, such as the imagination and the moon. Moreover, since the prevalent ideas on the body were governed by a theory of humours, it was clear that these physical manifestations had psychological implications.[20] The first mention of the 'abhorred pit' in *Titus* is made by Tamora:

> They told me here at dead time of the night
> A thousand fiends, a thousand hissing snakes,
> Ten thousand swelling toads, as many urchins,
> Would make such fearful and confused cries
> As any mortal body hearing it
> Should straight fall mad.
>
> (II.iii.99–104)

The Empress suggests that it is herself who will fall victim to this fate. The womb of the ultimate mythic female body – the earth – threatens to make Tamora mad, as in Renaissance beliefs any woman's uterus weakened her mind and made her susceptible to lunacy.[21] But in *Titus* this is not the case; on the contrary, Tamora fabricates the tale of injury and is in no danger of madness. And although Demetrius and Chiron threaten to rape Lavinia in this 'secret hole' (II.iii.129), they take her offstage rather than incarcerating her in the pit, which remains in full view of the audience. Instead, the cave consumes Bassanius's corpse and the bodies of the doomed Martius and Quintus. The 'swallowing womb' does carry the promise of death, but for men and not women. Its power is to castrate, not to madden.

The womb is not only the centre of female sexuality, but also the repository of familial descent. Michel Foucault, in *The History of Sexuality*, writes that the rules governing sexuality in the early modern society in France and England were determined by blood relations, and that it was through them that the mechanisms of power were able to function.[22] Control of the womb was paramount to determining a direct patrilineal descent, and when this exercise of power failed and women determined their own sexual appetites regardless of procreation, the social structure was threatened with collapse. This is exactly what happens in *Titus* when Tamora seeks amorous gratification with Aaron, and the subsequent presence of the half-caste child menaces 'Our Empress' shame and stately Rome's disgrace' (IV.ii.60). The 1597 rape legislation, with its suggestion of female self-determination, is a parallel validation of this same independent sexual control. Although it manifestly did not bring about the collapse of Elizabethan society, its very existence suggests a need to answer the same worrying concerns about women's identity as those evinced in *Titus Andronicus*.

The control of the female subject is not achieved only through the policing of her sexuality, since orality too is an important aspect of self-construction.[23] The pit in *Titus* functions as both a womb and a consuming mouth. As the play attempts to repress female sexuality through rape, so it denies female speech when Lavinia has her tongue cut out. Tamora's unheeded plea for her sons is likewise a reminder of women's muted state.[24] Yet it is through the 'consumption' of a pen that Lavinia regains the power of communication, and at the end of the play Tamora will literally eat her children. The play persistently empowers its female characters with a hard-won freedom of self-expression, only to have it rebound in a final reassertion of male dominance.

I have already suggested that the act – rape – and the acted upon – the womb as sign for the female body – pursue, through metaphor, multifarious and often uneasy incarnations. These fields of rhetorical play serve to test the limits of dismemberment and thrust before the audience a series of almost unacceptable collusions. The issues so pinned down are not solely concerned with the female subject, but she penetrates several of them.

III

In one respect, familial, social and political stability in a patrilineal society resides in the policing of a woman's womb. The essentiality of this premise recurs throughout the Shakespearean canon from Gratiano's comic recognition that

> while I live, I'll fear no other thing
> So sore as keeping safe Nerissa's ring.
> (*The Merchant of Venice*, V.i.306–7)

to the destructive and ultimately tragic actions of the base-born Edmund in *King Lear*. The pervasive impact which occurs when this control breaks down is traced by Robert Miola who, perhaps rather tellingly, translates the bloody rape of Lavinia into 'a direct assault on the Andronici family and the Roman virtue which it represents [and an expression of] the perversion of normal familial relations and values in Rome's royal household.'[25] The fundamental issue is assurance of blood descent, a point clearly indicated by pre-1597 rape legislation, but in *Titus* the issues are divided. Lavinia, who signifies the blameless victim and eradicated subject, remains barren, whereas Tamora, who acts as a symbol of aggressive female sexuality, bears the subversive blackamoor child. By emphasising the illegitimate fruits of female rather than male sexual transgression, the play appears to hold guilty the lust of women rather than of men for any social breakdown.

The extent of Tamora's vitiosity is evident in the metaphoric import of her child's black skin as well as in her displacement of the father in relation to her sons, Demetrius and Chiron. It was the Empress who 'unadvised' gave her sons swords, rather than the more acceptable gift of a book which young Lucius receives from his mother and which is read by his aunt.[26] Military activity is a masculine trait to be passed between father and son, culminating in honourable triumph such as is enjoyed by Titus and his sons at the start of the play. The sword given by Tamora, even as its distorted source prefigures, leads only to the debased dismembering of Lavinia. The privileging of paternal over maternal value systems is most persuasive in the comparison of Tamora's and Titus's pleas for their children. At the beginning of the play the Empress begs Titus not to sacrifice her son:

> Stay, Roman brethren, gracious conqueror,
> Victorious Titus, rue the tears I shed,
> A mother's tears in passion for her son;
> And if thy sons were ever dear to thee,
> O, think my son to be as dear to me.
> Sufficeth not that we are brought to Rome
> To beautify thy triumphs, and return
> Captive to thee and to thy Roman yoke;
> But must my sons be slaughtered in the streets
> For valiant doings in their country's cause?
> O, if to fight for king and commonweal
> Were piety in thine, it is in these.
>   (I.i.104–115)

Titus is forced to make a similar request when his sons are condemned for the murder of Bassianus:

> Hear me, grave fathers. Noble tribunes, stay.
> For pity of mine age, whose youth was spent
> In dangerous wars, whilst you securely slept;
> For all my blood in Rome's great quarrel shed,
> For all the frosty nights that I have watched,
> And for all these bitter tears which now you see,
> Filling the aged wrinkles in my cheeks,

> Be pitiful to my condemned sons,
> Whose souls is not corrupted as 'tis thought.
>   (III.i.1–9)

The physical actions of mother and father are the same: both prostrate themselves and shed tears. Both begin their speech in a commanding tone with brief phrases, and with a similar call to familial sympathies.[27] Both refer to honourable battle and ask for pity for their offspring. Moreover, Titus's poignant plea for his sons is as vain as that Tamora addressed to him earlier in the play. But the narrative construction appears to deploy the audience's sympathy, even if it leaves those on stage unmoved. Although both sets of progeny are innocent, we have been party to the events of the Andronici's condemnation and are aware that deceit and treachery have been involved, not impersonal militarism. After the Goth is put to death Tamora improves her position and becomes empress, whereas our sympathy for Titus is wrenched still further in our foreknowledge, and then experience, of his meeting with the mutilated Lavinia. The audience seems to be tacitly aligned with a familial discourse which enshrines male power. We are still left, though, with the disconcerting pictorial response of the Peacham manuscript, which depicts the plea of Tamora and not of Titus.

The deconstructive power of this single image is reinforced by the ambiguous elevation of Aaron's love for his son. The Moor, who repudiates all moral standards and stands in the play as an incarnation of evil, will risk everything for the sake of his child:

> My mistress is my mistress, this myself,
> The vigour and the picture of my youth:
> This before all the world do I prefer.
>   (IV.ii.107–9)

The sympathy aroused by Aaron in this scene can hardly be reconciled with the Moor's demonic role, and it results in a simultaneous humanisation of the individual character and a devaluation of the paternal value systems of the play.[28] The imaginative and ideological shifts required of the audience to encompass both a fatherly and a devilish Aaron fissure the patrilineal dominance irretrievably. Doubts about Titus's function as the archetype of fatherhood lurk around his sacrifice of his own son, Mutius, in the name of imperial loyalty, and about his conference of the kingship on grounds of primogeniture rather than election and individual worth. Both acts are in error and set in motion a series of familial and royal deaths which culminate in his own. When set in a dualism of mother / Tamora and father / Titus the value of a patrilineal society seems at first unquestionable, but the play slides into unexpected similarities and contrasts which compel a reworking of expected and perhaps accepted gender identities.

IV

Primogeniture not only determined familial inheritance but was the basis of royal descent in the early modern period. Ensuring that there was a male heir to further the line was a persistent concern of the monarch and his / her statesmen. However, in late sixteenth-century England the determining of a successor was a paramount source of disquiet and a promise of, rather than an insurance against, future political turmoil.[29] The first scene of *Titus* opens upon similar political worries, with an ungoverned Rome and the decision of the tribunes, through Marcus, to offer the crown to Titus:

> **Marcus** ... help to set a head on headless Rome.
> **Titus** A better head her glorious body fits
> Than his that shakes for age and feebleness.
> ... this suit I make,
> That you create our emperor's eldest son,
> Lord Saturnine, whose virtues will, I hope,
> Reflect on Rome as Titan's rays on earth,
> And ripen justice in this commonweal.
> Then if you will elect by my advice,
> Crown him and say, 'Long live our emperor!'
> (I.i.186–8, 223–9)

The Roman citadel and state are envisaged as a headless feminine body, a motif which is repeated at the end of the play when the contrasting office of governorship is offered to Lucius (V. iii. 66–75).[30] Nor is the image of a dismembered female body singular within the play. The horrific violence which is enacted upon Lavinia demands by analogy a brutal visualisation of an otherwise common metaphor for the body politic. In *Titus*, as in the best traditions of horror, the figurative tends to become the actual.[31] Apart from forcing a brutal vision of a political future without an assured and worthy ruler, the speech also calls into question the adequacy of public discourses to handle the impending crisis. If Rome begins and ends the play as a mutilated female form, then Titus's resolution of primogeniture can hardly be adequate.

The importance of public and political ideologies to the play is evident from the opening scene, with its panoply of the most renowned physical structures of civic Roman life: the Capitol, the Pantheon, the city walls and gates.[32] The action occurs in a series of ceremonies, public orations and almost pageant-like entries.[33] The females are acted upon within this formal setting, allotted according to the wishes of the patriarchy: Titus gives both Lavinia and Tamora to Saturninus, with as much proprietorial assurance as he gives away Rome. His doctrines are strikingly redolent of the pre-1597 act, when rape was a law of theft against the family, the women being regarded as possessions of their dominant male relations rather than as autonomous beings. Still, his actions in the play will prove misguided, and previously unquestioned ideologies are disrupted within the subsequent lack of moral or social determinants.[34] *Titus* presents us with a conundrum: the civil dismemberment endemic upon a female body politic set against the total inadequacy of the formal patriarchal solution of primogeniture. In contemporary allegory, how can one ensure the inheritance of the throne by a non-existent eldest son of a virgin Queen? This was not a question located solely in literary discourses, and the active public debate which accrued about the succession had far-reaching implications for a more general understanding of what constituted a state.[35] [...]

Shakespeare's use of Roman political history to enact the conceptual debate between imperialism and republicanism is commonly accepted. What *Titus* contributes is a disturbing gender dialectic.[36] The metaphor of the body politic here gives us a female state and city governed by a man whose inheritance rests on primogeniture and not on personal worth. This combination fails utterly. By analogy, if Marcus was right in suggesting self-determinism for the state, and indeed it seems he was, then the female body, human rather than civic, also has a valid right to independent choice. It was just such a freedom from the patriarchal ownership of their own sexuality that the 1597 rape legislation gave women, while our own horror at Lavinia's fate subtly nurtures the audience's complicity with this judgement.

The use of Rome in the context of contemporary political discourse also raises the spectre of imperialism. For an Elizabethan audience accustomed to the propagandist panoply of Tudor myth, which claimed dynastic descent from Aeneas, the legendary founder of Rome, the political resonance of empire would have been readily imparted to the sixteenth-century diplomatic arena.[37] When Titus first appears on stage in a triumphal entry bearing with him the conquered royal family of the Goths, he encapsulates an image of military triumph and imperial domination. The contemporary parallels of nationalistic victories are overt; Titus procures for the audience a parallel self-image dependent upon the defeat of the Spanish Armada in 1588, together with the territorial claims of Drake in California in 1579 and Raleigh's in Roanoke in 1585.[38] On stage the terms of conquest would have been transformed into a gender dialectic of Titus and Tamora, male and female. The importance of this association may be seen from its elision in the comparable text, *The Tragical History of Titus Andronicus*, where the Goths are led by their king, Tottilius, who is not even mentioned in Shakespeare's play.[39] Coppélia Kahn draws a similar gender parallel from *The Rape of Lucrece*: 'The heroine becomes an image for two fields of political conquest, the expanding Roman empire and the New World.'[40] Tamora and Lavinia fulfil equivalent functions: Tamora as the conquered Queen of the Goths, a slave 'brought to yoke', and Lavinia as an imperial treasure to be disputed over by rivals for the imperial throne (I.i.69, 52). Enslaved nations must always act as the identifying 'other' of imperial expansion; Tamora's gender accentuates this difference, while Aaron's race removes the Goths still further from the Roman victors and their signification in contemporary allegory. The interweaving parallels and contrasts which abound in *Titus* also occur between Aaron and Tamora, for not only are both captives of Rome, they are also mutually enslaved in physical passion:

> **Aaron** So Tamora;
> ... whom thou in triumph long
> Hast prisoner held, fettered in amorous chains,
> And faster bound to Aaron's charming eyes
> Than is Prometheus tied to Caucasus.
> (II.i.9, 14–17)

The use of slavery as a metaphor for binding love in *Titus* belongs to a romantic discourse, but it must also provoke political associations of power, even as the hunt scene, while evoking Petrarchan parallels, ends in rape.[41] Through the forced awareness of jarring affinities, the ownership and control of women – here Aaron's of Tamora – are seen to permeate the play. The hell-like associations of the womb and Tamora's bond with the demonic Moor confirm this identification.[42]

While using the audience's repugnance at, and fascination with, dominance and violence, *Titus* explores the idea of the independent subject, both corporal and metaphoric, but it never entirely over-throws the patriarchal values of the political system. Although Lavinia and Rome may be pitied, Tamora almost stands for a misogynistic stereotype of the scheming woman perversely taking political power and sexual freedom. Nor is she alone, for as Lavinia is set against the Empress, so the natural world of the forest with its 'swallowing womb' may be contrasted with Rome.

V

The concept of the organic body politic with its acceptance of blood descent carries, in the Elizabethan period, overtones of the femi-nine, and this is reinforced in *Titus* by identifying the organic and elemental images in the play with the quintessentially female earth.[43] The disturbing and threatening associations of the forest scene, with its 'swallowing womb' centre stage, are made through-out the play, as for example when Titus tells Chiron and Demetrius their fate:

> Hark, villains, I will grind your bones to dust,
> And with your blood and it I'll make a paste,
> And of the paste a coffin I will rear,
> And make two pasties of your shameful heads,
> And bid that strumpet, your unhallowed dam,
> Like to the earth swallow her own increase.
> (V.ii.186–91)[44]

Titus's metaphor is conventional and refers to the idea of the earth assimilating her children, that is humankind, when they are buried. But although Tamora is once more linked to the powerful otherness of the natural body, both are here perverted so that the consump-tion is *un*natural; a precipitous doom, rather than humankind's allotted and inevitable return to dust.

The symbolic signification of the forest and its female associations can, however, be read in quite another manner: Albert Tricomi in his article on 'The mutilated garden in *Titus Andronicus*' acknowledges that 'the forest ... eventually becomes synonymous with barbarism and chaos', but he also points out that it is initially described in pastoral and romantic terminology.[45] More significantly, he shows, through the repetition of lily, deer and fountain motifs, that 'Lavinia and the forest in *Titus Andronicus* are imagined as one or nearly one throughout the play.'[46] The chaste Lavinia cannot easily be reconciled with the overt and intimidating sexuality of the 'swallowing womb' and Tamora, but her close ties to the natural imagery of the forest demand that such an association be made. This fusion of opposite female stereotypes is compounded by Aaron's 'rape' of the earth, thus linking it in turn to the violated Lavinia. Mining for gems and precious metals is often described as rape; and this occurs in *Titus* when the Moor digs for gold in Act II, scene iii.[47] The earth is both castrating and raped, consumed and consuming.

The slippage between nurturing and disordering organic symbols still resides within the feminine, but Titus's famous 'I am the sea' speech to Lavinia, when he has been cruelly deceived by Aaron into sacrificing his hand, self-consciously dissolves all delineations of difference:

> If there were reason for these miseries,
> Then into limits could I bind my woes;
> When heaven doth weep, doth not the earth o'erflow?
> If the winds rage, doth not the sea wax mad,
> Threat'ning the welkin with his big-swoll'n face?
> And wilt thou have a reason for this coil?
> I am the sea. Hark how her sighs doth blow!
> She is the weeping welkin, I the earth;
> Then must my sea be moved with her sighs;
> Then must my earth with her continual tears
> Become a deluge, overflowed and drowned;
> For why my bowels cannot hide her woes,
> But like a drunkard must I vomit them.
> (III.i.218–30)

This speech is one of the cruxes of the play, set at a point of narrative crisis where the audience realises Titus has been duped, but where he remains hopeful. Moreover, the mythic language and solemn tone make it one of the most powerful and poignant speeches of the play. When our pity and sympathy become overwhelming this figurehead of patriarchy, whose stubborn adherence to the most conservative ideologies initiates the tragic action of the play, turns to his mutilated daughter and denies difference, elemental and gender. The complexity of Titus's identifications and the rapidity with which he changes them are sufficient to commingle the elements in the audience's imagination. But as the speech moves towards its end, a fatalistic sense of total breakdown becomes apparent. Titus's sea 'must' be affected by Lavinia's wind, but then his earth loses its separate identity and becomes liquid like her tears; he is 'overflowed and drowned'. The stark inevitability of this merging is emphasised by the biblical resonances of 'deluge'; there is no mystical metamorphosis into an idealised hermaphrodite. Instead we are faced with the appalling consequences of tragedy, which perforce takes identity beyond its limit to a point where gender overflows itself into another. Then as Titus returns to the body imagery this excessive unity becomes unbearable, as it must in a material world, and gender returns to otherness. The female is perceived as within and belonging intimately to the male, but only until disgorged.[48] Limits are breached in their connotation of dividing different forms as well as in the sense of containment and control. The overburdening and excessive nature of events – familial and social tragedy figured in the elemental symbolism – collapses the hierarchical and differential structures which retain order. Like the central image of the 'swallowing womb', Titus's speech evokes the utter and unquenchable forces of nature. In its biting evocation of grief it comes to the very brink of allowing the 'deluge' full sway, before retreating behind the sandbags of conventional gender difference. The utter pathos of this speech, which gives authenticity to this desperate immersion in the magnetic power of symbolism, lies in the knowledge of the audience that events will indeed get worse.

VI

[...] This essay has taken as its premise the containment and repression of women, and has dealt with the tensions and challenges to this convention as dramatic appurtenances. Woman as a physical entity to be possessed and controlled within sexual, familial and political discourses, as well as in the metaphoric figures of city, state, empire and the earth itself, is seen to be consumed by the patriarchal ideologies of late sixteenth-century England. Yet at the same time the strain produced by the pathologically strict adherence to these determinants necessitates a modulation of demarcations. Titus's 'I am the sea' speech suggests a way in which this collapse of differentiation may be attained, a way in which division might be unified, the female incorporated into the male. But it would be wrong to assume that the female characters of the play lack self-expression or fail to make claims for independent subjectivity. The play does not rest solely upon the father–daughter relationship of Titus and Lavinia.

The importance of authoritative women is refracted through the character of Tamora. She resembles Venus from *Venus and Adonis*, is related to the all-powerful mother earth, in political allegory recalls Elizabeth I, and it is she whom Peacham depicts at the centre of his drawing. In addition she is compared in the play to Dido, Hecuba and Semiramis (II.iii. 22; I.i.36; I.i.22), and Waith traces her name to Tomyris, a Scythian queen.[49] Yet Lavinia does not stand as an unambiguous sign for female repression either; she too is compared to Hecuba (IV.i.20), and she is the foremost instrument in the initiation of revenge against her rapists.[50] Further links occur between the two women through associations with Virgil's *Aeneid*; Tamora is related to Dido, and Lavinia suggests her own namesake who founds the imperial Roman dynasty. But the most curious textual semblance is drawn from Ovid.[51]

The account of Lavinia's rape and the method of its discovery are taken from the tale of Philomela, a debt which is acknowledged several times in the play. A copy of *Metamorphoses* is even brought on stage in the fourth act.[52] Ovid's story tells of how Philomela is raped by her brother-in-law, Tereus, who tries to conceal the assault by cutting out her tongue. However, she portrays the events in a tapestry and sends it to her sister, Procne. The two sisters are united and revenge themselves upon Tereus by killing his son and serving up the flesh for him to eat. Tereus tries to slay them but all three are metamorphosed into birds. The resemblance to Lavinia's experiences is manifest, but those of Tamora in the last scene of the play also recall the Ovidian text.

The final speech of *Titus* is given to Lucius, who heralds the new age of order and expunges the old. Lavinia is buried in the family tomb, and

> As for that ravenous tiger, Tamora,
> No funeral rite, nor man in mourning weed,
> No mournful bell shall ring her burial;
> But throw her forth to beasts and birds to prey;

> Her life was beastly and devoid of pity,
> And being dead, let birds on her take pity.
> (V.iii.194–9)

The threat posed by the Empress is such that she must be expurgated altogether from Rome to the organic and inherently feminine world of the earth, with its 'swallowing womb'. Her fate seems an almost inevitable return to that with which she has been so closely associated, and the method of her expulsion recalls Titus's vomiting up of feminine woes. It is the excess of Tamora's subversive signification which demands that she be finally removed and the breach repaired, while Lavinia is disempowered by being safely interred within the patriarchal vault. A choice of destinies awaits the aggressive woman: if she may be reintroduced into the patriarchal value system, then she will be awarded an identity within that structure. But if her irregularities prove too virulent, too ingrained, then she must be ejected from the system altogether. The last speech thus enacts a final circumscriptive locating of women in relation to the dominant male body – corporal and politic; they can either be consumed or, if they prove indigestible, they can be 'disgorged'.

Yet even at the close of the play *Titus* remains ragged and uncontainable, refusing to rest upon such formulaic dialecticisms. The birds are left to consume Tamora's carrion, thereby metamorphosing her body into the creatures which subsequently proceed to pity her; their actions recall for the audience the heavy indebtedness to Ovid. Tamora and all she represents may be eliminated from the public and political voices of Rome, but in the last line she accesses a literary discourse which perforce takes the audience back to one of the most dramatic moments in the play.

The scene where Lavinia takes the staff in her mouth and writes the names of her violators in the sand is the narrative fulcrum of *Titus Andronicus* (IV.i). From this point the revenge of the Andronici has purpose and the play's conclusion can be foreseen. In a text so redolent with images of eating and sexual penetration the act is startling. She takes in her mouth – that is, she consumes – the means of self-expression, thus encompassing what has been a masculine prerogative of subjectivity, and transmutes it into a feminine rhetorical practice. That she relates herself to the Ovidian text simply affirms our expectations of change and difference. But the action is also threatening, for the female mouth in *Titus* must also signify the womb, and the link between pen and phallus inevitably follows.[53] Lavinia's mouth appears to re-enact the swallowing womb of Act II when she consumes the masculine signifier, whether pen or phallus, and takes over the textual discourse, thereby castrating the source of male power.

The action does not convey this simple message of liberated female language, however, for Titus reads what Lavinia has written; he transmits her text to the audience, thereby once again attempting to confuse the issues of gender and production. The words – '*Stuprum. Chiron. Demetrius*' (IV.i.77) – become the location of mutual production and consumption, rebounding between Lavinia, Titus and the audience. The breakdown of traditional actor / audience response is redolent of Titus's elemental speech, where limits likewise collapse under the pressure of personal grief. Yet in this instance the audience wills the rapid pursuance of complicity, the union of minds, so that, when recourse to official channels fails, the injured can enact vengeance for themselves.

This essay began with a discussion of the injustices of rape legislation from the medieval period to the present day and, more particularly, the relevance of the 1597 rape act to the contemporary location of female sexual identity. *Titus Andronicus* participates in a corresponding discourse of disruption and revision; it draws upon the horror of rape and throws into sharp relief the difference between the sexual constraint and sexual self-determination of women. Like the legal encodement, the play at times appears to offer women control over their own corporal identities, but it reaches beyond the confines of the formal document into a multiplicity of interpretations and consequences. At times the play politically empowers Tamora, offers Lavinia a means of self-expression, weights the play with contemporary allegory which privileges an aged queen, allows the audience to focus upon the symbolic centre of the 'swallowing womb' and promises redemption for women through the metamorphosing power of Ovidian rhetoric. Yet at the same time as proffering an independent subject position for women, *Titus* shores the very fissures that it has mined. Moreover, it achieves this retrenchment through its figurative depiction of the violation and destruction of women. What both legal and dramatic discourses open is a distorted image of female sexuality, where its very independence is bound up in the brutal denial of its existence, where women can be both consumed and consuming. While the language of the parliamentary act remains coolly impartial, what the play forces recurrently before our eyes is an evocation of rape so horrific that, while we recognise its ideological location, we cannot help but question the values of a society which allows such a violation to occur.

From *The Matter of Difference: Materialist Feminist Criticism of Shakespeare*, ed. Valerie Wayne (Ithaca and London, 1991), pp. 129–51.

NOTES

[A slightly longer version of this essay first appeared in *The Matter of Difference*. Marion Wynne-Davies is engaged in the feminist project to uncover the history of early modern women, including women writers. Essays such as this one examine theatrical representations of women in terms of social and legal practices in early modern England. See also Wynne-Davies' edition (with S. P. Cerasano), *Renaissance Drama by Women: Texts and Documents* (New York and London, 1996). Ed.]

1. Christine de Pisan, *The Book of the City of Ladies* (London, 1983), pp. 158–64; see especially pp. 160–1.

2. Joan Smith, *Misogynies* (London, 1989), p. 3.

3. Here I am happy to follow the arguments of Eugene M. Waith in the Oxford edition of *Titus* (Oxford, 1984), where he suggests a date shortly before 1592 for the original composition, and late 1593 for the revision (pp. 4–11). Stanley Wells, in his review of Deborah Warner's 1986 production of the play, confirmed that it is a part of the Shakespearian canon in need of revaluing: Wells, 'Shakespeare performances in London and Stratford-upon-Avon 1986–7', *Shakespeare Survey*, 41 (1988), 159–81.

4. Elizabeth I, Cap. ix, *The Statutes of the Realm* (London, 1819).

5. A description of the benefit of clergy may be found in Sir William Holdsworth, *A History of English Law* (London, 1935), 4th edn, Vol. III, pp. 293–302.

6. Roy Porter, 'Rape – does it have a historical meaning?', in Sylvana Tomaselli and Roy Porter (eds), *Rape: An Historical and Cultural Enquiry* (Oxford, 1986), p. 217. For a discussion of the relationship between revenge and the law see Catherine Belsey, *The Subject of Tragedy* (London, 1985), pp. 113–16; for the relationship between revenge and violence see Huston Diehl, 'The iconography of violence in English Renaissance tragedy', *Renaissance Drama*, NS 11 (1980), 27–44.

7. The history of the rape laws is discussed in Susan Brownmiller, *Against Our Will: Men, Women and Rape* (New York, 1975), pp. 6–22; and in Barbara Toner, *The Facts of Rape* (London, 1977). There is a discrepancy over the dating of Henry VII's 1486 or 1487 law, 'The penalty for carrying a woman away against her will that hath lands or goods', between *Statutes of the Realm* and *Statutes at Large* (Henry VIII, cap. ii, *Statutes of the Realm* (London, 1816), and Henry VII, cap. ii, *The Statutes at Large* [London, 1770]).

8. It is important to note that men also rape other men; Brownmiller, *Against Our Will*, pp. 285–97.

9. Brownmiller, *Against Our Will*, p. 5.

10. All quotations are taken from the Oxford edition of *Titus Andronicus*, ed. Waith.

11. The use of Ovidian rhetoric in Marcus's speech is discussed by Albert H. Tricomi in 'The mutilated garden in *Titus Andronicus*', *Shakespeare Studies*, 9 (1976), 89–105.

12. There is a discussion of how women function as signs in an exchange system in Elizabeth Cowie, 'Woman as sign', *M / F*, 1 (1978), 49–63. The masculine confines of revenge tragedy will be discussed more fully later on in relation to Tamora. However, it is worth pointing out here that there are numerous parallels between Lavinia and the Empress, which link them firmly as women despite their other differences.

13. 'Rape': I.i.404 and 405; II.i.117; IV.i.48, 49 and 90; IV.ii.9; V.ii.37, 45, 62, 94, 134 and 156. 'Rapes': IV.i.57; V.i.63. Rape is also mentioned in *King John*, II.i.97; *Troilus and Cressida*, II.ii.148; *All's Well That Ends Well*, IV.iii.233; and *Lucrece*, ll.909 and 1369. All references to Shakespeare's works, other than *Titus*, are taken from *William Shakespeare: The Complete Works*, ed. Peter Alexander (London, 1951).

14. Coppélia Kahn, 'The rape in Shakespeare's *Lucrece*', *Shakespeare Studies*, 9, (1976), 45–72; quotation from p. 45. Kahn also has an interesting section on rape in *Venus and Adonis* in *Man's Estate: Masculine Identity in Shakespeare* (Berkeley, CA, 1981), pp. 547–58. See also Katharine Eisaman Maus, 'Taking tropes seriously: language and violence in Shakespeare's *Rape of Lucrece*', *Shakespeare Quarterly*, 37 (1986), 66–82.

15. Tricomi discusses the relationship between *Titus* and *Venus and Adonis* ('Mutilated garden', p. 94).

16. Thomas Nashe, *The Unfortunate Traveller*, ed. J. B. Steane (Harmondsworth, 1972), pp. 331–41.

17. For a reproduction of Peacham's drawing and a discussion of its authorship, see Waith's edition of *Titus*, pp. 20–7.

18. Kahn, 'The rape in Shakespeare's *Lucrece*', pp. 45–6; Alan Sommers, '"Wilderness of tigers": structure and symbolism in *Titus Andronicus*', *Essays in Criticism*, 10 (1960), 275–89.

19. Kahn, *Man's Estate*, pp. 101.

20. Ian Maclean, *The Renaissance Notion of Woman* (Cambridge, 1980), *passim*.

21. Ibid., p. 42. The uterus was also supposed to predispose women to revenge, as at V.ii.36.

22. Michel Foucault, *The History of Sexuality*, Vol. I, trans. Robert Hurley (London, 1978), p. 147.

23. Susan Rubin Suleiman, *The Female Body in Western Literature* (Cambridge, MA, 1986), pp. 1–29.

24. An analysis of the theory of women's muted state may be found in Shirley Ardener, *Defining Females: The Nature of Women in Society* (London, 1978), p. 21.

25. Robert Miola, '*Titus Andronicus* and the mythos of Shakespeare's Rome', *Shakespeare Studies*, 14 (1981), 88; see also Kahn, 'The rape in Shakespeare's *Lucrece*', p. 55.

26. II.i.38.

27. Although Titus has every reason to refer to the tribunes as kin, Tamora's plea to brotherhood seems markedly inadvisable in such a patriarchal society.

28. The popularity of Aaron as a stage character is traced by Waith in his introduction to the play, pp. 43–58. See also Waith, 'The appeal of the comic deceiver', *Yearbook of English Studies*, 12 (1982), 13–23.

29. For a discussion of civil turmoil in the play see Ronald Broude, 'Roman and Goth in *Titus Andronicus*', *Shakespeare Studies*, 6 (1970), 27–34. Several Elizabethan plays evince similar concerns about civil disruption: *Gorboduc* (1561); George Gascogyne, *Jocasta* (1566); Christopher Marlowe, *Tamburlaine* (1590); Thomas Lodge, *Wounds of Civil War* (1586–7).

30. Elizabeth I can be seen as a representation of the country: Roy Strong, *The Cult of Elizabeth* (Wallop, Hampshire, 1977); and Peter Stallybrass, 'Patriarchal territories', in M. W. Ferguson, M. Quilligan and N. J. Vickers (eds), *Rewriting the Renaissance* (Chicago, 1986), pp. 123–42; see especially p. 129.

31. Albert H. Tricomi, 'The aesthetics of mutilation in *Titus Andronicus*', *Shakespeare Survey*, 27 (1974), 11–19.

32. Lavinia is herself referred to as a 'ruin' at III.i.206, and this metaphor is discussed in Bernd Jager, 'Body, house, city, or the intertwinings of embodiment, inhabitation and civilisation', in Dreyer Kruger (ed.), *The Changing Reality of Modern Man* (Nijerk, 1984), pp. 50–8.

33. The pageant-like entries occur when Titus first enters, at the beginning of II.ii. and at V.ii.1–3.

34. A. C. Hamilton, *The Early Shakespeare* (San Marino, 1967), pp. 63–89; see especially pp. 74–5.

35. A detailed description of the debate on hierarchical and social contract forms of state can be found in David Hale, *The Body Politic* (The Hague, 1971).

36. Broude, 'Roman and Goth', pp. 27–34.

37. Sidney Anglo, 'The British history in early Tudor propaganda', *The Bulletin of the John Rylands Library*, 44 (1961), 17–48.

38. S. T. Bindoff, *Tudor England* (Harmondsworth, 1950), pp. 277–307. Similar triumphal scenes may be seen in Thomas Lodge, *The Wounds of Civil War* (1586–7), III. iii.

39. Waith's edition of *Titus* includes both history and ballad on Titus Andronicus, pp. 196–207; the reference here is to pp. 196–9.

40. Kahn, 'The rape in Shakespeare's *Lucrece*', p. 57.

41. Edgar Wind, *Pagan Mysteries in the Renaissance* (Oxford, 1958), pp. 89–90 and Figure 77 (Francesco Cossa, 'Mars Enchained by Venus'); and Tricomi, 'Mutilated garden'.

42. The significance of Aaron's blackness is worthy of another essay in itself. It must suffice here to point out that black men were seen as demonic (Aaron as Pluto: IV.iii.13), partly because of their colour but also, in the late sixteenth century, because of the merciless exploits of an actual Moor, Abd-el-Malck; these permutations are discussed by Eldred Jones, *Othello's Countrymen* (London, 1965). Evil Moors became stage commonplaces, as with Barabas in Marlowe's *The Jew of Malta* and Muly Mahamet in George Peele's *The Battle of Alcazar* (1588).

43. Merchant, *Death of Nature*, pp. 1–27.

44. Similar images occur at II.iii.194, 232, and V.ii.191.

45. Tricomi, 'Mutilated garden', p. 92.

46. Ibid., p. 91.

47. II.iii.280; Miola, 'Mythos of Shakespeare's Rome', p. 92.

48. See Suleiman, *Female Body*, pp. 1–2, 262–87.

49. Waith's edn, note to I.i.69.

50. Tamora becomes a personification of revenge in V. ii.

51. See Waith's edn, p. 36.

52. References to Philomela: II.iii.43; II.iv.26–7, 38–9; IV.i.47–8, 56; V.ii.194–5. *Metamorphoses* is brought on stage in IV.i.

53. This recalls the famous opening line of Sandra Gilbert and Susan Gubar, *The Madwoman in the Attic* (New Haven, CT, 1979).

11

'Funeral bak'd meats': Carnival and the Carnivalesque in *Hamlet*

MICHAEL D. BRISTOL

The action of *Hamlet* takes place against two contrasting back-drops. One of these is a world of international politics, charac-terised by diplomatic missions, intellectual and cultural exchange, and geopolitical struggle.[1] All of the young men in this story are engaged in this dynamic and cosmopolitan world that echoes the in-tellectual and political dynamism of Shakespeare's actual society. Claudius belongs to this world as well, but, as the representative of an older generation, he takes care to place himself and the activities of his court in a quite different social and cultural milieu when he proclaims a period of festive celebration that will honour simultane-ously his dead predecessor and his own marriage to the widowed queen. The funeral for Hamlet's father is combined with a wedding feast, and this odd mingling of grief and of festive laughter is typical of the play as a whole.

The personal struggle of Hamlet, his profound doubts about what to do and his agonised, sometimes hilarious reflections about his own uncertainty are the aspect of the play that modern audi-ences find most accessible and sympathetic. But this very private and personal tension is both clearer and more meaningful when it can be understood in the context of larger movements of social and cultural change. Hamlet has internalised strong oppositions in basic social values; he has a passionately felt loyalty to the traditional ethos of his murdered father and yet in some ways he more closely resembles his archenemy Claudius in his understanding of a more typically modern political reality. These fundamentally historical differences are experienced by Hamlet as psychological conflicts. Hamlet's question, 'What must I do?' can be usefully reinterpreted as the question of 'Where do I belong?' or even 'How can my life make sense within a social landscape of irreconcilable social difference?' The most effective critical strategy to adopt in this context, therefore, is to concentrate on the way Shakespeare has deployed the resources of Carnival to represent and at the same time to criticise important beliefs and practices in the official culture of his own time. Carnival is a vivid, intense, and highly dramatic way to make the complex social dialogue that is *Hamlet* much more audible.

Hamlet is a play that typifies Shakespeare's use of Carnival as the basis of his dramatic art. It is a text in which the language of popular festive form is deeply embedded in the structure of action and where the meanings privileged in the culture of Carnival are fully actualised. Although the play is filled with tragedy and horror, many of the scenes are extremely funny, and indeed for much of the action Hamlet and Claudius stalk each other like two murderous clowns attempting to achieve strategic advantage over the other. Claudius adopts certain popular, carnivalesque attitudes as a way to conceal his aggressive, rational calculation of self-interest behind a mask of traditional pieties, folk wisdom, and festive distractions. Hamlet's 'antic disposition' is also a kind of carnivalesque disguise or camouflage, although Hamlet is much more genuinely in touch with the popular festive sources of Carnival than Claudius, especially in his understanding of the corrosive and clarifying power of laughter. For Hamlet and for the audience as well, however, the larger meaning of Carnival emerges only gradually and is fully revealed in the grave-diggers' scene as a powerful transformation downward, or 'uncrowning', of the world of official culture, geopolitical conflict, and royal intrigue.

Carnival was observed throughout Europe during the early modern period, reaching its climax on Shrove Tuesday or Mardi Gras, just before the beginning of Lent. Traditionally this is a time of hedonistic excess and transgression. Carnival permits and actually encourages the unlimited consumption of special foods, drunkenness, and a high degree of sexual licence, which often leads to street violence and civil commotion. The custom of masking and disguise makes it easier for the participants to get away with these violations of social order, and indeed it is typical of Carnival that social order is literally turned upside down. Despite its notoriety as a time of excess, licence, and derangement, the word *Carnival* actually refers to and marks the beginning of a period of lenten renunciation; the word is derived from the Latin expression *carnem levare*, the taking away of meat or 'farewell to the flesh'. It is precisely this ambivalent, paradoxical, and unstable character that gives Carnival its social importance.

Misrule, inversion, and travesty are the typical strategies of the carnivalesque. A Carnival masquerade embodies an alternative set of rules for interpreting social reality. In these participatory celebrations traditional religious and political symbols are combined with humble objects from the kitchen and the workshop, and with images of bodily functions, especially those relating to food and eating. In Brueghel's painting *The Battle of Carnival and Lent*, the personification of Carnival rides on a wine barrel instead of a horse, and the combatants brandish cooking utensils instead of weapons. Various figures in Carnival's entourage wear articles of food or kitchenware on their heads – a kettle, a hat made of waffles – and Carnival himself is crowned with a meat pie that someone has bitten into.[2]

The comprehensive rethinking of the social world in terms of common everyday material and physical experience is central to the practice of 'uncrowning' – the fundamental transformation downward of popular festive imagery. Here the kettle or meat pie takes the place of the crown or helmet as the 'topmost' principle. In this way Carnival brings our knowledge of social reality down to earth and substitutes the body, its needs, and its capabilities, for more abstract and restrictive 'laws' of society and its organisation. Carnival draws attention to the relative and arbitrary character of official versions of political order. In this way the experience of Carnival opens up alternative possibilities for action and helps to facilitate creativity in the social sphere.

Although Carnival specifically refers only to festivities that immediately precede Lent, the typical Carnival experience of excess and social derangement is not limited to a single annual blowout. In fact, during the early modern period there were many regularly occurring feasts with typical carnivalesque features of material abundance, licence, and social effervescence.[3] In a further extension of the term, Carnival may also take in a class of social occasions held together by broad family resemblance – fairs, theatrical performances, public executions, and even spontaneous 'social dramas'. Carnival in this broader sense is characterised by its negativity and in-betweenness. It is the liminal occasion par excellence, something that happens betwixt and between the regularly scheduled events of ordinary life.

The combined sense of ambiguity and exteriority (or marginality) points to a further meaning for Carnival, not as a specific feast, a general type of celebration, or even a class of social occasions, but rather as a mode-of-being-in-the-world or mode-of-being-together-with-others. This is what Mikhail Bakhtin refers to when he speaks of Carnival as a 'second life of the people', with its own liturgy and its own system for the production and distribution of the good things of this life.[4]

Bakhtin's theories of Carnival are central to a more comprehensive and ambitious set of theories of human action, social initiative, and collective authority, all based on Bakhtin's highly original and distinctive theories of human language. For Bakhtin, language is not limited to verbal behaviour but encompasses gestures, physical actions, and even the organisation of space and time. Furthermore, language is characterised by a social diversity of 'speech types', the distinctive idiom, slang, or 'shop talk' of groups and communities. The visual, verbal, and gestural repertoires of Carnival are of particular importance as a kind of expressive resistance to the authorised and permitted languages of official culture. It is this possibility of purposeful opposition to injustice and oppression that gives the carnivalesque a particular importance for the many variants of Marxist critique or for any type of criticism that puts social struggle or conflict in the foreground of its concerns.

In Bakhtin's account, Carnival is very much more than just a particularly boisterous and extended holiday. For Bakhtin, Carnival expresses a fundamental truth about the world; its down-to-earth vocabularies, its affirmation of the body, its grotesque exaggeration and aggressive annihilation of all reified modes of legitimation in fact interpret the world in a more comprehensive, universal, and practical way than the official world-views and serious philosophies of elite culture. Furthermore, the knowledge of the social world sedimented in carnivalesque symbolic and participatory practice is available to the people as a resource to be used in defence of their own values, practices, and their own version of the 'good life' against the expropriations of a colonising social structure, whether feudal or capitalist. Carnival may inform actual strategic deliberations aimed at correcting specific injustices, but there is an even more fundamental tendency in the carnivalesque to abolish class difference and social inequality. Carnival both interprets the world and acts upon it, even when the participants cannot fully articulate what they are doing.

According to Bakhtin, then, Carnival constitutes a second world, or second culture, outside the world of official culture and political authority, where ordinary, unprivileged people act out a distinctive pattern of values. These values are generated out of the practical details of everyday life, and in particular from the various activities such as agricultural labour or the preparation of food by means of which human life is produced and reproduced. A central feature of this symbolic regime is a way of interpreting the human form in terms of what Bakhtin calls the grotesque body. Classical aesthetics represents the body in terms of closure, integrity, and rational proportion. In contrast to this, the grotesque body is open, unfinished, and unrestrained. The intact surfaces and well-defined contours of the classical body give way to a celebration of growth and bodily expansion. Instead, exaggerated shapes and openings – fat bellies, swollen breasts, open mouths, enlarged genitals – are affirmed and celebrated, but also ridiculed. The body as represented in its grotesque aspect is involved in continual exchange of materials with its environment; the enjoyment of food and sexuality, as well as the satisfactions of copious excretion, are represented as ambivalent. The grotesque interpretation acknowledges the body as both desirable *and* disgusting. The openness, vulnerability, and transience of the body are typically occasions for laughter. The ability of life to reproduce itself through eating and through sexuality are privileged metaphors that overturn formal ideologies based on rigid categories of status and privilege. In this pattern, death and physical dissolution are part of a system of symbols that represent a social and biological process of continuous rebirth and renewal. In this context, death may even be treated as an occasion for both laughter and grief.

The first scenes of *Hamlet* take place during a period of mourning for a dead king, Old Hamlet. His brother and successor Claudius proclaims a period of ambiguous festivity that serves as both funeral and wedding celebration. Dramatically, this gesture appears to be very similar to Duke Theseus's in *A Midsummer Night's Dream*. For Theseus the celebration of his wedding called for the banishment and exclusion of melancholy – a unison and concord of emotions that parallels the social unity of the various ranks and functions in the community. Claudius's call to the wedding feast reveals a deep ambivalence, however. The marriage is in many ways scandalous, tainted by intimations of incest, adultery, and indecorous haste. And, as the play very quickly reveals, there is no real and enduring social unity in Denmark that Claudius can appeal to. Nevertheless, Claudius tries to establish the legitimacy of his situation by a careful balancing of two evidently contradictory forms of celebration.

> **King** Though yet of Hamlet our dear brother's death
> The memory be green, and that it us befitted
> To bear our hearts in grief, and our whole kingdom
> To be contracted in one brow of woe,
> Yet so far hath discretion fought with nature
> That we with wisest sorrow think on him
> Together with remembrance of ourselves.
> Therefore our sometime sister, now our queen,
> Th' imperial jointress to this warlike state,
> Have we, as 'twere with a defeated joy,
> With an auspicious and a dropping eye,
> With mirth in funeral, and with dirge in marriage,
> In equal scale weighing delight and dole,
> Taken to wife.
>
> (I.ii.1–14)

Where Theseus wished to banish melancholy, Claudius must embrace it; his revels require a mixed decorum, the unification of contrary impulses. Claudius compares the mortality of a king as a specific human being with the immortality of his office, and affirms that the continuing vitality of society is independent of the transience of contingent individuals. The death of the old gives scope to the new and emergent. The marriage to Gertrude expresses this idea of succession and renewal at a sexual and bodily level; the disturbing candour with which that sexuality is expressed on stage is essential to the situation, since it 'brings down' the projects and ambitions of kingship to the material and earthly level of appetite and desire.

Taken out of context, Claudius's speech expresses a truthful intuition about death, change, and human individuality that is in many ways typical of the folk wisdom embedded in the carnivalesque. Individuals are never static entities but instead experience manifold changes and transformations. Communal life and its institutions create a background of relative permanency against which the multifarious transformations, substitutions, and surprises of each individual life must be played out. The transgressive character of Claudius's marriage to Gertrude expresses this carnivalesque understanding of death both in its affirmation of sexual appetite and in its endorsement of shifting social identity. In a sense, Claudius functions here as a complex variant of the Lord of Misrule. He violates decorum and makes a mockery of kingship by appearing in the usurped finery of the 'real' king. As a Lord of Misrule Claudius is no doubt intended to prompt our derision by virtue of the falseness of his claims, but he is also likely to encourage our mockery both for the office he usurps and for its rightful holder. He has killed his predecessor and replaced him in the queen's bed. His coronation and marriage, a kind of joke at his victim's expense, can be an occasion of Carnival mirth – an affirmation of continuing sexual, as well as political, life.

In the specific context of *Hamlet*, however, Claudius cannot really embody or represent the values of Carnival and plebeian culture in any simple or straightforward way. The link of death with marriage and sexuality as well as the affirmation of misrule are carnivalesque themes that Claudius appropriates in order to make legitimate his own questionable authority. Although he appears to understand popular culture, he is in fact both the agent and the beneficiary of a social order that excludes the popular element and expropriates its resources. Furthermore, his use of the carnivalesque is intended only as a mask for the strategic advancement of private goals and ambitions. Such a 'privatising' of carnivalesque transgression and sensuality is a fundamental distortion of the collective and communal orientations typical of plebeian culture. There is no sense in which Claudius acts in the interests of the excluded plebeian culture and although he is associated with misrule he is neither a popular king nor a champion of the popular element.

Claudius does not rely exclusively on a vocabulary of carnivalesque celebration of change as the source of his legitimacy. He also employs more conventional philosophical rhetoric to disguise the aspect of misrule in his claim to kingship.

> King   'Tis sweet and commendable in your nature, Hamlet,
> To give these mourning duties to your father.
> But you must know your father lost a father,
> That father lost, lost his, and the survivor bound

In filial obligation for some term
To do obsequious sorrow. But to persever
In obstinate condolement is a course
Of impious stubbornness, 'tis unmanly grief.

(I.ii.87–94)

This is a traditional language of Christian patience and resignation that is linked to the language of Carnival in seeing death as 'a part of life as a whole – its indispensable component, the condition of its constant renewal and rejuvenation ... Death is included in life, and together with Birth determines its eternal movement'.[5] Of course Claudius's appropriation of Christian doctrine is no more 'truly legitimate' than his appropriation of the spirit of Carnival. And there is a further irony in all of this. Claudius evidently wants to use Carnival as a means for reinforcing and making legitimate his otherwise dubious political authority. But Carnival typically mocks and uncrowns all authority. And, as the action will make clear, Carnival cannot be controlled 'from above'; Claudius's scheme to consolidate his power by means of a carnivalised variant of kingly authority will be fatally compromised by other versions of a downward carnivalesque movement articulated by Hamlet, the players, and the grave-diggers.

Although the Danish court participates in the traditional festive observance of political succession and regal hospitality, Hamlet sees himself as excluded from the conviviality of this society. The custom of excessive drinking, evidently a traditional practice in the Danish court, is viewed by Hamlet as corruption and decadence. His initial rejection of all forms of carnivalesque derangement, whether traditional or not, is symbolised by his black suit and his mournful attitude. The motivation of that exclusion is his revulsion toward the ambivalent and contradictory decorum of the festive practices of the Danish court. His perception of the feasting and revelry is expressed in his first greeting to Horatio, where he complains of his mother's haste in remarrying.

> **Hamlet**   Thrift, thrift, Horatio, the funeral bak'd-meats
> Did coldly furnish forth the marriage tables.
>
> (I.ii.180–1)

It is a bitter jest about the unseemliness, the indecorousness of the situation, that is at once a moral judgement on the behaviour of Claudius and Gertrude as well as a philosophically principled objection to what he takes to be a scandalous adherence to certain carnivalesque customs within the court. He has already explained how the outward presentation of self ought to correspond to the inner state. His own suit of woe, he insists, bears a constant and natural resemblance to the grief that excludes all other feeling in Hamlet. But conventional signs of grief are not enough in themselves to '[denote] [him] truly' (I.ii.83); since others dissemble and falsify outward symbols, strong action – but of a kind he may not yet recognise – will be required to reinvest signs with their true meanings.

In the strained and deceptively festive atmosphere of Claudius's court, Hamlet stands firmly for the values of seriousness; as the action begins, he does not perform nor play nor dissimulate. His laughter is satiric and judgemental, the laughter of rational evaluations. He feels particular revulsion about eating and drinking; the funeral meats that grace the wedding banquet are offensive to Hamlet in the way they actualise a process of continuity oblivious to the distinctions he wishes to make. Meat is the link between the living and the dead; in the wedding feast / funeral banquet, the continuity of social life is affirmed over the finite individual.

Claudius then can be interpreted as an individual representation of the grotesque body – incomplete, unfinished, deeply implicated in the lower functions of sexuality – and of its appetites, yet the full implications of carnivalesque uncrowning never enter his self-understanding. Carnival laughter, acknowledgement of the body in its open and festive manifestations, ambivalence of emotion, and mixed decorum have all been co-opted by power and authority, without the recognition that these strategies necessarily entail a critique of authority that is inimical to the interests of power. Hamlet's deliberate self-exclusion from the festive rests upon hunches and suspicions about the real meaning of the feasting in the Danish court that are more fully developed later in the play. He cannot return to Wittenberg and to the life of rational clarity it evidently represents for him; he must instead become part of and in a sense accept the complex and ambivalent world of courtly and popular festivity in order to understand it.

The environment of Denmark's court is dominated by dissimulation and intrigue; Hamlet defines his problem as the penetration of this intrigue, the unmasking and exposure of all dissimulation.[6] And yet neither his own rhetoric nor the interrogation of others is sufficient to consolidate his knowledge, let alone persuade others.

Even his counterfestivity – the antic disposition, the dumb show, and the re-enactment of the murder – falls short of producing knowledge. A more decisive act is required and this comes finally with the killing of Polonius. This murder is a mistake, but Polonius's identity is fixed at last, and, for Hamlet, words begin to have more solid meanings, as he laughs the guts offstage.

The killing reveals to Hamlet the clarifying possibilities of violence, the way in which the identity of a thing may be known by killing it and removing it from the changes of living experience. It also forces Hamlet back to the issues of the body and to a new understanding of 'funeral bak'd-meats'.

> **King**   Now, Hamlet, where's Polonius?
> **Hamlet**   At supper.
> **King**   At supper? where?
> **Hamlet**   Not where he eats, but where 'a is eaten; a certain convocation of politic worms are e'en at him. Your worm is your only emperor for diet: we fat all creatures else to fat us, and we fat ourselves for maggots; your fat king and your lean beggar is but variable service, two dishes, but to one table – that's the end.
>
> (IV.iii.16–24)

Here the rhetoric Hamlet uses is carnivalised; emperors are uncrowned so as to be used as food while worms have become 'politic' and imperial.

By opening Polonius's body with the sword, Hamlet has fixed his identity in the endless circular process in which life devours life and individual pretension is brought down to earth by the constant struggles for existence of 'worms' human and natural.

> **Hamlet**   A man may fish with the worm that hath eat of a king, and eat of the fish that hath fed of that worm.
> **King**   What dost thou mean by this?
> **Hamlet**   Nothing but to show you how a king may go a progress through the guts of a beggar.
>
> (IV.iii.26–30)

According to the principles of rationality by which he tried to operate at first, Hamlet was required to make distinctions between father and uncle, between Hyperion and satyr, king and beggar, human and worm. Using the logic of grotesque Carnival equivocation, he can now see an equivalence between Old Hamlet and Claudius. The royal 'progress', which affirms hierarchy, social superiority, and

political power, is brought down to the lower functions of the body –
a king's pretensions are devoured by the unprivileged.

Hamlet has learned the language of grotesque equivocation and
its critique of power as an outsider in the intrigues of the court, but
he is not yet acquainted with the popular sources of that language
within the everyday life and practical conscious of the common
people. The fullest elaboration of the carnivalesque pattern of uncrowning is presented in the grave-diggers' scene. Here actual representatives of the unprivileged appear as clowns who give direct
articulation to the perspective of a culture in which the meanings of
Carnival are most fully and accurately understood. The opening dialogue of the clowns anchors the graveyard scene in a concrete
social milieu; the clowns typify unprivileged labour in their work,
their language, and the social attitudes they express.

> **First Clown** Will you ha' the truth an't? If this had not been a
> gentlewoman, she should have been buried out a' Christian burial.
> **Second Clown** Why, there thou say'st, and the more pity that great
> folk should have count'nance in this world to drown or hang
> themselves more than their even-Christen.
>
> (V.i.22–7)

Christian burial is, of course, given in accordance with the spiritual
condition of the deceased at the presumed moment of death. The
clowns perceive very clearly, however, how wealth and privilege
influence such determination, so that social distinction seems to
persist into the afterlife. But the joking about suicide as a privilege
reserved for 'great folk' is extremely complicated. There is the direct
implication of resentment over privilege of any kind, resentment
grounded in the principle of 'even-Christen', the belief that all men
are equal in God's sight. At the same time the grave-digger expresses a certain grim satisfaction with the particular privilege in
question – let them all drown themselves if that's the privilege they
insist on.

The preoccupation with privilege and social class is given even
more direct expression in the grave-diggers' discussion of the
ancient origins of 'gentlemen'.

> **First Clown** There is no ancient gentlemen but gard'ners, ditchers,
> and grave-makers. They hold up Adam's profession.
> **Second Clown** Was he a gentleman?
> **First Clown** 'A was the first that ever bore arms.

> **Second Clown**   Why, he had none.
> **First Clown**   What, art a heathen? How dost thou understand
> the Scripture? The Scripture says Adam digg'd. Could he dig
> without arms?
>
> (V.i.28–36)

This is a clear and explicit critique of the basis for social hierarchy in gentility and the privilege of 'bearing arms'. The grave-digger's reference to Adam digging restores a subordinated meaning for 'arms' not as the signifier of social difference, but rather as the sign of social equality. All men and women have real arms, as opposed to a symbolic 'coat of arms', and all men and women thus share the capacity to work so as to create subsistence. The grave-digger's speech clearly echoes the nascent egalitarian ideology expressed in the following anonymous verse that was popular in various early modern protest movements such as the diggers or the levellers.

> When Adam delved
> And Eve span
> Who was then
> The Gentleman?

Gardeners and grave-makers, and by extension everyone who does productive labour, are the true descendants of Adam and thus the only real 'gentlefolk'.

Against the perspective of death and burial all claims to hierarchical superiority are nullified, all the 'serious' claims of economic, political, or moral systems become the objects of laughter. The doomsday image of the grave is from this perspective not something grim and gloomy but, on the contrary, the occasion for 'drink' and merriment. The grave-diggers' jokes reflect an alternative hierarchy of ontological categories in which death and change are sovereign and permanent, while such symbolic edifices as church, state, and society are killed, buried, dissolved back into the earth by the patient and persistent labour of the grave-digger.

In the grave-diggers' world-view, doomsday is a horizon that corresponds to the overthrow of social inequality. The grave-digger enacts this philosophy by staging the grotesque exchange between life and death as he tosses various skulls and bones out of the grave. Hamlet and Horatio enter as he works; after some extended raillery, the clown shows Hamlet a particularly interesting skull.

> **Clown** Here's a skull that hath lien you i' th' earth three and
> twenty years. ... A pestilence on him for a mad rogue! 'a poured a
> flagon of Rhenish on my head once. This same skull, sir, was, sir,
> Yorick's skull, the King's jester.
>
> (V.i.161–9)

There is no reason to doubt the grave-digger's assertion about the
skull's identity – but there is nothing to confirm it either. A skull
presents no identifying features, no countenance, that allows us to
recognise individuality. As far as the audience can tell, Yorick's
skull looks just like the other skulls that have by now been tossed
about onstage. But this absence of individual features does not
make the grave-digger's identification of the skull less cogent. The
entity known as 'Yorick' consists of a relationship between social
integument (guise, false-face, persona) and a 'viewer' or 'spectator'
(social Other) to acknowledge it.

Using the prop to focus his imagination Hamlet reconstitutes the
social meaning sedimented in a grinning skull.

> **Hamlet** Alas, poor Yorick! I knew him, Horatio, a fellow of infinite
> jest, of most excellent fancy. He hath bore me on his back a thou-
> sand times, and now how abhorr'd in my imagination it is! my
> gorge rises at it. Here hung those lips that I have kiss'd I know not
> how oft. Where be your gibes now, your gambols, your songs,
> your flashes of merriment, that were wont to set the table on a roar?
>
> (V.i.172–8)

The genuine 'community' the prince remembers is dead and buried,
but this is the moment of its resurrection as an object of nostalgia.
The old jester is dead, but the power of laughter is indestructible.
Even a dead jester can make us laugh; here the 'dead' mock the
'living', by reminding us that there is a kind of equality between 'a
pestilent rogue' and 'my lady'. The contemplation of mortality
becomes funny.

> **Hamlet** Imperious Caesar, dead and turn'd to clay,
> Might stop a hole to keep the wind away.
> O that that earth which kept the world in awe
> Should patch a wall t' expel the [winter's] flaw!
>
> (V.i.199–202)

All the categories of social existence, gender, rank, metier, and so
on, are relative and impermanent; the skull is the negation of

identity, an ominous parody of the human face. The imperial image of glory and majesty – Caesar, Alexander – is uncrowned by plebeian consciousness that views power as a bloody and farcical masquerade. In addition, the scene fundamentally disrupts the genre to which the play nominally belongs.

Hamlet is a tragedy, and the story the play tells happens long after the jester has died. In a sense this might be taken as an exemplary definition of tragedy, that is, as a story in which the skull as a memento mori replaces the actual jester. But in this play the jester's absence is more than offset by the appearance of a number of other clowns, including most notably Hamlet himself. The image of a man in a graveyard contemplating a skull is the typical representation of *memento mori*, but here this dark, forbidding symbol of the values of seriousness and penitential self-renunciation has itself been carnivalised. The sense of the tragic is not, however, diminished or 'subverted' by this; instead the laughter typical of the carnivalesque takes on greater philosophical depth and complexity.

The complex 'knowledge' Hamlet achieves at the edge of the grave does not stop with Caesar's return to dust, for at this moment the funeral procession for Ophelia comes onstage. The scene is a counter-statement to the grave-diggers' laughter. Ceremony is preserved, social convention is affirmed because even in these unhappy circumstances the value of the person remains. Imperious Caesar, whose function now is to stop a bunghole, is a suitable object for laughter and derision, but Ophelia's death is no joking matter. The ceremonies at the grave link death and marriage again, but in a more obviously disturbing way than before, for here death does not give birth to new possibility – death proscribes marriage and forestalls possibility of renewed life. A moment earlier the prince reflected on the impermanence of individuality; now he 'goes down' into the grave, to give himself a definite name and title, to struggle with an enemy, and in spite of the lessons in equivocation he learned from the grave-digger, to proclaim his love in heightened and theatrical rhetoric.

> **Hamlet**   'Swounds, show me what thou't do.
> Woo't weep? woo't fight? woo't fast? woo't tear thyself?
> Woo't drink up eisel, eat a crocadile?
> I'll do't. Dost thou come here to whine?
> To outface me with leaping in her grave?
> Be buried quick with her, and so will I.

And if thou prate of mountains, let them throw
Millions of acres on us, till our ground,
Singeing his pate against the burning zone,
Make Ossa like a wart! Nay, and thou'lt mouth,
I'll rant as well as thou.

(V.i.260–70)

To experience the grave is to pass beyond all histrionics; having seen this, Hamlet now indulges in a moment of exaggerated theatricality, reaching for the grand gesture, challenging Laertes to 'outface' him. Even standing in the grave Hamlet cannot stop acting, he cannot refrain from 'making a scene'. The laughing or grinning skull may objectify or represent an existence that is beyond dissimulation, it may instruct us in the impermanence of social categories, it may even humble us by dissolving our claims to status in a grim and frightening laugh – but the knowledge offered by the skull is never actualised on this side of the grave. This knowledge applies to everyone, whether aristocratic or plebeian. What typifies plebeian consciousness in this respect is the blunt and fearless acknowledgement of death as a process of social levelling.

At this point it is useful to raise a question about staging. What happens to the grave-digger when the coffin of Ophelia is brought on stage? The text provides no answer to this question, since the stage directions indicate only that all exit after the king's speech to Laertes. The director is faced with a number of choices – the grave-digger can retire discreetly, or he can remain onstage in a visible position without joining the mourners – in effect upstaging the entire proceeding. The director, in making this decision, must commit herself on the question of social distinction, dramatic tone – that is, on the entire complex of issues related to social degree and social hierarchy.

If the grave-digger discreetly exits during the burial sequence, his function as a popular chorus interpreting the values and the conflicts of the dominant culture is weakened. Plebeian values and popular critique would be given only limited expression in order to return with great assurance to the 'real' or official problematics of the court. But if he remains onstage throughout the burial, the grave-digger can gather up the skulls and prepare for the next scene. The grave-digger's resulting presence through Ophelia's burial would then amplify his function as a Plebeian chorus. He is the man whose houses last till doomsday. His presence would alter the audience's perception of Ophelia (who has the privilege to kill herself), of Laertes, of Hamlet, of the whole court. He can watch the grief, the ambition, the anxiety over privilege, decorum, and ceremony with an attitude of amused indifference.

The pattern of festivity is completed in the final scene, where Claudius again presides over a scene of revelry. The main festive sequence is from ritual to dramatic entertainment to game and sport: Claudius celebrates a marriage and a funeral, Claudius views a play, Claudius welcomes home a nobleman and enjoys a bout of fencing. In each of these scenes the king acts as host at a feast. We see him display the gestures and attitudes of merriment, or holiday, turning away from serious business, to indulge his appetites. Hamlet refuses participation in the festive process at the stage of ritual; he commits himself to partial but conditional involvement through dramatic artifice; when festivity opens into game, when genuine hazard and exercise of skill create a series of dynamic possibilities, his participation in the festive scene is complete.

But what does it mean to be fully engaged in a 'festive process' in the world of this play? The logic of everything that has come before is by now transparent; the stage must be piled high with slaughtered 'meat'. The two most powerful families have been completely exterminated; old kinship relationships are eliminated, traditional claims to the throne are cancelled and the situation is open for whatever is new and emergent. The redundancy of Claudius's assassination (execution) by Hamlet is of course entirely appropriate here; both aspects of Claudius's kingship – the active and the festive, the sword and cup of wine, are turned against him.

An important tendency in Carnival is fulfilled in this final scene. While it would be unusual for an actual Carnival to result in an organised insurrection of the common people, violent social protest was not uncommon and sometimes this violence could take the form of large-scale class warfare.[7] In *Hamlet* the violence and bloodshed latent in a Carnival arises from factional antagonism rather than class conflict, but it really does bring about a change in the political order. However, the regime of Fortinbras hardly represents the overthrow of aristocratic authority in favour of a popular and egalitarian redistribution of power. To the contrary, it seems likely that a stringent administrative and social discipline amounting to martial law will be imposed.

The party's over. The festive process we witness here does not move from rigidity through release to clarification, at least not in the basically reassuring sense of a controlled and exceptional 'holiday' turning us back to an unquestioned harmony. The real

logic of festivity is the dissolution, and finally the extinction of identity, the annihilation of the individual in the historical continuum.
The process, on the other hand, does not come to an end, and so
witnesses must be implicated in what has been acted out.

> **Hamlet** You that look pale and tremble at this chance,
> That are but mutes or audience to this act,
> Had I but time – as this fell sergeant, Death,
> Is strict in his arrest – O, I could tell you –
> But let it be.
>
> (V.ii.316–20)

Hamlet is about to leave the stage and his concern with how his
story will be told to the 'mutes and audience' suggest that there is
no real end to the histrionics. Horatio will 'stand in' for him, so
that Hamlet must compel his friend to 'refuse festivity' just as he
has done before.

'Mutes and audience' may be passive, they may be excluded from
privileged knowledge, and yet somehow the record of one's deed
vis-à-vis this witnessing body remains crucial.

> O God, Horatio, what a wounded name,
> Things standing thus unknown, shall I leave behind me!
>
> (V.ii.326–7)

Fortinbras enters to the sound of drums and trumpets; melancholy
joins with mirth again as Hamlet becomes a prop in someone else's
political pageantry – pageantry offered to an audience of ordinary
men and women in the 'yet unknowing world'. The play opens
toward a future that is not all that different in certain respects from
the events so far acted out, at least as far as the tension between
'high' political drama and a 'low' audience of non-participating witnesses is concerned. The grave-digger represents that 'low audience'
on the stage and serves as a chorus expressing their way of seeing
the events of high political struggle.

Carnival, with its ambivalent and contradictory language, uncrowns the shifting rationales used to explicate political intrigue
and supplies an alternative reading of history based on the
arbitrariness and transience of political authority.

> And so they said that these matters bee Kynges games, as it were
> stage playes, and for the more part plaied upon scafoldes. In which
> pore men be but lookers on ...[8]

These 'pore men' know and understand the action through the Carnival linking of life and death, their rhythmic alternation, and the mixed emotions this rhythm brings forth.

From *Hamlet: Case Studies in Contemporary Criticism*, ed. Suzanne L. Wofford (New York, 1994), pp. 348–67.

NOTES

[Michael Bristol's *Carnival and Theatre: Plebian Culture and the Structure of Authority in Renaissance England* (London, 1985), was a major stimulus in prompting analyses of Shakespeare's works, particularly his comedies, in terms of Bakhtian's concept of Carnival. Bristol's essay on *Hamlet* demonstrates the relevance of Carnival, as a mode of social inversion and misrule, to the analysis of tragic structure. Ed.]

1. See Thomas Metscher, 'Shakespeare in the Context of Renaissance Europe', *Science and Society*, 41 (1976), 17–24.

2. See Claude Gaignebet, 'Le Combat de Carnaval et de Carême de P. Breughel (1559)', *Annales: Economies Sociétés, Civilizations*, 27 (1972), 313–43, and Natalie Z. Davis, 'The Reasons of Misrule', *Society and Culture in Early Modern France* (Stanford, CA, 1975), pp. 97–123.

3. See Claude Gaignebet, *Le Carnaval: Essais de mythologie populaire* (Paris, 1974).

4. Mikhail Bakhtin, *The World of Rabelais*, trans. Hélène Iswolsky (Cambridge, 1968).

5. Ibid., p. 50.

6. See Maynard Mack, 'The World of *Hamlet*', *Yale Review*, 41 (1959), 502–23, and Rosalie Colie, *Shakespeare's Living Art* (Princeton, NJ, 1974).

7. See Emmanuel LeRoy Ladurie, *Carnival in Romans*, trans. Mary Feeney (New York, 1979).

8. Thomas More, *The History of King Richard III*, ed. Richard S. Sylvester, *Yale Edition of the Complete Works of St. Thomas More* (New Haven, CT, 1963), p. 81.

12

The Ideology of Superfluous Things: *King Lear* as Period Piece

MARGRETA DE GRAZIA

> [O]ur basest beggars
> Are in the poorest thing superfluous.

Born in the same year (1818), Jacob Burckhardt and Karl Marx together (though quite independently) gave birth to the Renaissance. Not to the Renaissance as the rebirth of antiquity but to the Renaissance as the birth of the Modern – the Renaissance, that is, as *Early* Modern – the period that anticipated the future rather than recovered the past.[1] In Burckhardt's 1860 *The Civilization of the Renaissance in Italy*, that birth took the form of individualism; in Marx's 1867 *Capital*, it took the form of capitalism. In broad terms (periodisation requires them), Burckhardt's cultural history provided Renaissance studies with its working notion of the subject – the individual; Marx's economic theory provided it with its working notion of the object – the commodity.

The differences between Burckhardt and Marx are vast. They wrote two different kinds of history (Burckhardt's cultural history juxtaposed synchronic Nietzschean fragments while Marx's economic history unfolded a diachronic Hegelian continuum) and had two different politics (Burckhardt feared levelling progressive reform while Marx envisioned a revolutionary classless society).[2] There is one thing, however, which Burckhardt's subject and Marx's object have in common: each excludes the other. Burckhardt's individuated subject is cut off from objects; Marx's commodified object is cut off from subjects.

INDIVIDUALS AND COMMODITIES

To attain autonomy, Burckhardt's subject must be removed from objects, both those it might own and those it might make. Indeed, the break between the two serves to differentiate the Renaissance from the Middle Ages: 'In the Middle Ages both sides of human consciousness – that which was turned within as that which was turned without – lay dreaming or half awake beneath a common veil.'[3] Only after the great Renaissance awakening was the subject able to assume its proper distance from objects: 'an *objective* treatment and consideration ... of all the things of this world became possible.' The subjective side also asserted itself: 'man became a spiritual individual, and recognised himself as such.' It is precisely this distancing of the subject from the object that conferred upon the subject a new power over the external world.[4] Burckhardt's exemplary individuals are often set apart from objects, by low and illegitimate birth like Alberti or by exile like Dante.[5] The same distance, however, can also be cultivated, as it is by the artist who stands apart from his material, the ruler from his state, the humanist from his texts. Like Descartes who begins his *Meditations* by abstracting himself from objects – from the winter cloak he is wearing, from the paper on which he is writing – the subject must remove himself from the world of objects in order to be fully conscious and capable.[6]

Marx's Early Modern object, the commodity, denies its relation to persons by effacing its origin in social production. It is precisely this denial that distinguishes a commodity from any other kind of object: the product of the medieval artisan, for example. The table the artisan makes is a product but no commodity because it retains a relation to him, either through his use or that of his feudal lord. But once that table is exchanged for something outside the maker's domain (money, for example), it enters a system of value in which its relation to social labour is misrepresented as a relation between objects. Objects then give off the false (and fetish-producing) impression that their value is intrinsic to them rather than the result of the social labour that produced them: 'The social character of labour appears to us to be an objective character of the products themselves.'[7] A wry little allegory in *Capital* has the table taking on airs, standing on its own four feet as if it had come into the world free-standing, and, more pretentiously still, standing on its head, as if to give the Hegelian impression that metaphysical ideas are the basis of material reality rather than the other way around.[8] Footloose and fancy-free, as it were, the table is alienated from its maker – indeed estranged, to the point that it turns on him like a menacing stranger or foreigner: 'the object confronts him as something hostile and alien.'[9]

Untrammelled by inherited objects, the Burckhardtian individual can flourish on the basis of his own talents. Disengaged from productive subjects, the Marxist commodity can circulate on the basis of its exchange value. In both cases, the Early Modern subject / object schism allows for mobility. Defined by intrinsic merit rather than extrinsic goods ('relying solely on his personal talent'),[10] the bourgeois subject can rise through the social ranks. Valued in its own right ('Could commodities themselves speak, they would say: ... What ... does belong to us as objects, is our value'),[11] the capitalist commodity can circulate freely in the market. Each has to deny the other in order to move freely, the precondition for Modern politics (bourgeois democracy) and Modern economics (capitalism). Indeed it is precisely this movement, this breaking away from an inert feudal period or 'Dark Ages', that gives the Renaissance pride of place as the onset of the Modern: the beginning of Modern man for Burckhardt, the beginning of capitalism for Marx.[12] It is at this point that history starts its inexorable progress forward, from Early Modern, through Modern, Late Modern, to Postmodern and perhaps onward beyond that.

The Burckhardtian and Marxian accounts have, without notice, come together in recent discussions of late sixteenth- and early seventeenth-century English theatre. Jean-Christophe Agnew has emphasised the importance of the traditional geographical proximity of the theatre and the marketplace, the stage and the stalls; the success of both institutions, he argues, depended on fluidity: 'the practical liquidity of the commodity form and the imaginative liquidity of the theatrical form.'[13] For Douglas Bruster, it is not simply that the theatre is *like* a market, it *is* a market ('London's playhouses were, of course, actual markets') based on the same mechanisms of commodification and consumerism:[14] as the market converted money into, say, a slab of bacon, so too the theatre converted the price of admission into, say, a fantasy of revenge.[15] The London theatre, then, emerges as a locus of double convertibility:

where actors change into characters (who often change into other characters) and where money converts into spectacle. The theatre thus seems the perfect site for observing the Renaissance as Early Modern: the fluidity of both identities and commodities.

The fluidity that characterises the Early Modern period is also seen to characterise not only what is arguably its dominant cultural institution, but also the productions of that institution, particularly its most memorable ones – those by Shakespeare. Criticism for the past two generations has tended to situate Shakespeare in history rather than assume his universality. This has generally meant locating him at the start of the ever-receding Modern; what most concerns us here-and-now is seen as having its origins in him there-and-then. Shakespeare thus comes to mark the passage into the modern age, often serving as a transitional figure between Medieval and Modern, his chronology itself often seen to display the break in the historical continuum, his shift from comedy to tragedy coinciding with the break from old to new (coinciding too with the turn of the century), from feudal collectivity to bourgeois individuality, from manor production to market commodification.[16]

In recent years *King Lear* in particular has been read in relation to this historical divide. Numerous readings have removed the play from its indeterminate once-upon-a-time frame (not to mention its wooden Tillyardian frame)[17] to situate it in the historically specific context of its writing (*c.* 1605–10). The play has accordingly been read as dramatising any number of relations to that momentous transition from one social formation to another (feudal to capitalist) and from one type of individual to another (loyal to self-interested). We thus have readings that, empowered by Lawrence Stone's *Crisis of the Aristocracy*, see *Lear* tottering on the brink between old and new, Hooker and Hobbes, nostalgic for receding social ties and values and wary of emergent selfish drives and impulses.[18] Other readings see *Lear* clearing the way for this break by dramatising the exhaustion of older structures and beliefs (absolutism, supernaturalism, spiritualism) that cave in from the very weight of their own contradictions in unwitting preparation for their supersession.[19] *Lear* has also been read as venturing a brief sortie into capitalism, only to retreat back to a familiar feudalism – an advisedly 'retrograde movement'.[20] Still other accounts find the play more impetuous, rushing headlong into the Modern, almost a half-century ahead of its time in anticipating such radical sects as the Levellers and even the Ranters and Diggers, pushing ahead

toward the upset of the Civil War, 'moving toward something genuinely new' that looks precipitously like the rise of the proletariat –
which, it must be said, as portrayed in Lear's invocations and
Tom's simulations, look more like the *lumpenproletariat*.[21] Finally,
Lear has been read so progressively as to extend right into the
Modern, specifically that of 1930s sharecroppers and New Deal
reform, demonstrating its precocious capacity to engage, especially
through the voice of Lear himself, in 'an emergent structural analysis of power and class relations'.[22] In all these readings, the
influence of periodisation is at work, predisposing criticism to see
the play's issues in terms of the great historical shift from the
Medieval to the Modern. Each reading sees the play as more or less
intrepidly gesturing toward (or away from) the future, as if it were
doing its part to start (or forestall) the rolling historical ball on its
teleological course into the Modern.

So what we have is a range of readings positioning *King Lear*
in relation to the Early Modern: pre-, proto-, retro-, avant-garde,
and ultra / trans-early Modern *King Lear* respectively. As Fredric
Jameson concludes, it may be that we have no other way of being
historical than by periodising; some division of the vast historical
span is necessary in order to have an object for historical study.[23]
The question is, then: in our eagerness to make the Renaissance relevant to the Modern, have we not been precipitous in identifying it
as the onset of the Modern? This is not to say that nascent individualism and capitalism cannot be found in England around
Shakespeare's time. Yet it is to ask, does it make sense to make the
nascent dominant before history does?[24] For that is surely what we
do, even by intensely focusing on it as such. There is a way in which
seeing the Renaissance as the Early-Now commits itself to the very
universalising tendency that historicising set out to avoid in the first
place. As if *the* relevant history were a prior version of what we
already are and live. It is a dynamic universalising to be sure, rich
with gradations and nuances, but a universalisation all the same. It
is what Foucault following Nietzsche would avoid by replacing a
teleologically driven continuum with proliferative genealogies or ar-
chaeologies.[25] The reading that follows below makes no pretence
of avoiding periodisation, however, for it too exists in relation to it.
Set resolutely *against* the Modern, it could easily be added to the
list compiled above, with a new prefix: *anti*-Early Modern. The
essay is about how *King Lear* blocks the mobility identified since
the nineteenth century with the Modern – through its locking of

persons into things, proper selves into property, subjectivity effects into personal effects – in an attempt to withstand flux or fluidity, superflux or superfluity.

THINGS AND PERSONS

Traditionally it has been Gloucester's experience that has been seen to double Lear's. The title pages of the early quartos, however, suggest that it is Edgar's life rather than his father's that makes up the subplot: 'True Chronicle Historie of the life and death of King Lear and his three Daughters. With the unfortunate life of Edgar, sonne and heire to the Earle of Gloster and his sullen and assumed humor of Tom of Bedlam.'[26] When character is dominant, Gloucester's plight seems more like Lear's: both are old men suffering at the hands of their children. Once objects are admitted, however, Edgar's story makes the more compelling counterpart: both men are detached from their possessions. Lear and Edgar both comment on their shared experience: Lear imagines that Tom too must have been stripped down by his daughters ('nothing could have subdu'd nature / To such a lowness but his unkind daughters', III.iv.69–70); and behind Edgar's sympathy for Lear is his own experience of being cut off ('that which makes me bend makes the King bow: / He childed as I fathered!' III.vi.109–10). Through the lives of both titular and subtitular characters, the play dramatises the relation of being and having. As we shall see, removing what a person *has* simultaneously takes away what a person *is*.

If having is tantamount to being, *not* having is tantamount to *non*-being – to being nothing. Edgar disentitled concludes 'Edgar I nothing am' (II.iii.21); Lear divested is, in the Fool's words, an 'O without a figure ... nothing' (I.iv.192, 194). And yet both of these descriptions prove too absolute. Though Lear believes that Tom has given away all – 'Couldst thou save nothing? Wouldst thou give 'em all?' (III.iv.64) – he misses something; as the Fool points out, Tom 'reserv'd a blanket' (l.65). So too when he claims he himself has given all – 'I gave you all' (II.iv.248) – he forgets something, his 'reservation of an hundred knights' (I.i.132). Both king and beggar by holding something back (in reserve) hold on to themselves, however fragmentarily. What they cling to (or in Edgar's case, what clings to him) is hardly necessary for subsistence. Lear, as his daughters point out, does not need his train in a household staffed with twice as many to attend him. Nor does Tom's blanket serve his needs; if Regan's gorgeous gown scarcely keeps her warm (because of silk? because décolleté?), it is no wonder 'Tom's a-cold' (III.iv. 57, 170, and IV.i.52) in his loincloth. As Lear argues in defending his right to keep his retainers, need – subsistence – is not the point:

> O, reason not the need! our basest beggars
> Are in the poorest thing superfluous.
> (II.iv.264–5)

All persons, from highest to lowest, must possess something beyond need – a superfluous thing. Tom's blanket is such a thing, the beggar's equivalent of the king's train, a dispensable item that is all the same constitutive.

Tom's and Lear's superfluous things have more in common than might first appear. Loincloth and retainers encase the body, like clothes generally which at once protect and suit their wearer, like codpieces particularly in their accent on phallic power: Tom's loincloth protects and highlights his generational loins; Lear's entourage 'enguards' (I.iv.326) him while exhibiting his chivalric might ('men of choice and rarest parts', I.iv.263).[27] More important than their functional similarity, however, is their material likeness. The retainers would have been liveried in cloth – the cloth that distinguished them as Lear's servants;[28] hence the appropriateness of their being also referred to as the king's 'train' that follows him like the trail of a majestic robe (that can, like both tail and garment, be 'cut off', II.iv.174). When enlisting Tom as one of his knights – 'You, sir, I entertain for one of my hundred' – Lear criticises his attire, perhaps preferring to see him in livery: 'only I do not like the fashion of your garments: you will say they are Persian, but let them be chang'd' (III.vi.78–81). Loincloth would be changed to livery, one superfluous thing becoming the other.

With the addition of Regan's unnecessarily gorgeous robes ('If only to go warm were gorgeous, / Why, nature needs not what thou gorgeous wears't, / Which scarcely keeps thee warm', II.iv.268–70), clothes rank as the play's representative superfluous thing. Practically useless – unable to protect the body from the storm's invasive cold and wet – clothes are expendable and transferable layers to be sloughed off like extra skins ('Off, off, you lendings!' III.iv.108). Like *traps* and *paraphernalia*,[29] clothes refer to property in general as well as cloth articles in particular.[30] The play's unusual use of 'accommodations' to refer to clothing rather than lodging reflects its primacy in the play's economy.[31] Valuable in itself, it also represents value, both immobile property like houses (and houselessness)[32] and mobile property like money (or impecuniousness). As the play's two gestural acts of redistributing wealth or shaking the superflux demonstrate, clothes and coins are interchangeable: Lear shakes the superflux by disrobing, Gloucester by disbursing.

Though property, coins, and jewels belong only to the rich, all persons possess some cloth item, whether sumptuous or scrappy. Cloth then is the universal superfluous thing, the one touch of nature that makes the whole world kin.[33] While for Plato it is the possession of reason that makes a creature human, for Heidegger hands, and for Bergson laughter, for Lear it is the possession of something beyond need. Whether on top or at bottom of the social hierarchy, a person must have some extra thing beyond subsistence in order to be more than an animal: 'Allow not nature more than nature needs, / Man's life is cheap as beast's' (II.iv.266–7). Lear's conclusion upon observing Tom that 'man is no more than such a poor, bare, fork'd animal as thou art' (III.iv.107–8) is based on a false premise much plainer than the frequently noted metatheatrical one (that Tom's nakedness conceals Edgar which in turn conceals an actor): for Tom is not quite 'bare'. Wrapped around his salient fork is a blanket, the superfluous thing that by Lear's own reasoning secures man's superiority to beasts.

Yet the main function of superfluous things is to mark not ontological distinctions but social ones. Lear pleads for the retention of his unnecessary retainers as if such holdings were a human right, for beggars as much as kings. Yet his defence rests on something less high-minded and anachronistic than natural rights. Sumptuary laws devised to regulate excess were based on the same allowance of excess according to rank. Sumptuary legislation proliferated throughout the sixteenth century, in theory regulating expenditure on attire, partly for economic reasons and partly to avoid what Elizabeth termed 'confusion also of degrees'.[34] However limited in practice, sumptuary laws were a system for fastening identity onto materiality, persons into cloth, in stratifications ranging from '[loop'd] and window'd raggedness' (III.iv.31) to gorgeous 'Robes and furr'd gowns' (IV.vi.164).[35] So too Lear's superfluous things would maintain not simply the difference between man and beast but, more critically, what Goneril terms 'the difference of man and man' (IV.i.26). This is the difference made by 'blood and breeding' (III.i.40) that manifests itself in 'countenance' (I.iv.26–7), though in giving the Bastard the sexual place proper to the Duke, Goneril shows small regard for this 'difference', much to Edgar's disgust upon discovering her adulterous relation with the Bastard – 'O in-distinguish'd space of woman's will!' (IV.vi.271).[36]

Possessions then are the superfluous things, superfluous because unnecessary for subsistence: as Poor Tom's existence proves, at least theoretically, survival is possible with no more than a hovel for shelter, straw for warmth, 'the swimming frog, the toad, the tadpole, the wall-newt' for food (III.iv.129–30), 'the green mantle of the standing pool' for drink (133–4). Yet they are absolutely nec-essary for upholding social and personal identity. Lear unhinges when his retainers are denied him, as if his retainers held him rather than he them. The disquantitying and abatement of his train dimin-ishes him too, so that his status as both man and king drop dramat-ically. Like a beggar, he falls to his knees pleading for raiment, bed, and food. Like a woman, he suffers 'hysterica passio', unmanned from within by the classic gynaecological disorder.[37] He himself admits to losing his shape, vowing to

> ... resume the shape which thou dost think
> I have cast off for ever.
>
> (I.iv.308–9)

His retainers function as containers, so that their removal makes him incontinent: his sides break, his eyes weep, his hysterical heart leaps up. Lear's retainers are, then, anything but dispensable, as is indicated by the many attempts to replace them, both in Lear's mind (through his induction of Poor Tom, his coining to impress soldiers, his commanding that his subjects wildly copulate to provide him with soldiers) and in reality (as 'five or six and thirty questrists' race to join him at Dover, III.vii.17; as Cordelia sends out a compensatory 'century' or sentry to rescue him, IV.iv.6).[38]

Subjects and objects are so tightly bound in the play's economy that a subject cannot survive the loss of his or her possessions. 'To change one's copy' in this period was a common expression for changing one's demeanour, the result of having gained or lost copy-hold, the commonest form of land tenure.[39] Kent banished becomes Caius, Cordelia disowned is instantly reinvested by France as Queen of France, and Gloucester disentitled (by Cornwall's charge of treason) attempts to end himself (an act that would have led to the legal confiscation of his property).[40] The opening action of the play puts this principle to test when that paradoxical entity, the sovereign subject, rids himself of his property: the kingdom itself.[41] Lear's 'will to publish' is in effect the making public of his will, the dividing of his property among his heirs.[42] One of the sovereign's privileges was, in theory, to will his property as he would, without thought to 'the plague of custom' and 'curiosity of nations' (I.ii.3, 4) constraining nobles like Gloucester.[43] What is striking about Lear's testation, however, is less *how* he divides his kingdom than *when*. It is a pre-mortem settlement, occurring before rather than after death. In his desire to anticipate the future, Lear is not unlike Edmund. Both cannot wait for nature to take its course, Edmund as eager to inherit as Lear to disinherit. In this respect, *Lear* could be described as a play about a man's attempt to outlast his property – the risks of living testate, as it were. It is not a healthy desire, to be sure – indeed, it could be said that Lear's suicidal desire to undo himself is as unnatural and illegal as Edmund's patricidal desire to undo his father.

Lear's initial attempt to disburden himself of his property might also be reconsidered in light of popular and medical lore on insanity. In Michael MacDonald's discussion of madness in the seventeenth century, numerous symptoms involve forms of self-destruction in which the 'self' includes personal property as well as person.[44] Neglect or damage to one's house and clothes were considered as symptomatic of madness as forms of self-affliction. Particularly common was the tearing and the tearing off of clothes, 'valuable property', as MacDonald notes.[45] In this context, each of Lear's acts of divestment might signal madness, beginning with his divestment 'of rule, / Interest of territory' (I.i.49–50), followed by his abjuration of all roofs, his unbonneting, the removal of his garments and, later, of his boots.[46] Edgar stages the familiar symptoms by stripping down and following the 'president / Of Bedlam beggars' (II.iii.13–14) who stick their arms with 'Pins, wooden pricks, nails, sprigs of rosemary' (l. 16).[47] Divestment, disrobing, disaccommodating are all acts of exposure that like self-inflicted wounds betray an unsound mind. According to this criterion, the strongest sign of Lear's sanity is his desire to keep his retainers.

Both plot and subplot dramatise the impossibility of the severance Lear attempts. Persons and things cannot be alienated from one another. Lear's kingdom cannot be given away; Gloucester's estate cannot be taken away. The land seized from Edgar returns to him; so too the kingdom given away by Lear comes back. And the course by which both return is remarkable. The removal of property is dramatised as an act of aberrant (unnatural) will: Lear's premature disposal of his property before death and Edmund's subversive desire to overturn 'the plague of custom' and 'curiosity of nations' (I.ii.3,4). Yet its return ostensibly happens on its own, in the natural course of things, rather than through any act of human exertion. Lear disposes of the kingdom with great pomp and circumstance and a battle is waged to keep it from him; but it returns to him quietly (almost imperceptibly) through Albany's modest resignation ('we will resign, / During the life of this old majesty, / To him our absolute power', V.iii.299–301). We twice overhear Edmund boldly contrive to dispossess his brother –

> Well then,
> Legitimate Edgar, I must have your land
> (I.ii.15–16)

– and 'Let me ... have lands by wit' (II.ii.183) – and witness his success, first with his father (**Glou.** 'I'll work the means / To make thee capable', II.i.84–5), and then after his father's disentitlement, with Cornwall (**Corn.** 'True or false, it hath made thee Earl of Gloucester', III.v.17–18) so that Goneril, Oswald, and Albany all address him by his appropriated title. But we never hear an antiphonal response from Edgar, 'Well then, illegitimate Edmund, I must have back my land'. (Indeed his re-entitlement gets lost in the pomp and circumstance of the duel that achieves it.) Removal involves disruptive human agency, while return occurs surreptitiously, as if the gods were not so boyishly wanton after all, responsibly returning what was lost, like so many Perditas from another dramatic genre.[48]

As estate clings to person so person clings to estate. That is why, to answer the Fool's pertinent question, 'a snail has a house' (II.i.27–8). Disowned (and therefore dispossessed) by his father, 'Edgar I nothing am' (II.iii.21); deprived of his 100 knights, 'This is not Lear' (I.iv.226). Expropriation fractures identity – with 100 knights gone in a clap, Lear dissolves into tears, breaks into 100,000 flawed pieces. Madness ensues, actual for Lear, feigned by Edgar. Identity dissipates with disentitlement. During the period Edgar is without property, he has no proper name ('my name is

lost', V.iii.121), only a generic one – Poor Tom. Edgar's two narratives both involve simultaneous loss of property and identity. His
own: dispossessed of his land, he disguises himself. And the one he
assumes: dispossessed of his 'three suits to his back, six shirts to his
body – Horse to ride and weapons to wear' (III.iv.135–7), he drops
from courtier / servingman to Bedlam beggar. A series of acquisi-
tions – of clothes and purses – enables Edgar to recover himself in a
series of linguistically marked upward gradations from 'Madman
and beggar too' (IV.i.30), to 'A poor unfortunate beggar' (IV.vi.68),
to 'A most poor man' (221), to 'bold peasant' (231), to ceremoni-
ous messenger (V.i.38), to chivalric 'champion' (V.iii.121) – until he
is finally in the position to reclaim his title (his name and land),
'My name is Edgar' (V.iii.170), a title which connects him to Lear
as well as his father, for, as Regan allows, it was Lear who named
him.[49]

It is the identity not only of those born into kingdoms and earl-
doms that is contingent upon possessions, but also – quite astonishingly – those born into nothing whatsoever. The given names of all
the highborn male characters in the play are dropped so that person
and property are synonymous: Gloucester, Albany, Cornwall,
France, Burgundy, Kent. The nameless poor are christened in Lear's
apostrophes after both their lack of clothing, 'Poor Naked
Wretches', and their lack of estate, 'You Houseless Poverty'
(III.iv.28, 26, capitals added). The beggar possesses a generic rather
than a proper name, 'Poor Tom' or 'Tom of Bedlam'; the latter
form, like a title (compare Earl of Gloucester), affixes person to
property (a madhouse for a house) and then collapses the two in
just plain 'Bedlam' (compare Gloucester). The speech prefixes of the
Quarto and Folio distinguish Edmund with no proper name but
rather with his legal status – Bastard, short for 'unpossessing
bastard' (II.i.67), identifying him with his incapacity to inherit land
(except by special dispensation).[50] The steward of another's property, having no land of his own (unlike his near namesake Osric
who is rich in the possession of much dirt), the hybrid Oswald ('son
and heir of a mungril bitch', II.ii.22–3) is called names that associate him with a hodgepodge of movables rather than a stable estate:
'three-suited, hundred-pound, filthy worsted-stocking knave'
(II.ii.16–17). Servants possess no names at all, even those distinguished by such memorable deeds as the slaying of Cornwall.
Regan exclaims 'A peasant stand up thus?' (III.vii.79) and Cornwall
commands 'throw this slave / Upon the dunghill' (ll.96–7) as if to

bring him as low as possible for standing up, combining his remains with offal, with filth rather than land. Oswald also calls a peasant (or Edgar's impersonation of one) 'dunghill'; this peasant too is uppity, daring to defy the steward's sword with his rustic costard.[51] Oswald – 'super-serviceable' (II.ii.18–19) in the Folio or 'superfinical' in the Quarto – is himself a social climber, at this very encounter hoping preferment will fall on him for cutting off Gloucester. It is fitting, therefore, that he be put down by the same association with excremental waste in Kent's threat to 'daub the wall of a jakes' (II.ii.66–7) with his remains. Those remains, appropriately enough, end up uninterred, just as those of the rising peasant are put upon the dunghill rather than underground, despite Oswald's dying request – 'Bury my body' (IV.vi.247).

SUPERFLUX

Oswald is associated with lexical excess as well as alimentary waste: 'Thou whoreson zed, thou unnecessary letter!' (II.ii.64) referring to the absence of 'z' from dictionaries. Both types of superfluity underscore his social dispensability. As Kent's 'additions' (l.24) indicate, Oswald is a supernumerary, the one thing the tight world of *Lear* could do without precisely because he stands for the possibility the play abhors (despite its own generic hybridity) – of hybridisation, mongrelisation, heterogeneity teeming its way into the hierarchy. Ideally, selfhood from top to bottom would be securely locked into possession, from extravagant to paltry, so that nothing would be left over to throw off the balance – or the imbalance.[52] Yet the balance *is* thrown off, or, in the hydraulic terms invited by the play, the water level spills over – in superflux. The first sign of overspill is the uncontrollable effusion of tears 'which break from [Lear] perforce' (I.iv.298), the water drops displaced by the passionate hysterics that threaten to drown or suffocate him in his own fluid. Concurrently another outburst makes itself heard – of cosmic, indeed cataclysmic, proportions: 'Storme and Tempest' reads the Folio stage direction. The storm magnifies Lear's lachrymal superflux with a deluvian downpour from above: floodgates and waterspouts, cataracts and hurricanoes, a torrent that raises the water level, as Lear bids the wind 'swell the curled waters 'bove the main' (III.i.6). The effect of the overflow is to collapse high into low as the firmament drops to land level, drowning and drenching

uppermost steeples and weathercocks, flattening the global sphere
into a liquid mass. 'Pour on' (III.iv.18), urges Lear, hoping to con-
found human generation as well as physical creation, bidding that
Nature's female receptive moulds be cracked, her masculine insemi-
nating germens spilled – so that all distinctions would dissolve in an
amorphous muddle.

It is appropriate that Gloucester should appear during the storm,
bearing a torch, heralded as 'a little fire in a wild field' like 'an old
lecher's heart' in a cold body (III.iv.111–12), for Gloucester admits
(even boasts) himself a spiller of germens: 'the whoreson must be
acknowledg'd' (I.i.24). While Gloucester may well, as he claims, be
reconciled to his past promiscuity, the play certainly is not.
Gloucester is 'the superfluous and lust-dieted man' (IV.i.67), in that
very epithet combining what are not yet two discrete words: luxury
and lechery, lavish spending and dissipate fornicating.[53] From the
first to the last, the play stigmatises him as the indiscriminate dis-
penser of both economic and sexual purses, coin and seed.[54] In the
opening scene, he boasts that he is 'braz'd' (I.i.11) – hardened like
brass – to his illicit deed. His blinding in Act IV, however, makes
him (and us) agonisingly sensitive to it. In the play's final scene,
Edgar retroactively makes the loss of his father's eyes the price
of his adultery (and not, as Cornwall charges, of his treason),[55]
explaining to the Bastard:

> The dark and vicious place where thee he got
> Cost him his eyes.
>
> (V.iii.173–4)

Gloucester pays for his whoring with his eyes, forfeiting those 'precious stones' (testicles and jewels), leaving 'cases' like empty purses.
'The dark and vicious place' where the whoreson was begotten was
the whore or whorehouse (person and house interchangeable here
too);[56] but it was Gloucester who found his way to that 'forfended
place' (V.i.11), failing to heed Poor Tom's caveat: 'Keep thy foot
out of brothels, / thy hand out of plackets' (III.iv.96–7).

In a grotesquely displaced recurrence of Gloucester's deed, the
foot and hand reappear together, making their way into sexually
charged openings. Cornwall uses first his foot (**Corn.** 'Upon these
eyes of thine I'll set my foot', III.vii.68)[57] and then his hand (**Serv.**
'Hold your hand', l.73) to put out Gloucester's eyes, called 'jelly'
(l.83), a synonym for sperm.[58] The sexual act could be recognised in

a gruesome blinding only in a culture steeped in the connection between lust and eyes.[59] Stephen Booth notes the ubiquity of eye for genitalia, male and female.[60] Medical lore attributes loss of eyesight to lechery[61] (and we already know that Gloucester's eyesight is dim – he needs spectacles to read [I.ii.35], and has to squint to see [III.iv.117] or fail to see [IV.vi.136–7]). Iconography makes the same causal connection, as in an image of voluptuous Lechery / Luxury piercing a man's eye with a spear.[62] Gloucester's sexual and optical history follows the same cultural links, as if there were no escaping the sadistic justice Edgar attributes to the gods.[63] Gloucester's punishment subjects him to the violation he committed; it ravishes him so that he is left with 'bleeding rings' (V.iii.190), hollow cases as Lear calls them, Gloucester's jewels or stones now gone, as if he were castrated and barren.[64] (The blanket around his legitimate son's loins takes on a new necessity.)[65] Eyesight and lust are again combined when Lear hails Gloucester as 'blind Cupid' (the sign of a brothel, IV.vi.137)[66] and hints at the sexual and financial expenditure that has unmanned (emasculated and impoverished) him:

> No eyes in your head, nor no money in your purse.
> (IV.vi.145–6)

After his repeated identification with Lechery / Luxury, it is more than likely that it is Gloucester and not Man in the abstract whom Lear tries for adultery in IV.vi. (It is, after all, Gloucester to whom he is speaking both before and after the arraignment.)

> When I do stare, see how the subject quakes.
> I pardon that man's life. What was thy cause?
> Adultery?
> (ll.108–10)

Lear's sentence endorses the crime rather than condemning it ('To it, luxury, pell-mell', IV.vi.117), invoking the demise of social order just as he invoked the end of natural order during the storm ('Crack nature's moulds', III.ii.8). He rewards the defendant rather than penalising him ('There's money for thee', IV.vi.131), as if to replenish his empty purse (with eyes, coin, and seed) and thereby legitimise further promiscuity, to the end of producing a mongrel, bastard population of Oswalds and Edmunds, the result of spilling germens into cracked moulds.

In effect, Gloucester is 'tried' twice for the same crime, first punished by Cornwall and then acquitted by Lear. Lear extends his forgiveness of Gloucester to all persons ('None does offend', l.168) though the flip side of that blanket pardon is his sweeping indictment at Cordelia's death, 'murderers, traitors all!' (V.iii.270). Either way, Lear would collapse differences between man and man, so that hierarchy would be engulfed by anarchy – the anarchy of 'handy-dandy' and 'pell-mell' in which justice and thief, dog and beggar, women and horses, rich and poor, guilty and innocent are indistinguishable.

Tears, rain, sperm – are the play's overflowing liquids, representing the superflux that disorders psyche, cosmos, and polis respectively.[67] The play also entertains economic superflux, the spilling over of possessions from the top that would raise the bottom.[68] Lear disrobes during the storm ('Expose thyself to feel what wretches feel, / That thou mayst shake the superflux to them', III.iv.34–5) in order to redress the gods' unjust distribution, an act he repeats a few moments later ('Off, off, you lendings! Come, unbutton here', ll.108–9). Gloucester repeats this gesture twice in the next act, giving away first one purse ('Here, take this purse', IV.i.64) and then another ('Here, friend,'s another purse', IV.vi.28). Moreover, he repeats it in the same spirit of evening out inequity:

> So distribution should undo excess,
> And each man have enough.
> (IV.i.70–1)

It is no small irony that both his purses should fall right into the very hands which stood to receive the handout in the first place: those of his legitimate first born. As if charity ended at home and the nature of revenue were to come back.

Indeed, since Lear has no male heirs and has disowned his female heirs, Edgar – Lear's godson – may be the designated beneficiary of Lear's handouts as well. If Nicholas Rowe had in his 1709 edition inserted the stage direction 'Tossing off his clothes' rather than 'Tearing off his clothes' it would have better corresponded to the act of shaking the superflux. For Lear is not just taking them off but flinging them away, to the poor naked wretches who inspire the gesture. It is in the middle of this shakedown that Poor Tom makes his first appearance, entering with a reference to the deluvial superflux: 'Fathom and half' (III.iv.37). If he were to snatch up

what Lear tossed off, it would be the second item in an expanding
wardrobe (beginning with his blanket) that will include the best
apparel owned by the man who has served his father for eighty
years and the 'war-like' garb (V.iii.143) in which he appears to
challenge Edmund. In the right place at the right time, Edgar might
also be the recipient of Lear's donation when he imagines recruiting
soldiers (he did, after all, enlist Tom into his retinue): 'There's your
press-money' (IV.vi.86–7). All the superflux comes Edgar's way as
if by fatal attraction – until the end when (Folio) Edgar, Lear's
godson, inherits the kingdom itself. 'Who gives anything to poor
Tom?' (III.iv.51) indeed.

There is nothing 'handy-dandy' or 'pellmell' about the shaking
of superflux, the undoing of excess: it follows the precise course of
primogeniture and succession. In the superflux, there is no spilling
down from the top that raises the bottom. Things end up passing
from father to son; and when there is no son (or daughter), from
godfather to godson.[69]

What I have called the ideology of superfluous things holds the
status quo in place by locking identity into property, the subject
into the object. What movements there are towards modern fluidity
of persons and things snap back into the same old moulds and
germens. The Apocalyptic storm only briefly holds out the millenar-
ian promise that 'things might change or cease' (III.i.7), evoking a
long tradition that associates the end of the world with radical political change.[70] Yet like Lear's and Gloucester's token acts of redistribution, nothing changes or ceases as a result of what turns out to
be, like the (Folio) Fool's utopian prophecy before the hovel
(III.ii.80–94), no more than a chiliastic tease.[71]

LUXURY

That the play restrains superfluity at the top – that it can only
imagine 'superflux' or overflow in the horrific terms of madness,
cataclysm, and anarchy – returns us to our starting point, this
essay's epigraph, Lear's principle of universal excess:

> [O]ur basest beggars
> Are in the poorest thing superfluous.

Far from being self-evident, the axiom contradicts itself: how can
the *basest* have something *super*fluous, over-the-top[72] – have extra

without having enough? How could those caved in by need – panged by 'Necessity's sharp pinch' (II.iv.211) with 'houseless heads and unfed sides' (III.iv.30) – have a surplus of anything?[73]

There is a grim illogic to Lear's theory, both semantic and social. For if the poor *did* have more than they needed, they would not still be poor, just as the rich would not be rich if they had less than they needed.[74] The axiom keeps the poor poor and the rich rich by relativising both need and excess: a man has more or less of both depending on his social position. In *The Needs of Strangers*, Michael Ignatieff refines the axiom by proposing a distinction between *natural need* (food, raiment, clothing) and *social due* (honour, regard): while there may be a universal modicum for the former, the other must be determined by 'rank, position and history'.[75] The distinction, however, seems applicable only to the rich. It explains why Lear could want more though his needs were met, but not how a beggar could have more than enough when cold and hungry. It would seem that the only excess beggars could know would come from the handouts of the rich, though in their hands gratuitous waste would instantly convert to necessary subsistence. Of course, there is always the possibility that the transferal might be motivated from the bottom rather than the top: that the beggar might enforce the charity of the rich (to paraphrase Poor Tom, II.iii.20) or 'take the thing she begs' (to quote Goneril, I.iv.248). Indeed this inversion was threatened annually on St Stephen's Day, the day after Christmas on which (according to the 1608 Quarto title page) *King Lear* was performed at court.[76] On this day, the poor were entitled to the hospitality and charity of the rich: it was, to borrow Ignatieff's distinction, their due as well as their need. 'Stephening' constrained charity, demanded instead of begged it, threatening violence if it were withheld. In this ritualised instance, distribution of the superflux hardly undid excess: it prevented it from becoming undone.[77]

It is not just in *King Lear* that superfluity remains at the top. According to Ferdinand Braudel's extraordinary *Capitalism and Material Life, 1400–1800*, it was not until well into the eighteenth century that luxury ceased to be the exclusive privilege of the rich.[78] For the 400-year span covered by his book, material life at the broad base of society remained essentially the same. Food, drink, houses, clothes, and fashion remained for the masses virtually unchanged for the simple reason that sufficiency made do with what it had.[79] Only at the narrow top where superfluity could afford change was there fluctuation. Sufficiency settled into a static 'omnipresent *vis inertiae*', whereas superfluity sought out dynamic variety and change. Once luxury dropped to the lower reaches of society, the *longue durée* of the Ancien Régime ended, and the 'fantastic changes' of capitalism were set rapidly afoot. It is Werner Sombart's thesis in *Luxury and Capitalism*, an important work for Braudel, that luxury itself gave rise to capitalism, stimulating production to satisfy desire beyond need.[80] A new ideology of superfluous things then came into being in which surplus (Lear's superflux) was seen to benefit all classes of society, trickling down (instead of spilling over) from the top to raise the standard of living at every level (rather than to level the whole), distribution determined by the mechanistic drives of an 'invisible hand' (rather than the charitable handouts of a Lear or Gloucester).

John Sekora provides the long and complex history that leads up to this surprisingly recent tenet in *Luxury: The Concept in Western Thought*.[81] As he shows, until the eighteenth century luxury was condemned as a civic and religious vice rather than commended as an economic stimulus. Until then, it was synonymous with 'lechery', both words designating excessive fleshly desire; sometimes it was Lechery, sometimes Luxury, who paraded among the seven deadly sins.[82] Posing a threat to both social hierarchy and the state of the soul, the terms were also interchangeable in sumptuary laws and admonitory sermons. The word decisively split in two during the eighteenth century: while lechery continued to refer to inordinate sexual appetite, luxury, in the context of expanding commercialism, came to designate an excessive appetite for pleasurable goods. It came to designate too the market's commodification of this appetite in the form of pleasurable goods themselves – luxury items. Yet luxury items are hardly Lear's superfluous things, for the simple reason that they presuppose the very identity that *Lear* makes coextensive with possessions. For individuals (it is now safe to call them that)[83] must *precede* the luxury items through which they project and indulge themselves. If, to return to the opening binaries of this essay, the commodity is an object removed from the subject, then the luxury item is the commodity *par excellence*: both estranged from its producers (who are even less likely to use it than any other product) and expendable to the consumer (who flaunts its expendability by conspicuously consuming it). One might go so far as to say that the luxury item is what the play (as in a dream) fears the superfluous thing will become, without having the historical vantage to know exactly what it is.

What *King Lear* cannot know, however, we know quite well. For we have no trouble conceiving of a self anterior to and independent of objects – constituted in such non-objective realms as biography, language, ideology. What we do not know and what *Lear* knows very well, is how – to deploy a common Renaissance homonym lost to modern pronunciation – what *one* is depends on what one *owns*. How can property be basic – even prior – to personhood?

In several important essays, J. G. A. Pocock has emphasised the long struggle extending well into the eighteenth century to keep the two aligned, to keep what he terms 'personality' grounded in changing forms of property.[84] As he points out, in our eagerness to make 'liberalism' triumphant, we have allowed Locke's model of autonomy and appropriation too early and too pervasive a sway, largely under the influence of C. B. Macpherson's *The Political Theory of Possessive Individualism*.[85] There is, however, another view of the relation of person to property extending back to Aristotle which Locke far from pre-empted. According to this classical tradition, 'Property was both an extension and a prerequisite of personality'.[86] As Pocock points out, this ancient view (a long-time basis for the franchise) was challenged by an increasingly mercantilised society in which stable land was converted to movable and variable money and goods. Yet the real challenge came from the conversion not of immobile to mobile, but of material to immaterial property. From the end of the seventeenth century on, property took on the speculative, even fantastical, form of credit or stock:[87] 'Property – the material foundation of both personality and government – had ceased to be real and has become not merely mobile but imaginary.'[88] Locke's 'possessive individualism' figured as tense alternative to what might be termed 'propertied individualism' and the two remained in contest through the eighteenth century.[89]

History has treated what Pocock has demonstrated to have been a strenuous and urgent dialectic as a steady development of only one of its positions. We therefore have lost sight of the long cultural project involved in having to reconceptualise personal identity once its basis in property had begun to shift.[90] Because we live the resolution – understanding ourselves through such dispropertied structures as Freudian childhoods, Lacanian signifiers, Althusserian interpellations – it is hard to imagine both the effort and cost once involved in preparing the way for it. This is precisely what we lose when Renaissance is seen as Early Modern, for – while we are quite sophisticated in our understanding of earlier versions of what we presently are – we have little sense of what the alternatives once might have been.

From *Subject and Object in Renaissance Culture*, ed. Margreta de Grazia, Maureen Quilligan and Peter Stallybrass (Cambridge, 1996), pp. 17–42.

NOTES

[Margreta de Grazia's essay examines the postmodern tendency to interpret the early modern period as the incipient modern, that is, to privilege the 'modern' in 'early modern' so as to read the past in terms of the present. This issue is the central concern of de Grazia's forthcoming book, *Counter Modern 'Hamlet'*, and can be seen as an extension of her earlier interest in the historical development of critical imperatives for the analysis of Shakespeare's works: see *Shakespeare Verbatim* (Oxford, 1991). Ed.]

1. On 'Burckhardt and the Formation of the Modern Concept', see Wallace K. Ferguson, *The Renaissance in Historical Thought: Five Centuries of Interpretation* (New York, 1948), ch. 7, pp. 179–94. On Burckhardt's frequent substitution of 'modern' and 'modern man' for 'Renaissance' and 'Renaissance man', see Felix Gilbert, *History: Politics or Culture? Reflections on Ranke and Burckhardt* (Princeton, NJ, 1990), p. 61. For Marx's identification of the sixteenth century with the collapse of feudalism and the beginning of modern bourgeois society, see *Manifesto of the Communist Party*, in *The Marx–Engels Reader*, ed. Robert C. Tucker (2nd edn, New York and London, 1978), pp. 474–5, and *Capital*, pp. 431–5. On the relation between Burckhardt and Marx, see William Kerrigan and Gordon Braden, *The Idea of the Renaissance* (Baltimore and London, 1989), pp. 3–35, and esp. 44–7, and Margaret W. Ferguson, Maureen Quilligan, and Nancy J. Vickers (eds), *Rewriting the Renaissance: The Discourses of Sexual Difference in Early Modern Europe* (Chicago and London, 1986), pp. xvi–xvii.

2. For Burckhardt's antipathy to progressive reform, see Gilbert, *History*, pp. 5–6, and David Norbrook, 'Life and Death of Renaissance Man', *Raritan*, 8:4 (1989), 95–7; for Marx's commitment to reform, see Engels's 'Speech at the Graveside of Karl Marx', in *Reader*, p. 682.

3. Jacob Burckhardt, *The Civilization of the Renaissance in Italy*, trans. Ludwig Geiger and Walter Götz (2 vols, New York, 1958), I, p. 143.

4. Kerrigan and Braden discuss Burckhardt's belief that 'detachment earns a new power over the external world', *Idea*, p. 13.

5. On Alberti's humble origins, see Burckhardt, *Civilization*, I, pp. 148–50; see also his praise of the humanist teacher and scholar, Pomponius Laetus, pp. 276–8. On the toleration of bastards generally, see pp. 38–40; on the benefits of banishment, particularly in relation to Dante, see pp. 145–6.

6. *Meditations on First Philosophy*, in Elizabeth Anscombe and Peter Thomas Geach (trans. and eds), *Descartes: Philosophical Writings* (Berkshire, 1986), p. 62.

7. Marx, *Capital, Reader*, p. 322.

8. Ibid., pp. 319–20.

9. Marx, *Economic and Philosophic Manuscripts of 1844, Reader*, p. 72.

10. Burckhardt, *Civilization*, I, p. 229.

11. Marx, *Capital, Reader*, p. 328.

12. 'We are situated at the close of the cultural movement initiated in the Renaissance; the places in which our social and psychological world seem to be cracking apart are those structural joints visible when it was first constructed', Stephen Greenblatt, *Renaissance Self-Fashioning: from More to Shakespeare* (Chicago, 1980), pp. 174–5, quoted by Greenblatt in *Learning to Curse: Essays in Early Modern Culture* (New York and London, 1990), p. 182, n. 4. On how this division marginalises the Middle Ages, see Lee Patterson, 'On the Margin: Postmodernism, Ironic History, and Medieval Studies', *Speculum: A Journal of Medieval Studies*, 65: 1 (1990), 87–108, and David Aers, 'Rewriting the Middle Ages: Some Suggestions', *The Journal of Medieval and Renaissance Studies*, 18 (1988), 221–40, and *Community, Gender, and Individual Identity: English Writing, 1360–1430* (London, 1988).

13. Jean-Christophe Agnew, *Worlds Apart: The Market and the Theater in Anglo-American Thought, 1550–1750* (Cambridge, 1986), pp. 11–12.

14. *Drama and the Market in the Age of Shakespeare* (Cambridge, 1992), p. 9.

15. Of course, another transaction precedes the audience's payment for a play: the acting company's payment to the playwright(s) for a play, as documented in Henslowe's *Diary*. See Neil Carson, *A Companion to Henslowe's Diary* (Cambridge, 1988), pp. 48, 56–7.

16. On the temptation to make Shakespeare's career correspondent to period divisions, see de Grazia, 'Fin de Siècle Renaissance', in Elaine Scarry (ed.), *Fins de Siècle: English Poetry in 1590, 1690, 1790, 1890, 1990* (Baltimore and London, 1995), pp. 37–63.

17. For an offsetting of Tillyard's world picture with a cultural materialist dynamic of social process, see Jonathan Dollimore, *Radical Tragedy:*

Religion, Ideology and Power in the Drama of Shakespeare and his Contemporaries (Chicago, 1984), pp. 6–8.

18. For two direct applications of Lawrence Stone's *The Crisis of the Aristocracy, 1558–1641* (Oxford, 1965), see Rosalie Colie, 'Reason and Need: *King Lear* and the "Crisis" of the Aristocracy', in R. L. Colie and F. T. Flahiff (eds), *Some Facets of King Lear: Essays in Prismatic Criticism* (Toronto, 1974), pp. 185–219, and Paul Delaney, 'King Lear and the Decline of Feudalism', *PMLA*, 92 (1977), 429–40. For an earlier treatment of *Lear* as transitional, see John Danby, *Shakespeare's Doctrine of Nature: A Study of 'King Lear'* (London, 1951), pp. 18–53, and Marshall McLuhan, *The Gutenberg Galaxy: The Making of Typographic Man* (London, 1962), pp. 11–18.

19. Franco Moretti, 'The Great Eclipse: Tragic Form as the Consecration of Sovereignty', in *Signs Taken for Wonders: Essays in the Sociology of Literary Forms*, trans. Susan Fischer, David Forgacs, and David Miller (London, 1983), pp. 42–82, and Stephen Greenblatt, 'Shakespeare and the Exorcists', in his *Shakespearean Negotiations: The Circulation of Social Energy in Renaissance England* (Berkeley, CA, 1988), pp. 94–128.

20. Richard Halpern, '"Historica Passio": *King Lear's* Fall into Feudalism', in his *The Poetics of Primitive Accumulation: English Renaissance Culture and the Genealogy of Capital* (Ithaca and London, 1991), pp. 215–313, p. 247. Halpern is acutely aware of the problems of reading for a pre-capitalist history and of his own precipitous inclination – 'my own book tends to lean forward' – which he counteracts with a genealogical fanning out into 'other areas of the social formation – political, cultural, ideological', p. 13. I am much indebted to Halpern's remarkably smart and thoughtful book.

21. Walter Cohen, *Drama of a Nation: Public Theater in Renaissance England and Spain* (Ithaca, NY, 1985), pp. 327–56, p. 345. On Marx's subclass, see Peter Stallybrass, 'Marx and Heterogeneity: Thinking the *Lumpenproletariat*', *Representations*, 31 (1991), 69–95.

22. Annabel Patterson, '"What matter who's speaking?" *Hamlet* and *King Lear*', in her *Shakespeare and the Popular Voice* (Cambridge, MA, 1989), pp. 93–119.

23. '[A]ll isolated or discrete cultural analysis always involves a buried or repressed theory of historical periodisation'; Fredric Jameson, *Postmodernism, or, The Cultural Logic of Late Capitalism* (Durham, NC, 1991), p. 3. For New Criticism's unvoiced presupposition of history, see Jameson's *Marxism and Form: Twentieth-Century Dialectical Theories of Literature* (Princeton, NJ, 1971), pp. 323–4. On the question of dividing history into temporal units, especially the 'century', see Daniel S. Milo, *Trahir le temps (Histoire)* (Paris, 1991).

24. See Raymond Williams's important essay, 'Dominant, Residual, and Emergent', in his *Marxism and Literature* (Oxford, 1992), pp. 121–7.

25. Foucault, 'Nietzsche, Genealogy, History', in *Language, Counter-Memory, Practice*, trans. Donald F. Bouchard and Sherry Simon (Ithaca, NY, 1977), pp. 139–64.

26. Quoted from the facsimile of the 1608 Quarto in *The Complete 'King Lear', 1608–1623: Texts and Parallel Texts in Photographic Facsimile*, prepared by Michael Warren (Berkeley, CA, 1989). All subsequent quotes from Shakespeare are from *The Riverside Shakespeare*, gen. ed. G. Blakemore Evans (Boston, 1974).

27. On 'train' as 'phallus', cut and shortened by his daughters, see Frankie Rubenstein, *A Dictionary of Shakespeare's Sexual Puns and their Significance* (London, 1984).

28. On the maintenance of a liveried retinue by great nobles in the sixteenth century, see Stone, *Crisis*, pp. 201–17. According to Stone, 'By the mid-eighteenth century it was generally accepted that "a livery suit may indeed fitly be called a badge of servility"', p. 214.

29. For *trappings* and *paraphernalia* as personal belongings, specifically dress, see *OED*.

30. Their symbolic centrality within the play matches their importance outside of it, for the theatrical company itself and for society generally, as Peter Stallybrass argues in 'Worn Worlds: Clothes and Identity on the Renaissance Stage', in *Subject and Object in Renaissance Culture*, ed. Margreta de Grazia, Maureen Quilligan and Peter Stallybrass (Cambridge, 1996), pp. 289–320. Clothes are the basic prop or property of the theatrical company, the attire of the tiring house, its largest investment is vestments.

31. Lear's reference to 'unaccommodated man' refers to his nakedness; Edgar's observation upon seeing Lear draped (crowned?) with weeds that a sane man would not so 'accommodate' himself also refers to his garb. According to Kenneth Muir, Shakespeare never used the word 'in the modern sense', *King Lear*, ed. Kenneth Muir (London, 1985), p. 115, n. III.iv.104–5.

32. For *house*, as 'a covering of textile material', see *OED*.

33. For a sharp critique of how Lear posits a need that is both universalised (and therefore egalitarian) and hierarchised (and therefore elitist), see James Kavanagh, 'Shakespeare in Ideology', in John Drakakis (ed), *Alternative Shakespeare* (London and New York, 1985), pp. 158–9.

34. 'The aims of the attempt to impose state control on dress are more apparent than the effects'; N. B. Harte, 'State Control of Dress and Social

Change in Pre-Industrial England', in D. C. Coleman and A. H. John (eds), *Trade, Government and Economy in Pre-Industrial England* (London, 1976), p. 143. See also Frank Whigham, *Ambition and Privilege: The Social Tropes of Elizabethan Courtesy Theory* (Berkeley, Los Angeles, London, 1984), pp. 155–69.

35. See the class restrictions on wearing various types of furs in the 1580 Proclamation reproduced by Whigham, that begins with 'fur of sables' forbidden to anyone 'under the degree of earl'. *Ambition*, Fig. 1, pp. 164–5.

36. Her servant Oswald, the issue of cross-breeding (like Edmund), 'the son and heir of a mungril bitch' (II.ii.22–3), has the same difficulty recognising distinctions of blood and breeding, to the outrage of Kent who describes himself as 'a gentleman of blood and breeding' (III.i.40). Hence his rebuke to Oswald, 'I'll teach thee differences' (I.iv.88–9). For an account of Oswald's status as 'a class and sexual *hybrid*', see Halpern, *Accumulation*, pp. 244–5.

37. See Janet Adelman's remarkable reading of Lear's ailment in her book named after it, *Suffocating Mothers: Fantasies of Maternal Origin in Shakespeare's Plays, 'Hamlet' to 'The Tempest'* (New York and London, 1992), pp. 113–14; pp. 300–1, ns. 27–8.

38. The Quarto reads 'century' (a subdivision of a Roman legion) and the Folio 'Century' (often modernised as 'sentry'). The two forms work together, suggesting both the number of men (100) dispatched by Cordelia and their function (to guard Lear).

39. I owe the reference to 'changing one's copy' and copyhold to Agnew, though he uses it to argue for the capacity of identity to, in effect, forge itself, becoming as ambiguous as falsified copyhold claims. See *Worlds Apart*, p. 58.

40. By saving his father from despair, Edgar also saves his inheritance, for suicide or *felo de se*, like felony of any kind, was punished through the confiscation of property. See Michael MacDonald, *Mystical Bedlam: Madness, Anxiety, and Healing in Seventeenth-Century England* (Cambridge, 1981), pp. 132, 166.

41. Lear's kingdom in this play, like Gloucester's estate, is represented primarily in terms of land, on the model of feudal property law. See Halpern, *Accumulation*, pp. 221–2, 229.

42. For a stunningly informative account of the changes in testamentary practice during Shakespeare's time, their complex dramatisation in his plays, and their shocking exploitation in his own will, see Richard Wilson, 'A Constant Will to Publish: Shakespeare's Dead Hand', *Will Power: Essays on Shakespearean Authority* (New York, London, Toronto, Sidney, 1993), pp. 184–280. I have also benefited from

Katherine Conway's discussion of 'dower' and 'dowery' as two distinct instruments for transferring property from males to females in
her unpublished essay, 'Shakespeare's "Material Girls"'.

43. On the fictive nature of this privilege, see Albert Braunmuller's discussion of 'Wills and the Crown of England' in his edition of *The Life
and Death of King John* (Oxford, 1989), pp. 54–61.

44. *Bedlam*, pp. 128–32.

45. Ibid., p. 130.

46. Halpern also notes Lear's 'improvident disposition of his own property' as symptomatic of madness, in *Accumulation*, p. 263.

47. On the histrionics of possessed madmen in Samuel Harsnett's *A
Declaration of Egregious Impostures* and *Lear*, see Greenblatt,
'Shakespeare and the Exorcists', *Negotiations*, pp. 94–128.

48. On the elements of pastoral romance in *Lear*, see John Turner, 'The
Tragic Romances of Feudalism', in Graham Holderness, Nick Potter,
and John Turner (eds), *Shakespeare: The Play of History* (Iowa City,
1987), pp. 85–118, and Maynard Mack, *'King Lear' in Our Time*
(London, 1966), pp. 63–6.

49. For a characterological reading of Edgar's progression in the role of Poor
Tom, see the introduction to Janet Adelman (ed.), *Twentieth Century
Interpretations of 'King Lear'* (Berkeley, CA, 1965), pp. 14–21.

50. On bastards and inheritance, see Alan Macfarlane, 'Illegitimacy and
Illegitimates in English History', in Peter Laslett, Karla Oosterveen,
and Richard M. Smith (eds), *Bastardy and its Comparative History*
(London, 1980), pp. 71–85, esp. p. 73.

51. For the class conflict staged by the costard and sword, see Mack, *'Lear'
in Our Time*, pp. 53–4. For 'the semiotics of execution' that would have
been applied to Oswald's death as well as that of Cornwall's servant
(stabbed in the back by Regan according to the stage direction in Q1–2,
IV.i.80, though simply killed by an anonymous 'harmful stroke' in the
messenger's report, IV.ii.77), see Stephen Greenblatt, 'Murdering
Peasants: Status, Genre, and the Representation of Rebellion', in
Greenblatt (ed.), *Representing the English Renaissance* (Berkeley, CA,
1988), pp. 1–29, p. 11.

52. On fixed land as the paradigm for *Lear's* 'Economies of the Zero
Sum', see Halpern, *Accumulation*, pp. 251–69.

53. See John Sekora, *Luxury: The Concept in Western Thought, Eden to
Smollett* (Baltimore and London, 1977), pp. 46–7.

54. The torch returns in Gloucester's desire for death, a smouldering
sexual consummation: 'My snuff and loathed part of nature should /

Burn itself out' (IV.vi.39–40). On venereal torches and their extinction, see Stephen Booth's prefatory comment to sonnet 153 and his gloss on 153.1, in *Shakespeare's Sonnets* (New Haven, CT, 1977), pp. 533–4.

55. Cornwall's punishment of treason with blinding appears to have no juridical basis. See John H. Langbein's discussion of models of torture in *Torture and the Law of Proof: Europe and England in the Ancien Régime* (Chicago, 1977), p. 67.

56. Adelman identifies the storm with the contaminating dark place of mothers, the rank 'sulphurous pit', *Mothers*, pp. 111–14.

57. On the sexual uses of *foot* and *hand*, see Rubenstein, *Dictionary*. See also Gary Taylor's discussion on the Folio's omission of the Quarto's profane and obscene expletive, 'Fut', 'Monopolies, Show Trials, Disaster, and Invasion: *King Lear* and Censorship', in Gary Taylor and Michael Warren (eds), *The Division of the Kingdoms: Shakespeare's Two Versions of 'King Lear'* (Oxford, 1983), pp. 77–8. Compare Katherine's French lesson that involves four repetitions of 'Le foot et le count' in *Henry V*, III.iii.51, 52, 56, 59. 'Foot' can refer to either female or male genitalia, through its relation to yard (penis) or to 'foutre' or fault, a woman's genital crack which is also her moral flaw. See Adelman, *Mothers*, p. 252, n. 26.

58. 'A female fishes sandie Roe / With the males jelly newly lev'ned was', Donne, 'Progress of the Soul', xxiii, *OED*.

59. Cf. the relation of blindness to castration in psychoanalysis as punishment for Oedipal crime, Sigmund Freud, 'The Uncanny', in *The Standard Edition of the Complete Psychological Works of Sigmund Freud*, Vol. XVII (London, 1955), p. 231.

60. *Sonnets*, p. 470, n. 2; p. 535, n. 9.

61. On the association of blindness and lechery, see William R. Elton, *'King Lear' and the Gods* (San Marino, CA, 1966), pp. 111–12, and Adelman, *Mothers*, pp. 295–6, n. 7.

62. On the synonymity of 'luxuria', 'fornicatio', and 'libido' through the Middle Ages, see Morton Bloomfield, *The Seven Deadly Sins* (Michigan, 1952), pp. 64–5, 69, 77. For an image of Lechery spearing a lecher's eye, see Rosemond Tuve, *Allegorical Imagery* (Princeton, NJ, 1966), fig. 51.

63. On the difficulty critics have had with Edgar's pronouncement, see Adelman, *Mothers*, pp. 295–6, n. 7.

64. On Gloucester's transformation from man (with stones) to woman (with rings), see Adelman, *Mothers*, p. 107 and p. 297, n. 11.

65. Edgar's generational powers are particularly precious in a play in which dynastic prospects have been blasted through Lear's acts of disowning ('degenerate bastard' [I.iv.254]) and cursing ('Into her womb convey sterility! / Dry up in her the organs of increase' [I.iv.278–9]).

66. See Muir, *Lear*, p. 167, IV.vi.136.

67. Language in this play is similarly inclined to superfluity, matching 'the extremity of the sky' (III.iv.102) by pressuring its own extremities: with superlatives and super-superlatives (Tom in an earlier life 'out-paramoor'd the Turk' [III.iv.91]), Oswald's offence of superservice-ability or superfinicality, Lear's superannuation ('the very verge / Of his confine' [II.v.147–8]) and with pejor-pejoratives ('the basest and most poorest', [II.iii.6–7] 'the worst is not / So long as we can say, "This is the worst"' [IV.i.27–8]). These locutions extend the superflux, pushing beyond the reaches of language, out-topping extremes, beginning with Regan's outdistancing of her eldest sister's superlatives; the base Bastard's resolve to '[top] th'legitimate' (I.ii.21); Edgar's exceeding the account of his father's death – 'Twixt two extremes of passion' (V.iii.199) – with another sorrow, which 'To amplify too much, would make much more, / And top extremity' (V.iii.207–8); Lear's body stretching out longer than the rack; the play itself finding a way to outlast even 'the promis'd end' (V.iii.264). The history of *Lear's* reception indicates that the play itself goes to extremes, pushing beyond the bounds of tragedy, particularly in its superfluous addition of Cordelia's death (not in the sources), an extreme that drove Tate to his uplifting revisions.

68. For the significance of the play's having been first performed (according to the 1608 Quarto title page) at court on St Stephen's or Boxing Day, a day on which the rich were expected to extend themselves to the poor, see Leah S. Marcus, *Puzzling Shakespeare: Local Reading and its Discontents* (Berkeley, Los Angeles, London, 1988), pp. 148–56.

69. On the substitution of god-relations for blood-relations, see David Sabean, 'Aspects of Kinship Behavior and Property in Rural Western Europe before 1800', in Laslett, Oosterveen, and Smith, *Bastardy*, pp. 248–95.

70. On *Lear* and doomsday, see Joseph Wittreich, *'Image of that Horror': History, Prophecy, and Apocalypse in 'King Lear'* (San Marino, CA, 1984). On the relation between 'the desire of the poor to improve the material conditions of their lives' and Apocalypse in Medieval and Reformation Europe, see Norman Cohn, *The Pursuit of the Millennium* (New York, 1961), p. xiii.

71. Cf. Halpern: 'The utopian strain, like the lightning that is its counter-point, flashes briefly in the night of the play and is then swallowed up – along, one assumes, with the concept of need that founded it', *Accumulation*, p. 261.

72. Cf. the *base* Bastard's intention to *top* the legitimate. Cf. too Gloucester's *defects* proving *commodities*.

73. In the face of the impossibility of such computations, Jean Baudrillard has argued that 'the "vital anthropological" minimum does not exist'. The level of survival is determined not by any essential human need perceptible at the bottom but rather by surplus expenditure from the top. 'In other words, there are only needs because the system needs them.' *For a Critique of the Political Economy of the Sign*, trans. Charles Levin (St Louis, MO, 1981), pp. 80, 82.

74. I owe my awareness of this fallacious logic to a painting by Peter Golfinopoulos, 'The Poor Have Never Lived Well'.

75. Michael Ignatieff, *The Needs of Strangers* (New York, 1986), p. 35.

76. I draw here on Leah S. Marcus's account of the play's liturgical context in *Puzzling Shakespeare*, pp. 148–59.

77. For an anthropological account of the complex strategies of giving to retain, see Annette B. Weiner, *Inalienable Possessions: The Paradox of Keeping-While-Giving* (Berkeley, Los Angeles, Oxford, 1992).

78. Trans. Miriam Kochan (New York, Cambridge, 1973). See especially Braudel's two chapters on 'Superfluity and Sufficiency', chs 3 and 4, pp. 121–91. See also Braudel, *The Structures of Everyday Life: The Limits of the Possible*, trans. Sian Reynolds (London, 1981), pp. 183–333.

79. On the tendency of pre-Industrial-Age workmen to work only to relieve want in an economic system that offered no incentives to work for more, see Edgar S. Furniss, *The Position of the Laborer in a System of Nationalism* (Boston, 1920), p. 234, and D. C. Coleman, 'Labour in the English Economy of the 17th Century', *Economic History Review*, 2nd series, 8 (1956), 289–95.

80. Trans. W. R. Dittmar (Michigan, 1967).

81. Sekora, *Luxury*, cited in n. 53.

82. Ibid., pp. 46–7.

83. On the mid seventeenth-century emergence of this word in its present sense, see Peter Stallybrass, 'Shakespeare, the Individual, and the Text', in Larry Grossberg, Cary Nelson, and Paula A. Treichler (eds), *Cultural Studies: Now and in the Future* (New York and London, 1992), pp. 593–612.

84. See especially 'Authority and Property: The Question of Liberal Origins' and 'The Mobility of Property and the Rise of Eighteenth-century Sociology', in *Virtue, Commerce, and History: Essays on Political Thought and History, Chiefly in the Eighteenth Century* (Cambridge, 1985), pp. 51–71 and pp. 103–23; 'Early Modern

Capitalism – the Augustan Perception', in Eugene Kamenka and R. S. Neale (eds), *Feudalism, Capitalism, and Beyond* (London, 1975), pp. 62–83; 'Neo-Machiavellian Political Economy; the Augustan Debate over Land, Trade and Credit', in *The Machiavellian Moment: Florentine Political Thought and the Atlantic Republican Tradition* (Princeton, NJ, 1975), pp. 423–61.

85. C. B. Macpherson, *The Political Theory of Possessive Individualism: Hobbes to Locke* (Oxford, 1962). For Pocock's critique of Macpherson, see *Virtue*, pp. 60–71.

86. *Virtue*, p. 103.

87. On the relation of fiscal and fictional credit and their unsettling effect on personal identity, see Sandra Sherman, *Finance and Fictionality in the Early Eighteenth Century* (Cambridge, forthcoming).

88. *Virtue*, p. 112.

89. '[T]here is no greater and no commoner mistake in the history of social thought than to suppose the tension [between the two relations of property to personality] ever disappeared', ibid., p. 122.

90. For the insight that 'property' gives way to 'psyche' after the Renaissance, I owe a long-standing debt to Stephen Greenblatt's 'Psychoanalysis and Renaissance Culture', in Patricia Parker and David Quint (eds), *Literary Theory / Renaissance Texts* (Baltimore, 1986), pp. 210–24.

Further Reading

RECENT COLLECTIONS OF ESSAYS

I have indicated which tragedies are included in each collection (in some instances there is more than one essay on a particular play), and have occasionally called attention to individual essays. The following collections also include essays (usually not cited here) which examine social or theoretical issues that are relevant to the tragedies.

G. Douglas Atkins and David M. Bergeron (eds), *Shakespeare and Deconstruction* (New York: Peter Lang, 1988). *Othello*, *King Lear*. See also Gary Waller, 'Decentering the Bard: The Dissemination of the Shakespearean Text', pp. 21–45.

Deborah E. Barker and Ivo Kamps (eds), *Shakespeare and Gender: A History* (London and New York: Verso, 1995). *Hamlet*, *Othello*, *Romeo and Juliet*. See especially Valerie Traub, 'Jewels, Statues, and Corpses: Containment of Female Erotic Power in Shakespeare's Plays', pp. 120–41 (*Hamlet* and *Othello*).

Jonathan Dollimore and Alan Sinfield (eds), *Political Shakespeare: Essays in Cultural Materialism*, 2nd edn (Ithaca and London: Cornell University Press, 1994). See Kathleen McLuskie, 'The Patriarchal Bard: Feminist Criticism and Shakespeare: *King Lear* and *Measure for Measure*', pp. 88–108; and see also Jonathan Dollimore, 'Introduction: Shakespeare, Cultural Materialism, and the New Historicism', pp. 2–17.

John Drakakis (ed.), *Alternative Shakespeares* (London and New York: Routledge, 1985). See Jacqueline Rose, 'Sexuality in the Reading of Shakespeare: *Hamlet* and *Measure for Measure*', pp. 95–118.

Margaret W. Ferguson, Maureen Quilligan, and Nancy J. Vickers (eds), *Rewriting the Renaissance: The Discourses of Sexual Difference in Early Modern England* (Chicago: University of Chicago Press, 1986). See Coppélia Kahn, 'The Absent Mother in *King Lear*', pp. 33–49; and Peter Stallybrass, 'Patriarchal Territories: The Body Enclosed', pp. 123–42 (*Othello*).

Shirley Nelson Garner and Madelon Sprengnether (eds), *Shakespearean Tragedy and Gender* (Bloomington and Indianapolis: Indiana University

Press, 1996). *Antony and Cleopatra, Macbeth, Othello, Timon of Athens, Titus Andronicus*. See especially Sara Eaton, 'A Woman of Letters: Lavinia in *Titus Andronicus*', pp. 54–74. See also Carol Thomas Neely, '"Documents in Madness": Reading Madness and Gender in Shakespeare's Tragedies and Early Modern Culture', pp. 75–104.

Jonathan Goldberg (ed.), *Queering the Renaissance* (Durham and London: Duke University Press, 1994). See Jonathan Goldberg, '*Romeo and Juliet*'s Open Rs', pp. 218–35.

Terence Hawkes (ed.), *Alternative Shakespeares, Vol. 2* (New York and London: Routledge, 1996). *Antony and Cleopatra, Othello, Hamlet*. See especially Dympna Callaghan, '"Othello was a white man": Properties of Race on Shakespeare's Stage', pp. 192–215; and see also Ania Loomba, 'Shakespeare and Cultural Difference', pp. 164–91.

Margo Hendricks and Patricia Parker (eds), *Women, 'Race', and Writing in the Early Modern Period* (London and New York: Routledge, 1994). *Othello*. See also Lynda E. Boose, '"The Getting of a Lawful Race": Racial Discourse in early Modern England and the Unrepresentable Black Woman', pp. 35–54.

Jean E. Howard and Marion F. O'Connor (eds), *Shakespeare Reproduced: The Text in History and Ideology* (New York and London: Methuen, 1987). *Coriolanus, Macbeth, Othello*. See especially Karen Newman, '"And wash the Ethiop white": Femininity and the Monstrous in *Othello*', pp. 143–62.

Ivo Kamps (ed.), *Materialist Shakespeare: A History* (London and New York: Verso, 1995). *Julius Caesar, King Lear, Macbeth, Othello*. See especially Alan Sinfield, '*Macbeth*: History, Ideology and Intellectuals', pp. 93–107.

Carolyn Ruth Swift Lenz, Gayle Greene, and Carol Thomas Neely (eds), *The Woman's Part: Feminist Criticism of Shakespeare* (Urbana: University of Illinois Press, 1980). *Hamlet, Macbeth, Othello, Romeo and Juliet*. See especially Madelon Gohlke, '"I wooed thee with my sword": Shakespeare's Tragic Paradigms', pp. 150–70.

Patricia Parker and Geoffrey Hartman (eds), *Shakespeare and the Question of Theory* (New York: Methuen, 1985). *Coriolanus, Hamlet, King Lear*. See especially Stanley Cavell, '"Who does the wolf love?": *Coriolanus* and the Interpretations of Politics', pp. 245–72; and Robert Weimann, 'Mimesis in *Hamlet*', pp. 275–91.

Valerie Traub, M. Lindsay Kaplan, and Dympna Callaghan (eds), *Feminist Readings of Early Modern Culture: Emerging Subjects* (Cambridge: Cambridge University Press, 1996). See Cynthia Marshall, 'Wound-man: *Coriolanus*, Gender, and the Theatrical Construction of Interiority', pp. 93–118.

Valerie Wayne (ed.), *The Matter of Difference: Materialist Feminist Criticism of Shakespeare* (Ithaca, NY: Cornell University Press, 1991). *King Lear, Othello, Titus Andronicus*. See especially Valerie Wayne, 'Historical Differences: Misogyny and *Othello*', pp. 153–80.

Susan Zimmerman (ed.), *Erotic Politics: Desire on the Renaissance Stage* (London and New York: Routledge, 1992). *Othello*. See also Bruce R. Smith, 'Making a Difference: Male/Male "Desire" in Tragedy, Comedy, and Tragi-comedy', pp. 127–49; and Valerie Traub, 'The (In)significance of "Lesbian" Desire in Early Modern England', pp. 150–69.

RECENT BOOKS (containing chapters or segments on Shakespeare's tragedies)

Harry Berger, Jr, *Making Trifles of Terrors: Redistributing Complicities in Shakespeare* (Stanford, CA, 1997). Analyses *King Lear* and *Macbeth* (as well as other Shakespearean plays) through poststructuralist strategies which uniquely encompass linguistic, psychoanalytical, and historical perspectives.

Linda Charnes, *Notorious Identity: Materializing the Subject in Shakespeare* (Cambridge, MA, and London, 1993). Examines the socio-political deployments of early modern legends of notorious figures, especially the relationship between notorious legend and the theatrical representation of subjectivity in Shakespeare's plays.

Kim Hall, *Things of Darkness: Economies of Race and Gender in Early Modern England* (Ithaca and London, 1995). Explores the role of colour in organising relations of power, in particular, the appropriation of tropes of black and white in imperialist/colonialist discourse, in poetry, and in drama.

Coppélia Kahn, *Roman Shakespeare: Warriors, Wounds, and Women* (New York and London, 1997). Examines the construction of masculinity in Shakespeare's Roman works, focusing on modes by which the 'wound' functions as a fetish, signifying masculinity as stoical and self-disciplined and evoking femininity as vulnerable and dependent.

Katherine Eisaman Maus, *Inwardness and Theatre in the English Renaissance* (Chicago and London, 1995). Interrogates early modern concepts of interiority, the modes by which interior states were theatricalised (particularly in Shakespeare), and the socio-political implications of these representations.

Michael Neill, *Issues of Death: Mortality and Identity in Renaissance Tragedy* (Oxford, 1997). Examines tragedy in relation to early modern practices for confronting death, such as the *Danse Macabre*, funereal rituals, and the new science of anatomical dissection.

Stephen Orgel, *Impersonations: The Performance of Gender in Shakespeare's England* (Cambridge, 1996). Examines the construction of gender in early modern English drama and society, focusing in particular on the significance of cross-dressing both within and without the theatre.

Lena Cowen Orlin, *Private Matters and Public Culture in Post-Reformation England* (Ithaca and London, 1994). Analyses early modern domestic tragedy in terms of political, economic and legal discourses on marital relations, household governance, and the status of women.

Patricia Parker, *Shakespeare from the Margins: Language, Culture, Context* (Chicago and London, 1996). Examines relationships between the linguistic patterns of Shakespeare's plays and the discourses of Shakespeare's culture, with an emphasis on representations of gender and sexuality.

Deborah Willis, *Malevolent Nurture: Witch-Hunting and Maternal Power in Early Modern England* (Ithaca and London, 1995). Explores the early modern construction of the witch as malevolent mother as represented in the records of witchcraft prosecutions as well as in Shakespearian tragedy.

Notes on Contributors

Janet Adelman is Professor of English at the University of California at Berkeley. Her publications include *The Common Liar: An Essay on 'Antony and Cleopatra'* (1973) and *Suffocating Mothers: Fantasies of Maternal Origins in Shakespeare's Plays: 'Hamlet' to 'The Tempest'* (1992).

Philip Armstrong teaches English at the University of Auckland. His publications include essays on the gaze, the uncanny, cartography, and psychoanalysis in relation to Shakespeare's works.

Catherine Belsey chairs the Centre for Critical and Cultural Theory at the University of Wales, Cardiff. She is author of *The Subject of Tragedy: Identity and Difference in Renaissance Drama* (1985). Her study of Shakespeare and the family is currently in preparation.

Michael D. Bristol, Professor of English, McGill University, is author of *Big-Time Shakespeare* (1997), *Shakespeare's America/America's Shakespeare* (1996), and *Carnival and Theatre: Plebian Culture and the Structure of Authority in Renaissance England* (1985).

Karin S. Coddon has taught Shakespeare, critical theory, and writing at the University of California, San Diego, and at Brown University. She has published widely in the field of Renaissance drama, including essays on *Macbeth, Twelfth Night,* and *The Revenger's Tragedy.*

Margreta de Grazia, Professor of English at the University of Pennsylvania, is the author of *Shakespeare Verbatim* (1991) and numerous articles on the early modern period and its periodisation. Her current project is entitled *Counter Modern 'Hamlet'.*

John Drakakis is Professor of English at the University of Stirling. He is editor of *Alternative Shakespeares* (1985), *Shakespearean Tragedy* (1992), the New Casebook *Antony and Cleopatra* (1994), and *'The Tragedie of Richard III' (1597)* in the Harvester Shakespeare Originals Series. He is also the general editor of the Routledge English Texts series, and the New Critical Idiom series, and has published widely in the areas of Shakespeare Studies, and Critical and Cultural Theory.

Jonathan Goldberg is Sir William Osler Professor of English Literature at the Johns Hopkins University and Professor of English at Duke University. His publications include *Desiring Women Writing: English Renaissance Examples* (1997), *Sodometries: Renaissance Texts, Modern Sexualities* (1992), and *Writing Matter: From the Hands of the English Renaissance* (1990).

Stephen Greenblatt is 1932 Professor of English at the University of California, Berkeley. He is the author of many books, including *Renaissance Self-Fashioning: From More to Shakespeare* (1980), and *Shakespearean Negotiations: The Circulation of Energy in Renaissance England* (1988), and he is General Editor of the Norton *Shakespeare* (1997).

Patricia Parker is Professor of English and Comparative Literature, Stanford University. Her publications include *Literary Fat Ladies: Rhetoric, Gender, Property* (1987), and *Shakespeare From the Margins* (1996). Her many collections include, with Geoffrey Hartman, *Shakespeare and the Question of Theory* (1985), with David Quint, *Literary Theory/Renaissance Texts* (1986), and with Margo Hendricks, *Women, 'Race,' and Writing in the Early Modern Period* (1994).

Peter Stallybrass is Professor of English and of Comparative Literature and Literary Theory at the University of Pennsylvania. With Allon White, he wrote *The Politics and Poetics of Transgression* (2nd edn, 1990), and he has co-edited *Staging the Renaissance: Studies in Elizabethan and Jacobean Drama* (1991), *Subject and Object in Renaissance Culture* (1996), and *Language Machines: Technologies of Literary and Cultural Production* (1997). He has just completed a book with Ann Rosalind Jones entitled *Worn Worlds: Clothes and the Constitution of the Subject in Renaissance England and Europe.*

Marion Wynne-Davies is Senior Lecturer in English Literature at the University of Dundee. Her publications include *The Bloomsbury Guide to English Literature* (1989) and *Women and Arthurian Literature: Seizing the Sword* (1996), and with S. P. Cerasano, *Gloriana's Face: Women, Public and Private, in the English Renaissance* (1992), and *Renaissance Drama by Women: Texts and Contexts* (1996).

Index